The Search for Good Government

Observers have frequently noted that Italians seem skilled at many things – but not at good government. As a people, Italians are said to have flair, panache, and tenacity, while as a polity Italy is in shambles. This paradoxical view of politics can be found in Italian history as far back as Guicciardini and Machiavelli. Nor is it unique to Italy, for the social dilemma of "rational individuals and irrational society" has, since Hobbes, produced a large literature on social theory and comparative politics, as well as numerous questionable suggestions for policy. In *The Search for Good Government* Filippo Sabetti examines Italian politics to reassess habitual presumptions in comparative politics, opening new territory in the art and science of institutional analysis.

Sabetti argues that poor government performance in contemporary Italy has been an unintended consequence of attempts to craft institutions for good – or democratic – government. He shows that, contrary to the conventional wisdom, a chief problem in contemporary Italy is not the absence of the rule of law but, rather, the presence of rule *by* law or too many laws. A principal conclusion of his study is that postwar Italian politics can best be understood as a laboratory for revealing how and why a search for good government can generate antithetical and counterintentional results. The Italian experience has important implications for all those who aspire to be self-governing – as opposed to state-governed – for it shows what people can do to enhance human cooperation in collective-action dilemmas and suggests the probable result if "democracy" continues to be identified with parliamentary government and representative assemblies rather than with the universality of the village or the local community.

The Search for Good Government changes our understanding of postwar Italian politics and provides new ways to evaluate the impact of the political changes that have occurred since 1992, arguing for a perceptual shift in the way we think about politics and the educative role of public institutions.

FILIPPO SABETTI is a professor of political science at McGill University.

Aosta Valley
Aosta

Verbano
Varese

Lombardy
Sondrio

Trentino-Alto Adige
Bolzano

Friuli-Venezia Giulia

Belluno

Biella
Como
Lecco

Bergamo

Trento

Pordenone
Udine
Gorizia

Novara

Trieste

Turin
Vercelli

Milan
Lodi
Brescia

Vicenza
Veneto
Treviso

Piedmont
Asti

Cremona

Verona
Padua
Venice

Pavia

Cuneo
Alessandria

Placenza
Parma
Mantua
Rovigo

Savona
Liguria
Reggio
Modena
Ferrara

Genoa
Emilia-Romagna
Ravenna

La Spezia
Bologna

Imperia

Massa Carrara
Pistoia
Prato
Forli
Rimini

Lucca

Pisa
Florence
Pesaro

Livorno

Arezzo
The Marches
Ancona

Siena

Perugia
Macerata

Tuscany

Grosseto
Umbria
Ascoli Piceno

Terni

Viterbo
Teramo
Pescara

Rieti
Chieti

Latium
L'Aquila

☆ Rome
Abruzzi

Frosinone
Isernia
Molise

Latina
Campobasso
Foggia

Campania
Apulia

Caserta
Benevento
Bari

Naples
Avellino

Salerno
Potenza
Brindisi

Matera
Taranto
Lecce

Sardinia
Sassari

Basilicata

Nuoro

Oristano

Calabria

Cagliari
Cosenza
Crotone

Catanzaro

Vibo Valentia

Messina
Reggio Calabria

Palermo

Trapani
Sicily

Caltanissetta
Catania

Enna

Agrigento
Syracuse

Ragusa

The Search for Good Government

Understanding the Paradox of Italian Democracy

FILIPPO SABETTI

McGill-Queen's University Press
Montreal & Kingston · London · Ithaca

© McGill-Queen's University Press 2000
ISBN 0-7735-2024-4

Legal deposit second quarter 2000
Bibliothèque nationale du Québec

Printed in Canada on acid-free paper

This book has been published with the help of a grant
from the Humanities and Social Sciences Federation of
Canada, using funds provided by the Social Sciences
and Humanities Research Council of Canada.

McGill-Queen's University Press acknowledges the
financial support of the Government of Canada through
the Book Publishing Industry Development Program for
its publishing activities. We also acknowledge the support of the Canada Council for the Arts for our publishing program.

Canadian Cataloguing in Publication Data

Sabetti, Filippo
The search for good government: understanding
the paradox of Italian democracy
Includes bibliographical references and index.
ISBN 0-7735-2024-4
1. Italy—Politics and government. I. Title.
JN5452.S22 2000   320.945   C99-901505-2

This book was typeset by True to Type in 10/12 Sabon.

In memory of
Rosina Sabetti, Nora Sabetti, Maria Filippa Pietrangeli

Contents

Acknowledgments

This book was truly a long time in the making. As work started, I felt compelled to learn what Carlo Cattaneo had to say about fundamental issues in the art and practice of self-governance during the Risorgimento, at the time of the creation of the Italian state; as my interest in Cattaneo grew, his political theory became another book project. While work on the present manuscript slowed down and proceeded fitfully, work on Cattaneo took me in directions in political philosophy and comparative inquiry I never expected. But it was only after several years, as I tried to contain the Cattaneo study within manageable limits, that I realized Cattaneo had given me a better grip on what observers have characterized again and again as "the paradox of Italy" – poor government performance in contrast with successes across a broad array of human endeavour. By providing an historical context to understanding contemporary Italian democracy, Cattaneo also freed me from having to do an entire history of the Italian state from the Risorgimento to the present. (My main focus is post-1946 politics.) I thus put aside Cattaneo and returned with renewed enthusiasm to the earlier project: to construct an argument for thinking differently about poor government performance in contemporary Italy.

A fortuitous encounter with Stephen L. Elkin at a Liberty Fund Colloquium on Robert D. Putnam's *Making Democracy Work: Civic Traditions in Modern Italy* (1993), organized by W. B. Allen in Oakland, California, in January 1996, led me to rediscover Elkin's book *City and Regime in the American Republic* (1987) and to invigorate the making of my own. Now Elkin's insistence on treating political institutions as formative and his emphasis on the place of urban political institutions in the larger American regime made perfect sense to me, and I took that revelation as an additional, independent confirmation that I was on the right track in pursuing the search for good government in Italy.

In short, I believe that the present work has better foundations than the version I planned to complete fourteen years ago. It would be nice but not quite true to justify the long gestation period simply in terms of intellectual pursuits. There were other more practical challenges that I have had to confront along the way, essential reminders that human life is worth living both as an adventure and a mystery.

The list of institutions and persons to whom I am indebted for assistance, criticism, and encouragement for this work has, therefore, grown to almost unmanageable proportions. The benefit I have derived from reading the authors listed in the bibliography is self-evident. As this book was completed in less than ideal – even adverse – circumstances, my greatest personal debt is to five people whose names I wish to keep *in pectore*. Their fortitude and cheerfulness kept my own alive. There are others whom I can acknowledge publicly, and I hope I may be pardoned if I fail to remember some.

Time to work out the basic scheme of the book and to undertake research was provided by several institutions. McGill University was twice generous with its sabbatical leave policy, as was the Social Science and Humanities Research Council of Canada. The Social Science Research Committee of the Faculty of Graduate Studies and Research of McGill University provided small but essential research budgets in 1983 and 1994. I spent the 1987–88 academic year at the Workshop in Political Theory and Policy Analysis, Indiana University, Bloomington, Indiana, as a recipient of its hospitality and generosity; Elinor and Vincent Ostrom, the workshop codirectors, opened a new intellectual world for me long ago and set, by example, standards of scholarship and collegiality not easy to emulate. The Società Siciliana Storia Patria of Palermo in the late 1980s, the Centro Studi e Documentazione sulla Criminalità of the University of Messina in the early 1990s, two Liberty Fund Colloquia on political economy in nineteenth-century Italy (organized by Domenico da Empoli in Reggio Calabria in 1991 and in Piacenza in 1995), the CENSIS Foundation in Rome in 1994, the Centro Studi e Documentazione sui Demani Civici e le Proprietà Collettive of the University of Trento in 1998 – all eased access to papers and people and provided additional opportunities for sustained fieldwork. Public officials in different parts of the peninsula graciously responded to what at times must have been impertinent questions. It would be invidious to single out specific individuals, but I cannot refrain from mentioning Antonio Anzalone of the Ufficio Stampa Giunta Regionale of Basilicata who in the summer of 1994 truly went to extraordinary lengths to help my work in Potenza. For their assistance over many years, I express particular gratitude to the staffs of the Biblioteca Provinciale di Foggia and the Interlibrary Loan of the Humanities and Social Sciences Library (McLennan and Redpath) at McGill University.

An extraordinary group of people helped at various stages of the project. In Bologna, Arturo Parisi of the Cattaneo Institute and Robert H. Evans and Thomas Row of the Johns Hopkins University Center offered hospitality to me and my research assistant, our son Leonardo, and provided insightful comments as the project was taking shape, as did Michelguglielmo and Wilma Torri in Rome and Turin. Francesco and Zina Brancato in Palermo put themselves and their local contacts in the world of academia and reform politics at my disposal. Alfio and Teresa Mastropaolo were gracious hosts in Turin; Alfio's own research on and participation in reform politics have stimulated my own investigations – all the more since we do not always agree. Maurizio Ferrera, from Pavia and Bocconi, was most generous in reading and offering comments on an early draft of the manuscript, while writing his own book in Montreal. Raffaella Nanetti came to Montreal with extensive written criticisms on portions of the manuscript, cheerfully sacrificing "tourist time" to make sure I understood them. Stephen E. Bornstein, Mark Donovan, Stephen L. Elkin, Miriam Golden, Margaret Levi, and Michael R. Smith made insightful suggestions on different chapters, helping me immensely to sort out confusions in my own thinking as the manuscript underwent rounds of revisions. Federico Varese's help was remarkable, considering that we have never met. He offered comments of extraordinary usefulness on several draft chapters and willingly shared some of the fruits of his own research, past and present; I do not just cite his work, I incorporate his own ideas in my narrative. Richard Alba, Mark Donovan, Diego Gambetta, Carlo G. Lacaita, Paolo Pezzino, Martin Rhodes, Andrea Simoncini, Salvatore Vassallo, and E. Spencer Wellhofer contributed to improving the argument and evidence by generously responding to my e-mail calls for help.

My heartfelt gratitude to Alfio Mastropaolo and Vincent Ostrom for commenting on the penultimate draft of the manuscript in its entirety. I did not ask Antony C. Masi to read any draft of the manuscript for fear of abusing his friendship and generosity: over the course of many years, in our once-a-week coffee break, he has been a gentle guide in the world of computers and comparative labour and industrial markets, and a sharp questioner of the theme of this book. Although none of the conferences organized by Daniel J. Elazar and Donald S. Lutz on covenant and politics, constitutionalism, and political thought that I have attended in the past fifteen years has directly dealt with Italian politics, they have served to sharpen the comparative perspective of this study; Dan Elazar has opened new lines of inquiries for me and enriched my understanding of federalism since we first met at a conference in Courmayer, Aosta, in 1978. Finally, the review process by the press and the Aid to Scholarly Publications Programme of the Humanities and Social Science Federation of Canada was most constructive and helpful; I wish to thank the reviewers for their valuable suggestions and critical judgments.

It has been a real learning experience to subject my work to critical scrutiny from so many colleagues. I may have borrowed their arguments in ways I am perhaps no longer conscious of, so much am I indebted to them. Where I have not accepted criticisms, I have had to amplify, and thus fortify, the argument to meet their objections.

McGill-Queen's University Press provided superb support. Joan McGilvray saw the book through its final stage with skill and care. I am especially grateful to Rebecca Green. Her careful copyediting made the book more readable and her thoughtful queries and suggestions helped to strengthen the narrative.

I dedicate the book to the memory of our daughters Rosina and Nora, and my sister Maria Filippa, who died in 1998.

Elements of chapters 2, 4, 6, and 7 were adapted and updated, respectively, from "The Making of Italy as an Experiment in Constitutional Choice," *Publius* 12 (Summer 1992): 65–84; "The Structure and Performance of Urban Systems in Italy," in *Comparing Urban Service Delivery Systems*, ed. Vincent Ostrom and Frances P. Bish, Urban Affairs Annual Reviews, vol. 12 (Beverly Hills: Sage, 1977), 113–45; "The Mafia and the Anti-mafia: Moments in the Struggle for Justice and Self-Governance in Sicily," in *Italian Politics: A Review*, vol. 4, ed. R. Nanetti and R. Catanzaro (London: Pinter, 1990), 174–95; and "Whose Law, Whose Justice? Of Crime and Punishment in Modern Times," in *Italian Politics: A Review*, vol. 7, ed. S. Hellman and G. Pasquino (London: Pinter, 1992), 129–44. An earlier version of chapter 9 was published as "Path Dependency and Civic Culture: Some Lessons from Italy about Interpreting Social Experiments," *Politics & Society* 24 (March 1996): 19–44. All translations are by the author, unless otherwise noted.

1 Italian Politics: School for Good Government

The search for good, or democratic government is approaching the status of a universal human aspiration and preoccupation. Yet, as many "transitions to democracy" demonstrate, state-citizens relationships and the complexity of governmental structures make crafting institutions of good government a daunting task. The task is made all the more vexatious by an inescapable fact of human existence: "All forms of human organization are artifacts that contain their own artisans" (V. Ostrom 1980, 251; see also Archer 1995, 1–30). When things do not work as they should, it is an empirical question whether Thomas Hobbes's conclusion that "the fault is not in men, as they are the *matter*; but as they are the makers, and orderers of [commonwealth]" always applies (Hobbes [1651] 1962, 237). Thus, it is not easy for people to move from one system of governance to another. The meaning of good government remains open to different social ontologies and constitutional designs; and, when people turn to academic knowledge for what it has to offer about the organizational terms and conditions necessary to craft institutions, they soon discover that academic knowledge contains some large doses of bad medicine. Exceptions like the Federalist Papers aside, "research grounded in a well-developed framework of scientific discourse that serves as a practical guide to the construction of stable democratic institutions is virtually nonexistent" (Ordeshook 1993, 198).

For all these reasons, much of the history of old and new democracies can be viewed as a continual search for a system of governance that is at once accountable, responsive, and efficient *as well as* formative of the autonomous citizenries that self-governing societies need. Because no single form of organization can be "good" for all circumstances, reform movements have become a perennial feature of modern societies. Several results can be observed.

One result is that the search for good government has proved to be as elusive as it is unceasing. When public institutions have not worked as they should, the standard practice among politicians has been to issue calls for "reinventing government," often with little or no consideration given to the government already invented. The work of social scientists has produced other kinds of results. One has been to generate considerable literature describing things that went wrong – corruption, or poor government performance, for example; the other has been to argue that institutional performance is not as bad as commonly assumed. There is merit in both these judgments, and they have in fact become a respectable part of the conventional academic wisdom. The problem is that social scientists have seldom, if ever, considered that poor government performance may actually be an unintended consequence of the attempt to craft institutions of good government. Indeed, when have people framed institutions with the intention of producing poor results? While it is possible to imagine foreign occupants of a certain territory willingly framing institutions in order to ruin the country, usually the bad results follow from good intentions, or gods that fail. This book considers these issues by focusing on Italy's political development.

To regard Italian politics as a school for good government may appear to be a provocation. After all, as a recent *Economist* survey of Italy put it, "despite its prosperity, Italy has never quite managed to be taken seriously as an advanced market economy and democratic state" *Economist* 1997a, 3). Nor have its people, if we are to believe Michael Lerner's account of "respectable bigotry." He cites "a brilliant professor in New Haven" who, at dinner "on the day an Italian American announced his candidacy for Mayor of New York," remarked that, "if Italians aren't actually an inferior race, they do the best imitation of one I've seen" (Lerner 1969, 616). Lerner's account is reiterated in Nathan Glazer and Daniel P. Moynihan's *Beyond the Melting Pot*, where the professor is further identified as "a world-famous Yale professor of government" (Glazer and Moynihan 1970, lxxiii). A recent survey suggests that Italophobia may be more than "respectable bigotry" – possibly even an "English-speaking malady" (Harney 1985). This malady may have historic roots in ambivalent British reactions to Italy, as a recent collection of essays on Italian culture in northern Europe in the eighteenth century reveals (West 1999). Indeed, the story told in these essays sharpens, in the words of a British reviewer, "our sense of the ageless polarity in British cultural attitudes towards Italy, between an envy of her resourcefulness on the one hand and a fear, on the other, of her sophistication as the vehicle of luxury, Popish intrigue and loose morals" (Keates 1999, 18). Douglas Johnson's survey of the practice of historians is no less revealing:

Historians of modern Italy are often pessimistic. When, like all other historians, they have sought to find a dominating theme, a key that would open all the locks, they have seized upon that of failure. Italy has been described as the country of failed revolutions, the *rivoluzione mancata*. The Jacobin revolution, the industrial revolution, the socialist revolution, the fascist revolution, the antifascist revolution – all have been seen as unsuccessful. And not only the so-called revolutions, but also all the other "turning points" where modern Italian history has failed to turn have been similarly described. The liberal parliamentary state, the resolve to make Italy an important imperial power, the intervention in two world wars, the membership in the European community, the evolution of the Italian Communist party: all these episodes, according to this interpretation, are part of a succession of betrayals, disasters, defeats, or disappointments.

In this melancholy catalog it is undoubtedly the Risorgimento and the Unification of Italy that have caused the greatest disillusionment. (Johnson 1985, 24)

The publicity posted on several Internet lists by the organizers of a two-day international conference on disasters in Italy since the 1860s, held at Yale University in June 1999, offers a variant on and explanation of standard views: "There is no European society whose modern history has been more deeply marked by disasters, both natural and social, than has Italy's." Successive Italian governing classes appear to have excelled, more than other Western governing elites, in the "manipulation of history," according to Denis Mack Smith – described by some as "the most distinguished living historian of the Risorgimento" (Beales 1995, 6). In a recent study, Mack Smith treats problematic episodes in Italian public life *sub specie mysterii* (Mack Smith 1998). It would be wrong to conclude that respectable bigotry, exalted pessimism, and debatable sweeping generalizations are confined to foreign observers. Such views can be found among Italians themselves, from Francesco Guicciardini to Cesare Lombroso to Antonio Gramsci, and among contemporary moulders of elite public opinion like Giorgio Bocca on the left and Indro Montanelli on the right. Mack Smith's most recent intepretation was, in the spirit of national self-abnegation, headlined in the "culture page" of a leading Italian newspaper as "Italians, artisans of deceit" (*Italiani, popolo di falsari*) (*La Repubblica* 1998a; see also a response by Nello Ajello on the same page).

There is not much else to say about Italian politics when failure, disillusionment, and deceit are said to dominate its proceedings and its history. At best, standard views of Italian politics continue to promote explanations based on a paradoxical view of Italians as a people with flair, resourcefulness, and tenacity, and Italy as a polity in shambles – in short, rational Italians, irrational Italy.

So runs the presumptive knowledge. But it is precisely these old prejudices, mindsets, or even respectable bigotry – in all their variations – that have prevented us from understanding and appreciating the search for good government in contemporary Italian politics. This volume seeks to show that the paradoxical view of Italy misstates issues and leads to wrong conclusions. It is perfectly possible to remove the shadows and false lights that obscure the general view of Italian democracy without falling into the other extreme of exaggerating its strengths or of adopting antireform rhetoric (Hirschman, 1991).

This volume traces poor government performance in present-day Italy and explains how it has been an unintended consequence of various attempts to craft institutions of good government since the Italian liberation and unification in the nineteenth century (Risorgimento). Let there be no misunderstanding. My work does not deny that the modern search for good or democratic government in Italy has a deep historical background; nor do I want to suggest that Italy's political problems began with the creation of the Italian state in the 1860s. My aim is to explain why crafting institutions for self-governance has borne particular fruits in our own time. This requires an examination of the constitutional knowledge and alternative constitutional designs available during the liberation and unification of Italy in the nineteenth century, without, however, the need to write either a history of modern Italy from the 1860s to the 1990s or a full historical account of the transition from liberal Italy to Fascism and from Fascism to republican Italy. Historians would be more appropriate writers of a history of the Italian state (e.g., Lanaro 1992; Romanelli 1995a). In fulfilling its aims, this inquiry follows another route.

The book is organized around four sets of interconnected issues at different levels of analysis. What institutional knowledge and alternative constitutional designs were available at the time of the formation of the Italian national state in the nineteenth century? What institutional learning shaped the creation of the republic in 1946, the accompanying institutional change and stability in the local delivery of public services and in problem solving by detailed planning? How can we see the government war on crime as a fight for good government? Since a strong impression exists abroad that the difficulties experienced by successive generations of Italian citizens and public officials in making governmental institutions work as they should are largely attributable to Italian culture, ethos, or a "vicious cycle" of distrust, the last part of the book examines the question of "cultural" and path-dependent explanations of poor government performance.

The organization of the book brings different levels of analysis together to see what kinds of social realities have come into being. How these realities might be modified to yield improvements in the way people live their lives and in how they come to understand the meaning of life is of rather basic importance. But the narrative stops *before* the political and judicial upheavals of the early 1990s that led to the collapse of postwar politics and, following the landmark national elections of 1992 and 1994, to the creation of what some analysts have arguably called the beginning of the Second Republic. Thus the book provides the historical context to the more recent reform efforts.

Why should we bother about the past? There is a broad agenda behind this question. The past is important for three simple reasons: 1) a large proportion of the reasoning employed in the analysis of post-1994 government and politics rests implicitly or explicitly on an interpretation of events that extend as far back as the Risorgimento: past political experience could discredit this current reasoning; 2) the modelling and remodelling of constitutional and institutional arrangements that followed Italian unification and republican Italy are well enough documented to suggest working hypotheses about the renewed search for good government after 1992; and 3) the new political order being established could be checked against the working hypotheses in order to predict the extent to which the new political order can resolve old problems.

By extending the analysis to Italian politics, the book seeks to open up new territory in the study of the art and science of institutional design, variously known under the rubrics of new constitutionalism (Buchanan and Tullock 1962; Elkin and Soltan 1993; Soltan and Elkin 1996), new economic institutionalism (M. Levi 1997a and 1997b); and institutional analysis and development (V. Ostrom 1997). This family of theoretical perspectives has considerable affinities with Giovanni Sartori's comparative constitutional engineering (Sartori 1994). Sartori's institutional engineering asks, How can constitutional mechanisms promote good government and obstruct bad government? It defines good government as "governments that are enabled to perform and encouraged to perform responsibly. *Per contra*, bad government consists of governments that are unstable, incompetent, inefficient and/or powerless" (Sartori 1994, 154). But Sartori's concern is centered too much on electoral laws and their consequences (see Sartori, quoted in Mariucci 1996, 42n28). The family of theoretical perspectives mentioned above differs from Sartori's institutional engineering in that they do not simply take the point of view of social engineers and experts or electoral law reform as their core concern. Rather, as Karol E. Soltan (1996, 3) has explained, analysts belonging to this family of theoretical perspectives consider institutions as instrumental in making both better decisions and better people; these analysts seek to understand the crafting of institutions from the point of view of persons, who, as noted earlier, are both artificers and matter of the commonwealth (see also Buchanan 1979, 93–112; Panebianco 1989).

Finally, by focusing on Italian politics, this book also explores more general themes connected with the search for good government in other democracies: the interplay of structural and cultural determinants; the place of past events and decisions in influencing current outcomes; and the ability of policy designs to effect the intended changes, including a desirable political way of life. As it will become apparent as the narrative unfolds, one of the volume's most important claims is that the sheer complexity of governmental structures, including the power of past decisions and the incentives that they provide in the present, makes it very difficult, if at all possible, to intentionally bring about "good government." Material from Italian politics is used to sustain this general proposition.

BEYOND ACADEMIC AND POPULAR KNOWLEDGE

In Canada, good government is generally understood as a system of governance whereby choices about basic policies and the availability of different organizational arrangements for pursuing new developmental opportunities reside with members of the executive (the cabinet), in control of the House of Commons. The transformation of provincial governments by 1927 from glorified municipalities into coordinate sovereignties amplified the domain of executive-determined facilities for constitutional arrangements and public policy. By the 1990s, this change brought into question parliamentary federalism itself, but did little to decenter the principle of executive paramountcy. Good government in Canada, Quebec included, remains grounded in the formula of "Peace, Order, and Good Government" used by British draftsmen in premodern times to express the full and general authority vested in the executive. By contrast, good government in the American political tradition means the opposite: limited government. As the authors of the Federalist Papers put it, the principle of limited government introduced in the American Constitution rests on the assumption that individuals are not angels. If they were, no government would be necessary. Though Italians have done much to foster the idea and practice of representative, responsible government, they have historically oscillated between omnipotent and limited government.

The political ideal of good government that shaped the early modern European states owes a great deal to the political theory and practice of Italian city states – "*el buon governo*," as reformers in Girolamo Savonarola's Florence liked to put it. Many modern scholars continue to debate what kind of liberty and republicanism actually existed in Renaissance Italy and to what extent Renaissance liberty and republicanism serve as models for "the invention of the modern republic" and for good government in our own times (e.g., Berman 1983, 356–403; Bock, Skinner, and Viroli 1990; B. Fontana 1994; see also M. Taylor 1996). Other scholars have been drawing attention to good government in the Kingdom of Naples. This is in sharp contrast to the standard view that "after the great days of the Emperor Frederick II, nobody, whether in Italy or elsewhere, looked to Naples for inspiration in politics or administration" (H.G. Koenigsberger, quoted in Calabria and Marino 1990, 1). As two American historians whose work has done much to broaden our knowledge of the Kingdom of Naples have reminded us, "Spanish rule in Italy was not the rule of decadence, but rather an attempt to continue the Renaissance ideal of good government under a universal emperor" (Calabria and Marino 1990, 7). This suggests that even foreign occupants of a certain territory may not necessarily frame institutions in order to ruin a country intentionally, as many have automatically assumed in the case of the Spanish occupation of Naples (and Lombardy).

Regardless of how we interpret the rich Italian historical and intellectual tradition concerned with the theme of good government, one irrefragable fact remains. Of all the things that come to mind when one thinks of present-day Italy, good government is not one of them. Whereas good or democratic government resonates positively in Canadian and American public discourse, the same cannot be said for Italian politics, which has been characterized as misgovernment, surviving without governing, or simply bad government. Some have even wondered whether postwar Italy had government at all (Cassese 1980).

The collapse of the postwar party system, hastened by the Milan Clean Hands investigations of the early 1990s, seemed to confirm what everyone already knew about "the art of government" practised in republican Italy (McCarthy 1995, 4). Even the city of Milan was not spared. Once viewed as Italy's "moral capital," it was now seen as its "immoral capital" (Della Porta 1993). But clientelism, corruption, and misgovernment are not unique characteristics of republican Italy. The Apulian socialist reformer Gaetano Salvemini (1873–1957) expressed the prevailing intellectual wisdom of the time when around 1910 he branded Giovanni Giolitti, whose government dominated liberal Italy, as "the leader of the underworld" (*il ministro della malavita*). Since then, even the Risorgimento, once hailed as "the most marvellous and difficult struggle for freedom recorded in modern times" (W.R. Thayer 1911, quoted in Romeo 1965, vii), has not been spared scornful and contemptuous reappraisals by Gramsci, Gramscians, and non-Gramscians alike. As we saw earlier, many foreign and national interpretations of Italian public life reiterate the old standard academic and popular stereotypes about Italy.

Against this backdrop, it becomes easier to understand why many commentators and analysts of present-day Italy have sought to explain poor government performance in terms of cultural backwardness and vicious cycles of distrust. This is thought to be the reason why Italy united so late, in spite of appeals by Dante and Machiavelli; this is also why, so the path-dependent argument continues, Italian citizens and public officials have been unable to cope effectively with many problems that plague their society. Matthew Arnold was reiterating the standard explanation when in 1867 he identified "a relaxed moral fibre" (i.e., Roman Catholicism) as Italy's "curse" and described the country's deficiencies as the absence of "*virtus verusque labor* of practical life" (Arnold 1867, 228). If only the inhabitants of the Italian peninsula and islands would become civic-minded or behave with a conception of "the public interest" in mind, observed Arnold, many "social pathologies," including poor governmental performance and the consequences that ensue, would disappear.

A chief merit of Robert D. Putnam's *Making Democracy Work* (1993) has been to challenge the paradoxical view of Italy somewhat and to place in bold relief the fact that, like good economy, good government does exist in contemporary Italy. Unfortunately, Putnam's challenge does not entirely succeed, because he offers only a partial theory and explanation. In fact, the path-dependent explanation of regional government performance has tended to entrench the prevailing culturalist interpretation of bad government with regard to southern Italy. *Making Democracy Work* stands as a refined and expanded version of Edward C. Banfield's *The Moral Basis of a Backward Society*, with one important difference. Whereas many analysts have tended to regard Italy across time and space as nothing but Banfield's "Montegrano" writ large (e.g., Bosworth 1979, 2; Gambino 1991, 1998; Hildebrand 1965, 310; Kogan 1965, 37; Pacini 1996, 16–7; see also Elster 1989, 147, 269), Putnam tends to see only southern Italy across time and space as "Montegrano" writ large.

One objective of this project is to challenge the received wisdom, including the versions advanced by Banfield and Putnam, by directing attention to the search for good government in the north as in the south of Italy. This can be done without calling up either good government in Renaissance Italy and in Spanish Naples or the associations and movements for good government in both parts of the peninsula that, in the March 1994 national elections, catapulted Forza Italia and its leader, the Milanese entrepreneur Silvio Berlusconi, to victory. After all, Salvemini himself had by 1945, when he was living in the United States, retracted somewhat his earlier characterization of pre-Fascist liberal Italy. His words may be quoted at some length:

I would have been wiser had I been more moderate in my criticism of the Giolittian system. My knowledge of the men who came after Giolitti in Italy as well as of the countries in which I have lived during the last twenty years has convinced me that if Giolitti was not better, neither was he worse than many non-Italian politicians, and he was certainly less reprehensible than the Italian politicians who followed him . . . Our criticism thus did not help to direct the evolution of Italian public life toward less imperfect forms of democracy, but rather toward the victory of those militarist, nationalist and reactionary groups who had found even Giolitti's democracy too perfect. It often happens that he who seeks only the best not only fails to get it but also plunges into the worst . . . If it were possible for me to live again in Italy between 1900 and 1914 with that modicum of experience which I have gained during these successive thirty years, I would not omit any of my censures of the Giolittian system, but I would be more indulgent and I would regard with greater suspicion those who found pleasure in my criticism. (Salvemini 1945, xxi)

After 1945, some others still went so far as to describe Giolitti as "the leader of the good life (or society)" (*il ministro della buonavita*), a play on words of Salvemini's pre-1914 description of Giolitti as "*il ministro della malavita*" (Ansaldo 1963; see also Giolitti [1922] 1967).

We will return to Giolitti in chapter 9; but the chief problem with statements like those of Salvemini and revisionist analysts is that they put too much emphasis on personality traits and sociological factors, without reference to the situations in which individuals find themselves and the constraints those situations impose on human behaviour in the pursuit of individual and joint opportunities. A more balanced, less Manichean interpretation of the Giolitti government and practice of rule came from the leader of the Italian Communist Party, Palmiro Togliatti, in 1950, when he recognized Giolitti's positive contributions to the affirmation and growth of Italian democracy (Togliatti [1950] 1973). Good as it is, Togliatti's interpretation does not quite succeed in moving the reassessment beyond sociological factors (Togliatti [1950] 1973, esp. 93). For the most part, revisionist analysis tends to give little or no consideration to 1) what constitutional and governmental rules govern the political game and public problem solving more generally; 2) how and by whom the rules are supplied; and 3) how and by whom the rules can be changed. Critical features of Italian public life have been glossed over or ignored. These features will be discussed in subsequent chapters but, as a way of illustrating the argument, let me allude to some of them here.

Some Core Features of Constitutional and Institutional Design

Risorgimento and republican leaders expected that the rules of constitutional design they advanced and promoted, (between 1859 and 1865 and between 1944 and 1948 respectively) would ensure representative, responsible government and efficient, responsive public services as well as be formative of the citizenry that each set of rules implied. The task of fusing Italy's heterogeneous areas and population into a single "reawakened" great nation was assigned to parliamentary monarchy. This is, in fact, what Massimo D'Azeglio meant by his much quoted and much misunderstood good-faith epigram of 1860: "Now that we have made Italy, we must make Italians."

The Fascist experience and the Gramscian scholarship that accompanied it have led many scholars to forget that Count Camillo Benso di Cavour's sincerely held view of institutions as instrumental both for better decisions and for better people owes more to Alexis de Tocqueville's *Democracy in America* than to Machiavelli's *The Prince*. Cavour personally knew Tocqueville, whom he had met in Paris and London, and admired his work, for in Cavour's own words, it "throws more light than any other on the political questions of the future" (Cavour, cited in Jardin 1988, 228). In a similar fashion, anti-Fascist leaders, motivated in part by the constitutional knowledge advanced by Carlo Cattaneo's republican and federalist constitutional design as an unsuccessful Risorgimento alternative to the monarchy, expected the republican and democratic ideals of the Resistance to operate through the post-1946 republic they helped to design (but see also Bobbio 1995, chs. 12–14; Ornaghi 1979; Ruffilli 1979).

In spite of many differences, most creators of the kingdom and later the republic of Italy shared other aspirations and judgments to the point that these can be taken as standard rules in the crafting of constitutional arrangements in modern Italy. One such rule involves the nature of political representation. The constitutional design of both the kingdom and republic of Italy required elected officials to represent the nation or town as a whole, not just a particular party, constituency, or district; consequently, elected officials were expected to carry out their duties without ties to party position or constituency mandate. Another feature shared by kingdom and republic goes back to what might be called the Cartesian rationalism of the Enlightenment and has to do with the concept of the *stato di diritto* (the state based on law).

The *stato di diritto* bears commonalities with what in English is understood as "the rule of law." Both are concerned with the *ways* governments operate rather than with the *form* that governments take; both are part of the primacy of the rule of law over the rule of men in the long-standing political debate of whether good government is one where the rulers are good because they govern in accordance with the established laws, or one where the laws are good because the rulers are wise (Bobbio 1984, 138–9; Ornaghi and Parsi 1994). But these concepts are not quite the same. The *stato di diritto* differs from the rule of law in its extreme rationality assumption: it is the rule of law taken to its logical conclusion. The *stato di diritto* stands to the rule of law in the same way that the nontuistic (i.e., *not* taking into account the interests of others), self-interested, rational actor approach stands to methodological individualism (V. Ostrom 1997, 89).

The "state based on law" in Italy was designed to do several things all at once: 1) to insure a centralized system of rational-legal authority; 2) to apply to specific government aims and tasks general, universalistic, context-free principles; and 3) to limit the area of executive and administrative discretion. In the post-1946 liberal, democratic constitution, the *stato di diritto* took on even stronger egalitarian connotations to take precedence over, and even override, all other considerations, including the pursuit of individual and collective opportunities in the market and voluntary sectors. This is why, as a perceptive British observer of contemporary Italy has noted, "there are few countries in Europe where the law plays such an invasive and complex role in the administrative system as in Italy" (Hine 1993, 233). And this is so for seemingly good, democratic reasons.

David Hine points out that "subjecting the exercise of public power to tight legal controls was a guarantee against arbitrary executive action, but it also gave explicit authority to the actions of even the lowest level of officialdom and provided a uniform system of administration throughout the national territory" (Hine 1993, 234). Modelling and remodelling the machinery of Italian government has generally proceeded on the assumption that the self-interest of individuals cannot or should not be made to serve and advance the commonweal – in the famous words of Vittorio Emanuele Orlando, "all political, socio-logical, economic considerations should be expunged from the pure science of law" (quoted in Ferraresi 1982, 8). By expunging such con-siderations, the law would theoretically enable officials to treat similar cases similarly across time and space, putting an end to the vicious cycle of favouritism.

This way of designing institutions stands in sharp contrast to the American view, expressed in *The Federalist*, that "ambition must be made to counteract ambition" and that "the interest of the man must be connected with the constitutional rights of the place" (*The Federalist* [1788] n.d., 337). There is another contrast worth emphasizing. The *stato di diritto* does not include the practice of restraining governments through judicial review. The legislator – once the monarch, now an assembly of men and women – remains omnipotent and omnicompetent in the Italian system. Legislators coming from most Italian parties have almost always been "centralist," especially on the left; the only exceptions are the Popular (Catholic) Party before Fascism and the Partito d'Azione during the Second World War. "Parliament sets up the administration to operate in particular ways, so that, even assuming the administrative system genuinely wants to escape from its excessive legalism, it has great difficulty doing so" (Hine 1993, 234).

The rules or norms that govern political representation are both stacked and nested in the configurations of rules of the *stato di diritto* – the ways governments operate. What results are likely to flow from such a system of governance in action?

An initial answer is that the "formation of individuals" (*la formazione degli uomini*) has been generally neglected, with priority given to the view that good democratic laws can solve everything. As a result, Italy has a lot of laws and very bad institutions for the formation of individuals, like universities and police academies. It is true that Italian law does disenfranchise convicted persons and serious offenders for the right reasons: to punish those who have manifestly demonstrated through their voluntary acts an inability to exercise self-control and good judgment required in a liberal democracy. The disenfranchisement law sends an important signal to the general public about what consti-tutes good citizenship (cf., Manfredi 1998), but it is not enough to com-pensate for other laws. As a consequence, virtuous social norms do not stick; there is no social ostracism against rational actors who pursue nontuistic self-interest within governmental arrangements – hence, the call for a "virtuous governing class" (Ornaghi and Parsi 1994).

A more carefully thought-out answer is hard to find in much of the literature on Italian politics. This literature has, for the most part, given little or no attention to the basic logic of the Italian governance system; the links between the constitutional, governmental, and operational levels of governance; the relationship between the structure and performance of the public service system; the recourse to problem solving by legislation; and the validity of the inferences drawn from those processes — whether we are dealing with, say, local public services, land reform, urban and physical planning, or successive "wars on crime." Reference is usually made to widespread illegality and corruption without much concern for their logic in different settings and the extent to which laws and regulations of government serve, in Hobbes's words, as "traps for money" (Hobbes [1651] 1962, 254); to bureaucratic inefficiency without a prior understanding of the politics of bureaucracy and the resultant "bureaucratic free enterprise" (Tullock 1965); and even to an "Italy without government" without much consideration of the properties of the political institutions that Italy actually has. As a result, most academic knowledge is unenlightening about what more casual observers have wondered: how is it that "while millions of private enterprises have long been flourishing and any espresso bar is staffed with untiring countrymen who serve customers quickly, expertly, and cheerfully, the Italian state has for generations proved unable to train and motivate its myriad employees" (Hofmann 1990, 69).

At the same time, the matrix of virtue and vice among Italian public officials is much more complex than many observers have generally assumed. This point is brought out most dramatically by recent research (Steinberg 1990) on why Italian military officers and diplomats refused to cooperate in the Holocaust while their German opposite numbers obeyed orders. This way "the state which ruthlessly deprived patriotic and distinguished Italian Jews of rights, property and position under the 'racial laws' of 1938 turned into the saviour of alien Jews by 1941" (Steinberg 1990, 8). Steinberg's research emphasizes the fact that the civic virtues which made the Nazi war machine work efficiently and responsively are secondary virtues and cannot be equated with the laws of humanity, a free society, or even good government. Civic virtues, disanchored from their proper transcendental moorings, can serve evil causes.

Some Core Assumptions about Individual Behaviour

Academic knowledge is even less enlightening about ordinary citizens. People in Italy are generally viewed as flouting the law, breaking the rules, and acting as if laws and regulations of government do not apply to them. At best, they are said to think only of themselves and their families. Edward C. Banfield's well known characterization of "Montegrano" (Chiaromonte) villagers in 1954–55 as "amoral familists" still resonates because it seems to confirm the standard view of Italian behaviour and to fit a general class of collective-action problems characteristic of the Olson-Hardin-Downs Prisoners' Dilemma literature. This literature suggests that it is impossible for rational, self-interested creatures to cooperate – "rational man and irrational society" (Barry and Hardin 1982). As the work of Elinor Ostrom (1990) makes clear, such a view of society would be deeply disturbing if it were true. Increasingly, it has become evident that there are empirical and logical difficulties with such a view and that much of the Olson-Hardin-Downs Prisoners' Dilemma literature is not fully consistent with observed facts. Self-interested individuals who repeatedly interact with each other (with an indefinite time horizon) may engage in cooperative behaviour if they can observe each other's actions and place a sufficiently high value on future transactions. At the same time, Banfield did not consider the possibility that residents of Chiaromonte (or Montegrano as he called it) could be moral familists, could think of themselves and others at the same time. As we shall see in chapters 8 and 9, his thesis is not fully consistent with the history of the town of Chiaromonte; it is an exalted generalization based on a misconstruction of local life (on peasant societies more generally, see Robert Wade 1988, 1–9).

Still, there is something to the reputation that Italians have of not following the law (see also recent research by CENSIS as reported in *Corriere della Sera* 1998a). But this is not the whole truth, or, rather, the matrix of virtue and vice among ordinary Italians is much more complex than the stereotype suggests. Again, one must go beyond prevailing academic knowledge to search for the full story.

As the one-time BBC Rome correspondent, Matt Frei, recounted, "(W)hen I first moved to Italy in 1991, I discovered to my horror that the Italians had been misunderstood and I had been misled. Italy turned out to be hair-splittingly legalistic, a country slavishly obsessed with petty rules and officialdom" (Frei 1995, 84). It was not long before Frei discovered that "even the enjoyable and deceptively simple act of drinking a frothy cappuccino" is in Italy "a minefield of [social] regulations" that outsiders tend to ignore at their peril. Frei found that enjoying a cappuccino in any Italian establishment involves at least six social norms. It is the tourists, and not the natives, who break those social norms. Frei's conclusion was that "the Italians distinguish [between] rules created by society, which are there to be observed, and laws imposed by the state, which are there to be broken" (Frei 1995, 86).

Frei's distinction is insightful. It is a useful reminder that the legislator is not the source of all laws in society, that rules of interpersonal conduct and problem solving exist apart from, and even prior to, state rules (*ubi societas, ibi ius*) and that even people in a unitary state like Italy generally live under a *multi*constitutional system of rules (e.g., Grossi 1996; E. Ostrom 1989). But Frei's reference to state laws needs the qualification suggested by Salvatore Sechi at a recent conference on "Deconstructing Italy" at the University of California at Berkeley. Sechi noted that, "together with a disregard for rules [of officialdom], Italians have a quasi-fetishistic cult for them" (Sechi 1995, 6). He further noted:

With a stupefying zeal, Italians line up diligently for long hours in front of those places of torture and insanity that are public offices and apply the laws and official regulations, including even those that are clearly iniquitous, such as the tax laws and the health regulations. In the summer of 1993, "they paid the tax for the family doctor, not only without knowing to whom this applied – the dead or living, newborns or ghosts – but also after having been carefully reassured by the ministry concerned that the omission of payment would not have led to penalties of any kind." They demonstrate the same attitude of indifferent heroism, a quasi-religious resigned acceptance, when faced with continuous tax increases on gas (already 77.5 percent of the price), scores of heavy property taxes, and an obligation to admit to possessing exotic animals ... Meanwhile, the minister of finance has made it known to the honest taxpayers, oppressed by an implacable treasury, that they can sleep easy because he has determined the taxability of the illegal income of architects not registered in the professional register, unlicensed merchants, professionals, business people employed in black market activities, and usurers. (Sechi 1995, 6–7; the inside quotation is from Eugenio Scalfari 1994)

Sechi is really asking why Italians do not revolt against the tax system. The answer is that some, like the Lega Nord, try to, while others, like Forza Italia, advocate a reduction in taxes and blame the left for not reducing them enough.

When all necessary allowances for the colourful language and the impressionistic and anecdotal nature of the observations, including the dubious reference to Italians lining up *diligently*, are duly made, one important fact remains. Both Frei and Sechi draw attention to pivotal distinctions not often encountered in the academic literature. In brief, the central question is not whether or not Italian citizens flout the law: they do. The central question is whether it is perfectly rational to follow the law or not, or why Italians sometimes comply with and sometimes disobey the demands of government.

Recent cross-national research by Margaret Levi suggests that citizens are more likely to comply and even give active consent when they perceive government as procedurally fair in both decision making and implementation processes and when they believe other citizens are also doing their share (M. Levi 1997a). Levi's work highlights the centrality of institutional design in understanding how the game of life is organized and played. As we shall see in chapters 8 and 9, this point has been almost completely overlooked in the Italian case, especially by culturalists, including Gabriel Almond and Sidney Verba in their famous study on civic culture (see Barry 1978, 48–52). We have allowed stereotypes expressed in abstract ideology or theoretics to prevent us from seeing what people do in constructing their own opportunities. If some concepts do not work, if the institutions are inefficient, why should people trust them? People will make their own adaptations. These may become rather perverse when officialdom thinks it can govern but people go their own way, as the history of the mafia suggests.

In the 1960s and 1970s, social scientists and historians spent a great deal of time constructing ideal-type models of mafia and other such groups. Evidently unconstrained by the lack of knowledge of how such groups actually developed in different towns, they gave scarcely any consideration to the nature of product illegality; the challenge of finding and maintaining "partners in crime"; the structure of criminal opportunities in the complexly nested areas of property rights, tenancy arrangements, law enforcement agencies, and communal and provincial rules; and, more generally, to governmental arrangements for determining, enforcing, and altering the legal basis of those social institutions. To borrow from what Richard F. Hamilton said about Michel Foucault's misrepresentation of the history of punishment, an entire school of "mafia history" has been based on patent nonfacts (Hamilton 1996, 178). As a result, the question that was to preoccupy Giovanni Falcone, the Sicilian antimafia magistrate killed in 1992, was beyond the grasp of this school: "Why is it that men like others, some even endowed with real intellectual abilities, are compelled to devise for themselves a criminal career in order to survive with dignity?" (Falcone 1991, 72).

With our empiricist epistemology, we have increasingly adopted a positivist, unproblematic view of the monopoly of state powers, misconstructing the social and political reality of Italian public monopolies and regulations. Thus we have, at times quite self-consciously, 1) declined to offer value judgments about the legitimacy and validity of those powers, in the north as in the south; 2) neglected to investigate the extent to which the basic objectives of the constitutional, institutional, and other policy designs and law contradict one another; 3) avoided considerations of the incentive structures of public institutions; 4) failed to consider the possibility that Italians may be "locked" into a system of governance that produces outcomes (e.g., corruption) that Italians themselves do not value very highly; 5) experienced difficulties in evaluating efforts of people to extricate themselves from or break the constraints of such vicious circles; and 6) ignored that people, in some basic sense, build their own social and political realities and that what officialdom in the formal regime may do is only part of the story. The political upheavals that followed the judicial investigations of the early 1990s exacerbated these intellectual difficulties.

Quite a number of chronological narratives now exist on the fateful events between 1992 and 1996. As I have argued elsewhere (Sabetti 1995), even some thoughtful attempts at blending comparative politics and chronology remain largely examples of the "instant replay of politics" in which journalists excel. A case in point is *The Crisis of the Italian State: From the Origins of the Cold War to the Fall of Berlusconi*, by Patrick McCarthy (1995), a professor of European Studies at the Johns Hopkins University Center in Bologna. In his preface, McCarthy alludes to four attempts to found or refound the state: the Risorgimento; the Fascist experience; the post-1943 experience leading to the First Republic; and the period between 1992 and Berlusconi's coming to power in 1994. Then he adds, "this obliges me to undertake the daunting task of defining what the 'problem' of the state is and how it emerged from the Unification period" (McCarthy 1995, xxiii). Unfortunately, he left this task largely undone.

Thus the other, more general objective of the book is to define exactly what is the problem of the state and to explain how it emerged from the unification period and continued with the birth of the Italian republic in 1946. That crafting (and recrafting) governmental institutions has often not produced the anticipated results in no way detracts from the attempt. Indeed, this is why the study of post-1946 Italian politics can be treated as a veritable school for good government. In tracing how poor government performance has been an unintended consequence of various attempts to craft institutions and policies of good government, we learn which factors facilitated or hindered the various efforts and appreciate that the paradoxical view of Italy is not fully consistent with observed facts. The entire inquiry is framed around these questions. Let us see how.

THE SCOPE OF THE INQUIRY

The objectives of this book require that we do three things. First, we need to pay close attention to the design characteristics of Italian political institutions – hence the need to go back to the making of a united Italy and consider the constitutional knowledge available at that time. Second, we need to examine the extent to which the working of those institutions yielded consequences consistent with the expectations of their founders, designers, or reformers – that is, persons with a strong interest in making those institutions work as they should. This in turn requires knowledge of the characteristic results that flow from institutional frameworks. If we can arrive at some initial assessment of these results and pursue an examination of why the institutional framework produced them, then we will be in a better position to account for how poor government performance can result from the search for good government.

It is here that the distinction between different levels of analysis offered by public, rational choice institutionalism is helpful. This school of thought, which draws in part on nineteenth-century Italian contributions to fiscal theory and public finance (Buchanan 1960, 24–74; Sabetti 1990; Weinberger 1940), provides the analytical tools to differentiate between the rules of constitutional design and the processes of government that come after, in order to better understand the structure of positive and perverse incentives of different institutional arrangements and to unpack the meaning of good government across time and at different levels of analysis – the constitutional, governmental, and operational levels of governance – all while maintaining the interrelatedness of the issues treated sequentially. It is in this sense that the book is organized like an intricate set of Chinese boxes, which in disassembling and reassembling reveals yet more features than previously anticipated. The search for good government by Italians is to be understood as embedded in several layers of institutional arrangements.

This inquiry does not confine itself to a "core" built on extreme rationality assumptions. Rather, it seeks to include different intellectual perspectives in the art and science of institutional design pursued in English over the last three or four decades and earlier traditions that can be found in the work of Carlo Cattaneo as well as other nineteenth-century Italian analysts like those belonging to the "Italian school of fiscal theory" (Buchanan 1960). In giving complementarity to diverse intellectual perspectives, the argument that follows is closer to that advanced by Tocqueville, Vincent Ostrom, and Stephen L. Elkin than to the analytical narratives advanced, through the use of rational choice and game theory models, by Robert H. Bates, Avner Greif, Margaret Levi, Jean-Laurent Rosenthal, and Barry Weingast in their most recent work (Bates et al. 1998; see also Golden 1997) – without, however, allowing the logic of inquiry to become disanchored from rational choice institutionalism.

The evidentiary basis of the inquiry draws on material of diverse sorts: archival historical research; primary sources, such as the memorandum to Cavour by the leading Sicilian political economist Francesco Ferrara, Cattaneo's texts, and government documents; the results of field work conducted through participant observation and elite interviews, especially in the regions of Sicily, Calabria, Basilicata, Apulia, Lombardy, Emilia-Romagna, Lazio, and Piedmont during the 1980s and 1990s; and the results of other people's research. The opportunity to take part in the third annual meeting held by the Center for Studies and Documentation on Common Properties of the University of Trento in November 1998 allowed me to round out my field research and to subject my argument to final scrutiny by colleagues, before closure. Some chapters, like 6 and 7, draw in part on newspaper accounts of the period. The study also draws on experience and knowledge accumulated over a sustained period of research in Italy, meeting one important methodological point, or "pressing need," raised by Graham T. Allison in his explanation of the Cuban Missile Crisis. He noted: "The use of public documents, newspapers, interviews of participants and discussion with close observers of participants to piece together the bits of information available is an art. Transfer of these skills from the fingertips of artists to a form that can guide ... students of foreign policy is ... [a] pressing need" (Allison 1971, 181). For this reason, the discussion in the text is not exclusively based on empiricist epistemology. It is also grounded in an interpretive and analytical epistemology of the kind that other intellectual artisans, including legal scholars, political theorists, and philosophers, often employ. The study, then, advances both an empirical and analytical argument about how and what to look for in comparative institutional analysis.

THE ORGANIZATION OF THE BOOK

The narrative is divided into four parts. Part 1 consists of chapters 2 and 3 and focuses on constitutional knowledge and the choice of one constitutional regime over other possibilities. These chapters examine how good government was understood at the level of constitutional design. By treating the creation of the Italian state as an experiment in constitutional choice, it becomes easier to understand the challenge confronting the protagonists of the Risorgimento and the extent to which the debate about what constituted a desirable political order articulated an awareness of the consequences associated with the different ways of organizing a united Italy. The presentation of Carlo Cattaneo's federalist ideas in chapter 3 affords an opportunity to appreciate why the "constitutional design that did not happen," with its emphasis on local as well as national democracy, has continued to have empirical and theoretical salience to the present day. Local self-governance constitutes an important feature of any larger democratic political order, both in the delivery of public services and in the political education and ways of life of free people. This analytical theme frames the analysis in part 2. In turn, parts 2, 3, and 4 will also serve to make even more self-evident why it is important to go back, as the starting point of this inquiry, to the original discussion about different ways to organize a united Italy.

Part 2, consisting of chapters 4 and 5, seeks to show the extent to which institutional learning and the accompanying post-1946 reforms are nested in the constitutional issues raised in part 1. These chapters suggest why there is reason to expect "pathologies" in the distribution of government services and in the political way of life of ordinary citizens. Institutional weakness and failure follow from contradictions in the basic objectives of the highly centralized state administration and decision making, and the politicization of local governments by national political parties. The comparison of Bologna and Naples and the use of detailed master plans for Rome develop and illustrate the argument, as do the various reform efforts aimed at improving services and increasing citizen participation.

Part 3 captures moments in the government war on crime as a "fight for good government." Chapters 6 and 7 suggest that the design characteristics of the administration of justice contradict one another and, in fact, defeat efforts to tackle big issues all at once. These problematics bring us back to the prediction in 1860 by the Sicilian political economist Francesco Ferrara, discussed in chapter 2; Ferrara advised Cavour that if questions of self-governance were not addressed properly in the making of a united Italy, Sicily could become "the Ireland of Italy." The narrative reveals the extent to which the war on crime is embedded in constitutional and governmental issues addressed in the previous chapters.

The resurgence of "political culture" and path-dependent explanations brought about by Robert D. Putnam's *Making Democracy Work* has lent additional credence to Edward C. Banfield's old thesis about determinants of backwardness. Chapters 8 and 9 in part 4 examine Banfield's and Putnam's studies and suggest why those efforts hinder rather than facilitate understanding of why public institutions do not work as they should. In so doing, part 4 also anticipates possible objections to the institutional emphasis of the entire project.

As noted in the beginning, one of the volume's most important claims is that the sheer complexity of governmental structures makes it very difficult, perhaps impossible, to bring about good government. Even so, we are left with the question, would the mess be even bigger than if people did not try at all to search for good government? Chapter 10 considers this question as it reiterates the principal claims of the study, examines those claims in light of evidence from other democracies, and speculates on how these claims might influence the current effort to reform Italian politics and administration.

PART ONE

Constitutional Knowledge and Alternative Constitutional Designs in the Making of Italy

2 The Creation of the Italian State

In examining the history of European state making, social scientists have increasingly drawn attention to the fact that the victory of unitary principles of organization has obscured the extent to which federalist and non-absolutist principles were alternative design criteria in the formation of states in modern Europe (e.g., Ertman 1997, ch. 4; Spruyt 1994, ch. 7; Tilly 1975). Centralized commonwealths emerged from relatively autonomous, uncoordinated, and lesser political structures; but as Charles Tilly is wont to recall, "nothing could be more detrimental to an understanding of this whole process than the old liberal conception of European history as the gradual creation and extension of political rights ... Far from promoting [representative] institutions, early state-makers struggled against them" (Tilly 1975, 37; cf., Scott 1998).

The unification of Italy in the nineteenth century was also a victory of centralized principles, but the Risorgimento differed from earlier European state making in several respects. First, the prospect of a single political regime for the entire Italian peninsula and islands generated considerable debate as to which constitutional design or model of government was best suited to a population that had lived under separate and diverse political regimes for more than thirteen hundred years. Second, the unitary system that emerged was the product of a conscious choice between alternative regimes. Third, the creation of the Italian state was indeed intended to realize, promote, and advance political liberation and good government, or what Tilly calls "the old liberal conception of European history"

(1975, 37). Finally, federalist principles of organization were such a central part of the Italian political tradition that the victory of unitary principles failed to eclipse them completely. Indeed, federalist principles gained renewed support well after Carlo Cattaneo's death in 1869, as government performance began to deviate radically from expectations. The establishment of regional and neighbourhood governments by the 1970s and the debate inside parliament and out by the end of the 1990s (about federalist solutions to the collapse of the postwar system of rule) attest to the enduring strength and validity of nonunitary political forms (e.g., Ciuffoletti 1994; Hine 1996a; Mariucci 1997; Miglio 1994; Newell 1998; Sabella and Urbinati 1994; Tremonti and Vitaletti 1994; Vassallo 1998). Cattaneo's defeated constitutional alternative is the topic of chapter 3. The rest of this chapter considers what constitutional knowledge was available at the time of unification and what resulted from the process of unification itself. Taken together, the two chapters allow us to begin to fulfil a central objective of the project sketched in the introductory chapter: to define the problem of the state and explain how it emerged from the struggle for the liberation and unification of Italy.

The analytical narrative begins with a discussion of what is gained by treating Italian unification as an experiment in crafting institutions of good government. This is followed by an overview of the question of Italian unity as it appeared in the early nineteenth century. We then examine the first phase of the constitutional discussion in terms of the proposals advanced by Giuseppe Mazzini and federalist writers. Next, we turn to the conditions that led to the eclipse of federalist alternatives. A discussion of Francesco Ferrara's memorandum to Count Camillo Benso di Cavour at the time of the liberation of Sicily from Bourbon rule in 1860 serves to convey the second phase of the constitutional debate. We conclude with a discussion of the triumph of centralization.

THE RISORGIMENTO AS LABORATORY OF CONSTITUTIONAL DESIGNS

Examination of what constitutional knowledge was available to Risorgimento leaders and opinion makers serves to extend our own knowledge of how the issues of centralist versus federalist arrangements were raised and what factors weighted the constitutional outcome in the direction of centralization. It enables us to explore what arguments were advanced in support of particular proposals for Italian unification and to indicate whether the process of constitutional choice articulated an awareness of the consequences associated with the different constitutional designs. The fact that certain modes of governing were *not* chosen by the creators of the Italian state sustains the argument that states and constitutional designs are created as the result of decisions, not by determined and closed processes – in essence, reviewing the choices made by Risorgimento leaders allows us to treat the making of Italy as an experiment in constitutional choice and design.

As noted in chapter 1, to treat Italian unification as an experiment in constitutional design accords well with a growing area of political inquiry in the art and science of institutional design variously known as new economic institutionalism, new constitutionalism, and institutional analysis and development (e.g., M. Levi 1988; E. Ostrom 1990; V. Ostrom 1997; Soltan and Elkin 1996; Sproule-Jones 1993). Italian scholars made important contributions to this tradition in the nineteenth century (see Buchanan 1960, 1975; Sabetti 1975, 1990; Weinberger 1940). Unfortunately, this is not how most students of Italian history and politics have approached the Risorgimento.

Most interpretations of the making of Italy can be grouped in two broad kinds of explanatory methodology, both of questionable merit. One has tended to give inadequate consideration to the relationship between the principles and forms used to fashion a united Italy and the consequences that followed. The other has tended to appraise the Risorgimento project in light of some variants of classic, rationalistic, liberal philosophy unconstrained by time and place contingencies and the complex situations in which individuals find themselves. For different reasons, then, the forms that the Italian political system took have been assumed to have had little effect on performance. As a result, most analysts have turned to cultural, social, or economic variables as the critical factors that explain gaps between expectations and performance – contributing to the paradoxical view of Italy. As we shall see in the subsequent chapters, this polarity between Italians as a people of resourceful individuals and Italy as a polity in shambles has generally been accepted with little or no appreciation of the difficulties of ensuring that political institutions work as they should.

Spencer Di Scala has observed that, "like all great historical events, the Risorgimento soon became a tool for different political groups," burdening that age with the mistakes and preconceptions that followed in subsequent eras (Di Scala 1995, 114). So the theme of failure and the resultant disillusionment have endured. Cavour's pragmatic liberalism has not fared well, either – especially in English (see Johnson 1985). It is easier to subject Cavour's pragmatic liberalism to harsh criticism and to describe him as "a cross between Peel and Machiavelli" than to study the institutional choices that government actors like him confronted – at the same time recognizing that "no doubt all successful liberal statesmen have something of this mixture [i.e., Peel and Machiavelli] and must sometimes be unprincipled in their liberalism" (Mack Smith 1971, 75). It has been much easier to reduce the Risorgimento to a Gramscian "failed revolution" than to understand whether or not at that time, in the 1850s and 1860s, there was even the prospect of a true agricultural and industrial workers' revolution capable of producing a united Italy. Equally, there is a need to understand why in 1860 a united Italy *à la* Cattaneo could not be established either.

The reflections of Denys Hays may be quoted at some length to indicate the paradigmatic problem that has plagued the study of Italian political development:

What do we mean by the history of a country? We mean the way that country has acquired self-consciousness, and the play of interests, political, social, cultural, within the perimeter established by language, by geography and by relations, acquisitive or concessive, with its neighbours. Put like that it sounds very vague indeed. But I think the statement covers Britain, France and many other sovereign states, where a territory, a language, and a tradition of government are all roughly coterminous with accepted or "natural" frontiers of some kind. It is, of course, true that we falsify the history of England and France in the eleventh and twelfth centuries if we concentrate our attention solely on the ultimate unity. At that time the realities of power were local or at best regional and there was no obvious linguistic or geographical frontier. But the distortion is less damaging in treating England or France than it would be if applied elsewhere, for by the thirteenth century a rough kind of political centralization was effective. This preface is, I feel, worth making before considering the problem of Italian unity.

Since 1870 Italy has been a country with a single more or less sovereign power (my qualification refers to the pope, not to the Republic of San Marino) and its history has been the story of central government, of regional reactions and regional influences within the framework of central government, and of a foreign policy backed by a single national army. No wonder that in preparation for this historians were active in proclaiming Italian unity and no wonder that since 1870 they have been writing Italian history in the way French or English historians write their history. Yet this approach does not in fact correspond with the realities. No history of Italy can be written on the French or British model which does not seriously distort the true picture. Thus, in a sentence, the basic problem of Italian history is that before the nineteenth century there is no Italian history, at least not in the same sense as we talk of English or French history ... It will be noted that I am illogically accepting the need to explain the diversity of Italy as though unity were the norm: so powerful is the influence of the model histories of sovereign states. (Hays 1961, 26–7; see also Lovett 1979, 102–4)

It takes a student of Renaissance Italy to recognize fully the danger of interpreting Italian history through the model histories of sovereign states – as though centralized government and administration were the norm, and political diversity antithetical to a common country (*paese*) and identity. To anticipate and dispel initial misunderstanding, let me emphasize a chief point made in this chapter and the next. The glaring contrast often perceived between the supreme cultural achievements of the Italians and their political weakness since the fifteenth century – pointedly portrayed by Francesco Guicciardini (1651) as by Jacob Burckhardt in 1860 – did not *necessarily* have to be resolved through the creation of a unitary system of government and administration in the nineteenth century. As we shall see in chapter 3, there are serious flaws in Guicciardini's and Burckhardt's arguments: a unitary system was not the sole model of successful government available to Italians, no matter what the model histories of European sovereign states suggested; patriots in the Risorgimento did not have to emulate the standard European great power model in the making of united Italy. More recently, Vincent Ostrom has put matters this way:

To adopt a strong central government because that was the key feature of the warring powers that threatened Italian autonomy would have been appropriate only if Italy sought to engage in imperial thrusts in relation to neighbouring countries in the Mediterranean world. Other European nations, including the Netherlands and Switzerland, also confronted much the same problem in dealing with the imperial aspirations of Austria, France, Germany, and Russia. Neither the Netherlands nor Switzerland chose the strong centralized government approach. Italy as a country of great cities had more in common with the Netherlands and Switzerland than the great imperial powers of the nineteenth and twentieth centuries. (V. Ostrom, 1998)

Thus, the discussion of the Risorgimento as a laboratory of constitutional design and choice represents a basic redirection in political analysis. It is a move away from what Giovanni Sartori once described as "a sociological reduction of politics" (Sartori 1969) to a consideration of political ideas and institutions as independent variables and determinants of human behaviour. To draw attention to the formative role of ideas and institutional arrangements, including property rights, is not to deny that the creation of the Italian state reinforced the political position of large proprietors, both rural and urban. Still, the inference found in much of the post-1946 historical and social science literature that Italian liberalism during the Risorgimento reflected a movement of the middle class to gain control of society is hard to sustain (see Greenfield 1965, 263). As we shall see later in this chapter, and in chapter 9, how the unification of Italy came about – and what consequences followed – was neither predetermined nor actually planned in advance (see esp. Mack Smith 1950). As this chapter makes clear, the making of Italy was not merely a debate between different schools of constitutional thought; the frame and context of the debate were as important as the alternative constitutional designs themselves.

There is considerable controversy among historians as to when the Risorgimento began and ended. Some analysts date the beginning from as far back as the writings on Italy by Dante or Machiavelli, and the end to the annexation of Rome in 1870, or even Trieste in 1918. But it seems clear that the movement for Italian unification reached its culmination with the formation of the Kingdom of Italy between 1859 and 1865. For our purpose, we can identify two broad phases in the debate about what system of government was best suited to a united Italy. The first phase, encompassing the period from the Napoleonic era to the revolutions of 1848, is associated with the spread of nationalism and liberalism. The second phase, ranging from the collapse of the 1848 revolts to the proclamation of the Kingdom of Italy in 1861, is associated with the hegemony of Piedmont in the unification movement. The first round of debate was followed by the eclipse of federalism; the second, by the victory of centralization. Before considering these phases, let us situate the question of Italian unity in the context of its own time.

THE QUESTION OF ITALIAN UNITY

Three distinct but interrelated issues made up "the Italian question" as it emerged in the nineteenth century. First, though Italy had always been a territorial unit as well as a country *(paese)* (Galli della Loggia 1998; Romano 1994), it remained divided into several states – often small and isolated – for many centuries. As late as the eighteenth century, the Italian peninsula was, in Franco Venturi's apt characterization, "still a sort of microcosm of all Europe" where, more than in Germany, it was possible to compare and contrast "a great variety of political forms and varying constitutions – theocracy, monarchies, dukedoms and republics, from Venice to San Marino. The Italian setting was fertile ground for examining the clash between kings and republics

Table 1
Italy after the Congress of Vienna

State	Ruler (in 1846)	Population
Piedmont-Sardinia (Kingdom)	Charles Albert of Savoy	4,916,084
Lombardy-Venetia	Emperor Ferdinand of Austria	5,000,000
Tuscany (Grand duchy)	Leopold II (first cousin of Austrian emperor)	1,534,740
Modena (Duchy)	Francesco IV (Austrian Este)	575,410
Parma (Duchy)	Empress Marie Louise (Napoleon's widow, Austrian)	497,343
Lucca (Duchy)	Charles-Louis of Bourbon	165,198
San Marino	Republic	7,800
The Papal States	Pope Pius IX	2,898,115
The Two Sicilies	Ferdinand II (Spanish Bourbon)	6,382,706

Source: G.F.H. and J. Berkeley 1936, vol. 2, 3

and the tension between Utopia and Reform in the Enlightenment" (Venturi 1971, 20).

During the Napoleonic period, the various monarchies, principalities, and republics vanished – either annexed by France or consolidated in realms ruled by Napoleon's relatives. In 1815, the Congress of Vienna redivided the whole peninsula into eight or nine states, according to "legitimist" and absolutist principles. The republic of Genoa was given to the Piedmontese ruler, the king of Sardinia. The republic of Venice was annexed by Austria into its north Italian province of Lombardy, making up the kingdom of Lombardy-Venetia. Much of central Italy was returned to papal rule. Southern Italy and Sicily became the Kingdom of the Two Sicilies under the Neapolitan Bourbons. The system of centralized government and administration introduced by the French became a useful instrument to solidify or extend absolutist rule. Only in the Austrian kingdom in northern Italy did there continue to be a large measure of local and even regional self-government after 1815. Table 1, showing Italian states as they appeared in 1846, indicates how the people of Italy were ruled by different sovereigns.

Second, the division of Italy reached at the Congress of Vienna was part of a larger settlement for the maintenance of European peace. The "trustee" of that European peace in Italy was Austria, which not only possessed Lombardy-Venetia, but also controlled the duchies of Tuscany, Parma, and Modena, and had its military forces positioned to suppress insurrections as far south as Sicily. Moreover, the central Italian states or legations held by the papacy were deemed essential prerequisites and signs of the universal patrimony of the church. The question of Italian unity was not just an internal Italian matter. It was a European and international question as well.

Third, the political divisions which had existed on the Italian peninsula for more than thirteen hundred years had given rise to and supported a strong attachment to community and regional affairs as well as an extraordinarily diverse set of social institutions, cultures, and languages. Estimates of the diffusion of the Italian language are contradictory. Some have suggested that, as late as 1850, Latin and not Italian was the *lingua franca* of Italy. One source suggests that, by the early 1860s, only about 160,000 out of twenty million people could speak the official language; another estimate for the same period gives a higher number, 600,000 (Asor Rosa 1975; Mack Smith 1974; 1968, 70–3). Still others have suggested a greater diffusion of Italian at the time, possibly as high as about two million (Romano 1994, 15). Less subject to dispute are the two most important dimensions of the political consciousness of the Italian people – in Antonio Gramsci's disparaging characterization, "municipal particularism and Catholic cosmopolitanism" (cited in Gerschenkron 1962, 92).

The complex and at times turbulent political experience in the different Italian states has led some foreign observers and rulers like Metternich to argue, often for self-serving reasons, that "the case of Italy was entirely different from that of Poland or Greece or any other of the nations fighting to win their freedom. Italy was not a conquered nation; she had never been a nation at all. The problem before her was to convert her into a nation" (cited in Berkeley and Berkeley 1936, xxii). This view has been dismissed by most Italian scholars as a misstatement at best. Historian Ruggiero Romano (1994) has put matters forcefully. He argues that the idea of "nation" as we have come to understand the term did not fully emerge until the eighteenth century, so it cannot be retrospectively applied to advance the argument about the absence of an Italian nation in history. Even in the eighteenth century, the idea of nation did not have the connotations it was to absorb in the nineteenth century; it was "a weak concept" used to characterize the Swiss, whose country was hardly the model of a nation-state. Italians have had an identity as a people and a *paese* for twenty centuries (Romano 1994, 3–29; see also Galli della Loggia 1998). As Luigi Salvatorelli put matters earlier, "centuries before the formation of a unified Italian state, there had existed an Italian people" (1970, 7).

What seems clear is that neither the nature of the country nor the political consciousness of its inhabitants could be ignored or denied without peril. A resolution of "the Italian question" that would respect and advance liberation and self-governance *all at once* was an exceedingly difficult undertaking. Whether Italians striving to end the long period of disunity and to live free of subjugation and even exploitation by absolutist rule should emulate the standard great power model of nation-state or not was problematic.

UNITARISM VS. FEDERALISM: THE FIRST PHASE OF THE CONSTITUTIONAL DEBATE

The Napoleonic hegemony over the Italian peninsula between 1796 and 1814 helped to foster political nationalism – the idea that some kind of Italian nation existed already, or ought to exist – but even in northern Italy, where French influence was most pronounced, pan-Italian nationalism had very few advocates. The Congress of Vienna, by treating the Italian peninsula as a convenient spoil of war, also generated dissatisfaction about foreign absolutist government. However, the rebellions against governmental oppression and the spread of liberalism did not necessarily coincide with or strengthen a single version of Italian nationalism. For example, as late as 1847, liberals in Naples and Sicily had little, if any, part in the development of a pan-Italian nationalism. Sicilian liberals wished to end absolutist rule and to free Sicily from "the yoke of Naples." Neapolitan liberals wished to end absolutist rule without, however, breaking up the territorial integrity of the newly established Kingdom of the Two Sicilies (Cortese 1956). The first phase of the constitutional debate took place essentially among Septentrionals who, with the exception of Giuseppe Mazzini (1805–72), may be described more as "men of ideas" than "men of action."

A Unitary Republic

In 1796, following Napoleon's occupation of Lombardy, the French administration at Milan offered a prize for an essay on what type of government best suited a united Italy. The prize was won by an advocate of a unitary republic, Melchiorre Gioia (extracts of his essay in Mack Smith 1968, 11–14; see also Ciuffoletti 1994, 11). His essay ruled out federal principles of organization because a system of government built on such design criteria was presumed to be conducive to bad, rather than good, government. A framework of government based on federalist ideas would be "inevitably slow when it comes to planning, slower still when it comes to carrying plans out, and only too ready for disagreement" (Gioia, cited in Mack Smith 1968, 14). A unitary republic was, instead, expected both to overcome disunity, understood as regional and municipal loyalties, and to act with speed and dispatch.

Mazzini proposed a system of government similar to that of Gioia. But unlike Gioia's proposal, Mazzini's was not just a literary exercise. In 1831, Mazzini founded a secret patriotic society, Young Italy, to prepare the grounds for "the Italian revolution" that would free Italians from the tyranny of princes. Though it was only around 1853 that Mazzini organized a "party of action" to continue the earlier work, he devoted his life to the cause of Italian independence and unification. From the perspective of federalist republican friends like Carlo Cattaneo ([1852] 1952, 2: 169), the problem with Mazzini was that he gave scant consideration to questions of constitutional design. This was largely because Mazzini thought that only "the world of action" – armed insurrection and politics – could automatically generate such a republic. For all his emphasis on the "rights of man" (cited in Mack Smith 1994, 129–30), Mazzini held firm to the view that the making of a united Italy and the realization of national sovereignty took precedence over a concern for what type of constitutional order could best foster liberty and self-government (see Della Peruta 1958, 14). Mazzini was a nationalist more than a republican; he was certainly not as committed a republican as Cattaneo. From this vantage point, it becomes easier to understand why by 1859 Mazzini and many of his republican followers could be found supporting unification efforts under the Savoy monarchy.

There is no denying Mazzini's substantial achievements, however. First, "the immediate result of Mazzini's teaching was to fan to a blaze the embers of Italian nationality" (King 1899, 1:132). Second, his nationalist teachings qualified the nature of the divine rights of Italian kings – so much so, in fact, that Victor Emmanuel II's eventual enthronement as king of Italy carried with it the recognition that this was so "by the will of the people" and not merely by an accident of birth, Deo gratias. Unlike British monarchs, the monarchs of united Italy styled themselves as kings by the grace of God and by the will of the people. Mack Smith has noted that this latter recognition was an affirmation, however diluted, of the principles of democracy and nationality that Mazzini had championed for thirty years (Mack Smith 1994, 143). The same principle was reaffirmed in 1946, when the will of the people was summoned, again, to decide in a referendum about the future of the Savoy monarchy.

A Confederation of Princes

Vincenzo Gioberti's book *On the Moral and Civil Primacy of the Italians*, published in 1843 at Brussels where the author (1801–52) lived in exile, challenged the idea of a unitary republic. Gioberti took particular issue with Mazzini's plans, as they appeared to promote or justify the forced creation of a united Italy:

It is madness to think that Italy, which has been divided for centuries, can be peacefully united in a single unitary state; and to want this brought about by force is a crime ... A united state would be almost impossible to create even at enormous cost, let alone keep in being. I would go even further and say that a centralized Italy is against the sheer facts of history and the character of our people; at least all the available facts go to show this. (Gioberti, quoted in Mack Smith 1968, 84)

Gioberti proposed a league of existing states under "the moderating authority of the pontiff" (quoted in Mack Smith 1968, 82). This neo-Guelph confederation was expected to achieve several goals: 1) to minimize and eventually remove foreign interference; 2) to make Italy a European power; and 3) to "eliminate or at least reduce the differences in weights, measures, currencies, customs duties, speech and systems of commercial and civil administration which so wretchedly and meanly divide the various provinces" (quoted in Mack Smith 1968, 83).

Unlike Mazzini's writings, Gioberti's work became very popular throughout the Italian peninsula. As a British historian observed, "the clergy were won by its Catholic tone; the nationalist statesmen by its praise of the Savoy princes" (King 1899, 1:155). It was, however, too much to hope that Italian nationalists and domestic and foreign princes would be prepared to accept an Italian confederation under the papacy. As a result, Gioberti's plan remained just that; before long, Gioberti himself abandoned it.

Yet Gioberti's work played an important part in advancing knowledge and encouraging debate over which constitutional design and framework of governance were best suited to Italy. First, the appeal to the "moral and civil primacy of the Italians" was not new (Romano 1994, 93–108), but Gioberti's work gave it renewed standing and, in the process, redirected adherents to the cause of the Risorgimento. Second, by challenging Mazzini's unitary republic, Gioberti's work oriented the constitutional debate toward nonunitary principles of organization.

A Customs Union

In his book *On the Hopes of Italy* (excerpts in Mack Smith 1968, 84–92), published at Paris a few months after the appearance of *On the Moral and Civil Primacy of the Italians*, Cesare Balbo (1785–1853) shared Gioberti's critical views about centralized government and adminstration. But Balbo rejected Gioberti's proposal of a neo-Guelph confederation, since the pope was likely to be the enemy of a larger Italian political union. Balbo's work was a kind of manifesto for a circle of Piedmontese intellectuals and politicians who held the view that independence must be sought before all else – even before unity and constitutional liberty – and that its attainment would come only when Austria voluntarily gave up her possessions and spheres of influence in Italy (King 1899, 1:157). In preparation for that event, Balbo, who was prime minister of Piedmont in 1848, pressed for free trade and a customs union among the Italian states as prerequisites for the peoples of the peninsula to share a common identity. Once some form of economic liberalism was in place, political liberation and unification were sure to follow in due course. A radically different variant was offered by Lombard analysts.

A Federation of People

The case for a federal union was advanced in particular by Carlo Cattaneo (1801–69), a Lombard publicist considered by his contemporaries as one of the leading figures in the republican, democratic, federalist current of the Risorgimento (e.g., Lovett 1972; Monti 1922). A recent *Times Literary Supplement* essay recalls some of the appellatives generally used to describe him: "the finest intelligence of the Italian Risorgimento"; "a polymath, an essayist of genius, a tireless publicist for scientific advance and technological improvement, in politics a liberal and a radical but also an advocate of federal governance" (Thom 1998, 25; see also Grossi 1981, 19–22).

Cattaneo was against the temporal power of the papacy. But he also disagreed sharply with Mazzini and Balbo. He suggested that Italian unification should not be obtained at any price – least of all at the price of liberty and self-government. As we shall see in chapter 3, Cattaneo liked to call up the French political experience in support of his argument that a forced creation of Italy through a unitary or centralized system of government and administration would hinder rather than facilitate self-rule and development. At the same time, Cattaneo rejected Gioberti's confederation of princes. His preference was for a federation of people.

This federation of people was expected to take the form of a polycentric system of government with overlapping jurisdictions – in effect, a multiconstitutional or "compound republic" (V. Ostrom 1987). Cattaneo coined the phrase "a United States of Italy within the United States of Europe" to denote how far his compound republic extended. Such a projected federal system represented, for Cattaneo, the theory of democracy in action, for it reconciled, preserved, and sustained order with liberty, union with diversity, and self-rule with shared rule. This was what the constitutional design of good government was about. As we shall see in the next chapter, Cattaneo insisted that the theoretical and material scaffold for this framework of governance derived from the principles of individual self-governance and extended, first of all, to the constitution of local self-governing units.

Like most modern institutionalists, Cattaneo had considerable appreciation for the genius of the eighteenth-century philosophers who recognized that the self-interest of individuals can be made to serve the commonweal, under appropriate institutional arrangements. Cattaneo also had considerable appreciation for the moral and cultural foundations of constitutional design and decision making. In his view, principles of human organization, including those that applied to the crafting of an Italian compound republic, are, above all, cultural endowments, the products of long-term historical development. Thus, *pace* Mazzini, "politics" alone – even armed insurrection – cannot generate such principles and the resultant constitutional regime. We shall elaborate these points in chapter 3, but enough has been suggested here that it should be easier to understand why Cattaneo disagreed so sharply with Mazzini and his fellow republicans, like Giuseppe Ferrari, who privileged direct, often violent action.

Cattaneo as well as other federalist patriots believed that a political economy of good government could be established in Italy on the basis of reflection and choice rather than through force or by accident. They drew particular inspiration and support for their national political program from developments taking place in Lombardy-Venetia. There, under Austrian rule, a veritable agricultural, industrial, commercial, and educational revival was taking place, and it had all the characteristics of a *risorgimento*. In his now classic work on economics and liberalism in Lombardy between 1814 and 1848, Kent R. Greenfield successfully captured the course of action that aimed at achieving the political economy of good government preferred by Cattaneo and others:

It is clear that in the inner circle of publicists who ventilated the public interests of Italy between 1815 and 1848 there was a common idea that even when cooperating with Austria they were working towards ends that were beyond the reach of Austrian policy, and also a common conviction that they were in conspiracy with the course of events, with the march of "the century"; in other words, that they had found a method of action which compelled even the national adversary to cooperate with them, in so far as that power was alert to its material interests. This was their "conspiracy in open daylight." They were right in their strategy: witness the confused and helpless opposition of Austria, whose rulers suspected but never fully comprehended their power. Metternich, with his germ theory of revolution, his persistent obsession that it grew solely out of a Jacobinical conspiracy which could be isolated and destroyed if the governments would only act in concert, proved incapable of meeting them on their own ground ... liberal journalists [like Cattaneo] saw at least a partial fulfilment of their hopes. By 1848, largely through their efforts, an Italian public opinion had been formed that could never again be governed successfully by the principles and methods of the *ancien régime*, less because the material interests of the Italian community had been revolutionized than because the public had been indoctrinated with a new conception of those interests. (Greenfield 1965, 286–7)

If such a conspiracy in broad daylight continued to grow and spread unhindered to other parts of the peninsula, the time would come when it would be extremely difficult for any absolutist government or army of occupation to defeat it. The revolts of 1848 swept away this possibility.

THE ECLIPSE OF FEDERALISM IN THE 1848 REVOLTS

The revolts of 1848 began with the Palermo uprising against Bourbon rule in January 1848, which forced King Ferdinand to give up absolutist rule and to grant representative institutions to Sicily as well as Naples. The Sicilian and Neapolitan revolts, together with the February uprisings in Paris, convinced King Leopold of Tuscany and Pope Pius IX to grant "constitutions" (Sartori 1962). King Charles Albert of Piedmont also yielded to liberal pressures, and on March 4, 1848, he granted the *Statuto*, which was to remain the basic law of Italy until 1946.

The pressures for representative institutions reached Vienna and led to the fall of Metternich. News of this revolt triggered revolts in the Austrian provinces of Lombardy and Venetia. Men of thought like Cattaneo were pressed to become men of action in the famous "five glorious days of Milan." Venetian revolutionaries and followers of Mazzini proclaimed the restoration of the ancient republic of Venice. The Piedmontese ruler supported revolutionaries by ranging his army against Austrian forces still in Italy. Soon afterward, the regular armies of Naples, the papal states, and Tuscany joined forces with those of King Charles Albert and with volunteers organized by Cattaneo federalists and Mazzini republicans in fighting against Austria. This unity of action among princes and patriots went far beyond any constitutional alternative heretofore contemplated. But the high probability of success suggested by this "federation of princes and people" in fact laid bare insurmountable contradictions in the movement for Italian independence, and these could not be reconciled in revolutionary times.

Charles Albert's insistence on the political fusion of Lombardy-Venetia with his kingdom disillusioned many Lombard and Venetian liberals. It also led other Italian rulers to desert the fight against Austrian domination. Soon afterward, the Neapolitan and Tuscan monarchs withdrew their constitutions and, with Austrian help, became once again absolutist rulers.

Pius IX soon faced dilemmas in his dual role as a temporal Italian ruler and spiritual leader of the Christian world. He could be neither a liberal pope nor an Italian nationalist ruler, since his temporal dominions stood for universalism rather than nationalism. For these reasons, Roman Catholicism could not be "the first political institution" (Tocqueville [1835 and 1840] 1962) in the national reawakening and political project, as it was in the case of Irish and Polish aspirations for national identity (see also Galli della Loggia 1996). As we shall see in chapter 9, this is not quite the same as saying that organized religion in Italy was an alternative to, or worked against, the civic community, although successive generations of Italian politicians and intellectuals who held strong rationalistic and secularist views denied the links between Roman Catholicism and the civic community (Galli della Loggia 1998, 124). For all his declared anticlericalism and secularism, Cattaneo cannot be easily situated in this group. He looked to the village priest as "the keystone in which all the lines of life (in the countryside) center." The parish organization was, for Cattaneo, a source of community strength and vitality – in his own words, "the most powerful and certain minister of the common prosperity" (Cattaneo, cited in Greenfield 1965, 33, 34).

Sicilian revolutionaries, who had joined the movement for a United States of Italy as a way of rejecting subjugation and insuring Sicilian independence from Naples, experienced other difficulties. They found that the revolutionary situation provided limitations to the making of a united Italy that could not be overcome in a short time span. They learned also that representative government itself was extraordinarily difficult to maintain in wartime (Romeo 1973, 317–45; Sabetti 1984, 73–6).

By 1849, all the uprisings collapsed; in retrospect they became "the first war of Italian independence." The failure of the 1848 revolts had several consequences for the making of Italy. First, it lent credence to Mazzini's view that the struggle for Italian unification and independence must take precedence over the issue of what framework of governance best suited Italy. The constitutional questions raised during the revolts – monarchy versus republic, centralization versus federalism, union versus unitarism – had impeded rather than facilitated the success of the uprisings. Second, the collapse of the revolts "ended neo-Guelph programs for Italian federation under the Papacy and greatly weakened any claims for federalism" (Grew 1963, 5). What happened also "established that all of Italy's crowned heads, except possibly Piedmont's new king, Victor Emmanuel II, were anti-nationalist" (Grew 1963, 5). After 1849, the Kingdom of Sardinia stood out in sharp relief as the only parliamentary monarchy in Italy. As a result, Piedmont "was left the one hope of Italian liberals, and for the next ten years the history of Piedmont is the history of Italy" (King 1899, 1:359–60).

CENTRALIZATION VS. DECENTRALIZATION: THE SECOND PHASE OF THE CONSTITUTIONAL DEBATE

The second phase of the constitutional debate occurred in the years immediately before and after the proclamation of a united Italy in 1861. At least four distinct but interrelated circumstances of the period are important for our analysis.

First, in 1857, a National Society was formed in Turin in support of the idea that Italian liberation depended on the actions of the Piedmontese government headed by Cavour. As Raymond Grew suggests (1963), this society attracted the support of Tuscan liberals as well as that of Giuseppe Garibaldi and other former companions of Mazzini.

Second, recognition of Piedmont as the principal agency of national liberation carried with it an implicit acceptance of its system of centralized government and administration as the model of government for all Italy. Some analysts allege, not unreasonably (e.g., King 1899, 2:22), that Victor Emmanuel II may have tended to view the movement for Italian unification as an opportunity for the dynastic aggrandizement of Piedmont. No matter how few grains of truth such an allegation carries, Cavour's contributions to the nascent liberal parliamentary system are readily acknowledged, even by some of the harshest revisionist historians. In the words of one such historian, "one of Cavour's finest constitutional achievements was to stand up against the king and habituate him to the practice of liberal government" (Mack Smith 1971, 61; see also Johnson 1985). Cavour's other contribution, no less important, was that, in the course of time, Cavour made parliament the very centre of government (Mack Smith 1971, 69), smoothing the transition from Savoyard Piedmont to liberal Italy (Romeo 1974).

Third, whereas before 1848 the Austrian presence in Italy had guaranteed European peace, after 1849 it became a threat to that very peace (A.J.P. Taylor 1934, 10–12, 236–9). At the same time, the French emperor, Louis Napoleon, sought to replace Austrian influence in Italy with French, and perhaps even to make Italy a satellite of France (Mack Smith 1968, 234). Finally, the suppression of the 1848 revolts in such places as Sicily generated a more diffused spirit of liberalism, which in turn encouraged more popular unrest against governmental oppression (Sabetti 1984, 69–77).

This interweave of national and international circumstances gave rise to several developments. In 1859, the Franco-Piedmontese war against Austria secured, among other things Lombardy for Piedmont. In the same year, uprisings in central Italy drove the various dukes out of power and prepared the ground for the annexation of central Italy by Piedmont (Hancock [1926] 1969). In April 1860, a popular revolt against Bourbon rule erupted once again in Sicily. The May 1860 landing of Garibaldi's "thousand men" at Marsala not only consolidated the revolt, it opened the way for the collapse of the Kingdom of the Two Sicilies and the unification of the south with the north. As this chain of events weighted the making of Italy in favour of a unitary and monarchical state, the constitutional debate shifted to a choice between centralized and decentralized conceptions of government. As chapter 4 will elaborate, decentralization implies an allocation of authority from the centre to a subordinate set of authorities, but the superior authority of the centre remains (see also Elazar 1971).

Perhaps nowhere else was the choice of rules that apply to the organization and conduct of government so hotly debated as in Sicily. Until 1816, when it was formally annexed by Naples, Sicily had been a more or less independent realm, with perhaps the longest continuous tradition of representative institutions in Italy (e.g., H.G. Koenigsberger 1971, quoted in Sabetti 1984, 30; 1999a). Chapter 9 will elaborate the challenge of reform before 1860 in Sicily and elsewhere. Suffice it to say here that the abolition of feudalism in 1812 did transform fiefs into allodial or private properties, and it gave Sicilian barons extensive proprietary authority over natural resources. But the abolition of feudal laws and privileges also reduced the barons' domain of authority and gave them very limited scope over the local population. A free labour market together with a communal government and parliament recast on the principles of self-government could have seriously "devalued" rural proprietorship as a determinant of the human condition and biased agricultural development toward a wider community of interests and a longer time horizon. The creation of the Bourbon state in 1815–16 prevented all this from happening. While the post–1816 central government dominated the structure of legal relationships (without, however, any effective legal remedies for government failures), the landowners, secure in their prerogatives as private proprietors, extended their control over the labour force and rural life more generally (Sabetti 1984, 229).

Sicilians had joined the cause of Italian unification only in 1848, when the possibility of creating a United States of Italy offered prospects for regaining independence from Naples, for securing a defence against the recurrent problem of war, and for being part of a larger political community which respected the need for local and regional self-governing capabilities. These political prospects had once again created the potential, through political action, for devaluing rural proprietorship as a determinant of the rural condition. In short, Sicilians had become Italian nationalists because of federalism. Now, while the Piedmontese saw themselves as coming to deliver Sicily from bondage, Sicilians came to fear the same process as exchanging the yoke of Naples for the yoke of Piedmont or of Italy (Brancato 1956, 69–153; 1963; Ganci 1968; Perez 1862).

Francesco Ferrara (1810–1900), perhaps the ablest political economist of nineteenth-century Italy (Buchanan 1960, 73; Weinberger 1940), was one of the Sicilians who took part in the debate about which rules and constitutional design were best suited for Sicily. In July 1860, as Garibaldi began to rule Sicily in the name of Italy and Victor Emmanuel, Ferrara wrote a memorandum to Cavour, whom he knew from his years in exile in Piedmont following the collapse of the 1848 Sicilian uprising. The memorandum, entitled "Brief Notes on Sicily," was written on about 8 July, 1860, and was circulated anonymously in

Sicily during that summer. The memorandum was eventually published in Cavour's papers, which is the source cited here (see Cavour 1949, 1:296–305).

The memorandum outlined several possible ways of uniting Sicily with the nascent Italian realm. In effect, Ferrara accepted the constitutional monarchy and, by implication, its system of government and administration – what Carlo Cattaneo, who had a stronger commitment to federalism and federal republicanism, steadfastly refused to accept. Still, Ferrara's memorandum remains important because it elucidates what constitutional knowledge was available and the problems that people confront in the design of governmental arrangements: namely, knowing what results alternative sets of principles articulated in correlative forms can be expected to yield.

Sicily in the Constitutional Design of United Italy

Ferrara began his reflections by noting that his analysis was grounded upon one fact and one principle: "The fact is that the Sicilian revolution springs solely from the irresistible desire to break free from Naples. The cries raised, the principles invoked – all simple phrases to which recourse is had – spring purely from reasons of political necessity, and these could be altered from one hour to the next as circumstances change. Words like 'nationality' and 'unity' therefore represent means and not ends." As for the principle, Ferrara continued, "Piedmont has an interest in supporting the present sentiment of annexation [among Sicilians] but has an even greater interest in bringing it about in such a way that annexation is transformed from a condition of necessity to a condition of willing consent [volontà]. It is important that we should prevent Sicily from becoming the running sore of the kingdom of Italy as she has been of the Bourbon state" (Ferrara [1860] 1949, 1:296–7).

On the premise that Sicilians wanted annexation as a means whereas Piedmont had an interest in transforming it into an end, Ferrara suggested four possible solutions or ways to unite Sicily with the rest of Italy. Let us follow his exposition of different political economies of good government and his reasons for preferring one alternative over the others.

The Swedish-Norwegian System
This constitutional design involved a union of Sicily with the Italian kingdom. Much as the king of Sweden was also the king of Norway, there would be no union of the institutions of each kingdom. Although this solution was one that "every Sicilian desires but no

one asks" (298), Ferrara suggested that it should be rejected. It would be less profitable to the interests of Sicily and even more damaging to the interests of Italy. Sicily would never have the certainty of being defended against invaders. The arrangement stood to weaken unity of action and to insure neither safety nor happiness. Indeed, the development of each country could proceed along radically different paths to the point that, Ferrara suggested, each would find it natural to go their separate ways. Their interests stood to push the two countries in opposite camps, though under the same monarch. Breakup of the system would follow. Hence, Ferrara reasoned, this system of government would not be appropriate to Sicily and Italy – as it eventually turned out to be equally inappropriate to Sweden and Norway.

The French System

A constitutional design patterned on the French political and administrative system meant complete fusion – Sicily would become just another province of Italy, as had happened to Lombardy and Tuscany. Ferrara informed Cavour that, though this solution was one that Sicilians asked for when they said "annexation," very few Sicilians, in fact, desired it. "The principle of fusion with the North now being preached is the very negation of liberty, concealed under the invocation of liberty itself: it is even a form of political socialism. It would be a fatal error if Italians showed that they could not emerge from the excesses of municipalism without throwing themselves into the other extreme, where unity is confused with absorption" (299). Ferrara rejected the view that, for such a people with such a past, the sole model of successful government that they had seen was the one imposed on them by "a fusion" from without. Couching his argument in a language that would appeal to Cavour's liberal sensibilities, Ferrara anticipated that this form of political socialism

is quite impossible to carry out in Sicily, simply because of the profound revolution it will involve for the customs and habits of Sicilians. Secondary laws ... will have to be changed without necessity but for reasons of assimilation ... A system of local government will be introduced quite different from that which has been the ideal and passion of Sicilians ... The public debt will perhaps have to be increased fourfold at one stroke in a country which would not have the resources for it. The system of taxation would have to be completely changed ... Apart from the difficulty of introducing military conscription, many unfortunate changes would be made in the system of administration, in money, weights, even in language: and the Supreme Court of Appeal would have to be abolished. Further difficulties would arise through the sheer distance away of

the new capital, and through the presence in Sicily of non-Sicilian officials.
(299)

Ferrara warned that "all these innovations would be found impossible
to apply in practice, however simple they may seem in the abstract"
(299).
    Ferrara reminded Cavour that the emulation of the standard great
power model was neither reasonable nor prudent:

Sicily has never in its history known such a fusion as this except with Naples
between 1838 and 1848; and on that occasion it was such a fusion that forced
the island into revolution ... The politics of a distant, vaster and more complex
government and, above all, if it is Parliament, however inspired by the most
benevolent of intentions, will never be so prompt, far-sighted and active as to
meet the needs of Sicily which will disappear in the great mass of Italian
national affairs. There seems no doubt that fusion would make Sicily the Ireland of Italy and this, instead of making our nationality more compact and
secure, would be a real and perennial source of weakness from which an enemy
could profit. (300–1)

By calling up the prospect of Sicily becoming the "Ireland of Italy,"
Ferrara added particular force to his argument – and a possible irritant
for Cavour. Here Ferrara was reminding the prime minister of Piedmont of his own essay on the Irish question. Originally written in
French in 1844, Cavour's essay was published in England (where it was
widely quoted) in 1845 under the title *Considerations on the Present
State and Future Prospects of Ireland* (Cavour 1845). While upholding
the political importance of the union for both England and Ireland,
Cavour attributed Irish suffering to the terms of the union and called
for changes in the structure of property rights and the political
supremacy of Protestantism there (Cavour 1845). Ferrara was now
anticipating for Sicily what Cavour had criticized in the British treatment of the Irish!
    For all these reasons, Ferrara rejected complete fusion as a desirable
constitutional alternative. He then turned to two other possibilities.

The Scottish System
This design of government meant that Sicily would, with the exception
of the authority of the national parliament, keep its secondary laws
and institutions. Ferrara was skeptical that the Scottish system could
work in Italy, revealing, in passing, something about his astute grasp of
British affairs.
    In his view, the problem in Great Britain had been one of how to

unite peoples whose traditions of individual liberty and local autonomy were historically entrenched. Parliament in London had not equated the happiness of subjects with the destruction of voluntary efforts and the erection of a Leviathan, but, Ferrara reasoned, it would be futile to entertain similar expectations from a general parliament of Italy "in our eminently Napoleonic epoch" (Ferrara [1860] 1949, 302). The dissolution of Tuscan autonomy, then ongoing, strengthened Ferrara's apprehension. For all these reasons, the solution applied to Scotland could not fit Italian conditions. This led Ferrara to consider a fourth alternative that appeared to have none of the shortcomings of the previous three constitutional designs: this was "the American system."

The American System

Applied to the kingdom of Italy, this constitutional solution meant decentralization of power from national to regional and local governments. It was a way of reconciling Sicilian and mainland political aspirations. Unfortunately, in the memorandum to Cavour, Ferrara offered a sketchy and inadequate portrayal of how this decentralization would actually take shape in Sicily. He did, however, indicate to Cavour the principle on which such an experiment could be carried out and some of the features that made it desirable.

The principle enunciated resembled very much the principle of subsidiarity: "nothing that is truly necessary for the expression of the Italian nationality should be taken away from the general parliament of Italy; nothing without proper cause should be taken away from the expression of Sicilian self-governance" (303). The application of this principle to Sicily would neither lower the dignity of the monarchy nor make Italy less of a nation. "It is," Ferrara averred, "a common error to attribute more cohesion to a state whose central government takes on tasks that subaltern bodies or individuals can do better" (304). He emphasized the importance that citizen consent and trust play in the creation and maintenance of a viable constitutional order, and advised Cavour that "whoever knows [Sicily] well must be convinced that annexation, on conditions which Sicilians might later regret, would soon generate sentiments not wholly Italian, which interested parties would not hesitate to nourish" (304).

The American system, Ferrara stressed, had two crucial advantages over all other constitutional designs: it secured the consent of the people of Sicily to the Italian union while reconciling both Sicilian and mainland political aspirations. In looking to the future, Ferrara anticipated a third, more long-term advantage accruing from the experiment of applying the American system of governance to Sicily. As he summarized it to Cavour, "who can ever tell that the solution currently being advanced for Sicily might not, some day, be extended to other parts of the peninsula? Certainly, ideas of rigid centralization are not native to Italy ... and no other part of Italy is as distinctive as Sicily. The Italian government could profitably carry out an experiment there which could do no harm. It might be a source of precious information for the future, if it ever came the day either to proceed to other annexations ... or to decentralize government in some of the regions already annexed" (304).

Ferrara's prognostication takes on new meaning when viewed in light of the search for new rules of constitutional design after the collapse of Fascism in 1943, a topic that we will examine in chapter 4. Cavour neither acknowledged nor answered Ferrara's memorandum directly; but, writing to a friend of Ferrara, Michele Amari, Cavour implicitly dismissed Ferrara's analysis with the observation that "(i)f the Italian idea has no influence in Sicily, if the idea of building a strong and great nation is not appreciated there, Sicilians would do well to accept the concessions offered by the king of Naples, and not unite themselves to people who would have neither sympathy nor esteem for them" (305). The problem was that, by this time, Sicilians could neither go back to the Bourbon monarchy nor turn away from the Savoy monarchy (e.g., Mack Smith 1954, 388–9, 402–3).

It is not entirely clear what influence the American Civil War had on the rejection of "the American system" well after Cavour had gone. Certainly, events in the United States, especially the polarization of states and the ensuing carnage of the American Civil War, helped to discredit the American system and prevent its extension to Italy, just as in the creation of the Canadian Confederation in 1867 (e.g., Sabetti 1982, 1999b). But other, less ambiguous and more compelling factors exist to suggest why Cavour and other creators of the Italian state rejected Ferrara's proposal.

The Italian System

Cavour and other creators of the Italian state were not unaware of the institutional problems that had characterized the Kingdom of the Two Sicilies since its forced creation of unity in 1816. A unitary system of government and administration was not necessarily a model of good, successful government. But, in their view, the critical difference after 1860 was that the ideological forces and political preferences that would work through and upon administrative structures were now liberal-parliamentary and not absolutist. The unstated presumption was that those institutional arrangements were *neutral* devices rather than fundamental determinants of behaviour in themselves; in proper hands, the arrangements of a unitary state would work accordingly.

Even historians generally hostile to Cavour recognize that he had always been a proponent of both local self-governance and reform of the Napoleonic system of prefectoral administration that many Italian states had inherited. As we saw in chapter 1, Cavour shared Alexis de Tocqueville's political ideas and assessment. Thus, another reason why he did not, or could not, act on Ferrara's proposal may be that events in 1859 had moved too fast for him. In spite of all his good intentions, Cavour may have "lacked the leisure to study the alternatives" (Mack Smith 1995, 249). This is, in fact, the main argument advanced by those who, like Raymond Grew, argue that "success spoiled the Risorgimento" with the result that, "in those very months of triumph, from April to December 1859, the Risorgimento itself came to be conceived in new and narrower limits" (Grew 1962, 38–9). Against this backdrop of success, it was much easier for Risorgimento leaders to assume that the reconstitution of political and economic activities as a function of Cavour's statecraft would have primarily beneficial effects. After all, Cavour genuinely believed that his "theory of the state [did] not imply either the tyranny of the capital over the rest of Italy or the creation of a bureaucratic caste that would subjugate all other bodies and would thus transform the position of the government into an artificial centre of an empire which the traditions and habits of Italians and Italy's geographic configuration would always be against" (Cavour 1949, 4:220).

Another factor in the creation of the unitary state is that most state founders, as well as postunification analysts, may have feared the centrifugal tendencies of Italians learning at their own expense, committing mistakes in governing themselves (see also Einaudi [1944] 1954, 53). The state founders certainly rejected an important but unarticulated premise that informed Ferrara's analysis – that in Sicily, as in other parts of the south, there were traditions of self-governance on which Italian unification could have relied (Sabetti 1999a). To be sure, by 1860 such traditions may have existed only in the microcosm of kinship and community and neighbourhood groupings (Sabetti 1984, 78), but such traditions could have been used to build the configuration of other enterprises and associations beyond the local plane to reach the nation as a whole. As we shall see in chapters 8 and 9, the weight of evidence about voluntary collective efforts after 1860 supports Ferrara's premise (see also Briggs 1978, 15–36; Bruccoleri 1913; Ivone 1979). People in Sicily, as in the rest of the south, found solutions to problems of organization when and where they were able to

engage in joint efforts and maintain reciprocity with one another. Theoretically, this is the argument that Cattaneo advanced, as we shall see
in chapter 3.

However compelling and persuasive these factors may be, they did
not provide a solution. In 1860 a united Italy *à la* Cattaneo or *à la* Ferrara could not be established. (There is great force in Grew's contention that "success spoiled the Risorgimento".) But the different factors together do strongly suggest an important conclusion: the second
round in the constitutional debate was as much affected by the politics
of the past and a chain of events beyond the capacity of anyone to
plan, stage, and direct as it was by misunderstanding and uncertainty
about the constitution of good government. The very success of uncoordinated action by Garibaldi and others, genuine worries about the
centrifugal tendencies inherent in the constitutional design suggested
by either Cattaneo or Ferrara, and a certain degree of optimism that
the new political system could be made to work as it should resulted in
a united and unitary Italy. Once the country was united, the institutions of liberal Italy would turn the king's subjects into good citizens,
or so the constitutional architects believed. Thus unconditional annexation followed, making Sicily a province in an indivisible Italy, under
Victor Emmanuel II as king.

PROMISES AND RESULTS OF UNITARY RULE

The law on administrative unification of 23 March, 1865 signalled the
defeat of last-minute efforts at decentralization and assured the triumph of centralized government and administration. The new nation-
state was organized with a single centre of authority having an exclusive monopoly on the ultimate use of physical force in the organization
of society. The monopoly over the supply of public goods and services
was accompanied by a single overarching system of public administration, with local elected officials and professionally trained personnel
who were hierarchically ordered and subject to direction by heads of
departments at the centre of government.

The creators of the Italian state anticipated that the forced creation
of unity through administrative measures under a common parliament,
backed by a national army, would produce both good policies and
good individuals by forging the diverse communities of peoples into
one strong and great self-governing nation, insuring a uniform provision of public services, and removing once and for all the spectre of foreign intervention in Italian affairs (e.g., Fried 1963, 72–119; Pavone
1964; Romanelli 1995b, 126–43). Their good intentions could be seen
in the crafting of specific institutional arrangements.

Unlike the French prefect, the Italian prefect was not given authority over all other field offices of the national system of administration for two reasons. The first is that the framers of the Italian system regarded the French system of public administration as oppressive and incompatible with their liberal values; they feared the accumulation of power in a single provincial official "of the vice-regal or proconsular type," like the French prefect (Fried 1963, 16; Romanelli 1995b, 126–31). The second reason is that the constitutional designers wanted to minimize the loss of control and information inherent in large-scale bureaucratic administration; they feared that the provincial prefect, already burdened with the task of being, *all at once*, the political representative of the national government, the chief of police, and the supervisor of local government, would be unable to provide expert direction and full-time coordination to the other provincial field services of the central bureaucracy, as was expected of his French counterpart. But let there be no misunderstanding. In departing from the French system, Italian leaders intended to *strengthen*, not weaken, their own unitary system. They believed they were crafting better institutions of government. A sympathetic student of the Italian prefectoral system conveyed their design intentions well when he wrote:

The drive for national uniformity was stronger than consideration for the special claims of particular areas. Local customs and interests were to be ignored, to be levelled out. National policies and obligations were to be imposed throughout the new nation over and against local demands for special treatment. If prefects were given greater authority, policies would vary from province to province with the amount and direction of prefectorial intervention. Prefects would be more susceptible to local pressures than functional specialists — the latter, it was contended would tend to have a more national, professional outlook. (Fried 1963, 118)

Hence, each field service had its own provincial director or "prefect" to minimize risk avoidance and goal displacement as well as to emphasize control rather than service.

Did such a framework of government attain the results that its crafters expected? Did the unitary rules of constitutional design triumph in practice as they had triumphed in theory, during the debate over alternative rules of constitutional design? Substantial data now exist about the performance of "the liberal project" acted upon between 1859 and 1865. It is hard to avoid the conclusion that many post-1946 historians have been unduly pessimistic about that project. Certainly, the theme of failure is exaltedly general and too sweeping for a proper characterization of what results obtained from the creation of the Italian state: how can this theme explain the success stories?

Gaetano Salvemini, the critic of Giovanni Giolitti's "new liberalism" mentioned in chapter 1, openly acknowledged in 1945 that Gaetano Mosca had been right. Tremendous improvements in all areas of public and private life had occurred between the period of the Risorgimento and the united Italy which succeeded it, between 1848 and 1914. It cannot be denied that the statecraft of the founders of the Italian state and the framework of government they left behind had something to do with this immense human and material progress (Salvemini [1945] 1960, xxi–xxii). Giolitti's ascent to power in 1901 solidified, during almost a decade of rule, the progress made in different areas of Italian life. The gap between the legal Italy and the actual Italy (*il paese legale e il paese reale*) was being bridged, even in government policies that required citizen compliance with a high degree of personal risk – military service (see M. Levi 1997a).

What has been found among Sicilian villagers fits the general tendency of the period. "By 1910, military service was no longer detested and had, in fact, become part of a young man's life cycle. Indeed, so dishonourable had desertion or draft evasion become that it was not unusual for young villagers who had emigrated to North America or Africa to return home just to do their military service" (Sabetti 1984, 119).

There is also something to Benedetto Croce's argument about the constitutional adjustment and the development of national life during this period. Croce took issue with those who argued that the source of all sorts of problems with parliamentary government (especially after the advent of the left in the late 1870s) and the "deep" cause of Fascist rule was *trasformismo*. The prime minister who originally used the term, Agostino Depretis, thought he was introducing "progressive government" when he suggested in 1882 that "anyone [who] wishes to transform himself" and accept these "very moderate programmes" would be welcomed (Seton-Watson 1967, 51). This "progressive" practice was a kind of consociational democracy that sought to conciliate clashing interests into parliamentary government – hence the verb "transform". The intent was clearly to fossilize the emerging two-party system; that success, however, also resulted in shifting governing coalitions and increased instability.

Transformism was a political strategy to obtain, maintain, and expand a national governing coalition. As Simona Piattoni has put it recently, like clientelism, transformism was "not the political expression of an ingrained social habit, but rather the most convenient power strategy of a social and political elite who was still unwilling to share its influence with larger social groups" (Piattoni 1998a, 49; see also S. Fontana 1998). The practice of transformism had close resemblance and affinity to the American practice of congressional politics and senatorial courtesy without, however, any of the other institutional arrangements that kept the American strategy of coalition building in check, or within manageable limits. This structural fault in Italian transformism doomed it, as time went on, to be worse than the ills it was supposed to remedy. No wonder intransigents on both left and right, as well as most intellectuals of liberal Italy and what came after, made *trasformismo* a term of political abuse. But Croce disagreed: "Italians had no reason to fear these frequent changes of ministry; to the historians they suggested the sick man tossing on his pillows, but they were rather the constant adaptations and re-adaptations which belong to all creative work, more especially to so intricate a work as the government of a great country" (Croce [1925] 1970, 22). There is more than a grain of truth in Croce's assessment, even if it is not the whole truth either.

Clearly the theme of failure cannot account for everything that followed the creation of the Italian state. There is more force in a less pessimistic, more positive assessment of liberal Italy, and this without denying the fact that the first sixty years of united Italy is also the history of a constitutional design that did *not* yield consequences consistent with expectations. The public service system excelled more in prevention than in action. As Ferrara predicted, Sicily slowly came to be viewed as "the Ireland of Italy." Still, at the fiftieth anniversary of unification, a British historian could observe that "nothing is more remarkable – though to believers in nationality and ordered liberty nothing is more natural – than the stability of the Italian Kingdom" (George M. Trevelyan, quoted in Romeo 1965, viii).

CONCLUSION

The creation of the Italian state was not merely a debate between different schools of constitutional thought. The issue of what kind of constitutional design would best suit a liberated and united Italy reflected not only the varying conditions in which patriots and politicians operated but also the changing fortunes of the disparate elements that pressed for unification over the course of about fifty years. Federalist and autonomist principles of organization led Cattaneo and Ferrara to believe that the nature of the country, the political consciousness of its people, and local and regional loyalties could be made to work for the commonweal under appropriate institutional arrangements. At the same time, alternative principles of organization, such as the standard great-power model, led Cavour and others to ignore or try to suppress federalist principles. From our vantage point, it becomes easier to see why the founders of the Italian kingdom reached different conclusions about what consequences were likely to flow from forced unity and the system of government and administration extended to Sicily and other parts of Italy. They reasoned that, as a liberal ruling class, they could make the institutions of government work as they should. In the end, unitary principles prevailed.

The creation of the Italian state was hailed, justifiably, as one of the most notable achievements of the nineteenth century. Rosario Romeo reminds us that "even as late as 1932 G.F.H. Berkeley could say of Italy that 'no other [nation] in Europe has made so much progress during the last seventy years'" (Romeo 1965, viii–ix). But no sooner had Italy become a nation-state than the consequences of its system of government brought into question the success of Risorgimento and permanently challenged Italian officials to search for news ways to bring about good government. (The stability noted by Trevelyan was not secure; liberal Italy won the First World War but lost the peace that followed.) As Luigi Einaudi, a Piedmontese political economist of international repute, governor of the Bank of Italy after 1944, and president of the Italian republic in 1948, was to note retrospectively, the creators of the Italian state "believed that they were establishing liberty and democracy when they were forging the instruments of dictatorship" (Einaudi [1944] 1954, 52). Einaudi devoted an entire book to show why "good government" as the dependent variable could not be achieved under such conditions. This also helps to explain why Cattaneo's federalist ideas, though eclipsed, could not be blotted out – for they were a reminder that good government might have proceeded less imperfectly through an alternative conception of rule. Let us, therefore, look at the underlying principles and building blocks of the constitutional design that did not happen.

3 The Constitutional Design That Did Not Happen

Carlo Cattaneo was born in Milan in 1801 to a Milanese artisan family with deep roots in the Lombard countryside. His modest origins give no inkling of the place that he was to occupy in the intellectual history of both Italy and Switzerland. By the 1840s Cattaneo was widely regarded by his contemporaries as a gifted publicist and a leading figure in the republican, democratic current of the Risorgimento. Following the collapse of the 1848 revolts, he took refuge and settled in Switzerland, where he is now regarded as one of the canton of Ticino's outstanding nineteenth-century figures. Cattaneo died in Castagnola, a Swiss hillside village overlooking Lugano and its lake, in 1869.

Cattaneo was four years older than the other great republican and democratic figure of the Risorgimento, Giuseppe Mazzini, whose national and international reputation completely overshadowed his own. Unlike Mazzini, Cattaneo did not see why the issue of national independence should dominate all other considerations, including the issue of freedom, nor why patriotism should require a centralized state. Cattaneo held firm to the view that the work of secret societies was antithetical to the creation of an open society, and that a preoccupation with sovereignty was inimical to the very principles of democracy. Furthermore, he saw no need for Italians to emulate the French and adopt a strong central government. So Cattaneo's ideas were doubly rejected in his own lifetime: first by the victorious liberal current of the Risorgimento and then by his own political circle, including close friends. Yet his ideas retained salience.

In spite of being relegated to oblivion by official culture, Cattaneo's ideas have had better fortune after his death. At critical junctures in the course of Italian public life – before and after the First World War, and during the debacles of both the Second World War and the First Republic in the 1990s – successive analysts and concerned citizens have turned to Cattaneo to rediscover a tradition of thought that could serve as a public philosophy, or program for laying new foundations to public life. As Norberto Bobbio, an Italian philosopher who has done much to make Cattaneo's work known, recalled amidst the ruins of the Second World War, "if we have to build bridges to the past, Cattaneo is a pillar on which we can safely lay our arch" (Bobbio 1971, 10). The flood of academic and elite-press interest in Cattaneo's ideas – not including the 1990s outpouring due in part to separatist tendencies in north Italy – is now a huge bibliography that fills a small book (Brignoli and Massagrande 1988). Resolutions to public sector problems invoked by the secessionist Lombard Northern League (Lega Nord) in the early 1990s helped to popularize again Cattaneo's alternative constitutional design. And yet, the enduring interest in Cattaneo has done little to alter the fortune of his ideas. By the end of the 1990s, the situation had changed little from what Bobbio acknowledged in 1971: "It is hard to find in the history of Italian political thought a writer who has been more admired and less followed than Carlo Cattaneo; who has achieved more recognition but exercised less influence; and whose relevance has been proclaimed and reproclaimed at various junctures, but each time without effect. Those who have encountered his ideas in their intellectual journey could do no less than stop and pay homage to his geniality, versatility, power and rigor of style, but they would each proceed to move away from them as quickly as possible" (Bobbio 1971, 182). This paradoxical situation stems from several problems.

One problem is the voluminous, broad, and fragmentary nature of Cattaneo's writings. He wrote notes, articles, and long essays on many theoretical and practical problems of his day (including the nature of chemistry and economics, the construction of railways, and the development of the study of languages and literature) across almost the entire fields of history, politics, philosophy, and law. Later in life, he regretted that he had scattered his ideas in far too many places, without bringing them together either in a single corpus or in the form of a "public science" (Cattaneo [1855] 1952, 2:239; all the subsequent translations of Cattaneo are my own, unless otherwise noted). Still, in spite of the sprawling, uneven nature of his work, there is a remarkable continuity both in his ideas and in his activities over the course of his life – enough to view him as a skilled intellectual craftsman, concerned with the way ideas and deeds complement each other to give meaning to human life and the civilizing process (*incivilimento*). It is fair to assume that he meant what he said, and therefore possible to reconstruct from his writing a theory of politics and history faithful to his intention.

Another problem is that many readers – including adherents of regionalist leagues present and past, separatist and nonseparatist – have turned to Cattaneo in the expectation of finding reinforcement for their own ideas, only to come away disappointed at Cattaneo's failure to lend complete support. Secularist analysts can find ample ammunition in Cattaneo for their salvos against the temporal power of the pope, "jesuitical and monastic obscurantism," and arcane metaphysical disquisitions, but not enough to discredit the importance of religion and local parishes for a democratic society. Idealists have been attracted by Cattaneo's treatment of the role of ideas in life, but Cattaneo belonged to a class of intellectuals who did not deal exclusively in the realm of ideas. Thus, in the end, idealists have judged him, with disappointment, as not idealistic enough. Positivists, lured by Cattaneo's concern for positive analysis, have soon realized that this is not sufficient to make him the first Italian positivist, or a positivist *à la* Auguste Comte. Materialists, too, have found some support in his economic writings, but Cattaneo still had, in Antonio Gramsci's colourful words (1978, 56n5), "too many fancies in his head" to be regarded as one of them. Cattaneo drew on Giambattista Vico to temper the extreme rationalism of Enlightenment doctrines, and, in the process, tempered Vico's own "antimodern" doctrines. It is true that Cattaneo could write rhapsodically about Lombard accomplishments, but his emphasis on the local as the essential foundation for a democratic society cannot be solely attributed to his attachment to Lombardy; thus his theory of politics does not quite support – or justify – secessionist tendencies in present-day north Italy. Cattaneo was rare among post-Restoration Italian intellectuals for his openness and support of science and technological progress, without either believing that one can, in principle, master all things by calculation, or by becoming "disenchanted" *à la* Max Weber. In brief, Cattaneo stands at the meeting point of several intellectual currents of his time but, if read selectively or in a segregated way, is apt to run counter to them all.

Another problem is that we have often tended not to read Cattaneo on his own terms and, as a consequence, have not always grasped his paradigmatic significance as a protagonist of a new science of politics. We have come away from his writings disappointed not to find in them a fully developed theory of the state, nor even of federalism. While impressed by Cattaneo's capacity to comprehend realities beyond the confines of his little world, we have often failed to treat his insights as essential ingredients in a general theory of politics and culture. This is so largely because of the tendency to approach his work through top-down, state-centred or simply wrong intellectual constructs. This helps to explain why, for example, Cattaneo's contribution to nineteenth-century liberal thought has been dismissed by nationalist writers or, when noticed, has not even been properly identified. For example, in Guido de Ruggiero's well-known text *The History of European Liberalism* (1927, 312–13), Cattaneo is identified as someone primarily interested in Lombard agriculture.

These problems help to explain why Cattaneo has been, sometimes all at once, both praised and neglected. Not surprisingly, he is hardly known beyond the small circle of Italian scholars and Italianists who have continued to keep alive a certain *tradizione cattaniana* (e.g., Armani 1998; Lacaita 1975; Lovett 1972). For all these reasons, there is still, in the words of a distinguished Risorgimento historian, "the need to recompose the fragments and to lay bare the structure of the theoretical analysis in Cattaneo's work" (Romeo 1977, 100).

This chapter has a more limited goal, however, namely, to present Cattaneo's federalist ideas as a way of advancing an alternative art and science of institutional design to the prevailing state-centred theory and practice. In so doing, we will discover why Cattaneo was so preoccupied with the political institutions of the city or commune and why he set for himself the task of recovering the forgotten tradition of Italian communal life. From this vantage point, the political history of the Italian people cannot be reduced to either some kind of tragedy of Hobbesian dimension (Guicciardini [1651] 1969), or to a paradox between unsurpassed success in every field of artistic endeavour and failure to create a sovereign state as early as the French (Burckhardt 1860). As it will become apparent later, the rejection of the standard great-power model offered by sovereign states does not mean that Cattaneo saw self-governing communes standing by themselves. He argued that the very survival of local self-government necessarily depends upon the extension of the principles of self-governance to the nation and to a united Europe. He conceptualized local self-governing units as parts of the larger political whole, crucial in producing good citizens for the maintenance of the larger political whole and a free society.

The chief argument in Cattaneo's work is that federalism as a constitutional and institutional framework for a self-governing society must start at the local level, with the commune as a fundamental unit of self-governance. Tracing why and how Cattaneo used this particular point of departure in his analysis gives added currency to the main argument of this study in two ways: it offers both an understanding of Italian history that challenges the paradoxical view of Italy and a mode of reasoning about the art and science of institutional design that remains applicable to Italian development long after Cattaneo's lifetime.

THE COMMUNE AS A FUNDAMENTAL UNIT OF GOOD GOVERNMENT

Cattaneo conceptualized the commune as a communal society – or a society of neighbours, the vital plexus of neighbourhoods – that exists beyond the family and prior to the consent of state legislators. Historical circumstances may help to explain, up to a point, the creation of cities and villages; contingencies of time and space may limit the design and practice of local democracy (Cattaneo [1864] 1965, 4:432). But, in Cattaneo's view, individuals have an inherent right, a kind of *ius nativum*, to constitute and reconstitute themselves into self-governing units or communal societies. Cattaneo showed an awareness of size constraints when he suggested that citizens' participation in communal affairs and access to public services could be realized most productively in communes not exceeding 100,000 inhabitants (Cattaneo [1864] 1965, 4:433). Institutional weakness and failure are most likely to ensue when that threshold is exceeded. By way of example, he noted that when individuals have to walk more than half an hour or, at most, one hour from their houses to school, to the midwife or public nurse, to the mortuary, or any other essential public service unit, then the commune loses meaning, and those who contribute to its maintenance and its affairs feel alienated (Cattaneo [1864] 1965, 4:431-2).

In Cattaneo's view, federalist principles offer important design criteria for crafting democratic institutions, but Cattaneo continued to be mindful that the size of self-governing units is an important constraint. He held firmly to the view that it is better to restructure or break up a commune than allow it to grow beyond manageable limits. As a way of legally justifying such a move, he suggested that dividing up a large commune could be treated like the break up of a commercial partnership venture that no fair legal system can prohibit or prevent. *Mutatis mutandis*, the commune as a communal society or society of neighbours can be treated just like any other provider of goods and services. Such a view of communal government may, Cattaneo continued, appear extraordinary to those who have not yet fully considered the art of association that underlies the meaning and purpose of democratic or good government. Consider the case of the United States, he told his readers. It was the extension of the art of association to all sorts of activities that gave rise to enterprises of various shapes and transformed that country beyond expectation (Cattaneo [1864] 1965, 4:435).

This is not the only place where Cattaneo echoed Tocqueville, whose book on America he, like Cavour, had read and liked. Cattaneo echoed Tocqueville when he noted that the commune seems to be a natural and spontaneous congregation of people that can be found anywhere, albeit under different names. Communal institutions are "the fundamental plant" of any national public service system (Cattaneo [1864] 1965, 4:436). At the same time, communal institutions can be organized so as to foreclose the possibility of local residents acting in concert on matters of the commonweal. Such is clearly the case, Cattaneo commented, when communal government is the lowest chain in a bureaucratic system of public administration, or when the only "inherent right" of communal institutions is that of obedience or tutelage to a superior authority. In such instances, the commune ceases to be a communal society, a joint local undertaking for a good society of better services and better individuals. The strength of superior authority or bureaucratic administration may be more so in name than in fact, however. Moreover, bureaucratic administration does little to foster a desirable way of life and civic virtues among citizens. The surface solidity of bureaucratic administration is misleading, Cattaneo reasoned, for it is inevitable that "those who sow servility usually reap betrayal" (Cattaneo [1864] 1965, 4:420).

For Cattaneo, then, the central theoretical and practical question is not, Is there local government? Local government can be found anywhere under all sorts of regimes. Rather, the central issue asks Is local government constituted so as to facilitate individual and collective efforts on behalf of common interests shared by local residents?

The worth of self-governing units goes beyond local matters, however. They are "the nation in the most intimate nursery of its liberties" (Cattaneo [1864] 1965, 4:422), for the skills and knowledge required for self-governance, like the art of harmonizing one's individual interest with that of others, can best be learned in the practice of everyday life. Self-government cannot be successfully achieved through force or handed down from above. "Only too well this is demonstrated by the examples of France and Spain where liberty won by blood constantly eludes people because of the overwhelming power accumulated into the hands of government" (Cattaneo, cited in Carbone 1956, 71).

Cattaneo was not unmindful of the French contribution to republican civilization and the civilizing process more generally. He observed, "when the American people proclaimed their independence and when the French people proclaimed the rights of man, they gave a lesson of philosophy to the rest of the world" (Cattaneo [1860] 1960, 1:371). But, unlike the American Revolution, "the French Revolution was unable to go beyond the centuries-old tradition of, and its own faith in, the omnipotence of rulers. The king's representatives gave way to the nation's representatives but the fervour engendered by discipline made them abandon liberty. The people had the land but not the commune" (Cattaneo [1864] 1965, 4:419). For such a system of government "no matter what it calls itself – kingdom or republic – will be made up of eighty-six monarchies [i.e., prefectures], with one king in Paris" (Cattaneo [1850] 1957, 2:178). Cattaneo anticipated that as long as provincial departments continued to be part of the prefectural administration, and as long as prefectural administration was combined with state militarism, rather than self-governing cantons with armed citizens, freedom understood as the theory of democracy in action remained an impossibility for the French (Cattaneo [?1848] 1965, 2:449). In other words, Italians should *avoid*, not emulate, the French political mistakes and weaknesses.

At the same time, Cattaneo insisted that communal self government is not enough. To succeed, the practice of local self-governance needs to be linked to and interpenetrate other larger self-governing institutions extending to the nation as a whole – what in the modern language of institutional analysis and development and economic institutionalism is referred to as "multiple layers of nested enterprises" (E. Ostrom 1992, 75–6). Cattaneo referred to "federal law" as the intellectual mechanism for designing and operating a multiconstitutional political system with overlapping self-governing jurisdictions. Through federal law, an innovative way had been found to organize multiple jurisdictions in relation to each other without recourse to a single chain of command and bureaucratic arrangement. This innovative way was for Cattaneo a fundamental discovery in constitutional analysis and design and is the leitmotif running through almost everything he wrote or taught. A federative polity so constituted was for Cattaneo liberty in action – liberty as "the plant of many roots" (Cattaneo [1860] 1965, 4:80).

Cattaneo rejected the standard definition of sovereignty. In his view, sovereignty referred first of all to individual sovereignty. As he put it, "the liberty of speech, press, association conscience, movements, etc., constitutes the antecedents of sovereignty. Sovereignty forms an equation with government. If we are not self-governing, we are not sovereign; sovereignty signifies mastery and mastery excludes the master: thus the suppression of privilege, thus the concept of [republican government] ... He who does his own bidding, he who determines the right of his own ideas and desires is said to be free; liberty is the will in its rational and fullest development; liberty is republic and republic is plurality or federation" (quoted in Carbone 1956, 69).

Like other federalist thinkers of his time, Cattaneo was wont to call up the examples of the United States and Switzerland in support of his proposal of a federative polity for Italy and Europe. But he was careful to point out that in no way did those examples represent the only expressions of federalist principles at work. It is possible to combine nonunitary principles and forms of governing in other ways – in ways specific to the political craftsmanship of particular peoples. True to this presupposition about constitutional design, Cattaneo does not presume to "construct" political arrangements for others; he only offers design principles. This way of reasoning exposed Cattaneo to the charge that critics since Mazzini have levelled against him: that for all his discussion of federalism and emphasis on federal law, Cattaneo did not compose a fully elaborated theory of federalism. There is something to this argument, but it is not the whole story if we keep in mind that Cattaneo was more interested in identifying the design criteria that should inform the crafting of a complexly nested self-governing system rather than constructing a ready-made system for others.

As we saw earlier, both Cavour and Massimo D'Azeglio held the view that institutional arrangements shape laws as well as individuals. This view was shared by Cattaneo, though he would have been appalled to be associated with these figures. Unlike Cavour and D'Azeglio and to some extent Francesco Ferrara, Cattaneo showed a stronger awareness of the differences that unitary and federal designs of government can make in shaping societies and individual character. His way of illustrating these differences was to search for examples of peoples sharing similar cultural traditions but dissimilar systems of government.

One example that Cattaneo liked to call up during the second phase of the constitutional debate during the Risorgimento was that of the French and Italians of France, Italy, and Switzerland. As he put matters at one point, "the inability of the French to maintain liberty for a long period under pressures from the unity of the state and the unity of the church is often attributed to French culture and character. But the fact is that the much calumnied French culture and character show themselves quite fit for the full and popular exercise of liberty in Genevà and Lausanne" (Cattaneo [1860] 1965, 4:80).

Cattaneo's microconstitutional perspective has two theoretical and practical implications for the crafting of institutions of good government in Italy. First, it offers a new key to understanding Italian developments across time and space, which, as we shall see in part 4, has gained renewed currency with the publication of Robert D. Putnam's *Making Democracy Work* (1993). Second, much like Ferrara's approach to decentralization in the last chapter, Cattaneo's perspective can be employed to anticipate consequences likely to flow from unitary systems of local public economies, as we shall see in part 2. For now, let us consider the commune in comparative perspective.

COMMUNES ACROSS TIME AND SPACE

Cattaneo's interest in world history and civilizations led him to explore the origins of communes beyond Italy. Central to this exploration is his concern for what made Italian history unique and what made it resemble that of other countries. In elaborating his concern, we can also see how Cattaneo's analysis challenges certain entrenched views about Italy's development experience.

Common Features

Cattaneo began his career by noting that, though the most ancient origins are lost in the memory of past generations, it is possible to highlight the changing nature of communes across long time periods if we turn to language "as the first element in social aggregation" (Cattaneo [1837] 1948, 1:210–11). Contemporary dialects are but remnants of earlier language systems. What we call dialects mark the indelible work of primitive human groupings and trace their multiform nature throughout Europe (Cattaneo [1836a] 1956, 1:116–18). Going against the official academic culture of his time, he argued that there was no reason to downplay the widespread use of dialects or treat them as sources of political disunity. Even in France – that land of unitarism, centralized administration, and cultural chauvinism par excellence – learned societies were increasingly recognizing the continued existence and use of several local and regional dialects (Cattaneo [1840] 1964, 1:157–8). The resilience of such languages is all the more remarkable when we consider that not even all the pressures of uniformity and homogeneity that linguistic nationalism and centralized government and administration could muster had extirpated them. Cattaneo speculated that the four languages most likely heard by Julius Caesar between the Adour and the Rhine had probably incorporated or eclipsed previous linguistic manifestations of communal life. Vestiges of those four languages were still being heard in nineteenth-century France (Cattaneo [1844a] 1957, 1: 341–432).

Cattaneo sought to chart the transformation of human settlements in ancient Europe from very large communal associations to increasingly smaller ones. He conjectured that the explanatory factors for the transformation must be traced back to the introduction, spread, and growth of Roman civil law and private property rights. Some common properties, he observed, were still functioning as communal associations in his own time, particularly in Alpine areas. In fact, recent scholarship (Grossi 1981) has emphasized the importance of Cattaneo's 1859 report on agrarian conditions in the Magadino plain, the Swiss portion of the upper valley of the Ticino River. Cattaneo, although a champion of private property rights, recognized that the Swiss commons "are not abuses, they are not privileges, they are not usurpations; [they are] another way of possessing, another system of legislation, another social order, one, which unobserved, has descended to us from centuries long past" (Cattaneo 1859, quoted in Grossi 1981, 21). For this reason, Cattaneo's 1859 report came to occupy an important point of reference in the post-1860s Italian debates about collective property as a viable alternative to private property.

There can be little doubt that Cattaneo was respectful of the commons as an enduring institution of self-governance. Without denying that importance, he speculated that the constant subdivision of ancient common properties could be taken as the juridical thread for charting the transition among large communities of people from uncertain cultivation to settled agricultural practices and private holdings (Cattaneo [1864] 1965, 4:427–8). He conjectured as follows: "It seems a paradox, but the fact is that the great communes came before the small ones. Ancient Europe lived in vast communal associations. Tribal chiefs lived in them in an open countryside. Over time, the term 'city' began to be used to refer to a specific locale (*vicus*), a country district (*pagus*), to a place of assembly, to a market, or to a fortified refuge in times of war" (Cattaneo [1864] 1965, 4: 428).

The transformation of large communal associations and corporate entities into smaller ones – cities, towns, and villages – was an evolutionary process that could still be observed in northern Italy in Cattaneo's time. In Lombardy it was still the practice of people to move from large to small communes or to constitute other smaller village communities.

The history of the long-term settlement of the Italian peninsula suggested to Cattaneo a paradox: cities came before villages and before the cultivation of the countryside as such; urbanization preceded the farmer and made the development of agriculture possible (e.g., Cattaneo [1864] 1965, 4: 428; see also Sabetti 1984, ch.3). What urban settlements in Italy did was to provide the necessary foundations for intensive resource capital and management expertise to build roads, canals, and the like. In this way they also provided the refinements of civilization. The Greek colonies in southern Italy, the *Magna Graecia*, and the creation of Rome illustrate the *urban* nature of Italians, their long-standing civic traditions, and the importance of the "urban frontier" as a positive force in Italian development. But it was not until the

1858 set of essays entitled "The City as the Organizing Principle for Understanding the Course of Italian History," that Cattaneo brought together the different strands of his argument.

To be sure, Cattaneo was neither the first nor the last analyst to attach great importance to cities for spearheading development. Writing around 1921, Robert Michels expressed Cattaneo's conclusions in the following way: "There is not in Italy any absolute separation between city and countryside. The Italian people in its entirety is in nature an urban people. The life of the Italian rural population develops in much more urban forms than that of the German or French inhabitants" (quoted in Fried 1967, 507–8). Nor is what both Cattaneo and Michels observed truly unique to the Italian development. In 1959, Richard C. Wade propounded a similar thesis for the rise of American cities as spearheads of the Anglo-American frontier between 1790 and 1830. This argument turned Frederick Jackson Turner's thesis about urbanization following agriculture inside out (Richard C. Wade 1959). Wade's thesis was innovative and revolutionized understanding of American development, but it would not have surprised Cattaneo.

It is possible to take issue with the way Cattaneo divided the history of Italian cities into different eras, to point out gaps in his grasp of that history, to question the importance he attached to cities in Italian development, and even to confuse his concern with free cities with a defence of the bourgeois class (see Puccio 1977; Romano 1994, 32–7, 49–52). What is important and distinctive about Cattaneo's analysis is that he used a microconstitutional perspective to offer a new key to understanding the Italian development experience and, at the same time, broadening the institutional knowledge of his contemporaries.

The Ontology of Italian Cities

Cattaneo wrote the 1858 set of essays to challenge two prevailing schools of thought of his day about how to understand the past and present search for good government in Italy. One school, whose leading proponent happened to be a friend of Cattaneo and a fellow radical republican democrat, Giuseppe Ferrari (see Lovett 1979), averred that the most productive way to make sense of the intricate vicissitudes of more than two thousand years of recorded history of Italy was to reduce it to an analysis of revolutions, or to the struggle between the universality of the papacy and that of the empire. Ferrari's macrohistory was national, with little or no regard for Italy's microconstitutional foundations. The other school called up the same vicissitudes to argue that what Italy really needed was a strong, centralized system of government and administration to bring an end to weakness, rivalry, and disunity and to bring about responsible and responsive government. Cattaneo found both arguments wanting.

In challenging the prevailing notions of his day, Cattaneo's analysis indirectly questioned Francesco Guicciardini's classic interpretation of the history of Italy (Guicciardini [1651] 1969) and Jacob Burckhardt's *The Civilization of the Renaissance in Italy* (1860), a work not yet published in 1858, but whose interpretation was destined to range alongside, and lend support to, Guicciardini's rendition of "rational Italians and irrational Italy." Cattaneo's mode of analysis helps us to see the extent to which Guicciardini mistook – understandably, given his own problematic government experience – the tumultuous events and personality clashes of the upper classes and their struggles of power during the Renaissance as *the* history of Italy. Cattaneo's analysis also suggests how inadequate Burckhardt's own rendition is. Burckhardt, for all his presumed matchless depth of historical analysis of different fields of Italian artistic endeavour, did not break free of the conventional view that Guicciardini helped to form; thus he did not – and could not, given his method of analysis – deliver what he promised; namely, to show that "Italian states were in their internal constitution works of art – that is, the fruit of reflection and careful adaptation" (Burckhardt 1860, 107). (Modern authors who come closest to Cattaneo in delivering Burckhardt's promise – without, however, accepting the paradoxical view of Italy he promoted – are Harold J. Berman (1983), who deals with basic principles of constitutional government as they were worked out in the free cities of Italy and Germany, and Scott Gordon (1991, ch.4), who focuses on the checks and balances devised by the Republic of Venice in an effort to reconcile the exercise of political authority with freedom and justice.) Let us turn, then, to how Cattaneo carried out the task he set for himself.

Cattaneo set out his point of departure in the first 1858 essay this way: "The city is the only organizing principle that allows us to make an evident and continuous exposition of thirty centuries of Italian histories. Without this organizing thread, the mind becomes disoriented in the labyrinth of conquests, factions, and civil wars, and in the frequent structuring and restructuring of states. Reason cannot see light in successive alternations of strength and weakness, virtue and corruption, good sense and imbecility, elegance and barbarism, opulence and desolation; and the mind becomes saddened and depressed by such dismal fatalism" (Cattaneo [1858] 1957, 2:383–4). The city was his organizing principle. With its help, it became possible for Cattaneo to reach some conclusions about whether the structures of basic local institutions had been the primary instrument for advancing human welfare or the essential source of human adversity among successive generations of Italians.

Cattaneo began by going back to ancient times – to the civic culture of *Magna Graecia* in the south, and that of the Etruscan communities in the centre and the north. He identified and discussed nine different eras of civic evolution since those early times, and ended his analytical narrative with the city republics of the fourteenth century. He used this history not to suggest a continuous, unbroken course of city development but rather to emphasize certain features that made the city, or the local, both an historical community in Italy and an appropriate level of analysis. Cattaneo sought to draw out features of the Italian cultural tradition that had theoretical and empirical implications for the problematics of political change and reform in his own time. The set of essays on the city can thus be read at different levels: the city as a conceptual variable, as an historical community, and as a manifestation of the struggle for self-governance – not just power struggles of upper classes over time. I discuss below some features of his narrative that reveal these different dimensions.

Civic Consciousness

One of the earliest discussions of the place occupied by the local in the consciousness or self-awareness of people can be found in a technical report on the projected rail line between Milan and Venice that was written by Cattaneo in 1836. There he noted that, "our cities are not only the fortuitous headquarters of a great number of individuals, stores, workshops, and warehouses, such as may be, for example, Birmingham, Trieste, Malta, and Gibraltar ... our cities are ancient centres of communications networks for each particular province ... They are like the heart in a system of veins. They serve as a point of intersection or, rather, as centres of gravity that cannot be arbitrarily moved elsewhere. Each is an action centre for a population between 200,000 and 300,000." Adding a cross-national perspective, he continued, "it is easier to attract all the large French landowners to Paris than to convince fifty or so gentlemen from Brescia to leave unattended their shops and their wheat harvests ... This condition of our cities is the work of centuries and of very remote events, whose causes are more ancient than memory remembers" (Cattaneo [1836a] 1956, 1:116–17).

In 1858, he extended his earlier observation to Italy as a whole: "From the very beginnings, the city in Italy is not the same as that in Asia or Northern Europe. The Roman Empire begins in a city, and it is the government of that city that expands to comprise all the nations surrounding the Mediterranean. Popular wisdom has the city of Rome originating from the city of Alba, Alba from Lavinius, Lavinius from the distant Troy. In this popular collective consciousness, different types of people appear with different types of cities" (Cattaneo [1858] 1957, 2:384). By contrast, "the empires of Cyrus, Gemshid, Genghis Khan, and Timur-Leng were not founded this way. Nor do they appear so in the collective consciousness of the people" (Cattaneo [1858] 1957, 2:384).

The term "colony" revealed some of these differences. Putting his grasp of early Latin texts to use, Cattaneo noted that *colonia* (colony) was understood by ancient Italians to stand for a people who move from one locality to another in order to constitute a new settlement and communal society – we might add, like the logic governing the constitution of Hutterite communes (Bullock and Baden 1977). Even in Cattaneo's own time, the term *colonia* continued to have that original meaning, without any of the pejorative connotations it was to assume later (Cattaneo [1858] 1957, 2:385).

Cattaneo reiterated another feature of Italian life that sharply differentiated it from its northern European counterpart. The tendency of most cultivators in northern Europe was to reside in the countryside, with urban settlements having no countryside of their own as such. This was not so in Italy, where each city continued to have a *contado*, a neighbouring countryside; together they formed an inseparable historical community. This situation had endured up to Cattaneo's own time:

Though now rural people have in large measure become small landowners, they continue to identify themselves with the name of their original city. In many provinces this is the only *patria* with which common people recognize and identify themselves. The people of Lombardy in their domestic and spontaneous usages have never identified themselves historically and geographically with Lombardy as such. Nor have they adopted the various administrative divisions of departments and provinces that transcend the ancient municipal boundaries. A shepherd from Val Camonica, now aggregated to one department, now to another, still sees himself as someone from the city of Brescia ... while no French peasant would call himself Parisian even when he has Paris in sight from his field. (Cattaneo [1858] 1957, 2:386)

Such is the importance of the communal society for successive generations of Italians that "this adherence of the countryside to the city ... constitutes a kind of permanent and indissoluble elementary state. It can be dominated by outside influences, crushed by force from another city state, incorporated by one lordship or another, and stripped of any legislative and administrative power. But whenever pressure and domination are, for whatever reason, relaxed, the native elasticity reemerges and the municipal fabric of the city regains its original vibrancy. Sometimes it is the countryside that regenerates a destroyed city" (Cattaneo [1858] 1957, 2:387). Thus, Cattaneo predicted that any legislator, entrepreneur, or analyst "who does not take this local patriotism into account will always sow in the sand" (Cattaneo [1836a] 1956, 1:118).

Municipal Institutions

The constancy and permanence of municipal institutions is another fundamental fact common to almost all of the history of Italy. The Roman Empire was originally constituted as the fusion of a military dictatorship and an association of cities. As the imperial bureaucracy slowly came to encroach on municipal institutions, the citizenship that accrued from membership in local communities became subordinate to membership in the empire. The increasing pressures for taxation and government control crushed the life of municipalities as the living cells of the nascent Roman imperial organization. City magistrates were replaced and supplemented by imperial officials. With the decline of the empire and the barbarian invasions of Italy, by the tenth century the Christian bishop replaced the Roman bureaucrat as city leader.

The municipal order provided the context for the diffusion of both the Latin Christianity and the study of Roman law that followed the Investiture Controversy (Cattaneo [1858] 1957, 2:424). In this way, municipal institutions proved to be more durable than successive waves of conquest.

Free Cities

The importance of municipal institutions was radically amplified with the growth of religious and legal consciousness in the eleventh century. Old and new cities constituted themselves as self-governing communes or city republics. Each town came to have laws and institutions peculiar to itself, but underneath differences of place and time, all the communities shared a capacity to make their own laws and to direct their own affairs and growth. This mode of governing became part of the culture and institutional knowledge of municipal life. Though it took root on the Lombard plain and other parts of Italy, this mode of governing and accompanying civic culture was especially strong in Tuscany where, according to Cattaneo, it reached even the lowest members of the common people (Cattaneo [1858] 1957, 2:434). The constitutional design of city republics fostered other positive features of governance as well.

First, there followed the spread of individual liberties. The Italian cities recognized the freedom of serfs. In doing so, they anticipated what emerged, by Cattaneo's time, as an imperative necessity in Russia and Poland. This freedom included the right to bear arms and to have a share in the common property resources of cities. One of the earliest recorded examples of this freedom took place in Bologna in 1236 (Cattaneo [1858] 1957, 2:425).

Second, Cattaneo attributed the growth of feudal and manorial law to the growth of urban law itself. As he put it, when Milanese consuls submitted feudal relations to the scrutiny of the law and wrote *De Feudis*, they proclaimed from the walls of a city a system of law whose influence was eventually felt in almost all of feudal Europe. In this way, feudal customs had the potential of evolving, as most did, from "a tradition of brute power to a tradition of reason" (Cattaneo [1858] 1957, 2:426; cf., Berman 1983, chs. 9–10).

Third, the growth of free cities also assured the growth and recognition of mercantile and commercial law amidst different peoples and across linguistic groups. For Cattaneo, this law possessed the characteristics of "a universal law of nations" (Cattaneo [1858] 1957, 2:426; cf., Berman 1983, ch. 11).

Fourth, Cattaneo pointed out that the "tenacious tradition of liberty and self-organization (*governo di sé*)" was maintained through "the continuous exercise of the art of association" (Cattaneo [1861] 1965, 4:182). The art of association ranged from the formation of artisanal guilds and schools among urban dwellers to the creation of an extraordinary number of commercial agricultural ventures among people from the *contado* and the city (Cattaneo [1858] 1957, 2:426–7; [1861] 1965, 4:168–209). To illustrate this observation, Cattaneo was fond of calling up the irrigation system in the Po River Plain, which encompassed several provinces and territories. Since he had a long and intimate association with those waterways, he could be lyrical in describing their enduring characteristics.

The origins of the irrigation system were lost over time, but it was clear for Cattaneo that what made the system endure until his own era was the set of evolving local rules, particularly the Milan statute known as *De acquis conducendis*. These local institutions furnished an evolutionary system of rules for the irrigation infrastructures (Cattaneo [1858] 1957, 2:427). Among other positive attributes, *De acquis conducendis* extended the principle of eminent domain to cover the specific needs of an expanding system of irrigation over and across territories of several cities, however fiercely citizens and officials of each city were determined to maintain their own local autonomy. By the sixteenth century, the laws and regulations that could be traced as far back as the eleventh century had become part of the common-law tradition of the Po River plain and of the institutional knowledge – what we would now call "social capital" – of the Plain people. In this way, the irrigation system created and maintained by successive generations of Plain people met changing conditions and requirements over many centuries, including circumstances when the Po River valley itself was the theatre of war and conquest. Not without a touch of pride in such long-enduring institutions, Cattaneo felt compelled to add, "there [were] some civilized nations that even [then, in his time, had] not yet learned how to reconcile the principle of eminent domain with the naked conception of absolute private property rights. It was for this reason that a Scottish engineer, using a phrase from the British experience, characterized the municipal statutes [of Milan] as 'the Magna Carta of irrigation.'" This Magna Carta was "the greatest gift" that the Lombard cities had given to their countryside (Cattaneo [1858] 1957, 2:427–8).

Finally, civic life contributed in a fundamental way to the growth of important centres of learning and, more generally, to the growth of a culture that privileged critical inquiry, disputation, and problem solving: "This way, we have come to experimental science that always looks ahead and seeks new discoveries. It does not bother to say *ipse dixit*. This is, in the final analysis, the true and hidden strength that distinguishes modern Europe from its past and from the immobile and fossilized reasoning of Indian Brahmins and Chinese mandarins, trained to fix their eyes only on ancient oracles ... The sources of a live science can be found to reside ... in the kind of tenacious consciousness and pursuit of discovery that led Galileo to say: *Eppur si muove!*" (Cattaneo [1858] 1957, 2:435).

Borrowing Vico's terminology, Cattaneo characterized the period of free cities as "an heroic era of cities" (Cattaneo [1858] 1957, 2:430). The importance of this period is better understood, Cattaneo observed, when we consider what happens when communes are so organized that their residents enjoy neither freedom nor self-governance. Look, Cattaneo said, to what has historically afflicted cities in Asia. Their chief problem is not that they lack commerce, industry, a certain tradition of science, love of poetry and music, gardens, perfumes, and the opulence of palaces and civilized lifestyle. What afflicts their public life resides in this: that people have had neither freedom nor autonomy; cities are without urban law and, as a consequence, without municipal consciousness and patriotism. Most urban dwellers have been conditioned to live as if they were inanimate beings, as if they did not have a capacity to reason and to take individual and joint initiatives.

European travellers who have depicted residents of Asian cities as resigned to their fate and unsolicitous about matters of common interest have been correct in their description, writes Cattaneo, but they have been seriously mistaken in explaining the causes. Communal apathy and inertia do not flow from personal characteristics, or even from community ethos. Whatever fatalism, inertia, and apathy can be observed, they do not derive from an innate incapacity or inability of Asians. Rather, they derive from the institutional arrangements that shape the political economy of everyday life for most ordinary people. Fatalism and inaction can and do become a way of coping with conditions of life devoid of chances to pursue individual and joint opportunities. Cattaneo seldom lost faith in the view that human beings in Asia, as elsewhere, could learn to break out of such vicious circles (Cattaneo [1858] 1957, 2:395).

Cattaneo then reinforced his argument with illustrations closer to his readers. He asked them to recall what happened in southern Italy. At one point in history, this area was the site of vibrant municipal institutions, flourishing civic culture, and rich associational life. So much so, in fact, that even in the aftermath of the fall of the Roman Empire and the resultant political disorder, residents of most southern Italian communes had continued to enjoy at least a modicum of civic life. This is all the more striking when we consider that civic life had by then become practically extinct in northern Italy. The contrast between north and south rapidly changed after the eleventh century, and Cattaneo dated the rupture to the Norman conquest of the south.

Cattaneo cast the rupture in bold comparative strokes. While people in Venice, Pisa, and Genoa were beginning their commercial ventures that would reach throughout the Mediterranean world to the Aegean and Black Seas, and while Milan city officials were waging their unequal fight against the emperor, Norman adventurers managed to extend their dominion as far south as Sicily. Invested with papal claims of jurisdiction, these adventurers presented themselves as defenders of the people. The Norman landing near Messina in 1060 signalled the end of two hundred years of Moslem rule in Sicily. The fall of the free cities of Amalfi in 1131 and of Naples in 1138 ensued. The Norman kingdom was created in this fashion and brought with it a rupture of major proportions in the civic culture of southern Italy.

Recent scholarship suggests that Cattaneo exaggerated the rupture in the civic culture of the south (Matthew 1992; Sabetti 1999a). But there was truth in his argument when Cattaneo recalled for his readers that "magistrates from southern cities were included in the three branches of parliament, but under the juridical fiction that cities were part of the domestic patrimony of the king. The kingdom recognized that cities could make laws, but both the constitution and the law-making powers of cities now became subordinate to the extraneous and adverse principle of royal authority" (Cattaneo [1858] 1957, 2:431). Certain consequences were said to follow: "Soon cities became powerless, servile, and dull, while their inhabitants became estranged from and indifferent to the places where they lived" (Cattaneo [1858] 1957, 2:431). Cattaneo summarized the long-term consequences this way: "And so it was that the Byzantine era lasted until modern times for a large part of Italy ... The land whose people had inflicted the greatest loss of life on the ancient Romans as they had tried to conquer them, now became the golden dream of every adventurer who hoped to gain a piece of real estate. What a difference between the vast and sick Kingdom of Two Sicilies ... and the humble set of lagoons from which the people of Venice resisted Charlemagne, Sulemein, and the League of Chambray!" (Cattaneo [1858] 1957, 2:431). The analytical narrative did not stop here. Cattaneo went on to discuss, alas too briefly, what people of his generation could also learn from the experience of free cities.

The Insufficiency of the Free Cities

There is some force in the contention, prevalent especially among foreign observers, that the insufficiency of northern city republics is attributable to the intense city rivalry that erupted in wars and led to foreign conquests (Cattaneo [1858] 1957, 2:421). Once free communes had constituted themselves into independent military powers, in part in response to imperial and papal designs over them, it was inevitable that they would be exposed to "the iron law of diplomacy" [i.e., war] that prevailed among the great powers (Cattaneo [1858] 1957, 2:419). This diplomacy, comprising a vicious and escalating system of threats and counterthreats, contaminated and, in time, destroyed established patterns of urban life, including mechanisms for the peaceful resolution of local differences. There is truth in this line of reasoning – and, we might add, in Guicciardini's and Burkhardt's accounts cited earlier – but, Cattaneo continued, it does not tell the whole story. Not only can such accounts not be generalized for the entire history of Italy, they do not go deep enough in understanding sources of institutional weakness and failure for the periods they treat.

The problem of the Italian republics, Cattaneo averred, lay in the very organization and practice of communal life and, above all, in the absence of knowledge about federative principles of organizations – what he called "federal law." True, the basic principles of constitutional government were worked out among the free cities of Italy (and Germany) long before the Americans confronted the problems of constitutional choice. The chief problem was that these basic principles did not extend to "federal law."

Cattaneo showed some reluctance to address these issues fully in his 1858 essays. After all, he was constructing an argument against two prevailing conceptions that justified unitary systems; he was not writing a history of free cities. But, throughout the course of his work, he did identify three sets of institutional weakness and failure. These were 1) the opportunities provided by the institutional design for the rise of self-perpetuating local oligarchies; 2) the practical absence of overlapping or federative arrangements between city republics; and, most importantly, 3) the absence of institutional knowledge about or the intellectual failure to conceptualize the possibility of a federative pan-Italian polity.

The discussion of each set of problems is of uneven quality in Cattaneo's writings, and one must turn to more recent scholarship to document fully his insights. His discussion centred on the absence of knowledge about federal principles of constitutional design among students and practitioners of urban law and republican government. Citizens and city officials knew a lot about local self-rule, but still they did not know how to organize multiple urban jurisdictions in relation to each other. They did not know how to combine self-rule with shared rule. It was the unavailability of a polycentric, federalist perspective to political craftsmanship and problem solving that, in the final analysis, deprived Italian city republics of the capacity to successfully manage local problem solving and exposed them to foreign domination and conquest. He characterized this lack of knowledge, or absence of learning, in this way: "The idea of equality of rights in the disparity of force, the idea of a federal constitutional law (*giustizia federale*), was a ray of light reserved to illuminate future generations" (Cattaneo [1858] 1957, 2:423). This ray of light shone above all on the people of the United States.

Cattaneo concluded by drawing some implications from the way Italy was being united during the Risorgimento. He noted that the institutional weakness of communal life was bound to persist as long as institutional change simply replaced local hegemonies with a national, more encompassing hegemony. A national public monopoly was apt to be just as deleterious to civic life and traditions as any of the old communal monopolies. The allusion to the negative consequences of public and private monopolies was censored by the publisher, who feared – correctly – that the argument when published could be extended to the creation of the Italian state itself (Cattaneo [1858] 1957, 2:423 n.1). Indeed, the making of Italy furnished new opportunities for Cattaneo to extend his analysis.

COMMUNAL LAW IN UNITED ITALY

As we saw in chapter 2, the creation of the Italian state from 1859 to 1865 led to a single, uniform, and overarching system of administration, patterned largely on the French system. It was presumed that this would serve the public interest of all citizens. A uniform pattern of consolidated local governments was extended to all parts of Italy, based on these underlying principles: 1) the organization of local government and intergovernmental arrangements was within the domain of the central government; 2) the choice of goods and services provided by communal and intergovernmental institutions was under the authority of the central government; and 3) supervision of communal government and of the provision of public goods and services by local government officials was the exclusive jurisdiction of the centralized government and administration.

Not satisfied with imposing a uniform system on all the communes, the founders of the Italian kingdom drafted legislation in 1864 to allow cities to annex small nearby communes and to permit other small communes to come together and form larger ones, encouraging larger units of government. The bigger the communal jurisdiction, the better local government was expected to be. In particular, communes below 3,000 residents were viewed as sources of impotence and disorder, an unqualified bad.

Cattaneo carefully examined the legislation in a series of open letters to a newspaper in Turin, then the seat of the central government (Cattaneo [1864] 1965, 4:414–40). His work must have had some impact, for the bill appears to have been withdrawn. Whatever the case may be, what is important here is how Cattaneo applied his microconstitutional approach to the proposed changes.

Cattaneo began by noting several problems in the very nature of the communal and provincial law. The transplanted administrative system had earlier subverted and negated the concept of the commune as a self-governing unit in France. Incorporated into the governmental framework of united Italy, the unitary system was now producing paradoxical results. All adult males had been allowed to vote in the various plebiscites leading to the proclamation of the kingdom. But once the kingdom had been created, the great majority of those who had constitutionally created it were deprived of a voice and treated as mere subjects. People in northern Italy had enjoyed more self-rule under Austrian occupation than they did once they were supposed to be free (cf., Rotelli 1976).

Cattaneo then turned to the major presuppositions of the bill. The first assumed that legislators, as the source of laws, can scan the horizon and ordain events and people as they wish: lawmakers know best. Second, bigger communes were presumed to stand for good government, while smaller communes were presumed to represent collective impotence, disorder, and bad government. Cattaneo took issue with these presuppositions.

He argued that no set of legislators can be omniscient and omnipotent. There were many historical reasons why villages, towns, and cities in Italy were of varying sizes and shapes; such diversity cannot be easily erased by legislative fiat and for the misguided goal of communal equality. Cattaneo deplored the unwillingness of Italian legislators to learn from the record of centralized systems of public administration experienced by large cities like Naples since 1816. We should not forget, he urged, that ordinary Neapolitans, including the poor, still had no more voice in a united Italy than they had before they were liberated. In addition, there was no evidence that the small size of communes per se was a source of bad government – or collective inaction, disorder, and inefficiency. Indeed, Cattaneo added, the test of experience suggests the opposite.

Compare communal life in Lombardy and in Sicily, he suggested. Lombardy had, in Cattaneo's own time, the greatest number of small communes in Italy. About half of the 2,242 communes were very small: 607 communes had not more 150 inhabitants; 746 did not exceed 1,000 inhabitants. There were only 151 communes of more than 3,000; even the populations of large cities did not exceed 150,000. By contrast, Sicily was the land of fewer but bigger communes. On average, there were 358 inhabitants per commune in Lombardy, while Sicily had roughly eighteen times as many – 6,681 inhabitants per commune.

The presuppositions of the 1864 legislation would lead us to believe that communal life and services in Lombardy were in poor health, while in Sicily they enjoyed good health. In fact, the reverse was the case (Cattaneo [1864] 1965, 4:424). Lombardy was first among all the regions to have a vast, overlapping public-service delivery system: local networks of public roads; communal schools, including daycare centres (*asili*); public health doctors; and many other essential public services that served almost all the mountainous areas and the plain. Sicily, the land of large communes, did not match by any measure the high standards of communal life achieved in Lombardy.

For Cattaneo, the features of good government found in Lombard communes were due to several interconnected factors that had historically worked together: the relatively small size and high number of autonomous communes; the degree of self-governance that applied within and beyond each commune since medieval times; and a rich mix of public and voluntary communal initiatives, including the Po valley waterways. Thus, Cattaneo rejected the argument that bigger communes lead ipso facto to responsive and responsible government. "Large size per se is not what gives meaning and purpose to human life" (Cattaneo, [1864] 1965, 4:425). Crafting his argument in language that would appeal to most readers, Cattaneo added, "it is better to live in ten separate houses as friends than to live in one in discord. It is true that ten families could prepare their soup in one hearth, but there are elements in the human spirit and in domestic desires that cannot be explained by the naked economy of arithmetic and material interests" (Cattaneo [1864] 1965, 4:426). The argument in favour of cities annexing neighbouring small communes was without empirical foundation (Cattaneo [1864] 1965, 4:426). Once again, the available evidence, drawn mostly from the suburbs of Milan, was used to reject the argument for big government and to reach opposite conclusions.

Consolidation and annexation would not automatically improve public services and communal life. Nor would they secure a stronger tax base to provide services to the annexed areas. Such institutional changes were not designed to foster either good citizenship or communal life (Cattaneo [1864] 1965, 4: 426–7). Most likely they would worsen the servitude that, in many ways, already weighed on the nation (Cattaneo [1864] 1965, 4:440). Once again, Cattaneo returned to his earlier conception of the commune as a society of neighbours.

CONCLUSION

The constitutional design favoured by Cattaneo did not happen. But his approach to crafting institutions of good government, which he understood to be the same as self governance, was as revolutionary as it was endurable. Revolutionary, in that it offered a radically new approach to Italian development experience, that reveals how partial were the histories of Italy (and even of the Renaissance) by Guicciardini and others, and shows that it is possible to incorporate such histories as "special cases" in a fuller, more articulated and reformulated understanding of constitutional government – emptying of meaning the strong-centralized-government approach to the question of Italian unity. Endurable, in that Cattaneo's mode of analysis did not end with his life. Many modern analysts have attributed remarkable intuition to Cattaneo and Francesco Ferrara for their capacity to anticipate patterns of development that occurred long after they wrote their works. Research by James M. Buchanan (1960) on the Italian political economy tradition suggests an alternative explanation, as does part 1 of this book. Cattaneo and Ferrara used a theory of institutional analysis and design that enabled them to reach important conclusions about the direction that the course of Italian political development would take. As we see in the chapters that follow, Ferrara's mode of reasoning about alternative constitutional designs and Cattaneo's perspective on institutional knowledge, choice, and learning might have anticipated the likely results of the reiteration of constitutional choice in republican Italy.

Italy had such a rich heritage that the meaning of the past already posed dilemmas in the nineteenth century about how to face the future. To try to do so by uniform rules of a "united" Italy did not allow a synthesis to develop by mutual accommodation in a world of great cities. This is where Cattaneo's and Ferrara's visions were of fundamental importance. The regional devolution that Ferrara suggested for Sicily in 1860 has now become a reality for Italy as a whole, albeit with mixed results. The nature of these results is open to different interpretations, as we shall see in chapters 4 and 9. Cattaneo's federalist principles continue to challenge the idea of sovereign states but offer little or no solace to secessionist movements in Italy and beyond. At the same time, they insist that the ecological conditions of Italy and much of the world are not uniform. In Cattaneo's view, we need to adapt to local ecological niches and leave room for variation in local and regional rules that fit within a law of municipal corporations and other types of associational realities. Serious problems are apt to rise when we identify "democracy" with parliamentary government and representative assemblies rather than with the universality of the village and community. We are also apt to forget, Cattaneo noted, that Italian pride is associated more with the local or the city than with the nation-state. The challenge in making of a united Italy was to built on that pride to extend to the nation the whole.

Though different in many ways, the Sicilian and Milanese analysts shared a common intellectual tradition in problem solving that is more concerned with underlying design principles for crafting institutions of self-government than with actual blueprints for the nuts and bolts of institutional arrangements. That mode of reasoning about ideas, institutions, and outcomes, about what system of governance is more conducive to self-rule and shared rule – what Machiavelli called *il vivere libero* – is what Cattaneo has to offer to the Italy of today. As we saw, the Risorgimento men of action par excellence, like Mazzini and other revolutionaries, did not quite understand this approach. Nor did they share Cattaneo's vision of the need to go back to the city and the neighbourhood as the basic human reality. The emphasis placed on underlying principles of self-governance, capable of reaching from the individual and the commune to the nation as a whole and even to a European union, explains why Cattaneo's ideas and method of analysis continue to be compelling in our own time.

PART TWO

How the System Worked in Republican Italy: Institutional Learning and Constraints

4 Expectations and Results in Public Service Delivery

The return to liberal democracy in 1946 after the Fascist period, assured the continuation of the public service system and, at the same time, led to renewed efforts to improve service delivery and the formative nature of public institutions. A number of changes in governmental policies and structures put in place during the postwar period aimed at improving how the public service system worked, and attempted to bring government closer to the citizens. Especially after 1950, professional training of police officers and other bureaucratic personnel increased; the expansion of public employment rolls was coupled with substantial salary increases for state officials; unprecedented expenditures for public works took place. These new policies were accompanied by institutional changes. During the 1960s, "little city halls" and district councils were established in large urban centres as part of communal decentralization. In 1970, regional government, already operative on the islands and in the border areas, was extended to the rest of the peninsula as part of the decentralization of the national bureaucracy. Most of these programmatic and institutional changes were already part of the 1948 republican constitution, but their implementation coincided with or was pushed for by the Opening to the Left in 1963, hailed as a new era in Italian public life.

Already by the 1980s, it had become apparent that this new era had not markedly improved government services, nor had it led to the sort of citizenry that is necessary if a republican regime is to flourish. In spite of the disparate efforts of citizens and public officials, many "pathologies" in the delivery of public services continued to exist. Why did crafting institutions for good government prove to be such an elusive goal in the postwar period? Why did the system not work as it should have? And if the empirical analysis of differentials in regional government performance by Robert D. Putnam, Robert Leonardi, and Raffaella Nanetti (1993) is accurate, what to make of the good government that does exist in Bologna and its regional government in Emilia-Romagna?

The work of Carlo Cattaneo and Francesco Ferrara suggests that there is good reason to expect "pathologies" in the way the system worked, especially in the distribution of government services. As we saw in chapters 2 and 3, Cattaneo and Ferrara predicted that the results of the public service system would radically deviate from those anticipated by the creators of the Italian state. In the aftermath of the Fascist regime, Luigi Einaudi, in his 1944 essay "Via al prefetto!" ("Away With the Prefect!") extended Cattaneo's analysis by arguing that major inadequacies in public service delivery follow from the form of government (centralized state administration) and the ways government operates (*stato di diritto*), as well as from the politicization of local governments by national political parties. Echoing Alexis de Tocqueville's analysis, Einaudi concluded that, in a system of bureaucratic administration with a government elected by democratic vote, there is a high probability that local officials "merely learn to obey, to intrigue, to recommend and to seek influence" (Einaudi [1944] 1954, 54).

At the same time, the work of North American scholars in new economic institutionalism suggests that the politics of bureaucracy in large-scale organizations and the infrastructure policies based on such units will be subject to serious problems (E. Ostrom, Schroeder, and Wynne 1993; Tullock 1965). Goal displacement and risk avoidance will be their characteristic features. In sum, these works suggest that a very large bureaucracy will "1) become increasingly indiscriminating in its response to diverse demands, 2) impose increasingly high social costs on those who are presumed to be the beneficiaries, 3) fail to proportion supply to demand, 4) allow public goods to erode by failing to take action to prevent one use from impairing others, 5) become increasingly error prone and uncontrollable to the point where public actions deviate radically from rhetoric about public purposes and objectives, and 6) eventually lead to circumstances where remedial actions exacerbate rather than ameliorate problems" (V. Ostrom 1974, 64).

On the basis of this analysis, we would expect the structure of institutional arrangements in postwar Italy to fail to supply all public services in relation to a uniform standard of performance within and between all the communes. We would expect the pathologies associated with large bureaucratic organizations to be the normal characteristics of Italian public service system. Moreover, we would expect administrative superiors responsible for insuring appropriate levels of performance in relation to uniform performance standards to experience loss of information and control in their efforts to monitor the output of public services. We would further expect citizen alienation to go hand in hand with poor government performance. In brief, we would not expect the system to work as it should.

Available evidence and inferential reasoning make it possible to estimate the warrantability of contending expectations about the relationship between structure and performance of institutional arrangements. This chapter examines the structure and performance of urban service delivery systems in postwar Italy; chapter 5 turns to problem solving by legislation. Both chapters seek to remove the false lights that obscure the constraints on the system and the institutional learning that followed from the design characteristics of the national state, especially the use of detailed central planning.

The two dominant factors influencing how the system worked in postwar Italy, including the delivery of public services, were the highly centralized state administrative and decision-making structure and the system of electoral laws that encouraged the active participation of national parties in the organization of local party activities. This chapter first considers these two factors as components of the basic design of Italian political institutions. Then we turn to an analysis of their consequences for the operation of the public service system, using the cities of Naples and Bologna as examples. In the last section, reforms in the 1970s at the communal and national levels designed to decentralize decision making are described, and the short- and long-run consequences of these reforms are discussed.

CONSTITUTIONAL CHANGE AND INSTITUTIONAL STABILITY

The post-1945 institutional arrangements for the public service system at the local level rest on the design criteria used to fashion a united Italy in the 1860s. As we saw in chapters 2 and 3, the nation-state was organized as a single centre of authority with an exclusive monopoly claim on the ultimate use of force in the organization of society. The monopoly over the supply of public goods and services was accompanied by a single overarching system of public administration with local elected officials and professionally trained personnel hierarchically ordered and subject to direction by heads of departments at the centre of government.

As was shown earlier, the unitary or monocentric solution to the question of Italian self-government in the 1860s was a conscious response by the artificers of unification to several perplexing problems. The new nation-state was forged through military victories. Previous rulers of Tuscany and Lombardy had allowed a large measure of self-government in internal affairs; roughly the same conditions had existed in Sardinia and Sicily until the Napoleonic wars. This tradition of self-rule had given rise to a strong attachment to community affairs as well as an extraordinarily diverse set of social institutions, cultures, and languages. To permit inhabitants of the peninsula to continue to exercise their self-governing capabilities, as Lombard and Sicilian publicists like Cattaneo and Ferrara urged, would have annulled the military victories and destroyed the very foundations of the state, or so it was assumed (Cavour 1949, 1:305). At the same time, it must be recalled that in 1860 a united Italy à la Cattaneo could not be established either. As we saw earlier, the forced creation of unity through administrative measures under a common parliament, backed by a national army, seemed – and not just to Piedmontese leaders – to be the only feasible option for both unification and good government. Consequently, the change from the old regimes to the Savoy monarchy made people "Italian" but the iron law of oligarchy continued to prevail.

The Fascist regime strengthened the forced creation of unity begun in the nineteenth century, but, just as Cattaneo had anticipated in 1864, the solidity of bureaucratic administration turned out to be false, for "those who sow servility usually reap betrayal" (Cattaneo [1864] 1965, 4: 420). The fragility of the Fascist state was revealed in dramatic proportions in the Second World War, and this helps to explain the call for some form of "regionalist state" to be enshrined in the republican constitution that followed.

The reopening of the question of Italian self-government after the Second World War was accompanied by the emergence of political groupings that claimed to represent the nation. The strategic positions assumed by the Christian Democrat and Communist-Socialist groups allowed their leaders to become the major artificers of "the second rebirth of Italy." These new artificers were confronted with the same perplexing problems that unification leaders had faced a century earlier. Changes in the authority and powers of the instrumentalities of the central government as some analysts were urging – in part recalling Cattaneo's ideas (Bobbio 1971; Ciuffoletti 1994, 101–65; Einaudi [1944] 1954; C. Levi 1963, 248–54; but cf., Lanaro 1994) – might have given support to localized groups intent on asserting an inherent right of self-government, thereby demolishing the work of the creators of unification. Moreover, the leftist and Christian Democrat leaders, who participated in the emerging postwar conflict between the two international superpowers, viewed the instrumentalities of the state as an opportunity to apply the principles of Marxism or Christian Democracy, and to advance or retard the causes of "Eastern" or "Western" civilization respectively.

For different reasons, then, there appeared strong justification for the reiteration of the basic unitary constitutional design, even though now the state would be divided, in the words of article 114 of the new constitution, into regions, provinces, and communes. A renewed commitment to liberal democracy, together with the emerging forces of Marxism and Christian Democracy and the prospect of a cold war, made it possible now both to ignore, for the most part, what Cattaneo and Einaudi had suggested and to anticipate that responsible, responsive, and efficient government would result from the *homines novi* of republican Italy. Aside from the need for a regionalist state, what the creators of "the second rebirth of Italy" learned above all from the Fascist experience was to craft a new parliamentary system that did not bias the policy process in favour of majority rule. Still, they put less faith in the independent utility of institutional design and more faith in "good" or "virtuous" men to make the system work. The holders of postwar republican sovereignty – the agents of constitutional choice and postconstitutional legislation – were the parties that made the First Republic of Italy. With this in mind, it is easier to appreciate what kind of institutional learning and "state project" accompanied the crafting of the republican regime between 1945 and 1948 (see also Legnani 1975; Mastropaolo 1991, 70–73; Ornaghi 1979; Pombeni 1995, 103–44; Rebuffa 1995, 52–7, 81–90; Romanelli 1995b, 161–6; Schiera 1993, 349–88).

The essential elements of the pre-Fascist parliamentary regime and "liberal state based on law" (*stato liberale di diritto*) were reintroduced, and extended to an unprecedented degree, especially in the declaration of "basic principles" in the new constitutional charter of 1948 (Fioravanti 1995; see also Quadrio Curzio 1997, 1101, 1108–9). The new constitution affirmed, among other things, the inviolability of fundamental human rights and "the task of the republic to remove all obstacles of an economic and social nature which, by limiting the freedom and equality of citizens, prevent the full development of the individual and the participation of all workers in the political, economic, and social organization of the country" (article 3, Constitution of the Republic of Italy, 1948). At the same time, it called for new institutions, such as a constitutional court and regional governments, aimed in effect at limiting central government authority. Secondary laws introduced during the Fascist era remained, however, and Fascist reforms, ranging from communal institutions to the judicial system, became permanent fixtures of republican Italy, impeding the full implementation of the new constitutional design. During much of the cold war, the central government thus retained authority through parliament over 1) the design of institutional arrangements at the local level, including the full implementation of the regionalist state as envisaged in article 114 of the constitution; 2) the choice of public services provided by these instrumentalities; 3) the exercise of governmental prerogatives in relation to the supply of public services; 4) the monitoring of the performance of public service systems; as well as 5) the removal of all economic and social obstacles to achieving full equality and freedom among citizens and workers. Given the range of these powers, it is not wide of the mark to suggest that the primacy of the national legislator seemed set, if not *in aeternum*, as Giorgio Rebuffa suggests (1995, 89–90), certainly in "concrete," to use Augusto Barbera's word (1991, 135–40, but cf., Mastropaolo 1991, 71).

Communal and Provincial Governments

After the Second World War, the Italian peninsula and islands continued to be divided into about 8,000 communes, or municipalities, of varying sizes. Each commune had the same governmental structure and authority originally granted by the central government. This general uniformity or "civic equality" derived from a mixture of the design principles of the unitary state and the *stato di diritto*: communes, not individuals, were the basic units for the fashioning and refashioning of the Italian state.

In 1934 a general law on local government had been promulgated to make communal and provincial institutions "more efficient and responsive to the demands of the central authority" (Steiner 1939, 315). This was achieved in two ways: consolidation and annexation. In 1920 there were 9,000 communes and a population of over thirty million people; by 1934 the number of communes had been reduced to 7,000, while the population had increased to forty million.

The trend toward consolidation or annexation was reversed following the Second World War, when approximately 800 communes were either reconstituted or established anew; by 1987, the number of communes had increased to 8,092 from 8,032 in 1960 (Rotelli 1991, 43–4). These changes, however, left unaltered the 1934 general law that had strengthened the authority of the central government over the organization and conduct of communal affairs. In fact, the principal difference in the structure of local government between the Fascist and the republican regimes was the election of local public officials (Rotelli 1973, 155). In the postwar period each commune served as 1) a local office for the vast bureaucracy of the central government; 2) the local administrative unit for the Ministry of the Interior; and 3) an expression of "local government" or "local autonomy" in the sense that elected communal officials were responsible for the production and delivery of communal services.

A characteristic feature of the post-1945 period was, *mutatis mutandis*, the close fit between the conduct of national affairs and that of communal or municipal affairs. The position of the mayor and members of his executive committee (*giunta*) vis-à-vis the communal council and the communal bureaucracy was exactly the same as that of the prime minister and members of his council vis-à-vis the national parliament and the national bureaucracy. Large cities such as Milan and Naples had fifteen or more communal departments ranging from sanitation to urban planning, but each department was organized in relation to a member of the communal executive council charged with general responsibility for the procurement and delivery of that service. The same principle applied to the operation of municipal enterprises. Since the turn of the century, municipal enterprises have delivered services ranging from public transportation to water and gas under the direction of administrative boards appointed by and responsible to the mayor and the executive committee.

The choice of which services were supplied by the central government and which by the communes depended historically upon the importance of each service *for* the central government as the chief provider, producer, and enforcer of good government. Services such as education, public health, public security, and fire protection have historically been supplied by the central government organized in terms of ministries or state services. Each ministry had a local production unit engaged in supplying a specific good or service that was jointly used by local residents. Each production unit was organized upon monocentric principles. The size of cities affected only the number of technical personnel: the larger the city, the larger the group of technical personnel (e.g., Baldissara 1998).

For example, a typical village for much of the postwar period was likely to have a medical health officer and veterinarian from the public health administration, a forest warden from the Ministry of Agriculture, a commandant of *carabinieri* in charge of the local garrison of the state police officers, and a "didactic director" in charge of elementary school instruction. With some differences, similar arrangements prevailed on a larger scale in cities. Fire protection service, for example, was generally supplied only to city residents. Inhabitants of small communes generally depended on the fire protection service of the provincial fire brigade. For every city and provincial capital the maintenance of public order or crime detection continued to be performed by two parallel state police forces: the *carabinieri* from the Ministry of Armed Forces and the public security corps (*polizia*) from the Ministry of the Interior. This is critically important for understanding the government war on organized crime, as we shall see in part 3. At the same time, in an effort to maintain the parallel system of police throughout the entire territory, mayors of small communes without *polizia* officials had the legal capacity to act as officers of the public security corps in relation to the commandant of the local *carabinieri* garrison. In this capacity, mayors of small communes could grant, for example, stay permits to foreigners wishing to reside in their communes.

Provinces served in part as an intermediate level linking local public service systems and the central government. By the First World War there were seventy-five provinces. During Fascism the consolidation of communes was accompanied by the creation of another nineteen provinces to improve the monitoring of the performance of communal governments and state technical services. After the Second World War, even though a number of old communes were reconstituted, the number of provinces that had been established during Fascist rule decreased somewhat, in part because of a loss of territory to Yugoslavia. The extension of regional government in the early 1970s increased the pressures within each newly created region – for example Molise and Calabria – for particular areas to constitute themselves as provinces. By 1992 these pressures had brought to ninety-five the total number of provinces. The number of communes attached to each province varied considerably, however; some northern provinces such as Turin still have as many as 300 communes. This change did not, however, drastically alter one historical fact: these territorial divisions were maintained, above all, for the convenience of the national bureaucracy. Each provincial capital historically reproduced in microcosm the state apparatus that existed at the national level.

During Fascist rule, the provincial prefect exercised general control over all the instrumentalities of government operating within the confines of each province. After the war, this power was withdrawn. The prefect remained, however, as the major representative of the central government at the provincial level and as the chief field agent for the minister of the Interior. In this capacity, each prefect still exercised general control over communal affairs. This control was strengthened by the authority granted to municipal secretaries or chief clerks, state employees who continued working in each of the communes. Often their position has been regarded as "anomalous," for as state employees in the 1920s they assumed the position of inside watchdogs of communal governments (Baldissara 1998, 121–94; Cappelletti 1963, 262). In addition, each prefect controlled the provincial fire brigade and was responsible for the maintenance of public order in the province.

In republican Italy, provincial officers of the state technical services functioned as intermediaries between local and central offices and they monitored the performance of local production units. For much of the postwar period, each province had, for example, a purveyor of studies, an intendant of finance, a provincial health officer, a chief engineer of the civil engineer corps, and a provincial agrarian inspector; each provincial state officer in turn assigned provincial inspectors to make periodic visits to local production units to monitor performance of subordinate officials. In this capacity, each provincial state officer acted as a surrogate prefect. In fact, each provincial officer, or field director, rendered account for the exercise of his authority only to his ministerial superiors. The delivery of public services that extended beyond the jurisdiction of a single "prefect" could thus be procured, for the most part, only through central directives aimed at coordinating provincial field services.

It is now possible to sum up performance expectations built into the system. Local governmental institutions were not designed to be responsive to the preferences of diverse communities of people. Serving the needs of localized or private interests was regarded as perverse or as "the first step to corruption" of the *stato di diritto*. For private citizens to take a serious interest in public affairs or local problems was regarded as improper and even illegal. As noted in chapter 1, according to the doctrine of the *stato di diritto*, only officials were presumed to be concerned with public affairs or local problems (see also Pizzorno 1971, 90–1). As we shall also see in detail in chapter 8, this point is rather important, and failure to take it into account has led to serious misconstruction of local realities, producing what students of institutional analysis and development call "truncated analyses" (E. Ostrom, Schroeder, and Wynne 1993, 154–5).

A uniform structure of governmental arrangements at the local level was presumed to serve the public interest of all citizens. The simplicity of the structure of communal government went hand in hand with the clearly defined and concentrated authority and responsibility of communal officials. The business of checking on these officials was the exclusive prerogative of higher officials. These higher officials were presumed to be in a position to monitor and evaluate the comparative performance of different communal governments and to determine the responsibility of communal officials if something went wrong. The hierarchical organization of communal officials and professionally trained personnel was assumed to be the least costly and most efficient arrangement 1) for excluding localized or private interests in public decision-making; 2) for providing a uniform supply of public services; and 3) for monitoring the comparative performance of local governmental units. But what ultimately determined the overall public interest was the central government. In this sense, institutional arrangements at the local level were designed to be responsive to the directives of central government authority (see also Baldissara 1998; Rebuffa 1995, 89–90; Raphael Zariski, quoted in Tarrow 1977, 124, 141).

After the Second World War, this particular set of institutional arrangements was still presumed to be a *neutral* device. The critical difference was a general recognition that the prevailing political concepts or the preferences of central government authority were "parliamentary" and not "dictatorial" in nature. Thus, the crafters of the Italian republican regime assumed that the system of public administration designed to be responsive to monarchical and Fascist leaders could now, by its very nature, be responsive to republican leaders: the basic presupposition was that the bureaucracy could serve any political master. The hierarchical arrangement that had been used to "unify" the country and "make Italians" – and, under Fascism, to "shape" people in the image of imperial Rome – could now serve to bolster the republican regime and to advance democratic, and even egalitarian, values. It was entirely consistent with this logic when Minister of the Interior Mario Scelba observed in 1960, in referring to the prefect as a symbol of that system: "If the prefect did not exist it would be necessary to create him. His function is essential; he cannot be replaced" (quoted in Adams and Barile 1972, 120).

Electoral Laws and Party Organizations

Before and after Fascism, access to the exercise of governmental prerogatives for the conduct of national and local government was dependent upon winning elections. The reiteration of the monocentric order after 1945 meant that those elected to exercise central governmental prerogatives would also be in a position to exercise a monopoly of authority over the supply of public services at the local level. The opportunities that derived from this structure of decision-making arrangements provided the conditions for political entrepreneurs to organize and maintain national party organizations for the purpose of capturing decision-making centres at the national and local levels. Electoral competition was in turn both enhanced and constrained by electoral laws. Thus party organizations and electoral laws, as well as being formative of the sort of citizenry necessary for the republican regime, provided the nexus between the structure of governmental arrangements and the procurement and delivery of public services at the local level.

The choice of electoral laws in the 1948 constitution reflected the agreement between the leaders of the major nongovernmental groupings that emerged during the Second World War. These major groupings were the Christian Democrat Party, the Communist Party, and the Socialist Party. These major parties were accompanied by small parties that represented Social Democrats, Republicans, Liberals, and, not before long, regrouped Monarchists and neo-Fascists. The strategic positions acquired by these parties at the national level (in their opposition to Fascism) together with the subordinate position of the communal government structure had the effect of insuring the dominance of these parties at the local level and of precluding the development of independent local organizations competing for municipal offices. In a study of grassroots politicians in Italy and France in the 1970s, Sidney G. Tarrow found that almost 90 per cent of Italian mayors were party members at the time of the interview, whereas only 45 per cent of the French mayors were currently party members; national parties were so central to local Italian political and associational life that voting in local elections for much of the postwar period merged with loyalism to national party organizations (Tarrow 1977, 127–8, 174–5, 209).

Before the First World War the electoral laws regulating elections to the chamber of deputies and elections for communal offices in large urban centres were based on a simple plurality vote in single-member constituencies and city wards. Elections in towns with less than 5,000 inhabitants, however, were based on a long party list with plurality vote; a winning party list automatically received 80 per cent of the seats on the municipal council. Following the Second World War, and after a brief experimentation, the electoral law for small towns, which contained about 25 per cent of the total population, was returned to majority voting. The electoral law for towns with more than 10,000 residents was changed, or *grosso modo* returned, to a 1919 at-large party-list system of proportional representation; in the early 1960s, proportionality was extended to *all* communes of more than 5,000 inhabitants, making this the most widespread electoral system for local elections (Romanelli 1995b, 184–6; Tarrow 1977, 74). Elections for the Chamber of Deputies were based on a party-list system of proportional representation in multimember districts or electoral colleges.

Proportional representation among party lists was in turn modified by a system of voter preferences within each party list that remained in force until its abolishment in the early 1990s. Voters would first choose which party they desired and then would be at liberty to choose not more than four of the names on that list as individual preferences. The number of seats assigned to each party would depend on the proportion of total votes received, but what determined the election of specific candidates from each party list in turn depended on the number of preference votes received. Party-list systems with proportional representation implied that representatives for a city in communal elections and for the Chamber of Deputies in national elections were elected at large. The appeal was to the voters of the city or of the nation as a whole. Elections became a popularity contest among the political parties. Candidates were successful by virtue of their being on a party list and within the winning proportion assigned to their political party. They were expected to represent the overall public interest, not the discrete interests of diverse constituencies or districts.

THE OPERATION OF PUBLIC SERVICE SYSTEMS

Having identified the rules of constitutional design and the governmental arrangements based on those principles, we now bring together the constitutional, governmental, and operational levels to consider how the system worked. What are the characteristic results which should flow from the postwar political process? Why is there reason to expect pathologies in the way the system worked, including the distribution of government services?

We begin with an examination of the impact of electoral laws and the structure of governmental arrangements on the procurement and delivery of public services. Next, evidence drawn from Bologna and Naples is used to examine the impact of differences between controlling parties on the conduct of communal governments. Institutional learning in the form of decentralization efforts will take up the last section.

Party Organizations, Elections, and Government Coalitions

Both national and local elections manifested competitive struggles among the postwar political parties. Similar issues and problems became the subject of local and national electoral campaigns (e.g., Pryce 1957, 1). As parties strove to distinguish themselves ideologically from one another, they appealed to "great issues" involving either the overall public interest of the nation or the intensity of some partisan commitment. A Turin newspaper noted during the 1951 local elections in that city that "no one has talked of the humble problems ... of roads, school buildings, health services ... everyone has preferred to concern themselves with the Atlantic Pact, Korea, peace and war, western and eastern civilization and even with religion and atheism" (*La Stampa* 13 May 1951, quoted in Pryce 1957, 11; see also Baldissara 1994, 116–22). Communal elections were not designed to allow for the articulation of different solutions to "humble problems." A study of party activities in central Italian communities indicates that, during the 1960s, communal electoral appeals changed little except in name – from the Atlantic Pact and Korea to Cuba and Vietnam (Stern 1974).

Voting served to emphasize the disjunction existing between participation in the electoral process and articulation of preferences for public services. In 1946 voting became universal, and an almost compulsory civic duty. Voting provided citizens with a certificate of good conduct or civic duty required for most employment and applications. Electoral laws under the party-list system encouraged citizens to choose parties on the basis of their ideological positions on "great issues" rather than to express their preferences for the humbler services. A logic of "polarized pluralism" came to dominate postwar Italian public life (Sartori 1966; cf., Farneti 1985).

At the same time, the introduction of preference voting with a party list provided some opportunity for citizens to express their preferences for particular candidates at least, but this undermined an essential rationale for long party lists. Candidates of the same list found themselves in competition with each other. In most parties two contests occurred in each national and urban election: an interparty contest and an intraparty contest. The intraparty contest created opportunities for successful candidates to use their influence to secure favourable decisions for electors from government authorities and administrative personnel and, once elected, to be more sensitive to the political entrepreneurship of local officials from other parties.

This situation helps to explain the combination of high partisanship and high entrepreneurship that researchers have found among Italian Communist who were mayors of about 10 per cent of the 8,000 or so communes in the 1960s and early 1970s (Tarrow 1977, 156–7, 180–2). The situation also made it possible that "not all roads lead to Rome," as Alberta Sbragia illustrated so well in the case of housing policy in postwar Milan (Sbragia 1979). But in the Italian setting, as in the French (Dupuy 1985; Thoenig 1978), where communal policies do not control official action in the bureaucracy, such local interventions have the potential to become perverse manifestations of responsiveness. The case of the bribe scandal *Tangentopoli* in Milan, which was brought into the open in the early 1990s, reveals how "a first step to corruption" can, over time, take on systemic features (cf., Della Porta 1996; for France, Mény 1997).

The complex mix of bureaucratic administration, party organization, and electoral laws facilitated one more postwar feature of Italian
politics: the rise of clientelistic politics and its eventual transformation
into forms of institutionalized corruption. The potential for Italian
governing parties to become, in the colourful language of Maurizio
Cotta and Pierangelo Isernia (1996), "giants with feet of clay" was
inherent in the very institutional design and dynamics of party government. Although the "enlightened" or "virtuous" party clientelism that
some analysts have found in Lucania and Abruzzo seems to be more
the exception than the rule in postwar Italy, as we shall see in chapter
7, it has transformed the social, economic, and political life of Lucania
and Abruzzo for the better (Piattoni 1996, 1998b; Zuckerman 1997).
The findings of Alan S. Zuckerman and Simona Piattoni, supported by
other research (Carboni 1998, Leonardi 1998; Leonardi, Putnam and
Nanetti 1987; Mutti 1994) have changed our understanding of clientelism and, by implication, earlier manifestations like transformism.

If the opportunities inherent in the electoral laws served to enhance
intraparty competition for most of the postwar period, the same
opportunities placed serious limitations on the ability of a *single* party
organization to secure a legislative majority and serve as the government. Forming and maintaining a winning legislative coalition required
different strategies than those used to appeal to the electorate. The different ideological positions emphasized during elections provided little
or no grounds to different party leaders to move forward to mutually
agreeable positions. Government coalitions were formed among leaders of different parties or party factions, but such coalitions were organized and maintained by unanimous consent of the groups involved.
Until the collapse of the postwar party system by 1994, intraparty factions, especially in the Christian Democrat Party (DC), would often
serve to bridge interparty differences (e.g., Mershon 1996; Zuckerman
1979).

Throughout the postwar years the exercise of central government
authority rested with a legislative coalition, headed by the DC as the
majority party, and was composed, until the Opening to the Left in
1963, of alternating small centre parties. The condition of unanimous
consent for the establishment and maintenance of these national coalitions gave rise to holdout strategies generally associated with this rule
(Buchanan and Tullock 1962; Sproule-Jones 1974). During the 1950s,
DC legislative leaders also relied from time to time on the "external"
and "uncovenanted" votes of Monarchists and neo-Fascists in efforts
to minimize their dependence on the small centre parties.

The formation of central government coalitions based upon unanimous consent was reflected at the local level where efforts were made

to replicate the same majority coalitions. Party and faction leaders needed to control both sets of coalitions in order to retain their strategic positions. The loss of a coalition at one level undermined the coalition at the other (see Allum 1973, 244; Barnes 1974; Fried 1973, 147; Rotelli 1991; see also Tsebelis 1990).

Following the 1956 local elections, for example, national party and faction leaders composing the central coalition faced the task of negotiating the formation of communal coalitions in more than 200 cities (Pryce 1957, 106–108). During the postwar period, party organizations both right and left were successful in capturing communal governments in cities such as Naples and Bologna. These communal governments took up countervailing positions vis-à-vis the DC Party and the successive national coalitions. Until about the end of the 1980s, the relationships between communal governments and the central government ranged from mutual support to mutual antagonism.

Administrative officials responsible for monitoring performance came to use the position of each communal government towards the central government as a critical performance variable. A condition of mutual support between the central government and the communal government was used to facilitate informal arrangements. A condition of mutual antagonism was an excuse to scrutinize the conduct of communal government. The degree of central control over local authorities was so substantial that if, for example, prefects "interpreted the law punctiliously and conscientiously intervened in the activities of local authorities in every case in which [they] are entitled to do so, local authorities could hardly operate at all" (Cappelletti 1963, 261–2). As we shall soon see, this situation turned out to be a positive "stimulus" for some local authorities.

The Conduct of Communal Governments in Naples and Bologna

It is hard to imagine two other Italian cities in the postwar period that offer sharper social, economic, and political contrasts than do Bologna and Naples. Both cities had a population size above what Cattaneo regarded as the threshold for communal self-governance. As late as the 1981 census, there were only thirteen cities with more than 250,000 inhabitants; the great majority of people still resided in communes of less than 10,000 people (Rotelli 1991, 44–6). By 1970 Bologna had a population of about 500,000, still relatively small when compared to Naples – with over 1,200,000 inhabitants, one of Italy's largest cities. While the population of Naples has continued to grow, that of Bologna has remained at 500,000 as late as 1998. From the point of view of

Cattaneo's "good government threshold," the population size of Naples is *ab initio* a condition for poor government performance, especially compared to the smaller population of Bologna. But city size is just one factor, though size itself may be construed as a product of government policy or lack of it. There are other factors that locate the two cities in widely different worlds.

The June 1999 local election produced a major political upset in Bologna. The Bolognese voters threw the left out of the commune and elected a right administration headed by the president of the local merchants' association and a one-time butcher shop owner, Giorgio Guazzaloca. Until then and continuously since 1946, Bologna was administered by successive Communist-Socialist coalitions led by Communist mayors. During the 1950s Naples was administered by a Monarchist-neo-Fascist coalition led by a Monarchist mayor, and during the 1960s it was administered by successive centre-left coalitions led by DC mayors. The DC coalition was shattered in 1975, when the Communists became the city's largest party at the polls, winning almost 33 per cent of the votes. This upset did not quite make Naples the Communist (PCI) stronghold that Bologna was, but it did lead to several PCI or left-sponsored communal administrations that continued after 1990.

In much of the popular and academic literature, Bologna has represented what the postwar Italian Communists could do, and highlighted what successive non-Communists in Naples could not or did not provide: efficiency in administration, responsive public services, lack of corruption, tackling of urban problems, quality of life. Recent research has placed in bold relief differentials in civic traditions that Bologna and Naples are said to typify (Putnam 1993; see also Nanetti 1988). Other studies have gone so far as to affirm that "there is no American city that does not suffer in comparison to Bologna" (Kertzer 1980, xxi).

By contrast, even a most sympathetic observer of postwar Naples has been forced to admit that "Naples has to be recognized for what it is: a challenge – and a thrilling challenge. Nowhere else are contrasts quite so violent – of sunlight and squalor, of grandeur and decay, pleasure and misery, gaiety and despair, the best and the worst – as in 'Parthenope' [as the Greeks who founded it called Naples]" (Seward 1984, 29). That the "gold of Naples", as the popular Neapolitan saying goes, is its human and social capital, the entrepreneurial and organizational skills of its citizens, there can be little question. Recognition that such "gold" has been applied to various forms of grassroots democracy is becoming increasingly common in academic knowledge (e.g., Pardo 1996). Grassroots democracy has been reinforced by the positive changes introduced by the administration of Antonio Bassolino, first elected in 1993 and reelected with overwhelming support in 1997. Such positive changes have been increasingly noticed to the point that some analysts suggest drawing lessons from Naples: "To many who are familiar with European cities, Naples may appear an unlikely case from which to draw lessons in planning, development and civicness. Yet, what is surprising is the degree of positive and purposive change which has occurred there over a few years period" (Nanetti 1998a, 111; see also Macry 1998). However, even when one-sided, stereotypical, negative views of Neapolitans are put aside and all allowances are made for a more calibrated view of the city, modern Naples cannot be described as it has been in earlier times. Writing in 1549, William Thomas described Naples as "one of the fairest cities of the world for goodly streets and beautiful buildings of temples and houses" (quoted in *Economist* 1996, 94). Today this description fits Bologna better than Naples.

In sum, there is no attempt here to gloss over differences between the two cities; those differences are not the issue. What is at issue is how to account for them. One way to proceed is to answer the question: What difference has the control of communal governments by different party organizations made, given that communal government authorities had, in general, no essential control over the delivery of public services supplied by the national bureaucracy? Available evidence on tax policies provides an entry into the question.

Evidence about communal tax policies comes from a Carlo Cattaneo Institute study. Investigators used the communal sales tax and the family tax as indicators of the effect of party control on communal revenue policies. Sales or consumption taxes fell largely on items of necessity and were considered instruments of conservative fiscal policy, whereas the family income tax was generally considered an instrument of progressive fiscal policy. Elected communal officials had discretion in the levying of these sources of revenue. Investigators expected that, given their leftist ideology, Communist communal governments would show relatively high per-capita family income tax levels and relatively low sales tax levels. The reverse was expected in the case of DC and right-wing communal governments (Galli and Prandi 1970, 241–3).

The research found, however, that "it was not possible to distinguish Communist from Christian Democrat taxation policies" (Galli and Prandi 1970, 242). Both PCI and DC communes showed a heavy reliance on family income tax. Communist-controlled Bologna, for example, had a higher percentage of revenues from the sales tax (35%) than the national average (33%) or the cities of Milan (30.1%) and Rome (30.4%), which were controlled by the Christian Democrats. This finding led the analysts to note that the "Communist party's program for increasing the family tax and reducing the sales tax had apparently not applied in Communist-administered cities" (Galli and Prandi 1970, 243). The general conclusion of this research was that "differences in budgetary policies were not associated in any systematic or consistent way with the control of communal governments by different party organizations" (Galli and Prandi 1970, 241; cf., Fried 1971).

A chief problem with this kind of research is that similar tax policies can mask quite different patterns of expenditures and quite different levels of performance (Baldissara 1994, 242–4; 1998). Indeed, much of the literature on grassroots politicians in France and Italy has found that Italian Communists were more radical and innovative in policy terms than their more sectarian French Communist counterparts (Tarrow 1977, 199). Equally, much of the literature on Bologna and other towns in Emilia-Romagna describes local budgetary politics in positive terms: efficiency in administration, responsive local public services, lack of corruption, effective tackling of urban problems through innovative institutional and other policy instruments, and a resultant high quality of civic life (Baldissara 1994; CENSIS 1982; Galetti 1975; Jaggi, Muller, and Schmid 1977; Putnam 1993). While such descriptions serve as useful correctives to conclusions drawn from taxation policies, the descriptions themselves gloss over other facts on the ground that point to a more complex, less flattering performance record of the Bologna government. For example, some research has strongly suggested that to understand performance in Bologna it is important to consider the political homogeneity of communes surrounding it (Nanetti 1988). Evidence drawn from, among others, Robert H. Evans' *Coexistence: Communism and Its Practice in Bologna, 1945–1965* (1967) and P.A. Allum's *Politics and Society in Post-War Naples* (1973) suggests that Bologna and Naples share operational characteristics overlooked by many observers. (To be sure, the purpose of these two works was not to highlight common operational characteristics, as I do here). What are, then, these characteristics?

Communal institutions that were expected to yield a uniform level of services were used instead as instruments of party organizations to indulge some people and deprive others. Regardless of party labels, elected officials of both communal governments took advantage of the opportunities inherent in the structure of communal government to enhance the objectives of their respective party organizations.

The use of communal institutions as instruments of party organizations took several forms in both cities. Both Communist and Monarchist mayors placed their respective party members in communal departments and enterprises (Evans 1967, 164; Allum 1973, 163–4) and provided their supporters with "letters of recommendation" for easy access to communal services (Evans 1967, 74, 204–6, 211–2; Allum 1973, 176–7). They also used their authoritative positions to grant "exceptions" to zoning regulations for private developers (Fried 1973, 254; Montanelli et al. 1965, 391; Allum 1973, 286) and to award municipal contracts ranging from food catering services to public works projects, to their respective party members and supporters (Evans 1967, 132, 134, 163; Allum 1973, 285; see also Passigli 1963, 729–30). Thus in both cities different party cards became "bread cards." Yet despite the similarities these practices did not negatively affect the overall policy performance of the Bologna government. What helps to explain differentials in performance are commitment to policy goals and to policy implementation shown in Bologna (Nanetti 1988; see also Baldissara 1994). From Cattaneo to Einaudi we saw that prefectoral tutelage and surveillance have been described as obstacles to local government initiative. The comparison of Bologna and Naples suggests that prefectoral influences could serve as stimuli for good as well as bad government.

The mutually antagonistic positions of the DC and PCI parties in postwar Italian politics and, more generally, in the cold war became reflected in "rigid" prefectural surveillance over Bolognese communal affairs (Evans 1967, 163). In a show of strength in the early 1950s, the central government dispatched a general as prefect of Bologna and its province; local officials labelled him "the little MacArthur of our province" (Baldissara 1994, 136–8, see also 180n109, 183n164, 375n92, 386–90, 403n4). Even though rigid control was exercised, it was difficult for the prefect or prefectoral officials to exert effective control over the conduct of *all* Bolognese communal affairs. This problem was especially evident in the case of municipal contracts awarded to PCI production cooperatives (Evans 1967, 314). In the building of an underground passage, for example, a contract clause required no traffic interruption and invoked a penalty of one million lire for every day of interruption. Yet this clause was waived after that public work contract was awarded to a PCI cooperative (Evans 1967, 163n31). In turn, cooperative leaders and individual members were required to turn over part of their earnings to party officials (Evans 1967, 110–11, 163; see also Passigli 1963, 729). By the late 1950s, control of the instrumentalities of communal government in Bologna and neighbouring communities had transformed the Communist Party into the largest private enterprise in the province (Evans 1967, 134; see also Galli and Prandi 1970, 162).

A different situation obtained in Naples. Between 1952 and 1953, the relationship between the Monarchist communal government of

Naples and the central government was characterized by partial antagonism. The 1953 national elections altered that relationship. In those
elections the Christian Democrat Party suffered a sharp loss of legislative seats; by contrast the Monarchist Party nearly trebled its legislative
representation from fourteen to forty deputies. In an effort to sustain
the legislative viability of the ruling coalition, national Christian
Democrat leaders came to rely upon the mayor of Naples, Achille
Lauro, for securing the "uncovenanted votes" of Monarchist deputies.
(Lauro was also a deputy and a national leader of the Monarchist
Party.) In 1954, DC provincial leaders also sought and secured Lauro's
help in order to wrest control from several left-wing communes in the
Neapolitan province (Allum 1973, 285–6; Fried 1963, 258).

Thus the legislative necessity to sustain the central government coalition and for wresting communal governments from leftist control
placed the mayor of Naples in a position to exploit the opportunities
inherent in the structure of communal government under a condition
of immunity from prefectoral control. In addition, the same conditions
gave the mayor of Naples easy access to special funds for public works
in Naples and to almost unlimited communal spending powers, as the
commune increasingly became a source of secure public employment
(Allum 1973, 286). These developments did little to improve performance, however.

Monarchist officials at the top of communal departments and enterprises found it relatively easy to procure funds for capital expenditures
on transportation facilities and water supply systems. However, they
experienced serious difficulties in checking on how their subordinates
discharged public services on behalf of the Monarchist Party. Once
faithful party followers had obtained secure, tenured, public employment, they sought to avoid being accountable to their superiors. In an
effort to reduce the frustration with bureaucratic unresponsiveness and
cynicism of both party members and supporters, the mayor of Naples
began to intervene personally in the conduct of communal departments
and enterprises. These "personal interventions" served to make Lauro
an extremely popular mayor. They also served to compound the problems already associated with the existing bureaucratic practices of city-
wide public organizations. The personal interventions as well as "general irregularities" were brought to the attention of judicial and prefectoral authorities by members of the communal opposition, but the
need to ensure legislative support of the central government coalition
sustained the Monarchist communal government.

By 1958, the approaching national elections served to alter this particular relationship of the central government with the Naples communal government, as efforts of DC leaders now shifted from legisla-

tive to electoral requirements. A few months before the 1958 national elections, the minister of the Interior dissolved the Naples communal government on grounds of "grave irregularities." While a prefect took charge of communal affairs, the Monarchist mayor was dismissed and faced criminal charges.

It was not until about three years later that communal affairs were again turned over to elected officials. Now DC leaders replaced Monarchist leaders in control of the Neapolitan commune, and the conduct of communal affairs during the 1960s once again became subject to the requirements of national politics. The previous communal "irregularities" were now magnified by the full correspondence between leaders of the central government and leaders of the communal government (Allum 1973, 307–24; Chubb 1982, 219–25). Under these conditions judicial proceedings against Achille Lauro were postponed indefinitely.

These events sharpened the general dissatisfaction already existing among ordinary Neapolitans about the instrumentalities of government and the provision of public services. Several surveys of citizens' perception of communal government conducted in the 1960s reveal that the high level of citizen alienation was grounded in the knowledge that ordinary Neapolitans have "no more control over the caprices of human authority than over the uncertainties of the physical universe" (Allum 1973, 98). As we have seen, public officials also experience serious difficulties in their efforts to exercise control over communal institutions. DC rule in Naples collapsed in 1975, but this collapse did not end difficulties in government services. As a leading Communist spokesman and administrator put matters in 1977:

At the institutional level, we have overemphasized the element of "good government" and "clean hands," of efficiency based on the rigor and spirit of sacrifice of our administrators ... without giving top priority to the question of participation and popular control ... This has generated a new form of delegation of responsibility and passive expectation on the part of the citizenry vis-à-vis those local institutions where our presence is determining ... The city government is a sort of island under siege, at the centre of all the social and economic tensions of the city, but without the capacity to give the responses which the people expect. In this way are created attitudes of extreme trust, which are then followed by extreme disillusionment. (Andrea Geramicca, quoted in Chubb 1982, 237)

By contrast, in Bologna the interweave between national and local Communist Party politics joined with the competitive relationship between the central and communal governments to subject the conduct of Bolognese communal affairs to quite different requirements of national party politics. For example, between 1946 and 1956 the Communist Party program included a revolutionary takeover of the country. However, the opportunity to transform the control of communal governments into positions of opposition, or counterhegemonic power, to the DC-dominated central government led national Communist officials to call for local self-rule and the abolition of prefects. Though it is not clear whether the local Communists had actually read Einaudi's 1944 essay "Away with the Prefect!" or even Cattaneo, they paraphrased Einaudi's words (Baldissara 1994, 159, 183n164) – albeit for different reasons. An eventual takeover of the country was expected to start from the communes.

In Bologna the application of this strategy took several forms. Communal officials identified the PCI with local self-rule. They now emphasized that the structure of communal government "suffocated" rather than facilitated municipal initiatives on behalf of common interests shared by urban residents (e.g., Mayor Giuseppe Dozza, quoted in Evans 1967, 151; and in Baldissara 1994, 161–2). In order to retain some measure of autonomy from the central government, Bolognese communal officials relied very little on state subsidies in meeting communal expenditures and in balancing the budget (Baldissara 1994, 242–81; Evans 1967, 37–8, 154). This may account for the relatively high communal sales tax cited earlier in the discussion of the Carlo Cattaneo Institute study of communal tax policies. Furthermore, "Bologna's status as one of the few Italian towns with a balanced budget provided excellent propaganda" for the Communist Party (Evans 1967, 38). It was because of this that by the early 1950s the Communist press began to portray Bologna as "Italy's model city," though the performance of communal government in other cities of Emilia-Romagna, like Modena, Reggio Emilia, and Parma, was not so dissimilar.

Bologna's reputation as a model city is not the only reason why "the achievements of the Italian Communists [were] nowhere more evident" than in Bologna (Sassoon 1977, 7). After 1956, in an attempt to minimize exposure to the vicissitudes of Eastern European Communism, PCI national leaders officially abandoned the call for a revolutionary takeover of the country in favour of an Italian Way to Socialism, which accepted the existing institutional arrangements. The switch in national party strategy led Bolognese communal officials who had earlier stressed the "suffocating" nature of the structure of communal government to recognize the same structure now as "the organic expression of the State" (Dozza, quoted in Evans 1967, 151). There were no more calls for the abolition of the prefectoral system.

The Italian Way to Socialism led to several changes in fiscal policy and in the organization of Bologna's communal government. The policy of a balanced budget, for example, gave way to a policy of state subsidies and deficit spending. Between 1958 and 1964 several capital projects were constructed and some 290,000 square meters of land were purchased for the construction of low-cost housing, and resold at a low price to Bolognese residents. The new public works projects provided capital intensive services for local residents and new employment opportunities for members of PCI cooperatives; these, in turn, brought Bologna to the same level of high deficit spending as Naples and most other Italian cities and towns. Deficit spending was accompanied by new central government constraints in the form of surveillance by officials of the central finance commission responsible for deficitary communes (Evans 1967, 38, 160–2).

In 1964, under a dormant 1915 national law, Bologna was divided into fifteen zones, each with a "little city hall" and a district council. Each little city hall was expected to serve as an administrative service centre. Each district council (composed of twenty members chosen by the municipal council according to the distribution of seats in the communal council and presided over by a mayor's representative) was expected to serve as a consultative organ between local residents and communal officials (Evans 1967, 158–9).

The establishment of district or neighbourhood councils reinforced the image of Bologna as "Italy's model city" by anticipating the establishment of similar councils in other cities. However, neighbourhood councils had originally been proposed for Bologna by Giuseppe Dossetti, the DC mayoral candidate in the 1956 local election (Baldissara 1994, 147–56). The program contained in Dossetti's "white paper on Bologna" was literally taken over by the Communists when the latter were reelected – adding to the perception shared by the citizens of Bologna that, underneath all the political rivalry, the chief Bolognese antagonists were committed to the same goals. (Dozza's published collection of speeches of the period was entitled "Good Government and the Rebirth of the City" [cited in Baldissara 1994, 179n107; Melloni 1997, 616].) At the same time, much of the prevailing knowledge about the operation of the district councils that emerged by the 1970s was based on interviews with the mayor of Bologna and on the first empirical study of neighbourhood councils in action, carried out by Raffaella Nanetti around 1974 (see Dragone 1975, 169–78; Jaggi, Muller, and Schmid 1977, 193; Nanetti 1977; but see Centro Studi Economici 1972). Evidence gathered by Nanetti suggests that the district councils did help to diminish the relative isolation of Bolognese residents from communal government reported earlier (Evans 1967, 185). By the early 1980s most local residents seemed familiar with neighbourhood councils (CENSIS 1982, 195). Additional reports since then do point to a great deal of citizen involvement in the Bolognese neighbourhood governments (Nanetti 1988).

These institutional changes in Bologna also served as a learning experience for other Italian communal officials on how to improve service delivery and to provide greater opportunities for citizens to shape events within their grasp. These and other reforms aimed at decentralizing governmental power in Italy are described below, but, as a way of summing up, some more general points are worth reiterating first.

This analysis of the complex interweave of party dynamics and local-national politics offers a more balanced account of variations in local government performance of both Naples and Bologna over time. It also points to the importance of variables and issues discounted by Robert D. Putnam (1993). Just as the Bolognese have not been hostile to the lure of patronage, so the Neapolitans have managed to overcome the lure of clientelistic politics. The very commitment to some form of good government, generated and sustained by a combination of ideological polarization and party competition, seems to account for critical variations and what might be termed Bolognese and Emilian exceptionalism. As we noted earlier, an identical commitment to some form of good government can – and did – lead to enlightened or virtuous party clientelism and what might be termed Lucanian and Abruzzian exceptionalism (Piattoni 1996, 1998a, 1998b; Zuckerman 1997 and works cited therein; see also Carboni 1998). Individual and party commitment to good government can lead to remarkable accomplishments – even in the tropics, as the recent study by Judith Tendler makes evident (Tendler 1997). Whether such a commitment can be sustained over time without appropriate changes in the institutional arrangements of the larger political regime within which people and parties work – in Italy as in Brazil – remains problematic, as the section below suggests.

INSTITUTIONAL LEARNING

During the course of the 1950s, calls for urban reform became part of a more general call for a reform of the state. These calls for reform raised the problems of 1) what knowledge parliament – the only governmental unit with the authority to make structural changes at all levels – had about how the system actually worked and 2) what reforms parliament could actually initiate when the parliamentary groups that formed governing coalitions had incentives to maintain the dominance of central authorities. The critical issue was whether changes contrary to the principles of centralized control over communal public services could be introduced in line with the original intention of the republican constitution. It seemed that only conditions that threatened, or appeared to threaten, the survival of the parliamentary regime itself could force parliamentary groups to accede either to basic reforms in the structure of government or to the full implementation of the 1948 constitution.

The Opening to the Left in 1963 was expected to initiate a policy of structural reforms. Instead, it extended the privileged position of the Christian Democrat Party to the Socialist Party. Although the so-called hot autumn of 1969 did not bring into question the very existence of the parliamentary regime, it did provide enough of a spark to generate the necessary consensus among leaders of the ruling coalition for institutional changes. This consensus resulted by 1972 in the establishment of fifteen regional governments in addition to those already at work on the islands and in the border areas.

Well before 1970, however, communal officials of large cities, faced with central government inattention to urban reforms, began to search for ways to meet local demands for structural changes. Communal decentralization in Bologna provided an example of what communal officials could do within the existing legal framework. By the early 1970s, one hundred cities, including at least sixty-six of the ninety-three provincial capitals, had learned from Bologna and adopted, with some variations, the Bologna model of communal decentralization.

Both types of institutional change (communal and central) were expected to improve how the system worked and to bring government closer to the citizens. Yet such expectations have proved difficult to meet – why? Unfortunately, there are not many before-and-after evaluative studies of the impact of communal and central government decentralization. However, a description of such institutional changes can reveal how these changes were expected to correct earlier sources of institutional weakness. We can then draw upon the evidence to discuss the effects that the changes had.

Communal Decentralization

The original enabling legislation for communal decentralization dates back to the 1915 law on communal and provincial reforms. By 1910, the failure of large communal governments to produce expected results had become a national concern, just as Cattaneo had anticipated more than fifty years earlier. The concern was expressed in a general recognition that 1) within large communes there were subcommunities with diverse interests and problems; 2) the structure of communal government was not sensitive to these problems; and 3) these problems might well be solved more effectively by local residents through some kind of neighbourhood government like those that had existed in the history of Naples, Siena, and most other Italian cities before 1860, and as far back as medieval times. National legislators, however, had difficulty reconciling principles and forms of local self-rule with the requirements of control by central authorities. The solution was to recognize the existence of smaller areas of common interests or *quartieri* (city districts) and to give them a voice through an appointed district delegate (*aggiunto*) acting as the mayor's representative – in essence, to create a "prefectoral" system at the communal level (Crea 1965).

The vicissitudes connected with the First and Second World Wars precluded the implementation of this legislation. The first application took place in Bologna in 1964, but during the latter part of the 1960s, other communal governments followed the Bolognese example. The essential characteristics of what became known as the "Bologna model of decentralization" were as follows:

(1) Each city was divided into zones or districts primarily on the basis of their historic district boundaries dating to before-1860. Each district had a set of "associates" or council, a "little city hall," and a mayor's representative (*aggiunto*).

(2) Each district council was composed of twenty local residents chosen by the municipal council according to the proportion of party seats on the municipal council.

(3) Each district council only had the power to make recommendations or suggestions to the municipal council on local problems, and these recommendations were not formally binding on city officials. District councils were not even permitted to hire their own clerk.

(4) Each "little city hall" served as a decentralized service centre for the municipal bureaucracy. The administrative director of each service centre was also the clerk of the district council.

(5) A mayor's representative, not necessarily from the same district, presided over each district council, and also had responsibility for coordinating and monitoring the activities of the decentralized municipal departments.

Thus, district councils reproduced in microcosm the composition of municipal councils. Mayors' representatives became known, among critics, as "the mayors' prefects" (Centro Studi Economici 1972, 12). Because administrative decentralization reiterated at each district level the hierarchic structure and operation of communal departments, there was no basic change in communal decision making authority (but see Stoppino 1975, 489–94).

Among the very large urban cities that adopted the "Bologna

model," with some variations, were Rome in 1966, Catania in 1967, Milan and Naples in 1968, and Genoa in 1969. In most cases, the districts had relatively large populations, because the use of historic boundaries for most districts did not take into account population increases. For example, the twelve historic districts of Rome now had, on average, 210,000 residents each; the twenty Milanese districts each had an average of 85,000. Naples did manage to have its increased population taken into account; three new districts were added to the twelve pre-1860 districts, but even with this increase, each district still had an average of 80,000 residents. Thus, the operation of communal decentralization still involved relatively large-scale organizations (Dente 1974, 184–5; Sinisi 1993).

A 1971 study of the operation of four Milanese district councils, three of which had fewer than 75,000 residents, suggests additional conclusions. The study found that district councils served neither to strengthen the strategic positions of party organizations nor to undermine or preempt neighbourhood efforts such as tenant associations and youth groups (Daolio 1971). The investigator also found that district councils were either not consulted on matters of district concern, or they were consulted, but their suggestions were not incorporated in communal policies. As a result of the lack of consultation, the four district councils presented "alternative proposals for the organization and operation of district councils" to the Milanese communal government (Daolio 1971, 30–1).

These alternative proposals included direct elections of district council members, power to hire district clerks and other officials, independent decision making authority in matters of district or neighbourhood concern, and "participation" with the communal government in levying and controlling communal taxes of district residents. These demands, however, went beyond the legal framework of the 1915 law and, as a result, were not adopted. The general conclusion of the 1971 study was that the establishment of district councils revealed both the existence of a large number of neighbourhood residents willing to act on behalf of common interests and the lack of governmental structures to facilitate such collective efforts (Daolio 1971, 31; see also Dente 1974, 194–6; Stoppino 1975, 504–5).

Critics from extraparliamentary groups charged that in general district councils simply served to strengthen the strategic position of party organizations and to undermine and preempt neighbourhood efforts by local residents (Della Pergola 1974). Local elected officials rejected these charges and contended instead that communal decentralization permitted a form of citizen participation that allowed public officials to respond more effectively to local problems (Dragone 1975, 13–28).

Nanetti's study of Bologna neighbourhood councils in the early 1970s found that there was merit in the local officials' argument – it was not entirely self-serving (Nanetti 1977). In fact, the argument advanced by local officials eventually prevailed with national legislators. In April 1976 the national parliament passed a law (no. 278) for the creation of *elected* neighbourhood or district councils. It was followed by a Sicilian regional law of 11 December 1976 (no. 84). Neighbourhood government seemed to have truly arrived – a point effectively made by Nanetti (1988).

There is no doubt that the 1976 law which led to the creation of elected neighbourhood councils was not without the usual trade-offs among parties in and outside parliament (see e.g., Hellman 1988, 72–6). But did neighbourhood elections make a positive change in the standing of district councils, as expected by the law and by many grassroots advocates and policy analysts?

Evidence about the operation of neighbourhood councils since the law was passed does suggest caution, but also optimism (Nanetti 1988, 146-50). Raffaella Nanetti's conclusion is supported by the comparative examination of municipal decentralization and neighbourhood democracy in Oslo and Bologna, carried out by Francesco Kjellberg in the late 1970s. Kjellberg found that what distinguished the Italian experience from that of Sweden and Norway was the greater influence of neighbourhood governments in Italy; in Sweden and Norway there have been only "a few short-lived experiments" (Kjellberg 1979, 109). Other evidence raised by more recent surveys of urban decentralization in different cities north and south between 1980 and 1990 is not as optimistic, however. Grassroots efforts since 1976 have done little to alter the hegemonic position of communal authorities (see Sinisi 1993). The general conclusion is that Italian communal decentralization did create a new layer of government that may actually be more responsive to local interests than similar experiments in Sweden and Norway. But whether this new layer favoured neighbourhood democracy or helped to improve the practice of municipal governance from Catania to Turin remains unclear (Sinisi 1993, 184; see also Hellman 1988, 72–6, 89, 148, 171). It may be that a longer temporal perspective is needed for a more accurate appreciation of communal decentralization in Italy. Moreover, it is still not clear what impact neighbourhood districts are having; since the new electoral laws and other decentralization changes of the late 1990s are simultaneously freeing local politics and services from the oligopolistic control of national parties, slimming down administrative activities and procedures, and centralizing the local policy making process in the mayor's office (see Baldini and Legnante 1998; Gilbert 1998; Nanetti 1998a, 5–8; Newell 1998).

Central Government Decentralization

The second major innovation in governmental organization undertaken in the postwar period was the creation of regional governments. Regional government was initially authorized in an effort to accommodate Sicilian claims to an inherent right of self-government that resurfaced during the Second World War (Sabetti 1984, 146–55). By 1944 central government officials had recognized the failure of efforts to create national unity through administrative measures and identified the existence of special regional problems in the provision of many public services. The same officials had serious difficulties, however, in meeting Sicilian claims to self-government without changing the unitary form of the state. The solution was a special provision for regional government in Sicily – leaving the basic structures of the unitary state unchanged.

The exceptional nature of this kind of central government decentralization was implied in the designation of the structure of Sicilian regional government as "extraordinary." This special arrangement was subsequently used to meet regional claims of independence or foreign threats of annexation in Sardinia, Valle d'Aosta, and Germanophone Alto Adige or South Tyrol. In 1963, following the return of the city of Trieste to Italian rule, a fifth extraordinary region was created, near what was once the Yugoslav border, with a Slovenian minority.

The organization of the five extraordinary regions was patterned upon a unicameral system of parliamentary government with proportional representation, long party lists, and preference voting. With some variations, such as the use of French and German, all five regional governments had the following powers:

(1) to exercise "limited exclusive" jurisdiction in such areas as land reform, public works, and urban planning and "complementary" or concurrent jurisdiction with the central government in such areas as public health and hospital care, commerce, and water resources;

(2) to adapt the details of national laws to the specific needs and conditions of each region whenever such "integrative" powers were delegated by the national parliament;

(3) to initiate proposals for submission to parliament concerning matters of regional interests outside their own legislative jurisdiction;

(4) to levy and collect regional taxes limited essentially to the use of public soil or property, to receive a share of certain national taxes collected in each region, and to borrow money for specific public works projects (about two-thirds of regional revenue, however, came from annual grants from the central government);

(5) to establish regional ministries or technical services;

(6) to monitor the performance of communal governments through the establishment of provincial control commissions responsible to regional ministers of the interior.

Regional autonomy did not, however, imply a diminution in the sovereignty of the national parliament. National legislation automatically took precedence over regional legislation. For example, regional "limited exclusive" jurisdiction could take place only when national legislation contained provisions limiting its sphere of application. General responsibility for monitoring the legality and merit of acts of regional governments rested with state commissioners or super prefects posted in each regional capital. The central government retained authority over 1) the substance of regional statutes; 2) the decision making powers assigned to regional governments; and 3) monitoring of the performance of regional governments. Perhaps more importantly – but seldom noted by analysts – there were no provisions in the constitution that allowed regional governments to engage in intergovernmental relations without the coordinating authority of the central government (e.g., Pizzetti 1996, 66–7; Woodcock 1967).

In fine, the structure of authority relationships inherent in the conduct of national affairs was reflected in the conduct of regional affairs. At the same time, the five regional authorities had no essential control over the national bureaucracy. Regional services would have to be carried out in relation to formal rules and regulations promulgated by the national government. In turn, communal authorities had no essential control over either the national or regional bureaucracies. Communal services would now have to be carried out in relation to formal rules and regulations promulgated by both the central and regional governments. Coordination between multiple jurisdictions was still expected to take place through hierarchic arrangements.

The establishment of fifteen "ordinary" regions in 1972 followed, with some variations, the essential features of the five extraordinary regions. Constitutional barriers to intergovernmental relations and exchange among regions remained unchanged. Variations between the two sets of regional governments involved primarily the assignment of different legislative powers. Ordinary regional governments were not, for example, empowered to exercise "limited exclusive" jurisdiction over some policy areas or to submit legislative proposals to parliament. As we have seen, however, "limited exclusive" jurisdiction by extraordinary regions could take place only when national legislation so allowed. At the same time, the new regional governments had no control over the national police system or the provision of public security.

Local *polizia* officers continued to be subject to a command structure in the Ministry of the Interior; prefects continued to exercise general responsibilities for peace and security in each province. Hence, the extension of regional government to the rest of the Italian peninsula appeared, in effect, to underscore the subordinate position of regional authorities vis-à-vis the central government and the national bureaucracy (Barile 1975, 401–11, 415; Pizzetti 1996, 56–84).

Leaders of the major political parties were confident, however, that this structure of regional government would correct the malfunctioning of the national bureaucracy and bring good government to the citizens. A student of Italian public service systems sought to clarify the basis of this confidence by examining the positions taken by the various political parties on the implementation of regional government (Villani 1972). A. Villani found that the national debate on structural changes was "burdened by ideological and self-serving elements [*politici*] that in many ways transcended the question of organizational efficiency designed to provide the maximum of collective goods to given resources and to match as closely as possible the preferences of consumers of those goods" (Villani 1972, 3). The optimism expressed by Communist, Christian Democrat, and Socialist officials rested upon an inadequate consideration of the potential effects of the institutional change being introduced. Sicilian exceptionalism was invoked to disregard the impact of regional governments there, even though they had been operational for some twenty years. But how exceptional was the Sicilian experience? Let us review some of its salient features.

As we have seen, access to the exercise of regional government authority was dependent upon winning elections. With the first regional election held in 1947, the Christian Democrat Party emerged as the principal ruling party in Sicily. As a result, the formation and conduct of successive Sicilian regional governments became subject to electoral and legislative requirements of national government coalitions. In turn, the formation and conduct of communal governments in such cities as Catania and Palermo became subject to electoral and legislative requirements of both national and regional government coalitions (Capurso 1964).

At the same time, the establishment of regional ministries to coincide with central government ministries was accompanied by a transfer of state administrative personnel to the regional bureaucracy. Most of these high administrative officials came from the disbanded Ministry for Colonial Affairs. By the 1950s intergovernmental relations between regional ministries and state technical services evidenced the same problems that afflicted intergovernmental relations between communal departments and state technical services. This national bureaucratic dominance was in turn compounded by resentment among Sicilian administrative personnel over the prominence of former colonial administrators in high bureaucratic positions (Serio 1966).

Faced with the requirements of national party politics and the problems of bureaucratic control, Christian Democrat regional officials proceeded by 1953 to transform the regional bureaucracy into a workplace for party functionaries (Sabetti 1984, 160–2, 185–91). Nevertheless, the informal and personal networks that developed cut across ideological and intergovernmental barriers and became fairly responsive to the articulation of demands for services by citizens and communal officials. Thus, interorganizational networks between central, regional, and communal authorities took on the appearance of a polycentric rather than a monocentric ordering – what scholars of French interorganizational networks have characterized as "the honeycomb system" (Thoenig 1987; see also Dupuy 1985). This polycentricity accrued, however, from a logic of corruption and machine politics, *not* from a design of self-governing, independent levels of government with overlapping jurisdictions (V. Ostrom 1972, 7). Some of the emergent properties of this state of affairs, including the practice of institutionalized corruption, will become apparent in chapters 6 and 7.

In 1958, some regional DC deputies refused to recognize the national party secretary's claim to designate the head of the DC regional government and were expelled from the party. These events led to a constituency revolt against party discipline, which in turn gave rise to an independent Sicilian Catholic Social Union (Unione Siciliana Cristiano Sociale). Leaders of this party proceeded to form a coalition government with Communists, Socialists, Monarchists, and neo-Fascists. Whereas on the Italian peninsula, this "unnatural alliance" or "vulgarity" (*inciucio*) – disparagingly labelled *milazzismo*, after the main protagonist, Silvio Milazzo – was seen as proof of Sicilian political immaturity, in Sicily it was seen as an expression of a common concern for Sicilian home rule (see also Corbi 1998). This identity of interests among ideologically diverse parties gave rise to the possibility of a political stalemate between the central government and the regional government that might have provided the conditions for a reformulation of the structure of Sicilian autonomy. By 1960 the "unnatural" practice of *milazzismo* collapsed, and in 1961 the legislative support of the Socialist regional party organization helped to reestablish control by the Christian Democrat Party in the formation and conduct of Sicilian regional government.

By the middle of the 1960s the organizational chart of the regional bureaucracy resembled an inverted pyramid. Some 400 technical personnel at the middle and bottom levels of this inverted pyramid expressed strong dissatisfaction about regional arrangements. Organized as a club (Associazione Culturale Funzionari Regionali), these regional bureaucrats supplemented work protests with reports about administrative practices. They proposed a system of democratic public administration based upon a restructuring of the regional bureaucracy in terms of "operative units" or "service bureaus" and a restructuring of incentives for administrative personnel that would follow from the less hierarchical and more service-oriented "operative units." The success of this alternative system of regional administration would depend in turn on the restructuring of the national public administration that was being proposed by the national minister for bureaucratic reforms. The resistance to change among other members of the regional bureaucracy and the absence of change in the national bureaucracy undermined these efforts.

Thus, even a constituency revolt within one party organization was insufficient to establish regional autonomy in the formation of regional governing coalitions. Work protest among some regional bureaucrats failed to change the operating characteristics of the regional bureaucracy. As long as the hegemony of central party headquarters prevailed over a majority of regional party organizations and as long as the central bureaucracy prevailed over the regional bureaucracy, it was difficult, perhaps impossible, to alter the structure of regional government. By the early 1970s, when regional government was being extended to the rest of Italy, the discrepancy between the public performance of Sicilian regional government and the public rhetoric about regional purposes and goals was difficult to reconcile. Other dimensions of this gap will be explored in some depth in part 3. But did the extension of regional government in 1972 bring about the good government that proved so difficult to achieve in postwar Sicily?

A few years after regional governments became operational, it was found that, in spite of some dissatisfaction among regional party officials about central party directives, the national party or faction leaders retained essential authority over regional party organizations. There was a tendency among central government leaders and bureaucrats "to treat regions as field offices of the national administration, executing orders and policies handed down from Rome" (Kogan 1975, 403). This impression was supported by a detailed study of the national ministries most affected by the extension of regional government (Amato 1974). The transfer of jurisdiction from the national ministries of the interior, public works, health, transportation, and tourism to their regional counterparts was accompanied by rules and regulations to insure the "imperial" position of the central bureaucracy (Amato 1974, 482, 485, 489). This state of affairs led the president of the Tuscan region to acknowledge, at one point, that "a truly regional government still remains to be constructed" (Lelio Lagorio, quoted in *Il Mondo* 1975, 67).

Research on the institutionalization of regional governments over the course of two decades suggests that the Tuscan official may have been too dismissive of what was being created (Putnam, Leonardi, and Nanetti 1985; Putnam 1993). It is now clear that, after two decades of institutional development, regional governments have put down roots. Certainly, elected regional representatives have worked to expand the political and administrative authority of regional governments vis-à-vis that of the central government – even to the point of taking of up the challenge of constitutional reform in the late 1990s and telling national legislators how best to do it (CINSEDO 1997; Mariucci 1997; Newell 1998; Vassallo 1998). There is no doubt that regional leaders have succeeded in extracting resources and other concessions from the centre. There is equally no doubt that they have successfully established a national presence through organizations such as the National Conference of Regional Presidents. Some regions do, in fact, work better than others. But whether *what they actually do* – including the introduction of technocratic innovations and modern management practices; mainly in the regional governments of the north and centre – has produced more responsive services and better citizens remains problematic.

Whether the legislative output is interpretable and explainable as Robert D. Putnam suggests is still open to debate, for at least two reasons. Differential behaviours in different regions cannot be explained unless one introduces the rich historical diversity that characterizes each region – and this Putnam is prevented from doing by the very method of analysis he uses; whether, in fact, the creation of regional government can be treated as a "natural" experiment is highly problematic. We shall return to these issues in chapter 9. At the same time, the validity of the inferences Putnam draws from the regional legislative process is also problematic. Of his twelve indicators of institutional performance, only one – budget promptness – can be reliably applied to all the regional governments (Masi 1998b). Some indicators, such as local health unit expenditures and the availability of universal daycare, skew the analysis *ab initio* in favour of some regions, without telling us much about the other ones. Other indicators, such as reform legislation, legislative innovation, and a bureaucratic responsiveness test are not reliable indicators of regional performance. We are still left with the question of what kind of regional government Italy has and how it actually works.

Other issues emerge: as Margaret Levi notes, it is still not clear how "government performance becomes a direct reflection of the cooperation it received from its citizens" in the northern/central regions (M. Levi 1993, 378; see also Goldberg 1996; M. Levi 1996). Equally problematic is whether, or to what extent, the poor performance of other regional governments can be attributed to a presumptive cultural backwardness, a millenary path-dependent explanation, or exceptionalism (mafia and the like). As we shall see in chapters 6 and 7, the war on crime is much more complicated than has been generally assumed; chapters 8 and 9 show that the cultural and path-dependent explanation that Putnam builds, in part on Banfield's earlier analysis, tends to hinder, rather than advance, understanding of differential performance among regional governments – and this without denying the fact that some regional governments do work better than others.

CONCLUSION

This analytical discussion has charted how the system worked in postwar Italy. In highlighting the constraints on public services that follow from the structure of the Italian state and politics, the discussion suggested why the characteristic results of the public service system radically deviated from those anticipated by its design principles. In brief, the main argument is that there is good reason *not* to expect the system to work as it should; pathologies in the distribution of government services are the more characteristic results of such a system. As Cattaneo, Ferrara, and later Einaudi anticipated, poor government performance is an unintended consequence of both the form of government and the ways centralized state administration and decision making and the politicization of local governments by the national parties work.

It must be quickly added, however, that the history of modern Italy is neither a story of unmitigated failure nor of unmitigated success, as the commitment to good government highlighted in the preceding analysis suggests. But the good intentions of legislators and the resultant success in places like Bologna, Potenza, and L'Aquila are not sufficient to override the design characteristics of the system as a whole. What shall we conclude, then, from the institutional learning that sparked the decentralization efforts?

In the course of the second half of the nineteenth century, publicists such as Napoleone Colajanni and Edoardo Pantano likened proposals to decentralize central and communal government authority to attempts to shorten the handle of a hammer when the hammer of central bureaucracy itself was the problem (Ganci 1973, 51). These analysts were sceptical that such efforts would correct the malfunctioning in the public sector. At the same time, they were aware that the transformation of a centralized state into a state based upon a different design could occur only over a long period of time.

In brief, those publicists did not share the fault that Barbara Geddes attributes to modern political scientists, who "spend much of their time explaining events that have not finished happening" (quoted in Trebilcock 1996, 9). Colajanni and Pantano came to view proposals to shorten the handle of the bureaucratic hammer as opportunities that might provide the conditions that would lead to a transformation of the Italian state into a different system of government. Not unlike Cattaneo and Einaudi, they anticipated that this different system of government would be based upon an extension of self-government to neighbourhoods, communes, regions, and the nation. Those southern publicists used the writings on democracy in America by James Madison, Alexander Hamilton, and Tocqueville, as well as the writings of Cattaneo and other Italian federalists, and their knowledge of local conditions to support the contention that such a design of government – which they equated with good government – was conceptually and operationally feasible in Italy (see Ganci 1973, 51–69, 261–85). Conditions developing since 1990 may lead to a gradual transformation of the Italian public service system to emphasize service rather than control and citizens rather than subjects (Zincone 1992). But if the search for good government in the new millennium is to proceed unhindered toward the institutionalization of the underlying principles of self-rule sketched by federalist publicists, other paradigmatic pathologies will have to be removed. Problem solving through central planning is one such obstacle and to this we shall turn in the next chapter.

5 Problem Solving by Central Planning

A legacy that Italy shares with other countries with representative systems of government is the presupposition of parliamentary sovereignty. Government policy making since the postunification period confirms the view prevalent among both Italian radical democrats and public finance specialists, at least since the time of Carlo Cattaneo and Francesco Ferrara – namely, that "the monopolistic process of legislation is a spontaneous product of parliamentary regimes" (De Viti De Marco [1903] 1965, 249). This process has produced two parallel, if contradictory, tendencies in problem solving by legislation: nationalization and privatization. As will be discussed at some length in chapter 9, the results have often been the same: disasters of major proportions. Such disasters have, however, tended to obscure the fact that they are the unintended consequences of attempts to craft institutions and policy instruments of good government.

Perhaps one of the clearest illustrations of the gaps between preferred solutions and the actual behaviour of government agencies, between good intentions and bad results, is the case of urban planning in postwar Rome. The design of detailed master plans and the effort to follow them have led to the inability to implement the plans *and* to their violations.

Consider the formulation of the so-called Roman plan of 1962. As an expression of good government, it needed to meet several goals: 1) to coordinate the large number of communal and state agencies whose own plans for public services had to be included in the Roman plan; 2) to resolve the large number of complexly nested issues evoked by the interorganizational process; and 3) to exclude citizen or "special" interests from public planning. Soon it became apparent that this kind of planning was its own major stumbling block, for it made unproblematic what the actual planning formulators, the people on the ground, found highly problematic. Because they could not see the whole picture, they could not know what was "good" for all Romans; hence they could not plan or predetermine the future course of events. It was impossible for a single master plan to relate comprehensively all the urban elements, as urban planning was expected to do. As a result, "the 1962 plan ... went the way of previous ones: abandoned in practice before it could be implemented" (Agnew 1995, 55). The rest of this chapter suggests why this was so; but first the empirical and theoretical setting helps to situate the importance of the Roman case for the thesis of this book.

THE EMPIRICAL AND THEORETICAL CONTEXT

During the postwar years and until the 1970s, the population of Rome increased from one and one-half to three million. The rising population, together with rising income and consumption, produced sharp demands for public services in such fields as water, sanitation, transportation, recreation, education, and in the demand for land use regulations more generally. However, land as such was never a problem. The vast territory of Rome, covering 600 square miles without major physical constraints such as mountains or canals, makes it one of the largest cities in the world. Yet despite a rising population, the city still occupied slightly more than 10 per cent of its legal territory by the 1970s. "Tourist Rome" covers only about 2 per cent.

The National Urban Planning Act of 1942 was the basic enabling act through which postwar communal and state officials in Rome were expected to meet rising demands for public services and to regulate private and public land use. The 1942 act extended an existing master plan for Rome – the 1931 Mussolini plan – until 1952, when another master plan was expected to take effect. The 1931 plan, which applied to about eighty of the city's 600 square miles, covered the existing built-up portion of the city and as much of the city's territory as was expected to be necessary for the predicted population increase. The master plan that was to be prepared in the 1950s was expected to coordinate elements of land use throughout the entire Roman territory. This plan, finally adopted in 1962, became known as the Roman plan.

As we saw in the previous chapter, beneath the name change from monarchy to republic in 1946, the Italian state retained a great deal of continuity in its institutional arrangements and laws and regulations of government (see also Pavone, cited in Duggan and Wagstaff 1995, 3). Thus, recourse to central planning to meet the changing conditions of the urban scene in Rome appeared to be a good fit with the structure of governmental arrangements. This fit also accorded well with most members of the National Institute of Planners, whose conception of planning as good government consisted in "identifying through professional doctrine what the community must have and presenting a plan designed accordingly" (Fried 1973, 96). Yet, like the three other central plans since 1883, the 1962 plan did not achieve its stated goals.

Robert C. Fried's *Planning the Eternal City: Roman Politics and Planning since World War II* (1973) provides an opportunity to assess the extent to which the institutional arrangements and master plans could be realized in practice. To be sure, *Planning the Eternal City* did not set out to show that collective action does not necessarily produce a collective good. Like more recent research on the topic (e.g., Agnew 1995), Fried's analysis did not question the assumption that urban growth can be satisfactorily met through master plans. Still, to his credit, Fried provided a rich database that allows us to understand how urban planning became, unintentionally, an expression of bad government. The empirical material provided by Fried is all the more useful more than two decades later for three additional reasons.

First, with the extention of regional government in the 1970s, area-wide urban planning was transferred to the regions. Since then, regional statutes have adopted a more realistic, less ambitious notion of planning as a process of discovery and problem solving (e.g., Nanetti 1988, 83–6, 131–45). But the fact is that present-day planning in Rome is still being set in the framework of the 1962 plan. As John Agnew in his own work on urban planning in Rome has noted recently, "debate over the future of the city has remained largely trapped in the terms [the 1962 plan] provided" (Agnew 1995, 55; see also Cervellati 1976, 345).

Second, that central urban planning produces the opposite of what it claims and builds cities that do not work is by no means a uniquely Roman or even Italian phenomenon. Such problems are more universal than we have supposed. Recent research on American, Canadian, and Danish cities and metropolitan organization reveals how widespread pathologies in the organization and distribution of government services can become (e.g., ACIR 1987; Flyvbjerg [1991] 1998; Fowler 1992; Jacobs 1961). The decline of North America's inner cities suggests that, once a spiral of disorder and decay sets in, it is extraordinarily difficult to break out of it – no war on poverty or community policing alone can check decay (Skogan 1992) – but neither Rome nor probably any other Italian city has experienced the spiral of decay observed in many American neighbourhoods.

Third, and in Robert C. Fried's defence, how many knew and accepted, when he published his research in 1973, what we know and accept now? The work of Friedrich A. Hayek ([1944] 1972; 1988), which questioned the wisdom and inevitability of central planning, had been rejected almost out of hand as a malicious and disingenuous right-wing attack on the finest ideals of modern human progress, and Jane Jacobs' analysis of the life and death of American cities (1961) was dismissed when it first appeared as contrarian analysis by most students and practitioners of urban planning. The recent fall of Communism has drawn attention to problems with centralized planning not fully appreciated by an earlier generation of analysts studying planning in Italy and beyond (e.g., S. Cohen 1969; LaPalombara 1966). Reflecting on what radical historical lessons to draw from that fall, Adam Przeworski observes that, "what died in Eastern Europe is the very idea of rationally administering things to satisfy human needs – the feasibility of implementing public ownership of productive resources through centralized command; the very project of basing society on disinterested cooperation – the possibility of dissociating social contribution from individual rewards" (Przeworski 1991, 7; see also Chickering 1976; Scott 1998). In brief, tracing what went wrong with the urban planning experience in Rome advances the argument of this book on several counts.

THE 1931 MUSSOLINI PLAN

Until the adoption of the 1962 master plan, post-1945 communal and central government officials were expected to meet the changing requirements of land use primarily through the application of the 1931 master plan. Prepared by urban planners and administrative officials in six months, the Mussolini plan, as it was known, sought, among other things, to retain the historic city as the centre of the modern city, to provide for a variety of housing needs, to insure adequate provisions of public facilities and services in the old and new districts, to improve the quantity and quality of parks and recreation facilities, and to guide and coordinate policy makers in various sectors of the city and national government (Fried 1973, 33–4). A separate communal planning department, detached from the public works department, was created for the implementation of the plan and the building code of 1934.

Planning and Fascism appeared "a natural pairing" (Agnew 1995, 47). Yet the 1931 plan had already been a disappointment by 1936, for, in the words of the governor of Rome, "though studied by eminent technicians and realized on the basis of norms representing the most advanced planning legislation, [the plan] is not sufficient to ensure a rational succession of initiatives on the part of the Administration or on the part of private citizens in the development and modification of the urban agglomeration" (quoted in Fried 1973, 38). Despite the "regular and generous" appropriations from the national budget, most public works projects did not produce the anticipated results (Fried 1973, 39). Why was this so?

No single set of factors could account for the radical differences between expectations and results, but unwieldy intergovernmental arrangements loomed large in the explanation, as they fell victim to the complexity of their own hierarchical and bureaucratic structures. In turn, the limits on control over the conduct of communal departments and state technical services engendered "bureaucratic free enterprise" (Tullock 1965) among subordinate administrative officials. At the same time, high government officials used their authority to approve a number of "exceptions" or unofficial amendments to the plan.

Relatively crowded districts were built with public facilities allocated for much less densely built districts (Fried 1973, 36–7). Moreover, the relatively cheap land available outside the plan perimeter, coupled with a rise in the city's population, provided incentives to those without access to government officials to circumvent public planning. By 1940 some two hundred thousand people were living in villages or shantytowns outside the plan perimeter but within the city territory (Fried 1973, 37–8). Thus it was difficult to bring about in practice the order and symmetry that institutional arrangements, Fascism and the master plan claimed in theory. Yet, this was the plan that in 1942 was extended until 1952, and remained legally in effect until 1959.

POSTWAR GOVERNANCE AND URBAN PLANNING

The reiteration of centralized government and administration after the Second World War facilitated the continuity of Fascist laws for postwar urban growth with little or no regard for the relative failure of urban planning in the 1930s (see Cervellati 1976). At the same time, in the immediate postwar years, the Christian Democrat mayor of Rome and the communal councillors of all the parties represented in the eighty-member council came to view such laws as threats to postwar recovery and impediments in meeting the increasing demand for public services. These officials thus engaged in "official illegalism" in several ways.

They first ignored the 1931 plan, and then made little or no prepa-
rations for a new one, even though required by the 1942 Urban Planning Act. At the same time, Roman officials directed their efforts
toward more pressing local problems such as relieving hunger, restor-
ing electricity and gas, and relocating refugees still temporarily housed
in schools and barracks (Fried 1973, 205–6). But they experienced
increasing difficulties in resisting pressures from the Rome branch of
the National Institute of Planners (Fried 1973, 305) and the "prod-
ding" by officials of the Ministry of Public Works (Fried 1973, 206).

The result was that Roman communal officials initiated the formulation of a new comprehensive plan before the expiration of the 1931
plan. In October 1951 the Roman communal council approved in principle the establishment of a new master plan to be formulated in cooperation with most of the state technical services and under the supervision of the Ministry of Public Works. But in order to become a legal
reality and to survive as a viable policy, this new plan needed to rely
upon largely the same governmental authorities that had experienced
serious difficulties in implementing the less comprehensive plan of
1931. Thus, calls for postwar urban planning revealed the extent to
which Italian legislators and administrative officials seemed locked
into an organization that closely matched Michel Crozier's characterization of bureaucratic structure: "an organization that cannot correct
its behaviour by learning from its errors" (Crozier 1964, 187).

The prospect of comprehensive urban planning served to foreclose
recourse to alternative strategies in meeting the changing requirements
of public services and land use. For example, the rising Roman population created a sharp demand for housing. Yet, in part because of rent
control, structurally sound buildings were allowed to deteriorate so as
to force out older tenants and permit either the conversion of these
buildings into luxury apartments or the construction of new more
expensive ones (Fried 1973, 56). But the initial challenge remained. A
1974 report in the news magazine *Epoca* highlighted the paradox:
Rome was the city where perhaps most postwar housing construction
had taken place, yet it remained without adequate housing (Baini
1974; see also *Il Mondo* 1969). The issue was not so much the building of new houses or public housing projects but how to devise institutional arrangements with appropriate incentives for individuals to
use and maintain the available housing stock.

FORMULATING THE POSTWAR PLAN

The postwar plan was expected to relate comprehensively all the elements of urban-based land use in their multidimensional, space-time

continuum throughout the entire Roman territory. However, the very formulation of such a plan proved to be an arduous task.

Party politics as such was not an impediment. Throughout the postwar years the relationship between successive communal and central governments was characterized by mutually supportive positions. Moreover, even during the cold war period, multipartisanship was the norm in communal decisionmaking (Fried 1973, 206–7); ideological warfare was generally reserved for elections (Fried 1973, 205, 210). Instead, the very nature of planning became a principal impediment to the formulation of a new master plan. Recall again what the formulation required.

As noted earlier, the formulation needed to meet several goals: 1) to coordinate the public services of communal and state agencies; 2) to resolve the complex issues caused by the hierarchic arrangements of government; and 3) to exclude interests of local individuals and groups from the planning process. Soon it became apparent that the sheer complexity of governmental structures – including past decisions and their ramifications – made it very difficult, if at all possible, to bring about good government in detailed planning. No one master plan could comprehensively integrate all the urban elements as urban planning was expected to do.

Thus, it was not until 1957 that a first plan was prepared, but the search for a "better or perfect master plan" gave way to another master plan in 1959. This was further "refined" in 1962 (Fried 1973, 52). After some revisions by the Council of State in 1965, this plan became law in 1966. It called, among other things, for stringent standards in the location and construction of public service centres. The problem was that the master plan was already obsolete. Most of the urban growth that the new plan was supposed to regulate had already taken place. As noted earlier, the 1962 plan was abandoned even before it was put in place (Agnew 1995, 55). What happened is not difficult to sketch.

PUBLIC UNPLANNING AND
PRIVATE PLANNING

The difficulties in formulating a "perfect master plan" served to extend the legal validity of the 1931 plan, set to expire in 1952, for the rest of the 1950s. As we have seen, the Mussolini plan was no more than a proclamation or pretence. Thus, public unplanning or official illegalism became a way of coping with the exigencies of postwar urban growth. At the same time, the preparation of another master plan that threatened to place severe restrictions on private property rights throughout the Roman territory added incentives for large and small private developers to proceed with their own planning (Agnew 1995, 56; Fried 1973, 153).

Overwhelmed by permit applications, the Rome Planning Department tended to act only on those applications backed by political influence. Falling back on the letter of the 1931 master plan became a polite expedient for rejecting building permits. A perverse emphasis on legality was accommodated by either neglect, or the wink of an eye. This situation echoed Alexis de Tocqueville's description of the practice of rule under the old regime in France: "rigid rules, but flexibility, not to say laxity, in their application ... Indeed, whenever the authorities fell back on the letter of the law, this was only a polite expedient for rejecting a petition" (Tocqueville [1856] 1956, 67–8).

Under such conditions, it is not surprising that most Roman citizens came to view land use laws and regulations as instruments permitting public officials to vex and victimize the public (Fried 1973, 258). When legalities become obstacles and people must find a way to cope with a problem, they usually find some way to ignore the law or get around it. Flouting the law by disobeying the demands of democratic government appeared to many modern Romans to be perfectly legitimate – a point raised initially in the first chapter (see also M. Levi 1997a). Thus, the denial of building permits failed to prevent individuals from proceeding with their own plans.

This situation became a source of personal embarrassment, creating a reluctance to turn to officials. Hernando de Soto's study (1989) of people who work outside the law in Lima, Peru, indicates a corollary to the Roman shantytowns and illegal land developments that emerged in full force in the late 1990s: an endless tangle of problems in establishing legal title and great difficulties in using present assets as security in making further investments. With no effective registration of property titles in shantytowns, a horrible mess is created. For example, many sites assumed to be vacant by urban planners designing the new master plan were later found to be filled by private buildings erected either as "legal" exceptions or as "illegal" exceptions to both the 1931 master plan and communal building regulations (Fried 1973, 184; see also La Repubblica 1998b). What is not clear from Fried's rich database is how policing, fire protection, water supply, sanitation, and the like were organized in such areas. In these conditions, illegalities can become an easy ally of organized crime because ways may be found to steal electricity and water as well as access to sewage disposal.

Embarrassment and difficulties were not confined to citizens. Under the Urban Planning Act of 1942, administrative officials of the Ministry of Public Works had authority to demolish or suspend construction of any structures built without a regular city permit. They also had the power to annul any permits issued by the Rome Planning Department that violated the 1931 plan. There were, however, no reported cases of such actions in Rome, or in other Italian cities. This puzzle cannot be explained simply in terms of bureaucratic incompetence or administrative difficulties in securing compliance. The explanation given by Minister of Public Works Fiorentino Sullo to the Chamber of Deputies in 1962 points to a much deeper source of poor government performance. As he put it, "the laws give [administrative officials] important sanctions, it is true, but since they cannot see and check on everything, to exercise these powers would be a form of discriminatory treatment" (quoted in Fried 1973, 275; see also Cervellati 1976, 358–9).

The very ideas constitutive of the Italian *stato di diritto* are themselves principal impediments to good government – sources of pathologies in government services. This also helps to explain the puzzle that has intrigued many observers, including those mentioned in chapter 1: Why is Italy both an excessively legalistic country and a place where rules of officialdom tend to be disregarded.

Against this backdrop it becomes easier to understand why the postwar attempts to enforce maximum public planning took on the characteristics of "discriminatory treatment" and why official illegalism and maximum private planning became, instead, a means to reduce exposure to potential discriminatory treatment. Unfortunately, these individual and collective strategies – however justifiable in each particular instance – added to existing problems in the use of urban roads, water, electricity, sewage disposal, air masses, open space, and the like. It comes as no surprise that, as a consequence,

one of the striking characteristics of postwar Roman development is not so much the inequalities among districts but the uniformities among them. One expects to find considerable variation in the services and environmental quality as between wealthier and poorer sections of the city, but instead one finds a lack of services and poor environmental quality in all districts, including the wealthiest. Many of the wealthiest districts built during the postwar period have no more street space, green space, or recreational facilities than the low income districts. The streets in upper-income districts are no cleaner than those in the less wealthy districts. There has been the same penchant toward maximum exploitation of property in both kinds of districts. The real inequalities have been those between regularly built districts – whether rich or poor – and the *bidonvilles*, or shantytowns. The better districts usually have basic infrastructure ... such as streets, sewers, water, and electricity, while lacking community facilities ... such as schools, markets, churches, parks, playgrounds and social centres. The *borgate* and *bidonvilles* lack both kinds of infrastructures. (Fried 1973, 275; see also Il Mondo 1973, 1974)

The sudden collapse of an entire apartment building in 1998 drew attention to another problematic aspect of the mess: the potential structural fragility of many housing projects built between the 1940s and the 1960s (*La Repubblica* 1998b). Private as well as public planning produced "public bads" (Buchanan 1970).

CONCLUSION

The case of planning modern Rome indicates the difficulties of bringing about in practice the order and symmetry that both Italian governmental arrangements and master plans claim to deliver in theory. Planning modern Rome lends support to the general proposition that problem solving through central planning is itself a source of institutional weakness. In such circumstances, private planning simply added to "the congestion on the common" (Buchanan 1968). At the same time, this chapter offers additional evidence that, for much of the postwar period Italians – both citizens and public officials – behaved in an institutional framework that produced outcomes that they themselves did not value highly as possible alternatives. The discussion of problem solving by central planning reveals that the paradox of rational Italians and irrational Italy is simplistic at best and does not quite capture how and why the postwar system worked as it did.

PART THREE

The War on Crime as a Fight for Good Government

6 The Mafia and the Antimafia

Perhaps no other situation illustrates more dramatically the inconsistencies between preferred solutions and the actual behaviour of public and elected officials – how crafting good government can generate gaps between policy intentions and policy outcomes – than the contemporary Italian government war on crime. At the same time, the chasm between popular and academic knowledge and the experience of participants in the fight for good government is probably nowhere wider than in this area of Italian public life.

Elsewhere I have dealt with successive government wars on crime before, during, and after Fascism, until the end of the 1960s (Sabetti 1984). This chapter and the next refine and extend more recent analysis (Sabetti 1990, 1992) aimed at unravelling what constraints were at work in the war on crime in the 1980s, before the political and judicial upheavals of the early 1990s. These chapters do not aim to be either exhaustive or definitive, but they do seek to capture critical moments in the war on crime as a fight for good government. These critical moments allow us to understand the challenge of the place of statutory legislation and administrative regulations as the core of legal processes whose perverse emphasis on legality, in turn, presents a serious challenge to the very concept of a rule of law in the *stato di diritto*. At any one point each aspect of a specific problematic situation is complexly nested within other problematic situations. More generally, the chapters help to situate the Italian government war on crime in a comparative context.

The rich mix of difficult scenarios that will be examined contains troubling and unavoidable facts. Reasonable people can disagree about the nature of the mafia problem and which strategy should prevail in the war on crime. Moreover, the *forma mentis,* or mindset, that goes with general statutory enactments – that of a state official oriented to universalities and uniformities – also leads to deep troubles. Agreement among state actors and agencies on what must be done ("fight organized crime") does not suffice to guarantee agreement on how to proceed; even when agreement on how to proceed is unproblematic, it does not, *ipso facto,* guarantee the anticipated action and outcome. The splits and rivalries within the Palermo police force and the Italian judiciary provide empirical force to the argument that the complex layering of issues and structures in organized crime investigations and prosecutions can defeat efforts to tackle big issues all at once. The chapters also reveal what challenges the instrumentalities of government face in trying to overcome their own problems all at once and to wage a successful campaign against a phenomenon whose very nature is ambiguous, porous, and contestable. In such conditions, as we saw in chapter 5, magistrates and police officials – no less than analysts – have an immense problem of deciding whether illegalities are crimes or the difficulties of ordinary people trying to solve problems. This distinction is compounded by the fact that the boundaries between organized crime and "ordinary crime" are fuzzy at best, so that illegalities can become an easy ally of organized crime.

For all these reasons, the internal world of government, including public administration, is much messier than popular and academic knowledge generally allow. But, it should be emphasized, to acknowledge this fact is no argument for scepticism – it merely guards against exaggerated generalizations and pretensions to omniscience. By seeking to understand why and how governments sometimes work and sometimes do not work, this and the next chapter try to give added coherence to what the previous chapters have sought to elucidate: the challenges and constraints that await the translation of universalistic statutory legislation and administrative regulations into outcomes and operational reality.

At this point, informed readers of current Italian affairs may be provoked to ask: If the world of the Italian central government and administration is so plagued with internal problems that fighting the war on crime was difficult to carry out, why did the mafia strike out so fiercely and effectively against symbols of state power like magistrates Giovanni Falcone and Paolo Borsellino in 1992? The methods of these leaders must have been very effective to spark such brutal retaliations. In fact, the prevailing wisdom since their deaths has been that the assassinations of Falcone and Borsellino were acts of desperation because the state, through them, was highly effective in fighting criminality. How does the analysis in this book square with these post-1992 developments? Is the prevailing wisdom mistaken?

Readers are entitled to an explanation. I urge them not to rush to judgment, but to hold their reactions in abeyance until they see how the analysis unfolds. In the concluding chapter, I address the post-1992 conventional wisdom and the questions it raises within the context of events of 1992 and after, but one point can be anticipated now. As I hope to make clear, there is no fundamental contradiction between the argument advanced here and the post-1992 prevailing wisdom that sees the murders of Falcone and Borsellino as an *ex adverso* confirmation of the successful government war on crime. I would argue, and hope to prove by chapter 10, that what happened to the government war on crime after 1991 can be better understood from the vantage point of the analytical narrative developed in this part. We need to be open to the possibility – without in any way detracting from their good intentions and actions and without implying irreverence to their memory – that magistrates Falcone and Borsellino may have been both right (in the method of investigations they used) and wrong (in the way they conceptualized mafia groups).

We begin this chapter with events that occurred in 1988. That year is important, for it marked a new direction in the response by national and local authorities to the mafia problem. These developments are simple in outline but complex in detail, as they are linked together in a simultaneous and sequential way. Understanding is complicated by problems both in the prevailing conception of the Sicilian criminal underworld and in the organization and conduct of the administration of justice, law enforcement agencies, and administrative and party politics. This chapter surveys this rich mix of problematic solutions by first sketching the principal events of 1988 that made the year stand out in postwar Sicilian history, then discussing the conception of the mafia that sustained much of the public initiative and response during the period. The remainder of the chapter unravels the response of the instrumentalities of government: first, by clarifying how and why law enforcement agencies acted as they did; second, by considering the extent to which the Palermitan government under Mayor Leoluca Orlando became a critical antimafia point of reference. Chapter 7 follows subsequent developments with particular attention to the issues of illegality, crime, and punishment.

The two chapters are based upon almost all the available public documentation of the period as well as field research, which included several background interviews – conducted in Palermo in 1988, and in Messina, Naples, Palermo, and Reggio Calabria in 1991 – with academics and public officials directly involved in antimafia activity. Additional field research in 1994, 1995, and 1998 opened up new possibilities for improving the argument and for reducing uncertainties and gaps in earlier fieldwork.

THE PUZZLING EVENTS OF 1988 IN CONTEXT

In the immediate post-1943 period, the primary and most visible response to the mafia problem in Sicily came from parties and groups on the left: these forces then constituted the antimafia. Elsewhere I have explained what kind of clash ensued between the mafia and the antimafia in the postwar life of Camporano, a notorious mafia town in western Sicily (Sabetti 1984, 1993, 31–41). There I also emphasize how the absence of judicial remedies for use by individual Sicilians and the need to win elections facilitated the exercise of a monopoly of central and regional authority by Christian Democrat (DC) leaders, which in turn fostered the transformation of that Sicilian commune into a sort of trading company of the local mafia (Sabetti 1984, 167–9). By the mid-1950s, this state of affairs had come to an end in Camporano, with the collapse of both the local mafia and antimafia (Sabetti 1984, 185–98). Nevertheless, mafia influence continued in the regional capital, reaching dramatic proportions by the 1970s. So much so, in fact, that Judith Chubb's analysis of Palermitan politics ended on a note of despair about the enduring strength of machine politics, boss rule, and violence (Chubb 1982).

Judith Chubb's work had hardly reached the cold finality of print when, in a radical move unprecedented in the history of republican Italy, magistrates in Palermo began a vigorous antimafia campaign. What would have been unimaginable a few years earlier – the very seat of the Palermo commune, the Palazzo delle Aquile, was being transformed into an institutional force for checking machine politics and boss rule, and under a DC mayor! (see also Alongi 1997, chs. 6–8; Varese 1994, 229–30).

By 1987 the vigorous judicial and police investigations led to over 300 guilty verdicts, as well as notable mafia repenters and their "confessions," a considerable reduction in drug trafficking between Sicily and the United States, the arrest and exile from Sicily of a once powerful DC leader and former mayor of Palermo, and the collapse of the economic-political empire of two financiers with reputed links to the underworld. The force behind these unprecedented developments was essentially a team of magistrates – all of them Sicilians – specializing in mafia investigations under the acknowledged leadership of Giovanni Falcone in the office of the investigating magistrate of the Palermo tribunal (*ufficio istruzione*), popularly known in Italy as the "antimafia pool." The very personalities of Falcone and his closest colleague and friend, Paolo Borsellino, appeared to symbolize a unity of purpose and direction reaching across the usual divides of Italian public life: Falcone, a lapsed Catholic, professed republican sentiments and cultivated strong ties to the moderate left; Borsellino, a practising Catholic, professed monarchist sentiments and cultivated strong ties to the extreme right, now known as National Alliance.

The year 1988 marked a turning point in the fortunes of the judicial team. As the killings on the island continued unabated, the antimafia parliamentary commission was resurrected and a new antimafia commissioner with apparently wider powers than those of his predecessors was appointed. But the very campaign conducted by the Palermitan team of investigating magistrates appeared to be flagging. Matters were finally brought into the open in July 1988, when a former member of the judicial team, Borsellino, then a Marsala prosecutor, declared in a newspaper interview that there were behind-the-scenes attempts in Palermo to weaken, if not dismantle, judicial and police investigations (cited in Bolzoni 1988a). The newspaper headline, appearing to come from Borsellino's own words, read: "The state has surrendered; the antimafia pool is in ruins." In August of that year, the president of the Palermo Court of Appeal, Carmelo Conti, was quoted as saying that "the state has abandoned Sicily" (cited in *Giornale di Sicilia* 1989a). As a result, the president of the Republic took the unusual step of asking the government for a clear explanation of what was taking place in Palermo.

A complex series of state initiatives and responses followed, accompanied by a heated, often public debate within the legal administration and law enforcement agencies and beyond. By the end of the year – and well before the 1989 legal reforms dismantling the *uffici istruzioni* began to govern criminal proceedings – not only had the antimafia pool practically ceased to exist, but the very concept of organized crime that informed and sustained its work, to the point of being nicknamed "the Falcone theorem," was being seriously challenged. Megatrials now seemed a thing of the past. Had the state really surrendered, by implication, to criminality? Had the state really abandoned Sicily?

During the same year, there were marked positive developments in civil society and political institutions in the two major Sicilian cities of Catania and Palermo. While reform activities were just under way in Catania, the Palermitan revolt against the hegemony of the national ruling coalition over the issue of local self-government was consolidated, making the Palermo commune a vital point in the antimafia campaign. By 1988, the mayor of Palermo, Leoluca Orlando, had become a highly visible representative of the renewal taking place in civil society and political institutions.

To paraphrase Antonio Gramsci somewhat, the old had died and the new was being born precisely in the Palermo citadel often taken as emblematic of what was wrong with Sicily – the Palazzo delle Aquile (city hall). The goal of the Orlando-led government coalition (like that of its newly established counterpart in Catania, led by Enzo Bianco) was to bring transparency to city hall, to isolate and reduce the mafia phenomenon in communal affairs, and to implement a system of politics in line with the realization of a "liveable city" – in effect, to break the rules by which many Sicilian communes seemed to be governed. Thus the year 1988 marked both a pause and an expansion in the response by national and local authorities to the mafia problem. The rest of this chapter seeks to show how and why.

THE ONTOLOGY OF THE MAFIA IN QUESTION

The prevailing conception of the contemporary criminal underworld, the conception that shaped the response of government instrumentalities in the 1980s, was grounded in much of the investigative work of Giovanni Falcone. He, in turn, appeared to have been influenced somewhat – or so it seemed to outside observers – by Pino Arlacchi's ideal-type models of organized crime (see Arlacchi 1987, xi; Falcone, cited in Galluzzo, La Licata, and Lodato 1986, 32–3). The extent of Arlacchi's influence on Falcone is more complicated than it was once thought. While Falcone's posthumous collection of essays written between 1982 and 1992 refers to Arlacchi, Falcone tends to disagree with him (Falcone 1994, 122, 320, 337). For instance, Falcone did not think that there were two mafias, an old mafia and a new mafia (*mafia imprenditrice*), as Arlacchi suggested (1987). Also, Arlacchi never thought that the mafia was a secret organization until Falcone told him so, pointing out that Arlacchi's studies were wrong on this crucial point (see Arlacchi 1992, vii; 1994, vii–xii).

In a paper presented at a conference in June 1988, Magistrate Falcone asserted that the real name of the mafia is Cosa Nostra (Falcone 1988, 6; cf., Arlacchi 1994, vii). This is the organization that, partly on the basis of confessions by mafia repenters, Falcone and other magistrates had earlier described as "organized with rigidly vertical structures and its epicentre in Palermo, the site of the directing body of the association called the *cupola* or the Commission" (Stajano 1986, ix). This organization was deemed "unique" as it was not strictly confined to the criminal underworld. It was said to encompass, sometimes by association and sometimes by organic participation, almost all elements in Sicilian society and to permeate all aspects of Sicilian life (see esp. Stajano 1986, xvi; cf., Arlacchi and Dalla Chiesa 1987, vii, 16–17, 36–49). Thus, in the words of Falcone, "the Sicilian reality is that there is a unitary criminal organization called Cosa Nostra, with thousands of followers. Given the cohesion, compactness, and ferocity of its members and the protection and connivance it enjoys at every level, its dangerousness is without equal in the world. This organization operates in Italy and abroad in every kind of illicit activity and, in particular, in the international drug traffic" (Falcone 1987 cited in Guarrasi 1988, 66).

This conclusion was strongly endorsed by the self-regulating body of the judiciary, the Superior Judicial Council (*Consiglio Superiore della Magistratura*), in a resolution of February 1988 (Carlo Smuraglia, cited in *Giornale di Sicilia*, 1989b). The confessions of another Tommaso Buscetta-like repenter – Antonino Calderone, a former *capoclan* from Catania arrested in France in 1986 – became known in the spring of 1988. Filling over 900 typewritten pages, these confessions lent weight to the common opinion, based on the Falcone theorem. But the accepted conception of the mafia and the exalted generalizations about its reach had problems in theory and substance.

First, to say that the real name of the mafia is Cosa Nostra tended to confuse matters rather than clarify them. Calderone was reported to have revealed that "Cosa Nostra has been in Catania since 1925" (cited in Bolzoni 1988b; see also Stille 1995, 229), but it is hard to see how Cosa Nostra could have been operating in Catania as far back as 1925, when that characterization was not then even part of the language and practice of North American crime syndicates.

The earliest evidence of the existence of Cosa Nostra is in the testimony of a minor underworld figure, Joseph Valachi, at the U.S. Senate hearings in 1963. This testimony has been found to be contradictory and inaccurate (Albini 1971, 221–62). In fact, Valachi's statements were so puzzling that, even among American law enforcement officials, there was some uncertainty as to whether the organization Valachi referred to was actually called Cosa Nostra, Causa Nostra, or Casa Nostra (Albini 1971, 224). Subsequent recorded conversations between underworld figures in New Jersey – the so-called De Cavalcante recordings – showed that terms like "Commission" and "Cosa Nostra" do occur. One should bear in mind that (as noted in Moore 1974, 252–3), the De Cavalcante recordings referred to New York-New Jersey underworld circles and did not establish the existence of a tightly knit national criminal organization. Furthermore, the greater number of references to the Commission in the De Cavalcante recordings occurred during the Bonanno War, after

Valachi's testimony; De Cavalcante appeared to be using the Valachi terminology to explain issues to a confused friend, which suggests the extent to which the underworld itself was influenced by press speculation and the dramatic testimony of witnesses such as Valachi. It is hard, therefore, to avoid coming to the conclusion that Sicilian and American criminals and the myths and half-truths that surround their activities subsist in different but contiguous worlds, making the task of distinguishing fact from fantasy exceedingly difficult. What made the Falcone theorem difficult to accept was that its characterization of Cosa Nostra as an omnipotent hydra sounded like the old myth of the mafia. This myth has a long and sad history in polemical writings on Sicilian criminality, including the published views of public security officials such as Giuseppe Alongi, Antonio Cutrera, and Cesare Mori.

Apart from definitional problems of the Falcone theorem, there were also problems that challenge the empirical strength of the concept. After noting that the testimony of Tommaso Buscetta and the Cosa Nostra trials in Palermo and New York strengthened belief in the idea of a criminal conspiracy, Christopher Duggan wrote:

Buscetta was more articulate and consistent than Valachi; but whether the Sicilian organization he described (which he also said was known as "Cosa Nostra") was indeed a formal one, is by no means certain. Like Valachi, he had a vested interest in providing the authorities with confirmation of their suspicions, and his collaboration has led to his own immunity, and the prosecution of many of his enemies. What was particularly unclear from Buscetta's testimony was what the organization existed for. At one point, he confessed to the Palermo magistrates that when it came to "business" activities (including drug trafficking) each "man of honour" was free to do whatever he wanted. (Duggan 1989, 6)

Then Duggan asked, "How organized, then, was organized crime?" (Duggan 1989, 6). The confessions by Calderone (cited in L'Ora, 1988) produced the same puzzle (cf., Lupo 1993a, 82, 184).

A chief problem with Duggan's line of inquiry is that it can be taken to suggest that the mafia as a secret, organized, and hierarchical entity does not exist, that the term mafia may be just a word of abuse that political factions of all sorts level at each other. In the process, we may forget that, though the mafia aspires to obtain a monopoly of protection in a certain territory, this does not mean that all mafiosi are involved in every illegal activity, that non-mafia criminals are happy to pay the mafia with protection, that mafiosi do not engage in criminal activities as individuals. Even if we were to treat Duggan's interpretation as unreliable, as some suggest (Gambetta 1993, 137–8, 288n11, 290–1n2; Varese 1996, 1997c), and Calderone's confession as self-serving, one important fact goes against the standard view. As Peter Reuter has noted so well, this fact applies to New York as well as Palermo. As he put it, "the orthodoxy, entrenched in both popular belief and official statement, is that illegal markets are typically dominated by a single group whose power rests on the control of corrupt public authority and the command of overwhelming violence. These are the forces of the 'visible hand.' But other forces are at work too. These are the influences usually referred to as the 'invisible hand,' the working of self-interest and technology that largely shape the organization of markets for legal goods and services. Often tension exists between the visible and invisible hands in illegal markets" (Reuter 1983, 20).

Like Gambetta's research (1993), Reuter's work helps us to recognize several issues: that there are incentives for the emergence of a dominant violent group; that the invisible hand precludes criminal groups from maintaining a monopoly of illegal markets; and that if a local mafia group does not have a monopoly over particular activities, this fact cannot be taken to mean that it does not aspire to have a monopoly over the protection of such activities. Gay Talese's *Honor Thy Father* (1972) casts a good deal of doubt on the "organized" character of organized crime in New York City. Still, even if the mafia did not, or does not, have a monopoly of illegal markets in New York City or Palermo, it is important here not to conflate very different things: organization (or firm), monopoly of markets, and protection of markets. Although it is difficult to have a monopoly without some organization, it does not follow that *not* having a monopoly correspondingly means not being organized and not aspiring to gain control over the supply of protection.

All this is to stress the danger that ontological, ideal-type models highlighting mafia involvement in drug trafficking and the like may hinder rather than facilitate understanding of the Sicilian criminal underworld. Moreover, we should expect the tension between the visible and invisible hands in Sicily to lead not to "the mafia enterprise," as some suggest, but, rather, to the formation of many small and relatively ephemeral underworld firms involved in a combination of licit and illicit activities. Research carried out by Raimondo Catanzaro (1988) on the variety of economic firms constituted to hide profits obtained from drug traffic in the Palermo region lends support to Reuter's argument.

Additional scepticism about the accepted ontology of the mafia phenomenon was borne out by the presence of twenty-two drug traffic rings found in Palermo in 1988; their presence was noted by the Palermo chief prosecutor at the formal opening of the new judicial year in January 1989 (Vincenzo Pajano cited in *Giornale di Sicilia* 1989b). These drug traffic rings suggested a relatively free and open entry to the drug trade by different entrepreneurs, which contradicts an earlier assertion by Magistrate Giuseppe Ayala – from the same office – who claimed that the Palermo drug trade was directed by a single monopolistic organization, Cosa Nostra (*La Repubblica* 1988a). Furthermore, the result of inquiries made by the antimafia parliamentary commission in November 1988, made public in a draft report prepared by the commission's vice- president in January 1989, strongly suggested the absence of a drug trade monopoly in Sicily. It claimed that the mafia phenomenon and drug trafficking, though sharing many common characteristics, did not necessarily overlap (Claudio Vitalone, cited in *Giornale di Sicilia* 1989c). The result of these inquiries did not, however, clarify what the work of Gambetta and Varese has since made clear: the mafia does not aspire to have a monopoly over drug trafficking, but over the protection of drug trafficking.

A far more damaging challenge to the empirical validity of the Cosa Nostra conception – which had direct consequences for the antimafia pool, as we shall see – came towards the end of 1988 from the Supreme Court of Appeal (*Corte di Cassazione*). Asked to rule on the allocation of judicial investigations surrounding the so-called Madonie police raid in the spring of 1988, the Supreme Court of Appeal partly rejected the unitary model in the following way:

The mafia, like the *camorra* and the *'ndrangheta*, have not each constructed a single organization with pyramidal and vertical structures to which the various associations operating at the national or international level can be tied. Rather they each constitute a plurality of criminal associations, often in conflict with one another. These criminal associations may follow the same methods and the same structures ... but are endowed with a wide decision-making scope, operate in different territorial contexts, and have a predominantly subjective differentiation ... [The mafia family of the Madonie is] an association autonomous of and distinct from Cosa Nostra. (cited in *Giornale di Sicilia* 1988)

In January 1989, another official interpretation suggested that the real name of the mafia was not Cosa Nostra and that Cosa Nostra itself was merely one of many crime syndicates. A widely circulated draft report of the antimafia parliamentary commission, prepared by its vice- president on the basis of almost ninety interviews conducted in

Sicily in November 1988, read in part as follows: "In Sicily there coexist today on the one side a vertical organization known as Cosa Nostra with a diffuse network on the island, in various regions of Italy and abroad, and, on the other, organizations of far more limited dimensions that, even if belonging to the mafia typology, can certainly not be identified with Cosa Nostra and that, very often, come in conflict with it" (excerpts in *Giornale di Sicilia* 1989c).

By the end of 1988, supporters of the original Cosa Nostra concept could still be found in the (now renamed) Communist Party (PCI), in the judiciary both at the Palermo *Procura* (district attorney's office) and on the Superior Judicial Council (see Di Lello 1994; *Giornale di Sicilia* 1989b), as well as on the Palermitan communal council (Alongi 1997). But that conception had lost standing as a guide and orientation for the state response to criminality.

Finally, there was a third, more general, transtemporal problem. Magistrates, the police, and politicians, not unlike academic researchers, were under pressure to make sense of a complex reality and to achieve quick results. They faced – but did not always overcome – the real danger to using Cosa Nostra or the mafia as a convenient explanatory *deus ex machina* for institutionalized corruption, illegal markets, and a host of other problems that beset Sicilian society. Assertions such as "the mafia has the face of public institutions" could be often heard in Palermo in 1988. Such assertions became important "plastic words" (Porsken 1989) for fuelling public debate, grabbing headlines, and promising to shake up the status quo, but – it needs to be added – they shed little or no light on the underlying processes that have continued to structure the mix of legitimate and illegitimate opportunities available to most Sicilians.

As noted in the first chapter, many historical accounts of the origins of mafia groups and the Fascist war against them reveal critical disjunctions between myth and reality (for the United States, see Di Bella, Sabetti, and Tremblay forthcoming; Kelly 1986, 29n6; and for Russia, Varese 1994). In my political-economic history of Camporano, I found that the local mafia had already ceased to be part of the Sicilian problem by the 1960s, when police officials resurrected it in order to wage the antimafia campaign in the town – with somewhat tragic consequences (Sabetti 1984, 208–16). This led me to conclude that the fight against criminality – no matter how well-intentioned – is apt to be counterproductive if carried out without due process of inquiry and without due regard for justice. On the strength of that fieldwork, I went as far as to conclude that, "appeals to the mafia to explain or account for governmental failures and even criminal activities in Sicily should be generally treated as mere confessions of ignorance because they avoid the investigation needed to show their empirical war-rantability. Such appeals may unwittingly serve both to misdirect public concern about the course that the fight against crime should take ... and to provide a handy cover for ignoring 'the practice of empire' or 'bureaucratic free enterprise' among those who occupy public positions" (Sabetti 1984, 234).

Generally, as we have seen in the previous chapters, public monopolies can pose even more difficult problems than private monopolies. Carlo Cattaneo and Francesco Ferrara, as well as subsequent analysts like Napoleone Colajanni and Luigi Einaudi, feared that public monopolists, without an appropriate structure of incentives and accountability, are not only less responsive and less efficient than private monopolists, but can also engage in a more effective practice of predatory rule and racketeering (see also Loveman 1973; V. Ostrom 1988). In fact, a logic of predatory rule, illegal markets, and violent crime can result directly from the practice of empire building and bureaucratic free enterprise among public monopolists who experience either difficulties with general statutory enactments and administrative regulations or transitions from one political and property-rights regime to another (e.g., Sabetti 1984, chs. 4–6; Varese 1994; in press). The kind of institutionalized corruption or clientelism that can emerge from a perverse emphasis on legality can transform the public sector into a diseconomy and a temptation for criminal syndicates. This is in fact what Colajanni had in mind when he provocatively noted in 1900 that "to combat and destroy the kingdom of the mafia it is necessary that the Italian government cease to be the king of the mafia" (cited in Sabetti 1984, 10).

Analysts who have adopted a positivist view of the monopoly of state powers have, quite self-consciously, avoided normative consideration or "value judgments" of the legitimacy of those powers in Sicily (see Blok 1974, 172). As a result, they have missed the opportunity to explore the extent to which the rise of outlaw groups and the practice of predatory rule and violent entrepreneurship may be a direct but partial outcome of the nature and exercise of public monopolies in Sicily. As noted in chapters 1 and 2, the lesson taught by Francesco Ferrara (and later by Sidney Sonnino, as we shall see in chapter 9) has been ignored by most of the academic literature on Sicily, at great cost.

For all these reasons, we still do not quite understand the role of crime syndicates and illegal markets in Sicily and elsewhere in southern Italy (cf., Varese 1994, 1997b). The most important ingredient in advancing understanding in this area is the sharing of concepts and theories. Without a common conceptual and theoretical framework, we face problems such as those noted by Diego Gambetta:

We know much and understand little about the Italian mafia. The amount of factual information surrounding it – what that "it" may be – is disproportionately and dramatically greater than our theoretical understanding of this elusive entity. We do not know everything it might be interesting to know, of course, yet in the monumental quantity of scholarly and judicial sources devoted to the mafia, we can find far more information than scholars have been able to make good, cogent sense of. Facts and anecdotes are not only numerous, but of the most diverse and seemingly irreconcilable kinds, and theoretical and analytical shortcomings have made it impossible to accomplish two fundamental operations: first, to discriminate between relevant information and contingent ethnographical detail, and between reliable and distorted evidence; second, to find a coherent thread linking whatever disparate pieces of information remain after the first screening operation. (Gambetta 1988, 127; 1993; see also Di Bella, Sabetti, and Tremblay forthcoming; Varese 1996)

In summary, the response of governmental agencies to Sicilian criminality in the period under review was hindered by ambiguous and contestable characterizations of the very phenomenon they sought to overcome. But the instrumentalities of government faced other difficulties to which we now turn. Let me first prevent a possible misreading of what follows.

Chapters 6 and 7 should not be construed as primarily aiming to demonstrate the existence of confusion and back-biting, splits, and rivalries within the Palermo police force and the Italian judiciary, or to suggest that centralized institutions and general statutory enactments requiring uniform application never work as their designers intended. Rather, what follows should, above all, be taken as evidence that a lot of poor results in various sectors of Italian administration are due to genuinely different views on what is best. The interests of different professional groups within certain sectors of the administration are represented by rational actors who invoke either the war on the mafia (*la lotta alla mafia*) or the universalities and uniformities of rules of procedure (*il garantismo*) to pursue their plans. Rational self-interest and genuine arguments intermingle with each other to create the situation traced below.

THE POLITICS OF BUREAUCRACY

Developments set in motion by the Borsellino newspaper interview in July 1988 meant that a host of other contentious issues with regard to the administration of justice and law enforcement agencies were relegated to the background. Even the question of whether or not Minister of the Interior Antonio Gava was still fit to hold office – after judicial investigators expressed concern about his alleged involvement in questionable dealings related to the release of a DC politician from Campania by kidnappers, "the Cirillo case" – seemed less pressing than what was taking place in Palermo. As events unfolded from the interview, the entire political, administrative, and judicial system was sucked into the Sicilian controversy, exposing the extent to which the politics of bureaucracy itself slowed down or deflected the antimafia war.

Borsellino declared that there were behind-the-scenes attempts to minimize Falcone's role in investigations, to dismantle the antimafia pool, and to "normalize" police inquiries (cited in Bolzoni 1988a). The state appeared to have surrendered – by implication, to crime syndicates – on its two most critical anticrime fronts: the office of the investigating magistrate (*ufficio istruzione*) and the police detective unit (*squadra mobile*). While Falcone publicly praised Borsellino for his "sense of the State and personal courage" (*Corriere della Sera* 1988a), the heads of these two offices, Antonino Meli and Antonino Nicchi respectively, strenuously rejected *in toto* Borsellino's charges. They denied that the state had surrendered.

The press had a field day with these developments. It is therefore not surprising that even some usually responsible editorialists like those at *La Repubblica* now unbridled their imaginations to picture the "mafia octopus" manipulating (often behind the scene and without the participants' knowledge) various judicial and other public officials as if they were marionettes. No doubt, developments were far more complex, far more fraught with *res incognitae*, than available evidence would suggest; but two irrefutably clear points emerged.

First, speculation as to the behaviour of the chief investigating magistrate (*consigliere istruttore*), Meli, and the police detective chief, Nicchi, turned out to be insubstantial. They were both state officials above suspicion and reproach. Moreover, both were right in insisting that they had not shirked their respective responsibilities in the antimafia campaign. Evidence from investigations of connections between crime syndicates and construction firms in Catania, disclosed during the latter part of the year, strongly supported Meli's often-repeated statement that his office had not surrendered to organized or disorganized crime. Indeed, that evidence suggested that it was Falcone and other magistrates in the chief prosecutor's office – and not Meli – who were more cautious in pressing criminal charges for those connections (see Di Lello 1994, 211–12; Mignosi 1988).

As for the police detective unit, Nicchi rejected as polemical the charges that his office had not produced any report worthy of the name on Cosa Nostra since 1982. He claimed that, since heading the detective unit in 1985, he had produced many reports on the mafia, on various gang murders, on drug trafficking, and on changes in crime syndicates (see Bolzoni 1988c).

Second, if the state response to the mafia problem had indeed slowed down and seemed without direction, the reasons were both more complex and less dramatic than they appeared either in the Borsellino interview or in statements by those who took issue with it. They related to factors intrinsic to the *ufficio istruzione*, the *squadra mobile*, and the administration of justice in general. Let us disaggregate these factors in some detail.

Ufficio istruzione

An issue that increased tension in the Palace of Justice "bunker" of the antimafia team in Palermo was Meli's appointment as the chief investigating magistrate in January 1988. This appointment revealed some of the most problematic qualities of the Italian system: the politicization of the judiciary and the judicialization of politics.

The previous holder of that post, Antonino Caponnetto, had come to appreciate Falcone's painstaking work and his ability to search for Sicilian crime syndicates in Italy and abroad (See Caponnetto 1993). Falcone had thus emerged not only as Italy's leading antimafia investigator but also as an important ally of the police in other countries and especially in the United States (see *New York Times* 1988). For most of his four-year term, therefore, Caponnetto had delegated his authority to the informal antimafia pool operating under Falcone's acknowledged leadership (Caponnetto 1993; see also Di Lello 1994, 169; Stille 1995). Thus, it is understandable why both Caponnetto and the other magistrates preferred Falcone and campaigned vigorously for him to be the new chief investigating magistrate (Di Lello 1994, 208–10). That these men fought hard for the candidate they judged to be right should not be surprising, but this did not make bureaucratic politics, the antimafia campaign, and the lives of Meli and Falcone less complicated.

Despite the efforts of Caponnetto and others, the Superior Judicial Council, in charge of the appointment, chose Meli. Like the judiciary in general, the Superior Judicial Council, especially by the end of the 1960s, had become divided along party lines and "ideological currents." This is not to suggest that matters were better immediately after the war, when, it is fair to say, "Italy was in the hands of a judiciary that was deeply conservative in its approach to the law and the role of the courts" (Spotts and Wieser 1986, 158). The point is that the judicial system, designed to be both independent of government and immune from politics, instead became highly politicized by the end of the 1960s, at the same time that it dramatically biased other branches of government in its favour (e.g., *Corriere della Sera* 1970; Gentile 1969; Maradei 1975; Mazzocchi 1974). The assessment of two leading students of the Italian judiciary may be worth quoting at some length to put in context the battle fought over Meli's appointment:

The political significance of our judiciary is today much higher than in other democratic regimes, even in those in which, as in the United States, the political role of the judiciary has been entrusted not only the power of judging, with complete independence, issues regarding the freedom and the wealth of the citizenry, but also the power of self-recruitment, self-evaluation, and self-discipline. Moreover, the Italian judiciary enjoys exclusive control of access to the criminal justice system, i.e., the monopoly of criminal initiative. In other words, it enjoys the power of defining and implementing a large part of criminal policy without the possibility of being held responsible, directly or indirectly – as in the case of all other significant democratic regimes – by the political community. (Di Federico and Guarnieri 1988, 178)

The matrix of choice tends to be more complex when we examine the facts on the ground. Support for the sixty-eight year old Meli – who had an unimpeachable reputation as a judge but was viewed as "a magistrate of the old school" – also came from members of the judicial faction to which Falcone then belonged, the Unity for the Constitution group (UNICOST). Meli was even supported by some members of the Democratic Magistracy (MD), the more left-oriented group on the Superior Judicial Council. Though ideologically close to Falcone, these magistrates apparently supported Meli's candidacy in order to uphold the principle and importance of seniority in such appointments (Di Lello 1994, 208–9; Stille 1995, 221).

Against this backdrop, it is not surprising that, upon taking up office in March 1988, Meli found the antimafia team of magistrates, if not hostile, at least cool towards him. But not one of these magistrates seemed to doubt – either privately or publicly (Di Lello 1994) – his skill, honesty, and competence. In fact, an American writer found that "even Meli's harshest critics have never questioned his good faith" (Stille 1995, 267). The younger magistrates just thought that he was not up to the job as *the* instructing magistrate for mafia cases; he did not seem sophisticated enough to handle the evidence. Meli, sensing the general feeling of the office, did not convene the team upon arrival. He met only with Falcone.

Following the inaugural ceremony to mark the transfer of authority from Caponnetto to Meli in mid-March, a newspaper correspondent noted prophetically that the new investigating magistrate had "a difficult inheritance to manage" (Viviano 1988). In fact, no sooner had Meli settled into his new routine that another series of difficulties arose to exacerbate personal and working relations.

This second source of internal tension revolved around the question of who actually directed antimafia investigations. In law, it was the investigating magistrate; but Meli's predecessors, though remaining officially in charge of all inquiries, had allowed the antimafia team to handle the inquiries – with the result that Falcone and the antimafia pool had acquired considerable autonomy and power. This de facto position rested on the de jure authority and discretion of the chief investigating magistrate; and as long as there was common understanding and agreement between the head magistrate and the team members, the de facto position of the pool posed no problem. Whereas in the past the murder of one magistrate was sufficient to bring investigations to a halt, the very existence of the pool assured now the survival of the investigations regardless of what happened to individual magistrates. It was more difficult to silence them all at once. But now, in part because of events connected with his appointment, including the way he had been received by his staff, Meli appeared to challenge the strategic thinking behind the judicial team by seeking to reclaim and exercise all the power and discretion that was legally and formally due to him. The stage was set for a confrontation.

Apparently, on 28 March 1988, less than two weeks after taking up office, Meli indicated that it was juridically incorrect or irregular to assign mafia investigations to several antimafia pool members simultaneously. This led the other magistrates to fear the dismantling of the antimafia judicial team. Thus they replied by asking him to share in the teamwork by working with them on all the cases. Meli refused and took over all the cases under investigation, as was his right. In the following weeks, he proceeded to assign some cases to magistrates outside the pool – in effect, expanding the antimafia team, a move that was resented by the original nucleus of magistrates.

In May the four magistrates of the original nucleus of the team sought to resolve the problem by asking, *inter alia*, to review all cases involving mafia activities in order to obtain an overview without which, they argued, it would be impossible to prepare adequate investigations for particular cases. Several days later, Meli rejected their proposal on the grounds that it would create anomalous and inefficient parallel investigations of similar facts. At the same time, Meli acceded to their earlier request to assign himself to investigations of the coming megatrial and proceeded to assign investigations to particular magistrates rather than to the pool as such.

At this juncture, the magistrates collectively rejected Meli's counterproposal on two grounds. First, they doubted whether Meli could have acquired, in his few months in office, a complete grasp of the mafia files so as to be, de jure and de facto, the head of proceedings, especially those not originally initiated by him. Secondly, they wanted work for the coming megatrial to be shared collectively by all the antimafia team magistrates and not to be assigned individually to a few at Meli's discretion. Meli disagreed. Frustrated, some magistrates contacted their former colleague, Borsellino, who, with the help of some eager journalists, brought matters into the open in July (see also Di Lello 1994, 209-13).

Between July 20 – the time of the Borsellino interview – and September 15 – the time of the announcement of the Superior Judicial Council's "final" decision on the controversy – there was a flurry of activity within the judiciary, in the Ministry of Justice, and elsewhere over what came to be known as the Meli-Falcone dispute. This flurry was fuelled in part by press leaks and counterleaks of what was purportedly taking place behind closed doors.

There is little point in tracing *ad plenum* this flurry of activities. What is important is that in September the Superior Judicial Council overturned its own interim majority decision, which had supported Meli's interpretation of events. Now it reached a unanimous decision emphasizing several points. First, in spite of some imprecision in his July press interview, Borsellino was deemed to be correct in indicating the existence of real problems in the judicial and police response to the mafia problem – a judgment widely interpreted to be in Borsellino's favour. Second, the differences that had emerged in the *ufficio istruzione* could in no way be interpreted as leading or intending to lead to the dismantling of the antimafia team, since no mafia trial had been withdrawn from the pool – a judgment widely interpreted to be in Meli's favour. And, third, the organizational arrangement of the antimafia pool and the wealth of experience gained through teamwork must be maintained, safeguarded, and further strengthened in light of the 1989 changes in penal reform – a point widely interpreted to concede the other magistrates' point (excerpts in *La Repubblica* 1988b; see also Di Lello 1994, 213–4).

Many newspapers headlined this ruling as a victory for all the parties concerned – Meli, Borsellino, Falcone, and the antimafia pool. The ruling had something for everybody, but this did not displease Meli, either. Some time later, as if to signal the end of hostility, the two principal antagonists, Falcone and Meli, met and embraced one another publicly. The president of the republic and nominal head of the Superior Judicial Council, Francesco Cossiga, appeared justified in hailing the Superior Judicial Council's decision as "resolutive" (*La Repubblica* 1988c; Di Lello 1994, 214–15).

If the decision in Rome appeared "resolutive" in ending tension in the internal operation of the *ufficio istruzione*, other developments in Sicily were unfolding to place in sharp relief a third and greater source of tension in that office: the conception of criminality that shaped the work of the investigating judicial team.

In the spring of 1988, the Calderone confessions led the *carabinieri* to take a close look at underworld activities in the Cefalù and Termini Imerese area, not far from Palermo. Eventually, the chief investigating magistrate for that district ordered several arrests that became known as the Madonie police raid. Since the antimafia judicial team in Palermo had assumed an investigative monopoly of all mafia-like underworld activities, the chief investigating magistrate for Termini Imerese declared that he was not competent to instigate trial proceedings. He turned over the Madonie crime syndicate files to the *ufficio istruzione* in Palermo.

Falcone and the other investigating magistrates welcomed the initiative. Meli did not. He argued, instead, that the dossier should be sent back to the Termini Imerese magistrate because the alleged crimes had been committed within that judicial district. The question was: which set of magistrates should prepare the case for the prosecution? The issue simmered throughout the summer and autumn. It was complicated by the knowledge that the Termini Imerese Tribunal was administratively ill-equipped to conduct trial proceedings of that magnitude.

To make the administration of justice work as it should could not be easily resolved. The issues were debated in the Palermo Palace of Justice throughout the spring, summer, and early autumn of 1988. They centred *grosso modo* on the following arguments and counterarguments put forward by the parties involved. We grant the importance we should attach to the Buscetta theorem of organized crime. But what if such a model doesn't fit all cases of criminality? Even if valid, some countered, should such a conception dominate all other considerations in the administration of justice? Should it, for example, override the jurisdictional competence assigned to particular judicial districts? But, others contended, what if some judicial districts are so administratively ill-equipped to instruct and stage lengthy criminal trials that to assign them trials is in effect to thwart justice? Should (still others argued) a judicial system go against its own legality, contravene its own jurisdictional arrangements, act *ultra vires*, in order to secure efficient results? And if so, who is competent to make that decision? In short, the magistrates were locked into a legal system that made it exceedingly difficult to reconcile different considerations bearing upon an efficient and just administration of justice.

Finally, in early October, the chief investigating magistrate sent the Madonie dossier to the Supreme Court of Appeal for a ruling. In November, the court upheld Meli's earlier suggestion to send the case back to Termini Imerese. In its opinion made public in December, the court – as was noted earlier – challenged the Cosa Nostra conception of the Sicilian underworld and, by implication, dealt a heavy blow to the very raison d'être of the antimafia pool.

News of the court's decision shook the "bunker" of the antimafia pool in the Palermo Palace of Justice. The magistrates asked Meli to disband the team, but Meli refused; he wanted the teamwork to continue. By the end of November, Meli and Falcone appeared to have reached a working arrangement that kept the antimafia pool alive without necessarily putting all the new criminal cases and investigations in the same file – the so-called "1817 envelope" or "container" – as had been the practice in the past. Some junior team associates bitterly resented this working arrangement and initiated steps to be transferred elsewhere (see also Di Lello 1994, 214).

The year ended with an announcement from the chief prosecutor's office that there would not be a megatrial of those seized during the Madonie police raid. This announcement gave rise to additional dissension, now among magistrates in the chief prosecutor's office. But by this time, productive relations seemed to prevail at the *ufficio istruzione*, if only between the main antagonists of the year, Falcone and Meli.

Squadra mobile

The Borsellino interview in July 1988 was also instrumental in focusing attention on internal problems within the most sensitive unit of the police force in Palermo, the *squadra mobile*. First, there were personality clashes between the chief detective, Antonino Nicchi, and those who supposedly were his closest aides – the two officers in charge of homicides and investigations, Francesco Accordino and Vincenzo Montalbano.

Second, the chief detective and his two aides differed sharply on how best to carry out their respective mandates. The investigation of the January 1988 murder of the former DC mayor of Palermo, Giuseppe Insalaco, was yet another occasion for personal and professional clashes between them. But differences between the chief detective and his closest aides date back to 1985, when Nicchi became chief detective, and they arose for almost the same reasons as those that affected Meli's appointment at the *ufficio istruzione*. Moreover, the internal management and operation of the *squadra mobile* was complicated by other factors.

The local police union branch came out in support of Nicchi and against his two assistants. At the same time, one aide, Accordino, received death threats on the internal police telephone system; the other Montalbano, was charged – by the same investigating magistrate who had, in the past, valued Montalbano's antimafia work – for abetting the killing of one of his own undercover agents in the *squadra mobile* in January 1988.

All these issues emerged in the open during the summer of 1988. They further demoralized an already highly demoralized police force. In fact, the force was in such disarray that the detective unit had no part in the Madonie police raid in April 1988. Not even its chief of detectives had prior knowledge of the raid. The operation had been conducted by a special police unit flown in from Rome especially for the occasion. By the end of August, Nicchi, Accordino, and Montalbano were replaced. New people were sent in to bring order and to restore confidence in the police detective unit, but the problems appeared to go much deeper than these events suggest.

Between 1980 and 1988, the *polizia* detective unit for the Palermitan area had more than seven chiefs. Two *squadra mobile* chiefs were killed in the line of duty. Most of the others were replaced: some for their apparent involvement in the quasi-Masonic Lodge P2; others because they appeared, like Nicchi, to have put more emphasis on good working relations with the police chief than with their immediate subordinates; and at least one other still for alleged collusion with some mafiosi. The police detective unit had also difficult working relations with the office of the investigating magistrate.

Over the years, the investigative functions of the police detective unit had been essentially taken over by the antimafia judicial team. These functions may have increased the efficiency of investigating magistrates, but they did little to bolster the morale of police officers. At the same time, since 1986 more officers had been added to the Palermo police contingent, with no apparent improvement in performance. By 1988 more than half (350) of the 600 police officers were employed as bodyguards and the like for public officials – but not always for security reasons. More often than not the assignment was to enhance the status of the public official involved. The structure of perverse incentives inherent in the maintenance of law and order in the tense Palermitan context had led some public officials to claim, and apparently receive, police protection as a prerequisite of their official status, regardless of whether or not they faced life-threatening situations (*Corriere della Sera* 1988b).

The Administration of Justice

The constitutional and institutional problems in the postwar administration of justice, highlighted earlier for the system as a whole (Di Federico and Guarnieri 1988; also Di Federico 1989; Guarnieri 1995), could be found in a magnified and exaggerated version in Sicily. By the late 1980s, as the administration of criminal justice struggled to wage a war on crime syndicates, problems relating to the peculiarity of Italy's judicial setting assumed critical proportions, especially when viewed in comparison with those of other liberal democratic regimes (Guarnieri 1995, 95).

First, mindful of the problems of justice in liberal and Fascist Italy, the new postwar constitutional order gave magistrates internal and external independence broader than that of magistrates in most other liberal democratic countries. On the strength of this de jure independence, magistrates in the *ufficio istruzione* had become the de facto protagonists of both police and judicial investigations (see also Falcone 1994, 3–9). As indicated above, this preeminence helped create considerable problems of coordination and morale with the police detective unit. But this situation equally created considerable dissatisfaction among those officials ultimately in charge of prosecution in the chief prosecutor's office. The creation of a parallel antimafia team at the *Procura* was intended to overcome problems of coordination and control in investigations between the two offices. By 1987 this move appeared to have added to the problems, rather than eased them. Changes at the top of the *Procura* and the *ufficio istruzione* early in 1988 did not help either. Little wonder that, throughout the year under review, those working in the Palermo Palace of Justice were wont to call it the Palace of Venoms (*Palazzo dei Veleni*) (cf., Di Lello 1994).

Second, many other killings were added in 1988 to the rather long list of unsolved cases. By the end of the year, some 7,000 criminal cases were awaiting trial in the Palermo district alone (Graldi 1988). Even when cases were brought to trial, it does not mean that they were resolved. This problem has to do with the very nature of both the inquisitorial trial system and the appeal system – what a leading scholar calls "the uniqueness of the institutional setting of the Italian judiciary" (Guarnieri 1995, 96).

In the Italian legal system there was then, and there is still, no clear separation between prosecutors and trial judges – which is why both are called "judges" in Italian. As one observer explains it, "in this scheme, the 'investigative magistrate' ... was a strange hybrid creature who, on the one hand, had vast powers of inquiry and, at the same time, was supposed to 'judge' his own evidence with serene impartiality" (Stille 1995, 268). The inquisitorial trial system could, when combined with the excessive and unconstrainable zeal of an instructing magistrate, easily lead to the making of a strong case for the prosecution irrespective of the people involved, their guilt, and the nature of the crime (see also Burnett and Mantovani 1998). Moreover, in marked contrast to other judicial systems where findings of fact are rarely at issue and only points of law may be appealed, Italian appeal courts, at least until 1989, treated each case as though it had never been tried before. Even when the length of time between trials is shortened by the good faith and herculean efforts of judges and other judicial officials, results can be surprisingly different and even sharply contradictory. A case in point was the 1988 trial for the Palermo massacre in June 1983, in which the then chief instructing magistrate, Rocco Chinnici, two *carabinieri*, and a janitor lost their lives.

The first trial in 1983, with Antonino Meli acting as presiding judge, found Michele Greco (the so-called mafia pope) and three others, guilty. Greco and another of the accused were sentenced to life imprisonment. The sentence was reduced in 1985 by an appeal court, presided over by a judge who in September 1988 became the seventh magistrate to be murdered in Sicily since Palermo prosecutor Pietro Scaglione in 1971. The sentence was subsequently annulled by the Supreme Court of Appeal on procedural and evidentiary grounds. At a sixth trial held in Messina in December 1988, an assize court dismissed the charges of murder against the accused for lack of proof. The court could only condemn Greco and his associates to several years of imprisonment for belonging to a mafia-type criminal association (see *Corriere della Sera* 1988c).

It has become part of the received wisdom to note that the threat of violence by criminal elements and the rule of silence (*omertà*) have been sufficient to thwart justice and to secure insufficiency-of-proof dismissals in Sicily. Especially in the course of the 1980s, the received wisdom was extended to the excessive judicial "rationalism" (*il garantismo*) or imputed corruption of some magistrates like judge Corrado Carnevale of the Supreme Court of Appeal. Judge Carnevale was sharply criticized as "the sentence killer" when he and his panel of judges failed to uphold the verdict of lower courts (see Bolzoni and D'Avanzo 1995). Before long, he was moved to other cases. Finally in March 1993, Carnevale was accused of mafia association by some state witnesses for having overturned sentences of some mafia bosses; in April of the same year, the Superior Judicial Council suspended him from his post at the Supreme Court of Appeal, but it was not until April 1998 that newspapers announced that his case would soon be brought to court. The case was not settled by 1999, and it is not clear if it will be settled soon. Whatever the case may be about Judge Carnevale, there is truth in the argument about silence and, possibly, even about corrupt judges in the past (Di Lello 1994). Even when proper allowance is made for these factors, however, they still cannot be used to account for all the difficulties in the administration of justice.

Sentences of lower courts were overturned by higher courts, even when Judge Carnevale was not presiding or was not even remotely connected with the proceedings. The different trials for the assassination of Magistrate Chinnici are a case in point. They serve as a useful reminder that what has helped to thwart justice in Sicily, as in the rest of Italy, has often been the perverse emphasis on legalism of the *stato di diritto* itself. Though judicial investigations generated highly publicized megatrials, many guilty verdicts reached in those trials could not survive the scrutiny of other courts, Judge Carnevale aside (cf., Stille 1995, 250–1).

Third, by 1988 there was a dramatic rise in public hostility towards magistrates and the judicial system more generally in Sicily. The anti-antimafia reactions became especially pronounced with the highly publicized comments by novelist Leonardo Sciascia, who inveighed in 1987 and 1988 against "antimafia professionals." Such reactions must be understood within the context of the malaise that afflicted the administration of justice in Sicily, and within the context, perhaps, of a resurgent *Sicilianismo*. The success of the 1987 referendum, opening the way for individuals to claim damages against judges and magistrates for grave negligence, revealed just how widespread the problem was. A dramatic example of the malaise – no less strong than the anti-antimafia reaction – were the events which took place in the resort town of Mondello, outside Palermo, in July 1988. A round-table discussion of the film *Mafia and* P2 was transformed into a sort of people's tribunal that condemned "a loyal servant of the state," the chief prosecutor of Palermo, for being soft on criminality (*Corriere della Sera* 1988c). Ironically, it was apparently this magistrate who had been one of first to introduce the system of teamwork in judicial investigation (but see also Alongi 1997, 129; Caponnetto 1993; Di Lello 1994, 156–63).

RESPONSES FROM CIVIL SOCIETY

Well before the events traced above took shape, participant-observers of Sicilian affairs, such as the Jesuit sociologist Ennio Pintacuda and

Redemptorist fathers associated with the periodical *Segno*, had been suggesting that the strong state response to the mafia problem in the form of megatrials was only a phase in the antimafia struggle. There was a need for citizens to join forces in civil society and carry the struggle to the local ramparts of the state (see Saladino 1988, 39; Alongi 1997). Certainly, opposition to machine politics, illegalities, boss rule, and violence had always existed among Sicilians, but what emerged during the 1980s, as perhaps never before, was a self-styled "antimafia coordination movement" that cut across party labels and affiliations. The growth of this particular "movement" was spurred in part by the vigorous judicial measures, the increase in lawlessness and disorder, and changes in the two principal forces in Sicilian politics and society of the time: the church and the DC.

Obviously, a few Catholic priests and a few DC reformers did not constitute the church and the DC in Palermo. Nevertheless, the cardinal archbishop of Palermo and primate of Sicily, Salvatore Pappalardo – however muted his public antimafia stand was to become later (Alongi 1997, 168) – offered in the late 1980s a sharply different kind of leadership from that exercised by Cardinal Ernesto Ruffini until the early 1960s (see also *Segno* 1997). The local parish priests and various parish associations were increasingly tending to their flock rather than serving political bosses (see Alongi 1997, 143–75). Similarly, the murdered DC regional premier, Piersanti Mattarella, and his younger brother, Sergio Mattarella, minister in successive national governments and the 1988 appointed trustee of the DC in Palermo, witnessed dramatic changes taking place inside the DC. In the immediate postwar period, their own father, Bernardo, had been often accused of underworld connections. The younger Mattarellas exemplified, as perhaps no others, the new attitudes of the DC party towards crime.

Local political institutions provided the antimafia groupings with an important opportunity to shape events within their grasp. By 1987, it had become evident that the Palermo communal government headed by Leoluca Orlando was an important vehicle for institutional renewal. Orlando appeared admirably suited to spearhead the renewal. Young and (mistakenly) thought by some to be of aristocratic lineage, he was open to new ideas, accessible to people and the press, at ease in the major languages and cultures of the nascent European Community, and, not unimportant, the first native Palermitan mayor in a long time (see also Alongi 1997, 242). Though Orlando's identification with the progressive wing of the DC was already evident in his earlier association with the Piersanti Mattarella regional government, the communal government coalition he led after the 1985 local elections gave little inkling of what was to follow by 1988.

The local coalition partners in 1985 were the standard national and regional coalition parties of the period. What prompted Orlando's sharp turn was a new combination of factors coming together in the late 1980s (Alongi 1997, chs. 5–8). The June 1987 national elections showed a relatively marked increase in Socialist (PSI) electoral support in Palermo – 16.4 per cent of the vote, as against 13.7 per cent in the 1986 regional elections, 13.3 per cent in the 1985 local elections, and 9.8 per cent in the 1983 national elections (Cancila 1988, 523). This strong showing gave impetus to the regional PSI, then vigorously led by an academic, Antonino Buttitta, to insist on replacing Orlando with a non–DC "lay" mayor. Relations between the DC and the PSI were not helped when Orlando dismissed the PSI electoral success in some of the low-income neighbourhoods as "mafia votes" (Cancila 1988, 523). Moreover, the then national DC secretary, Ciriaco De Mita, and his Palermitan counterpart, Sergio Mattarella, were not prepared to give in to PSI demands in Palermo.

An equally important set of factors emerged: the presence in Palermo since 1986 of the Pedro Arrupe Institute for Political Formation, founded by Bartolomeo Sorge, a former editor of the Jesuit journal *Civiltà cattolica* (Alongi 1997, 299). The thought and action of Sorge and his associates, then including Ennio Pintacuda (see 1986, 1988), furnished Orlando with a strong moral base and justification for breaking up entrenched patterns of coalitions and predatory rule.

For these reasons, the local administration that emerged in the summer of 1987 signalled a new kind of coalition governance. Orlando continued as mayor, but the vice-mayor now was a magistrate and an independent leftist councillor who, in the 1985 communal elections, had headed the Communist (PCI) party list. The new governing coalition consisted of Christian Democrats, Social Democrats, and a so-called cartel from the independent left elected on the PCI ticket – the two dissident Catholic-DC *Città per l'uomo* councillors and the only Green Party councillor. The administration could also count on the "external" support of the PCI both in and outside the city council. As a leader of the *Città per l'uomo* movement explained, "this is a new thing, not put together by the usual professional politicians. It is not the pastiche of *milazzismo*[1], but it breaks up the historical design that has always dominated Palermo, that which tied the DC to the so-called lay parties. In breaking up the old way of doing things, maybe we can also break up the 'affairs committee' that has dominated Palermo" (Nino Alongi, cited in Nicastro 1988, 38). If Palermo was not quite "the laboratory of democracy" as some partisans claimed, it had certainly become the laboratory of an almost unprecedented political-reform experiment.

The new Orlando administration had three main objectives. First, it sought to create an open political space, or public square, to serve as a focal point for citizens wishing to work toward the renewal of public institutions and political parties. Second, it aimed to isolate and reduce the practice of political corruption and boss rule in communal affairs – in Orlando's colourful language, to remove "the mafia from the face of public institutions." This declared aim assumed a tremendous importance in light of the anticipated huge expenditure for various public works projects, including the urban renewal of the old city. In order to minimize exposure to the old practice of rule, critical decisions involving the public works projects were assigned to a specially constituted board in Rome.

These two aims had been largely achieved by the end of 1988. Their realization was expected, in turn, to generate a third, more enduring goal: to transform the institutions of communal government into formative institutions for both better services and better citizenry. This was the way, finally, to overcome the impression of Palermo as an "unredeemable" city and to make it into a self-governing and liveable place for its residents.

In listening to Mayor Orlando in 1988, no outside observer could fail to acknowledge or be impressed by the dedication, sincerity, and passion he brought to his project (see also Orlando 1988, 1997). There is much truth in Orlando's claim about what his administration had accomplished during that year. It is doubtful that any right-thinking person could quarrel with the aims of his administration. How, then, is one to explain the stiff opposition that the Orlando *giunta* evoked in many quarters in Sicily, especially from regional and national Socialist leaders and the local news media like the *Giornale di Sicilia*?

It would be simplistic to turn to some kind of "Sicilianist" anti-antimafia reaction, though there is something to this. The Orlando administration, after all, made effective – some would say, obsessive – use of antimafia rhetoric as the catalyst for renewal. But an interpretation based largely on local contingencies – however important they are in the antimafia struggle – would not reveal the whole truth. Palermitan events must also be understood within the national context of the party politics of the 1980s. The rich interplay between national tendencies and local variables evoked by Orlando's mayorship was traced by Alfio Mastropaolo (1988), a Palermitan who was teaching political science at the University of Turin and was to become a Palermo councillor in a subsequent Orlando administration. Mastropaolo convincingly argues that a proper interpretation of the substance of the opposition – mostly but not exclusively Socialist – would have to include the following considerations.

The Orlando administration was viewed as another case of *trasformismo*, for Orlando's party, the DC, was the party that had contributed most to the deterioration of urban life in Palermo, and it was still the party ruling Palermo in the late 1980s. If the Orlando administration and the new communal majority really wanted to innovate public life, why did they rely on the support of the Social Democratic Party (PSDI), a party whose reputation was hardly unblemished? Why did the PCI formally remain outside the communal government? What was the hidden agenda of the DC and the PCI? The truth – so went this anti-Orlando, Socialist interpretation – was that under the protective cover afforded by an antimafia campaign, DC and PCI leaders were imposing their duopoly on Palermo as part of a long-term strategy aimed at securing a similar agreement at the national level. What was happening in Palermo was another way for the two major parties to continue their covert collaboration. This line of reasoning reflected Socialist fears of being bypassed by the DC and the PCI (see also Di Scala 1989). Such fears were not without foundation, however, if the context of the time is kept in mind. Consider the following.

If there was a city where the DC could, from a position of strength, experiment with an Orlando-type coalition with the PCI, it was Palermo. The DC there operated from a strong cultural and social position, in part, because of the supportive Catholic milieu and the relatively weak Communist base. And so it was – the Socialist interpretation continued – that a party most tainted with underworld connections was able to overcome those connections and to present itself as the party fighting for good government (Mastropaolo 1988, 49). To those reasoning this way, it did not seem at all clear whether what was emerging was new in the Gramscian sense (as Orlando supporters suggested), or whether the old practice of predatory rule was resurfacing (as Orlando opponents maintained).

As much force as there is in this kind of reasoning, it was, in retrospect, too grounded in the logic of postwar party politics to the point of seriously misinterpreting the new governing Palermitan coalition and its political designs. The Orlando experiment pointed to crucially symbolic and practical features of an emergent political order that constituted a sharp break with the past. It identified "democracy" with the city and its citizens, and not with parliamentary government and representative assemblies. By going back to the city as the basic human reality for Palermitans, the Orlando experiment pointed to the possibility of escaping from the tyranny of uniform legislation and party alliance and beginning to appreciate that universalities of democracy and citizenship are always subject to specificities of time and place.

It is not clear if Orlando and his closest aides ever read Carlo Cattaneo, but their thoughts and actions were close to his conception of communal society, sketched in chapter 3. What is clear is that the emergent order showed that there were people in Sicilian public life who, in spite of risks, could challenge illegality, machine politics, boss rule, and violence, *and* that local political institutions could be used to wage such a challenge by emphasizing transparency in public conduct without succumbing to excessive legalism. With the benefit of hindsight, we now know that this dramatic break with the past would have long-term consequences: Orlando's move away from the DC, the eventual collapse of the DC in and beyond Palermo, and the creation by Orlando of his own political movement called La Rete, or Citizens' Network (Alongi 1997). Still, several problems conditioned the extent to which the Orlando or any other reform-minded administration in Palermo could make the practice of good government an enduring Palermitan reality (Mastropaolo 1988, 52–5).

First, there was the challenge of what to do about local public monopolies – from transit systems and hospitals to sanitation and public works – that for years operated according to a logic of patronage or institutionalized corruption. The conceptualization of public offices as private property (or concessions allotted to those who belong to winning electoral coalitions, in the absence of effective institutional judicial remedies available to individual citizens) had the effect of converting public authority – and, therefore, public goods – into private goods and collective bads. The practice of rule through empire building and bureaucratic free enterprise had acquired over the years a strong organizational foundation in 1) an at-large electoral system; 2) patronage-filled bureaucracy; and 3) rebates on salaries and/or cuts to party and individual coffers (see also Loveman 1973). The memorandum of the former Palermitan mayor, Insalaco, was widely published in the popular press after his murder in January 1988. Even if self-serving, it revealed how difficult it is for public officials to withstand the established pattern of rule. Furthermore, the public service employees' strike that paralysed the entire city public service delivery system in November and December 1988 pointed to the difficulty of moving against entrenched bureaucratic interests. The Italian "system of guarantees," (*il garantismo*) formalized in the Workers' Statute of 1970, introduced rigidities in the labour markets and industrial relations practices, as well as employment in public services, parastate institutions, and large manufacturing and service firms that could not be overcome by the Orlando administration, nor by practically any other communal administration (see Masi 1987).

Another set of challenges was inherent in the nature of the "moral coalition" at the commune. One of the great merits of the Orlando administration was to demonstrate that it was possible to challenge the private empires over the local public economy and begin to break up the pervasiveness of illegality and criminality in everyday life. Many of the administration's messages and positions tended, however, to be too abstract and generic. For example, the progressive disintegration of the historical city centre and the increasingly dramatic failure of public services in the postwar period could not be attributed entirely to "the mafia." As we saw in chapter 4, these problems were also the result of the failure of the public service system to meet the demands and expectations of successive generations of urban and metropolitan residents, demands encouraged partly by the transformation of Palermo into the regional capital and partly by the rapid economic changes that took place in Italy as a whole. "Pathologies" had occurred not only in the production and delivery of essential public services, but also in the maintenance of institutional arrangements for the pursuit of individual and joint ventures in the market economy, and in reformist efforts to improve performance in both the public and private sectors. From such a vantage point, it becomes easier to view the informal and illegal economy in Palermo as largely a response to the rigidities and perverse emphasis on legalism introduced by both the Italian "system of guarantees" and the *stato di diritto*.

The fragility of the Orlando political project and its social-political base could easily have been challenged if much of the progressive local initiative had confined itself to symbolic politics. As Mastropaolo noted, "more than ever ... the struggle for Palermo must be conducted from the muddy trenches of the public service system of everyday life" (Mastropaolo 1988, 54). If not, public officials, not just reformist politicians, were in danger of becoming – in the famous words of a master of boss rule and "theoretician" of "honest and dishonest graft," George Washington Plunkitt (1842–1924) – "mornin' glories – who looked lovely in the mornin' and withered upon a short time while the regular machines went on flourishin' forever like fine old oaks" (Plunkitt [1905] 1963, 17).

CONCLUSION

The war on crime as a fight for good government continues in Sicily. The events of 1988 charted above reveal critical moments in that war.

For one thing, they highlight factors that help to account for the patterns of lull and expansion in the response of government to the mafia problem. No sooner had a particular conception of the Sicilian criminal underworld – for example, Cosa Nostra – become dominant than it began to disintegrate; whether it could regain the standing it once had remained an open question. But there is little or no doubt about one issue: the state had neither surrendered to crime nor abandoned Sicily. What other conclusions emerge from the analytical narrative?

One important conclusion is that central government action, even when sharply focused on "a war on crime," tends to be the result of relatively independent decisions and actions involving multiple agencies and actors that are difficult to coordinate through hierarchic arrangements. Just as important, the disputes in the judiciary point to an aspect of Italian public decision making that, unlike American practices (Allison 1971), has not been fully considered in the academic literature on Italian democracy: because of the type of office public officials occupy, differences in positions, responsibilities, perceptions, and priorities can privilege different facets of a complexly nested issue like the mafia phenomenon. As we have seen, this can allow each player, however hierarchically linked to each other, to judge his own course of action to be the right one.

Thus, all the leading protagonists – from Borsellino to Meli, from Falcone to Nicchi – were not wrong, despite the fact that their respective positions and actions conflicted with one another. That each fought hard for the course of action he judged to be right should, therefore, not be surprising. Translating the war on crime into outcomes and even actual behaviour of public officials cannot be easily accomplished. It is hardly surprising, though worth stressing, that public officials in Sicily, not unlike those in other parts of Italy, seemed locked into a system of governance that produced outcomes that they did not value very highly as viable alternatives. At the same time, the changes in civil society and politics initiated by Leoluca Orlando and his communal administration went beyond a mere symbolic response to crime.

Orlando's reforms suggest that it was possible for people to extricate themselves from a multiperson analogue of the prisoner's dilemma and to start playing a new political game. This is not to diminish or gloss over the fact that, after the local elections of 1990, the Orlando administration earnestly faced the challenge of how to overcome the perverse incentives inherent in government institutions, such as the entrenched practice of institutionalized corruption through empire building and bureaucratic free enterprise. The attempt to restructure the game of politics in Palermo was still going on by the end of the 1990s (Alongi 1997) – well after the old postwar governing class and practice of rule had been eclipsed and discredited by the *homines novi*. It seems clear, though, that Mayor Orlando and the group of reformers connected with the movement La Rete do not quite fit George Washington Plunkitt's characterization of reformers as "mornin' glories." Orlando's movement proved to be much more resilient; it opened up new and unanticipated vistas. Sicily could cease to be "the Ireland of Italy" after all! But the fight for good government in Italy cannot be won by one city government – perhaps not even by reformers in one generation and region – unless more attention is paid to the structure of crime and punishment more generally. And to this topic we turn next.

7 The Political Economy of Crime and Punishment

As we saw in chapter 6, by 1988 the mafia megatrials were becoming a thing of the past, culminating in mass acquittals by 1991. The "Palermitan experiment" also seemed short lived. In January 1990, the national leaders of the Christian Democratic Party forced the resignation of Mayor Leoluca Orlando in Palermo, putting an end to the local alliance of the Christian Democratic Party (DC) and the Communist Party (PCI). The political fortunes of Catania's reformist mayor, Enzo Bianco, appeared no more promising. From the perspective of events sketched in the previous chapter, the Palermo and Catania communes no longer seemed vital to the antimafia campaign and democratic movement that treated the city and the neighbourhood as the basic human reality. The people and coalitions that had transformed those communes into antimafia and democratic outposts were in disarray to the point that even some close observers and supporters of the Orlando experiment understandably took what we now know as momentary setbacks for final "epitaphs for a failed revolt" (Mastropaolo 1992; see also Alongi 1997).

Crime statistics went up, or were better reported. In any case, 1990 and 1991 seemed exceptionally violent years in some parts of Calabria, Sicily, and Campania. A recurrent pattern can be illustrated by what happened in 1991: the murder of a magistrate in Calabria, that of an industrialist in Sicily, and brutal mass killings in the Sicilian town of Gela and the Calabrian town of Taurianova. Within a few months in 1991, forty-five people were killed in Gela. In May 1991, five people were shot within a few hours in Taurianuova, but what horrified Italians was the news that apparently one of the victims had been beheaded by his assassins, who then used his head for target practice. Though this latter aspect could not be confirmed, "making the news" was enough for many to treat it a true story.

In response to these situations, government ministers and other functionaries from Rome would rush in, often separately, to affirm "the presence of the state" and the war against criminality. After the distinguished visitors had returned to Rome, two interconnected but analytically distinct facts on the ground would remain: 1) the range of effective choices open to state officials in a democracy was limited and could not fill the gap between the declared intentions of government officials and the result of government action; 2) evidence that a perverse emphasis on legality in people's everyday life was accommodated by either neglect, the wink of an eye, or the granting of exceptions carried little or no weight in this atmosphere and, indeed, was seldom viewed as a source of constraint to government initiative. Often enough, the only lasting outcome of these visits would be yet another controversy either about the demonstrated insensitivity of officials to the administrative feasibilities of law-enforcement agencies, or about the inadequacies of existing organizational capabilities and procedures of police and judicial officers in the field.

Even the move in February 1991 of Italy's perhaps best known crime fighter, Magistrate Giovanni Falcone, from the Palermo Tribunal to Rome's Justice ministry, seemed at the time to lend additional weight to the argument that the government was losing the fight on organized crime. In retrospect, we now know that Falcone's departure from Palermo signalled the beginning of a new police and legal policy whose main features emerged by the end of the year.

All these events help to amplify the analytical themes sketched in the previous chapter. First, these events remind us that the antimafia was part of a larger government war on crime and criminality, as the boundaries between organized crime and "ordinary crime" are fuzzy at best. Second, they reiterate the challenge awaiting government officials: how to reconcile the pressing need to respond to a wide spectrum of problems in a general war on crime with the knowledge that neither government fiat nor any available repertoire of action programs and policy instruments could easily eradicate crime, criminality, and the criminal underworld more generally. Third, they serve to spotlight some neglected aspects of the political economy of crime and punishment that situate the Italian experience in a comparative and theoretical perspective. A discussion of the strength of organized crime groups, the very issue of illegal markets, and events connected with such developments highlight basic issues in crime and punishment.

THE STRENGTH OF THE
CRIMINAL UNDERWORLD

Not unlike mass media people, academic researchers have, for the most part, virtually no independent sources for surveying organized criminality and illegal markets. What they generally cover is the police and judicial response to the criminal underworld: the investigations and their prosecutorial results. As we saw in chapter 6, there are reasons to be sceptical of police and judicial coverage (see also Ericson 1982, 203; Reuter and Rubinstein 1978; Santino and La Fiura 1990, 49–63). Nevertheless, such sources do provide a starting point for making sense of a world that has its own laws and demands.

The tendency among law enforcement agencies fighting organized crime in Italy, as in the United States, has historically been to focus more on the character of the criminals and less on the nature of the crime. This is understandable. Reputed professional criminals like mafiosi, endowed with high-visibility profiles, are easier to identify than transactions in illegal markets. The antimafia law no. 646 of 13 September 1982, also known as the Rognoni-La Torre Law, and the ensuing judicial investigations by the "antimafia pool" of Palermo magistrates, discussed in chapter 6, did much to direct attention to the nature of the crime. By 1991, however, there seemed to be no serious ongoing judicial investigations of illegal activities. According to a statement by Magistrate Falcone in 1991, the last serious investigation of money recycling from illegal markets had taken place in 1984 (Falcone cited in Manno 1991; see also Cecchini, Vasconi, and Vettraino 1991, 164–5).

Also by 1991, a big question mark hovered over the view of the Sicilian mafia as a single unitary organization and a synonym for organized crime itself (but cf., Falcone 1991, 1994; and Falcone cited in Arlacchi 1992, vii). What was emerging was somewhat of a consensus that the world of organized crime was made up of different and rivalrous groups – mafia, 'ndrangheta, and camorra in Sicily, Calabria, and Campania respectively – and that these groups were, in varying degrees, inseparable from most illegal markets in the business of protection and ordinary (i.e., legitimate) industries (see also Cazzola 1992; Coletti 1995; Di Lello 1994; Gambetta 1993; and Canosa 1991). People in such groups formed the core underworld population.

We know a lot about this core underworld population. In his April 1991 report to parliament on the state of public security, then DC Interior Minister Enzo Scotti characterized this underworld population as made up of 500 criminal groups (cosche) with a total of 15,000 soldiers, territorially located as follows: 186 groups with about 5,000 members in Sicily, more than 2,500 of them in the Palermo metropolitan area; 142 groups ('*drine*) with about 5,100 members in Calabria; 106 groups with more than 5,000 members in Campania, in and around Naples, Caserta, and Salerno. Scotti identified a fourth growing pole of criminality in Apulia: 30 groups with some 1,000 soldiers (cited in Chianura 1991). According to Falcone, only members of Sicilian gangs could be regarded as "the true professional criminals" to the point that "even when they describe themselves as 'soldiers,' they have the qualities of generals, or of cardinals of a church a lot less permissive than the Catholic one" (Falcone 1991, 60; see also Falcone 1994, 303–52). In October 1991, the weekly magazine *Epoca* published a leaked police document listing presumed core members and enforcers of different Sicilian groups, "the yellow pages of the mafia."

What was left out of these accounts was the total number of people actually employed in illegal or criminal activities, including extortion, cigarette smuggling, trafficking of drugs and weapons and wine adulteration. The total is probably much higher than the data reported by Scotti and *Epoca*. A 1985 CENSIS estimate suggested that the total number varied between half a million and one million; that is, between 2.5 per cent and 5.5 per cent of the Italian working population (cited in Santino 1988, 228). But even the CENSIS estimate – even when taken at face value, without considering the distinction between illegalities and crimes – must be a conservative estimate of those in Italy who do, in Peter Letkemann's words, "crime as work" (Letkemann 1973). As research on "common criminality" suggests, people do not have to be mafiosi to be experienced criminals (e.g., Barbagli 1995). It is true that the 1990 crime statistics reveal that the highest number of thefts were done by people born in Sardinia and Apulia, but the northern region of Liguria comes third; in fact there were more such crimes committed by people born in Piedmont, Trentino and Emilia than those born in Campania and Calabria (Barbagli 1995, 171–2).

Homicides give a particular portrayal of north-south differences. Eighty-two per cent of all the homicides committed in the south in 1990 were reported to have occurred in areas traditionally linked to organized crime: Campania, Calabria, and Sicily (SVIMEZ 1991, 289). Seventy-one per cent of all the reported homicides in Italy in 1990 took place in those three regions and Apulia (*Corriere della Sera* 1991a). Calabria, in particular, had a 40 per cent increase in homicides between 1989 and 1990: fifteen homicides for every 100,000 inhabitants, five times the Italian average (SVIMEZ 1991, 289). These crime statistics are significant for three reasons.

One reason has to do with the brutality and rapid succession of crime that occasionally occur. Second, and contrary to popular perception, the homicide rate for Italy as a whole has sharply declined since the 1880s; the rate has increased somewhat since 1968, though not enough to off-set the steady decline over time (Barbagli 1995, 45; Chinnici and Santino 1989, 34). Third, contemporary Italy actually has one of the lowest reported rates of homicides per 100,000 inhabitants in the world, especially among the advanced industrial nations – lower than those of the United States, Japan, France, West Germany, and Canada (Chinnici and Santino 1989, 33). The violent crime rate experienced in some American neighbourhoods is of such magnitude (5,812 violent crimes per 100,000 in the 25th Precinct of New York City for 1980 [C. Murray 1994, 66–7]) as to be practically unimaginable even for the worst crime-ridden neighbourhoods of Milan, Naples, Palermo, and even Gela and Taurianova.

Judicial authorities in Sicily and researchers at the Giuseppe Impastato Sicilian Research Centre in Palermo (Centro Siciliano di Documentazione Giuseppe Impastato) have carefully disaggregated crime statistics to be able to distinguish underworld murders from other killings. The available data come from the city and province of Palermo for 1960–66 and 1978–84.

Briefly stated, of the ninety-three mafia murders between 1960 and 1966, seventy-seven, or 83 per cent, were identified as "internal", that is, committed within and across different outlaw groups. Only 14 or 15 per cent of such mafia killings were deemed "external" to such groups and economic or political in nature. Between 1978 and 1984 the number of identified mafia homicides increased to 332. Murders involving internal settling of accounts still remained high, however: 203, or 61 per cent. "External" murders continued to be relatively low: fifty-seven, or 17 per cent (Chinnici and Santino 1989, 201–3). This kind of data does not seem to be readily available for other regions, but it seems safe to conjecture that most, if not all, of the violent crimes in Calabria for the same period were "internal" to the criminal underworld. For the most part, they involved settling of accounts within the underworld.

The findings presented above add to our knowledge of the criminal underworld in several respects. The largest number of homicides involves gangsters, either within or across particular groups. As in organized crime in Canada and the United States, professional criminals in Italy face higher victimization risks from other gangsters than non-criminals do. Like their Canadian, American, and Russian counterparts, Sicilians and Calabrians doing crime face considerable danger among themselves; the risk of being executed by fellow criminals is very high (Cordeau and Tremblay 1989; Di Bella, Sabetti, and Tremblay, forthcoming; Varese, 1994, 1997a, 1997b).

Why, then, do some people knowingly subject themselves to such high occupational hazards? Unfortunately, as we noted in the first chapter, postwar research on organized (or disorganized) crime in Italy has not directed much attention to this question, and has not always carefully distinguished between becoming an ordinary criminal (in Sicily or in Naples) and becoming a mafioso, even though the dividing line between the two is often blurred. Magistrate Giovanni Falcone raised these issues in his own fashion, as a Sicilian antimafia prosecutor. Reflecting on the question a year before his assassination as to why some people want to become mafiosi, he put matters this way: "In certain moments of sadness I allow myself to think about the destiny of 'men of honour': why is it that men like others – some even endowed with real intellectual abilities – are compelled to devise for themselves a criminal career in order to survive with dignity?" (Falcone 1991, 72).

At one point, Falcone answered his own question as follows: many modern Sicilians prefer to live as parasites because the fast lane of crime has considerable attraction as work and a way of life (Falcone 1991, 132). This seems so because most Sicilians have historically faced conditions of life devoid of many lawful opportunities. In this sense, Daniel Bell's characterization of crime as a form of upward mobility – "crime as an American Way of Life" (Bell 1960) – may apply to crime in Sicily. But Falcone's answer does not – nor, in fairness, did it aim to – go far enough in clarifying what underlying processes structure the mix of legitimate and illegitimate opportunities and resultant patterns of multiple job holding available to a socially disadvantaged minority. The chapters in parts 1 and 2 suggest that the notion of an independent officialdom is not a very good way to establish a "service" economy. The public sector can become an important aspect of a service economy. The problem – as Ferrara warned Cavour in 1860 – is that when it loads people with burdens, it becomes a diseconomy and a temptation for criminal syndicates. Elsewhere I have inquired whether the structure of basic institutions in a particular Sicilian community has been the primary instrument for advancing human welfare or the essential source of human adversity among Sicilian villagers (Sabetti 1984). Unfortunately, the nature of informal or illegal institutions is too complex to be captured in a single study of illegality and crime. In spite of the absence of more extensive "criminal opportunity analysis" in Sicily and southern Italy (for elsewhere, see Cloward and Ohlin, 1960; Di Bella, Sabetti, and Tremblay, forthcoming; Gambetta 1993; cf., Varese, 1994, 1996, 1997a, 1997b, and 1997c), it is possible to build on the previous work and preceding chapters to explain how the strength of the criminal underworld is largely grounded in the illegalities that result from a perfectionist conception of the rule of law (stato di diritto).

THE STRENGTH OF ILLEGALISM

An important change in perspective has occurred in organized crime research over the past twenty years (see the literature discussed in Di Bella, Sabetti, and Tremblay forthcoming). This change consists mainly in conceiving underworld participants as social actors who make purposive and intentional choices and in analyzing crime networks as the aggregate outcome of individual decisions. Whereas conventional literature on organized crime has assumed corruption opportunities as a plentiful constant over time and across settings, the work of Mark H. Haller on illegal enterprises in the United States has transformed this "constant" into a variable (Haller 1990). The implication is that an understanding of the strength of the Italian underworld requires some attempt to understand the depth of illegalism and availability of corruption opportunities. Haller shows that in the United States a significant decline in institutionalized corruption brought about by several political reforms has "depoliticized" criminal markets – in effect, isolating crime entrepreneurs more and more from the world of legal governments. Institutionalized corruption in the United States has also been contained by the federal system itself. Unlike what happens in a centralized system of government and administration, corruption in a federal system seldom envelopes the entire system. As Burnett and Mantovani have observed, "President Clinton's problems with campaign donations have not engulfed state and city Democratic parties nor endangered Democratic mayors and governors. And conversely Boss Daley's troubles in Chicago did not threaten the Truman administration. A strongly federal system has firebreaks, not always perfect but largely effective" (Burnett and Mantovani 1998, 260).

By contrast, depoliticization is happening in Italy at a much slower rate, despite all the antimafia legislations passed since the 1980s (e.g., Conso 1995; Fiandaca and Costantino 1986). This is so largely because there has been no decrease in the intrusiveness in Italian life of the *stato di diritto*. Hobbes argued that "the greatest liberty of subjects, depends on the silence of the law" (Hobbes [1651] 1962, 165). By contrast in Italy, notwithstanding claims to the contrary, legislators have proceeded on the assumption that "the greatest liberty of subjects depends on the intrusiveness of the law."

Descriptive accounts of widespread illegalism and bribe bargains in the public sector can be called upon (e.g., Cazzola 1988, 1992) as evidence of how efforts to enhance the integrity of the *stato di diritto* have increased, not reduced, the perverse emphasis on legalism and the availability of corruptible officials. But much work still remains to be done to uncover the choice-structuring characteristics of different illicit (declining and expanding) markets in Italy.

The structure of any given crime market transforms itself to attract a very different set of entrepreneurs as a result of a discrete but significant alteration of the legal and judicial constraints that regulate its scope. It is an established fact that illicit markets are complexly nested within the larger environment of crime opportunities, but several aspects are still unclear. As I have argued, boundaries between organized crime and street crime, professional crime and white collar crime are porous. Yet we still need to establish conceptual and empirical links between mainstream criminological interest in "ordinary crime" and research on organized crime. For example, contrary to the conventional wisdom noted in chapter 6 that sees organized crime everywhere in Sicily, not all the criminogenic field settings there may actually be accessible to underworld participants. Furthermore, it still remains largely unexplored why a given work setting suddenly or progressively allows underworld participants to bend the rules of "normal" criminality in Palermo as in Vittoria. While many aspects of the political economy of crime and punishment remain unclear, the state of research appears far more promising today than it did in the 1960s and 1970s. We sketch below some emergent properties of this research as a way of rounding out the narrative on the government war on crime as a fight for good government.

Crime Pays

In spite of the high risk of underworld victimization, one fact remains: crime pays, either in the form of illegal markets or private protection supplied to those markets. Supplying private protection and other illegal activities – ranging from theft, extortion, and blackmail to attempts on both private and public property – result in a transfer of wealth from one individual or group of individuals to others. But, contrary to what Daniel Bell suggested (1960), crime may be a ladder of highly constrained mobility, particularly for the ordinary "rank and file" underworld participants. The life of Tommaso Buscetta reveals another facet: even dealers and smugglers who reach upper levels in illegal markets are also active participants in the legitimate world of work. The patterns of multiple job holding that occur within the conventional and non-conventional labour markets, including the informal economy, are still not well understood (see Masi 1987).

The Italian National Association of Merchants (*Confesercenti*) suggested in 1991 that the extortion racket alone involves an annual redistribution of about thirty billion lire (Cecchini, Vasconi, and Vettraino,

1991). At the same time, trafficking in drugs, weapons, and contraband goods provides services to large groups of people in society. At least until the early 1990s, Naples alone appeared to have 2,500 "street corner counters" for the sale of contraband cigarettes. It was not unusual, even for casual observers, to spot uniformed police officers buying their preferred cigarettes – especially Marlboros and Merits – from such illegal street vendors, who most likely had other occupations in the conventional labour market. Also by 1990, there were at least 50,000 people earning a living in Naples from the running of illegal lotteries (Solazzo 1991; see also Mastrogiacomo 1991). Many Italian sources on the underground economy tell the story of the mayor of Naples lamenting to the press in the late 1970s that while something like 500,000 pairs of goat skin gloves had been shipped from the port with papers indicating that they were manufactured in that city, there was at the time not one factory officially registered as producing such items! (Masi 1999, personal communication). Whether this kind of illegal economy is always exploitative – as some allege (Warren 1994) – is open to serious question, especially if we keep in mind what other employment may be available. In the Italian case, the emergence of underground economic activities has been directly linked to the rigidity of labour market regulations and the heavy social burdens that they impose on legitimate employers. For example, the wage bill paid by the employer is twice the amount actually received by workers. In addition, overregulation of labour markets, including restrictions on legitimately holding second jobs, often leads to moonlighting by the employed to round out take-home pay (Masi 1987, 1989). These kinds of illegalism may be convenient to consumers, employees, and employers alike. Furthermore, we should not forget that what is considered criminal according to Italian law may pass as perfectly legitimate practice in other advanced Western industrial democracies. This point cannot be emphasized enough, so let me put it another way: labour market behaviours that in other advanced Western industrial democracies are considered legitimate practices are often defined as illegal in Italy.

Postwar Sicily adds other dimensions. By the middle of the 1950s many mafia groups in the towns and villages of western Sicily had lost their raison d'être and strength; in part as a result of intense opposition from local antimafia groups, they had either extinguished themselves or been extinguished (Sabetti 1984, 189–92; 1996, 479–82). By the 1960s, new opportunities in drug running and urban and regional development reinvigorated the pool of people in the business of private protection and in working illegally for a living more generally. Public works and forced industrialization (combined with intense intraparty rivalry for hegemonic positions in the ruling DC Party heading the regional government) generated a structure of perverse incentives, expanding individual corruption to what in an earlier chapter we referred to as "institutionalized corruption," an expression originally coined for corrupt practices in American life (Haller 1990).

The intrusiveness of statutory legislation and administrative regulations joined with the dynamics of intraparty competition to do three things: 1) to increase the availability of corruptible public officials; 2) to politicize Sicilian criminal markets to an unprecedented degree; and 3) to expand the range of illegal activities, including the business of protection and violence. As noted earlier, by contrast, during the same postwar period, there was a significant decline in corruption opportunities available to contemporary illegal entrepreneurs operating in North America, resulting from several factors including civil service reform, police unionization, and better pay. While specialists are still debating what factors best explain the decline, there is general agreement that the decline served, to a large extent, to "depoliticize" North American criminal markets (Di Bella, Sabetti, and Tremblay, forthcoming). For these reasons, crime entrepreneurs operating in the 1970s and 1980s in Palermo, the regional capital of Sicily, had more in common with the 1940s cohort of American mobsters, and even of earlier periods in "lusty Chicago," than with American crime entrepreneurs of their own time. When viewed from this vantage point, much of what has been written on postwar Palermo can be recast to make its "mafia and politics" less arcane.

Palermo is not unique, however. Consider Gela, a town of about 90,000 inhabitants in 1990, and the scene of many homicides in the late 1980s and early 1990s. Between 1987 and 1990 alone, settlings of accounts between rival criminal groups claimed more than one hundred lives there. But things were not always so in Gela. In the immediate postwar period, Gela was half the size it was to become by the 1980s, and not just in terms of inhabitants. The building of a refinery there almost thirty years ago radically changed the structure of employment opportunities in the construction industry, urban planning, and land use, while the rigidities of the laws governing those activities increased, especially after 1970. At the same time, national, regional, provincial, and local agencies experienced serious problems of bureaucratic administration as they tried to maintain some semblance of the earlier delivery of public services, to meet the demands of new residents in search of work, and to fashion urban planning instruments appropriate to a rapid, forced industrial growth. The problems of urban unplanning and private planning that, as we saw in chapter 5, emerged in postwar Rome were evident in Gela with a particular twist: ordinary criminality turned into organized crime and criminal markets became increasingly politicized. The potential for violent settlings of accounts increased, since much of the town that now stands was built, and probably operates, illegally.

Whether illegalities that result from the necessity to subject the universality and uniformity of statutory legislation to accommodations to time and place specificities in Gela – as in Palermo and Rome – is criminal remains problematic. Many of us would not consider shantytowns and illegal land developments criminal, but they did create a horrible mess, as they carried with them no effective registration of property titles. Not surprising in such contexts, illegalities became an easy ally of organized crime because ways had to be found to steal electricity, water, and access to sewage disposal on a regular basis. When he was prosecutor at Marsala in the late 1980s, Paolo Borsellino used to tell visiting observers how difficult and upsetting it was for him to have to prosecute illegalities of ordinary people who were trying to find ways to cope with problems.

The changes in postwar Gela can be treated as a microcosm of what happened in postwar Palermo, or Marsala, or elsewhere in the south. The logic of forced industrial growth, with its emphasis on government-financed public contracts and huge sums in specialized aids to poorer regions, became a chief source of corruption opportunities and considerable financial profit for the underworld. By the early 1990s, 80 per cent of the construction industry in Reggio Calabria was reported to be within the control of outlaw groups (antimafia parliamentary commission, cited in *Il Mondo* 1991, 35).

When legalities become obstacles and people must cope with a problem, they find some way to ignore the law or get around it. That illegality "pays" under such conditions seems clear, though the corollary may be an endless tangle of future problems. How much organized criminality actually pays in monetary terms remains ambiguous, however.

Some attempts to quantify how much crime pays suggest an estimated total value of at least 150,000 billion lire a year (*Il Mondo* 1991). The National Association of Chambers of Commerce (*Unioncamere*) reported in 1991 that the underworld criminal economy had by then reached about 12 per cent of the gross domestic product, while the annual earnings of mafia-type groups was greater than the combined annual earnings of the automobile company Fiat and the then state owned enterprise IRI (*La Stampa* 1991a). Such figures must, at best, be taken *cum grano salis*, for several reasons.

No distinction is made between gross and net revenues; so the *cost* of doing illegal business is left unclear. As for the wealth of particular underworld figures, we still know very little about the relationship between access to monies and long-term control over the sources of such funds. After all, as noted in chapter 6, a criminal enterprise cannot be sold, for example, to settle an estate. Property ownership and devolution in the organized crime environment can be exceedingly difficult to trace, as the Organized Crime Research Program at the Temple University School of Law in Philadelphia discovered (Libonati and Edelhertz 1991).

Still, the 1990s figures available for Italy, however out of date and unreliable they may appear, can, in the absence of careful analysis of questions of ownership, control, and fruits of operations, be taken as suggestive of the strong attraction that the fast lane of crime has as a way of life. Whether the working population employed in underworld activities actually profits from crime is not altogether clear.

Clientelism and Institutionalized Corruption

Clientelism refers to a social and political grouping of individuals who, while occupying unequal positions, are tied to one another (hence the idea of patron-client relationship) based on personal loyalty, obligation, and the exchange of unequal goods and services (i.e., clients trade votes, while patrons trade tangible benefits they have at their disposal, often as holders of legal positions of authority). Machine politics, patronage appointments, and the spoil system characterize North American clientelism, suggesting how widespread the phenomenon is beyond the Mediterranean. The chief point here is that clientelism as a practice of rule is not an inexhaustible resource, contrary to what elected officials making promises would have people believe. A central point that emerged from Judith Chubb's study of Palermo and Naples was that the scarcity of resources, rather than their availability, is what gave postwar politicians their bargaining power (Chubb 1982). But clientelist rule does not necessarily have to be rapacious, politicizing all policy decisions and government appointments and abetting institutionalized corruption. At least this is what emerges from the evidence about clientelism of DC leaders in Lucania (Basilicata) and Abruzzo over a period of thirty years (Piattoni 1996, 1998a; Zuckerman 1997; see also Carboni 1998; Leonardi 1998; Mutti 1994). As Alan Zuckerman notes, "in the absence of serious challenge to their power [including intraparty rivalries], DC leaders in Basilicata and Abruzzo were able to merge the roles of political patron, statesman and policy analyst" (Zuckerman 1997, 9, 14–16). This evidence demands revisions of the standard argument.

Clientelist rule can be "enlightened" and even "virtuous" when it offers a way of moving closer to the generalized benefits of the welfare system. Even if we accept the evidence from Basilicata and Abruzzo, the fact remains that well before 1992 – that is, before the collapse of the postwar governing class – many southern politicians had already lost their bargaining power to local criminal elements.

What factors worked to create propitious opportunities for institutionalized corruption and for criminal syndicates? At a most general level, the perverse incentives built into statutory legislation and administrative regulations presented a serious challenge to the concept of a rule of law itself; in other words, the state created opportunities for illegalities, informal economy, and crime by regulating too much (see also Masi 1987). More specifically, variations in the type and extent of such activities differ according to specific local and regional political factors. While much more remains to be done to uncover and map these processes, available evidence points to the importance of particular factors. Let us briefly examine some of them.

First, there was the highly competitive rivalry for electoral support and preference votes within and across governing coalition parties. As we saw in chapter 4, this rivalry gave postwar Italian political life a vibrancy unmatched by most other liberal, representative democracies, though it generated as a by-product other less positive consequences. One important long-term consequence was for party candidates to opportunistically scramble for votes (Sabetti 1984, 186–9). The press leaks of intercepted telephone conversations between Republican Party activists and candidates and underworld figures during the June 1991 Sicilian regional elections points to how widespread the dependence on criminal entrepreneurs had become in some regions.

The "Catania scandal," as it became known, involved a party long regarded as the standard bearer of political probity in Italian public life, the Italian Republican Party (PRI). The press revelations served as a vivid and ominous reminder of the individualistic practice many politicians had routinely come to employ in order to secure enough preference votes and electoral success (e.g., Bolzoni 1991a). Ironically, the June 1991 referendum, aimed at limiting the choice to only one preference vote, was successful. It did away with the legal structure that necessitated electoral clientelism, albeit coming too late to save the postwar ruling class from extinction (see *Corriere della Sera* 1991b).

Second, the chief problem with the (legal) practice of postwar clientelistic public employment was not the discretionary authority of elected officials as such. A spoil and patronage system operates in other political systems as well. In Swiss cantons, for example, almost everyone knows that "party membership frequently determines who gets which jobs"; clearly some firms engaged in public works projects receive preferential treatment, as they are not always awarded contracts through competitive bidding (Steinberg 1996, 82). A critical difference is public accountability of officialdom. In the design of the Italian system, public service employees were not expected, or motivated, to be public servants. Appointments to Italian administrative posts, boards and commissions often implied tenure with little or no public accountability. As noted earlier, this was justified as a way to prevent both the misuse of discretion and the abuse of favouritism. The opposite has generally occurred, though this does not deny the presence of very able and dedicated public servants among the functionaries at the Palermo and Naples communes, as Alfio Mastropaolo discovered when he became a member of the Orlando administration (Mastropaolo 1998) and as Raffaella Nanetti also discovered in the case of Naples when she worked on a public project with the Bassolino administration (Nanetti 1998b). Even when such qualifications are duly noted, it becomes clear why the difference between the service orientation and behaviour of espresso bar employees and state employees, presented to us in the first chapter as a paradox – by Paul Hofmann, a one-time *New York Times* correspondent in Rome – is no paradox at all.

Most public service delivery systems, including local health units (USL), had by 1990 become almost indestructible systems of bureaucratic free enterprise beyond the supervisory reach and control of elected and higher administrative officials (Ferrera 1996a, 1996b). Substantial evidence now exists to support the view that, below the pomp of mayoral offices and regional presidencies, was a vast network of public, non-elected officials who converted public authority into private concessions, practicing various forms of abusive rule and racketeering on citizens as well as on public administration. This situation helped to transform Italian ruling parties, as will be recalled from chapter 4, into "giants with feet of clay" (Cotta and Isernia 1996), lending credibility to Leoluca Orlando's often-repeated charge that organized crime had taken over public institutions.

The chief problem in Orlando's characterization was that it restricted perceptions of predatory rule largely, if not exclusively, to the south and to "the mafia" (cf., Alexander and Caiden 1986, 4–5). The bribe scandal in Milan uncovered in the early 1990s (*Tangentopoli*) was an example of what was often presumed to apply only to southern areas: namely, that a perverse emphasis on legality gives way to the practice of bureaucratic free enterprise among public monopolies in the north as well – just as a Sicilian newspaper article had predicted in 1991, before the bribe scandal in Milan became public knowledge (*Giornale di Sicilia* 1991a). *Tangentopoli* made it clear that rebates on salaries and cuts to party and individual coffers – institutionalized graft *à la*

George Washington Plunkitt – were not restricted to areas and people south of Rome. It also illustrated a more general point: public monopolies and their legislative and administrative complements, with a presumption of universality requiring uniform application, are much too arbitrary; they can pose even more difficult problems than private monopolies.

Third, the opportunities for institutionalized corruption opened the way to an increasingly dominant role of mafia-controlled firms in both the underground and the legal economies (see *Il Mondo* 1991; Santino and La Fiura 1990). The "privileged position of business" (Lindblom 1977), in society as in politics, can be all the more effective at stifling competition and market forces when it is backed by its own very effective protection mechanisms. To put matters this way does not deny Diego Gambetta's insistence (1993) that the chief distinguishing economic characteristic of the Sicilian mafia has been that it produces, promotes, and sells private protection and *not* other commodities (Gambetta 1993, 1; see also the work extending Gambetta's analysis by Varese 1994, 1996, 1997a, 1997b, 1997c, in press). Indeed, Gambetta's theoretical redirection does not preclude the possibility that mafiosi, manipulating their own mafia trademarks, could form other business enterprises to include protection from market competition, monopoly controls over illicit and licit markets, and immunity from state regulations secured through political connections. This is, in fact, what has happened in several instances. By the 1980s "mafia enterprises" could be found operating in many sectors beyond the business of protection, including tendering public works. As a result, in cities like Reggio Calabria, some local public officials themselves began to publicly question the wisdom of spending billions of lire for public works projects, since such works exposed local officials to all sorts of bribe bargains (Tucci 1991; see also Sergi 1991). The lack of "budget promptness" that Robert Putnam (1993, chp. 3) found among southern regional governments may be best understood either as a strategy to reduce exposure to pressures from criminal elements or as the result of deadlocked decisions among coalition parties.

The situation described in the preceding paragraph tends to support the standard version of businesses infiltrated by organized crime in both Italy and the United States. But let me quickly add that the standard version glosses over some fine details that merit further attention. What in Italy, as in North America, is perceived as self-evident – that mobsters (all-powerful by definitional fiat) have the resources and the ability to easily"'infiltrate" and control various legitimate markets – may not happen automatically, at least not always. It is reasonable to presume that work settings vary in "criminal liability." Some work settings are more criminogenic than others, while some provide the kinds of crime opportunities for which particular illicit entrepreneurs are searching. The "infiltration" model sketched in the previous paragraph assumes predatory outsiders (mafiosi) imposing patterns of illicit appropriation on otherwise honest and legal market participants. What is still less known is which already criminogenic field settings may or may not be accessible to underworld participants, and what possibilities exist for "outsiders" like mafiosi to be co-opted by willing "insiders" in particular settings – whether shipping docks, used-car wholesale businesses, or urban housing markets. We still do not know, except in much anecdotal evidence that has not yet been integrated in social science narrative, what criminogenic practices allow the entry of successful mobsters. What we do know is that consumers of most crime markets are largely composed of ordinary citizens.

As a way of summing up, much of the practice of clientelistic politics ultimately undermined its legal basis in the public sector, as it became a temptation for criminal syndicates. By 1991 the antimafia commissioner revealed that 15 per cent of all local, provincial, and regional politicians – 17,000 out of 124,000 elected officials – had broken the law or were living in the shadow of the law (*La Stampa*, 1991b). At least eighteen communal governments in three southern regions were suspected of collusion with outlaw groups and stood to be disbanded and placed under public trusteeship (*Corriere della Sera* 1991c; see also Della Porta and Vannucci 1995). These characterizations may not be bad as they seem. Illegalities may have helped people find ways to cope with problems, but illegalities also blur the standards that apply or ought to apply to the conduct of public affairs in a *stato di diritto*, thereby reducing the cost of doing crime.

The Price of Crime

Illegal activities, including the act of murder and extortion, may be approached like other commodities. This is why Gambetta's analysis of the "protection industry" in Sicily and Varese's analysis of the Russian mafia and its protection industry during the transition to democracy in Russia have brought about a paradigmatic shift in the comparative study of such clandestine and criminal entities (Gambetta 1993; Varese 1994, 1996, 1997a, 1997b, 1997c; cf., Della Porta and Vannucci 1995). Economic reasoning suggests that each commodity carries a price. What is the price of crime?

There is the human cost for the victim, of course. Offenders also face the risk of being executed by fellow criminals, as we saw earlier. For our purpose here let us consider other risk factors: the fairly low probability of being caught, and, after capture, the numerous legal opportunities for impunity available to the accused; the possible jail sentence, but the low probability that any particular punishment will actually be implemented as the price of crime (Miller, Benjamin, and North 1990). When this perspective is applied to an analysis of the structural and operational aspects of Italian law enforcement agencies and administration of justice, it becomes easier to understand why there continued to be profound dissatisfaction with the government war on crime, and why, as we saw in chapter 6, there was recurrent tension within the police and between the police and other instrumentalities of government.

The probability of being caught for illegal activities, including murder, continued in 1991 to be very low. This was due to a multiplicity of distinct and interconnected factors, two of which have been given primary explanatory power in public and scholarly debate. First, many judicial districts, especially in the so-called troubled areas of the south, continued to be chronically understaffed, often without even the bare necessities of judicial work. When efforts were made to fill judicial appointments or to create new tribunals such as that at Gela, the president of the republic, Francesco Cossiga, expressed concern about the value of appointing new largely inexperienced magistrates to such difficult posts – by implication raising serious questions about the professional formation of magistrates and the way judicial appointments are made in Italy.

Second, law enforcement officials themselves are to be blamed for many unsolved crimes. The antimafia commissioner, then Domenico Sica, publicly complained about the lack of professionalism among police and judicial officials, but in August 1991 the Interior minister removed him from office for practically the same reasons. While recognizing good intentions on both sides, *polizia* and *carabinieri* officials blamed each other for bungling investigations. Frustration for lack of results in the fight against organized crime became such that even magistrates with a reputation for being above reproach and suspicion were accused of being soft on both criminals and DC politicians "in odour of mafia." During 1991, the DC Interior minister himself joined the public debate by adding his name to the list of complainants. At one point, his public statements prompted a high magistrate to criticize him publicly for misrepresenting ongoing judicial investigations of extortion rackets. In turn, the Socialist Justice minister, Claudio Martelli, criticized both police officials and judges for being soft on criminals. In the fall, Martelli went as far as to ask the Superior Judicial Council to remove some judges from their positions in Sicily, evoking, in turn, sharp rebukes from the National Association of Magistrates and from legal scholars like Guido Neppi Modona. An immensely popular marathon television program on the mafia in September 1991 helped to sensitize viewers to the problem of organized criminality, but did little to clarify it.

Important as they may be, these two sets of factors do not fully explain the low probability of being caught for illegal activities. A chief problem is that a lack of comparative perspective has led many in Italy to have expectations about police work that cannot possibly be continuously met. Police officers of other industrialized countries do not generally fight organized or disorganized crime; in fact, the literature on police work suggests that police officers are ill equipped to do so (e.g., Alexander and Caiden 1986; Ericson 1982).

The situation in the province of Palermo in the early 1990s points to other bureaucratic constraints that created obstacles for translating intentions into outcomes. Agreement on what must be done about a problem does not suffice to guarantee action. According to the Interior minister and the Palermo police chief (cited in Scalfari 1991), in that province there were in 1991 at least 3,700 "dangerous subjects," while the total number of police officials – *polizia, carabinieri,* and *guardie di finanza* – was 8,525, divided into three shifts of a little more than six hours each. That is, at any one point there were 2,840 police officials on duty in the province's territory. Even on a nearly one-to-one basis, police officials could not keep a close watch on all the presumed or real dangerous subjects. Nor could round-the-clock police protection be physically extended to all those who refused the "protection" of gangsters and outlaw groups.

The recollections by Tommaso Buscetta of the early 1980s further complicate this situation: apparently Palermo mafiosi had noted that there was no police patrol work between 1:30 and 4:30 in the afternoon, the traditional mealtime; during this period even fugitive mafiosi like Buscetta could apparently move around the city freely and unhindered by police road blocks (Buscetta in Arlacchi 1994, 218–19). The absence of patrol work during mealtime in northern Italy – albeit much shorter, 12:00 to 2:00 p.m. – has also been noticed, and exploited, by others doing ordinary crime in northern Italian settings (Barbagli 1995, 213). Moreover, fighting organized crime was only one of the many daily tasks that police officers were called upon to do in Palermo as elsewhere. It has become a truism in American police studies to say that adding more officers to a police force does not necessarily mean increased output, less crimes, and higher arrest rates; and it is hard to see why the same "truth" should not apply to the Sicilian setting.

The case of the Palermitan industrialist, Libero Grassi, murdered in August 1991, dramatically illustrates this problematic situation. It was public knowledge as early as January 1991 (*Corriere della Sera* 1991d) that Grassi had rejected several times the "protection" of gangsters, but several stories exist. One is that he had paid for a long time but when the price of protection increased, he refused to go along; another is that he stopped paying for private protection when a new protector took over from the old. Regardless of which story is true, one thing is clear: his refusal to pay exposed him to mortal danger. Just as police officers had difficulties protecting him twenty-four hours a day, so the racketeers could not fail to kill him if he did not accept their "offer." After waiting at least seven months for Grassi to accept the offer, they could not wait longer; the credibility of their threat system was at stake.

Libero Grassi's murder placed in sharp relief another dimension of the price of crime specific to Italy's system of bureaucratic administration: two national police forces with the same territorial jurisdiction, as noted earlier in chapter 4, but without effective interorganizational arrangements for cooperative and joint efforts in overlapping matters at the field level of operation. The two police services can monitor each other's activities but this does little to advance law enforcement, since the two forces generally are reluctant to share information unless so ordered by their respective superiors at the top. Not surprisingly, parallel investigations of the Grassi murder led to parallel and antithetical conclusions.

The *polizia* attributed the murder to a particular crime group. On this basis, the Interior minister complained publicly in October that the Palermo magistrates were unaccountably slow in prosecuting the racketeers. This in turn compelled the Palermo chief procurator, Pietro Giammanco, to charge in a newspaper interview that the Interior minister had either been lied to or had been misinformed by his own staff (i.e., the police chief; *La Repubblica* 1991). While this controversy raged on, it became known that the *carabinieri* had, for their part, reached different conclusions from their own separate investigations. According to the *carabinieri*, the *polizia* and, by implication, the Interior minister had bungled the Grassi investigation. The *carabinieri* identified mafiosi from another protection gang as the authors (*mandanti*) of the murder (Bolzoni 1991b). As a result, the search for the racketeer-murderers gave way, in the words of a Palermitan newspaper, to "a hunt for liars of state" (*Giornale di Sicilia* 1991b).

When law enforcement officials and investigating magistrates did succeed in bringing underworld figures to trial, problems connected with jail sentences tended to emerge. These problems highlight another aspect of the cost of crime: whether or not the sentence will actually be implemented, as the accused or guilty parties pursue the legal opportunities afforded by the judicial system. Since this was discussed in chapter 6, a few illustrations will suffice here.

The view of the mafia held by Giovanni Falcone and other magistrates led inevitably to the belief that people at the top of the chain knew everything about what their "soldiers" were doing. This meant that people like Michele Greco, the so-called boss of bosses, were jailed on the basis of this "theorem," but with no evidence. In February 1991, Michele Greco and some forty other mafiosi were released from jail by a law which then allowed anyone who appealed a prison sentence to walk free unless the appeal was heard within a year. The government, spurred by the Interior and Justice ministers, rushed through a new law setting different rules for calculating the time spent waiting for appeal. The mafiosi were back in jail soon after their release. But the legislation, applying retroactively, was highly contentious. The contention went something like this: we might all be very happy that people like Greco are in jail, but the legislation involves the distortion of a fundamental principle of legality.

In short, the legislation did little to instill confidence in public authority and led to a protest strike by Sicilian lawyers. At the same time, it served to lend credence to a prevailing way of reasoning among mafiosi, expressed in the testimony of an ex-mafioso, Gaspare Mutolo, before a parliamentary commission in 1993 as follows: since whenever someone is killed, police and magistrates throw us in jail even when we have nothing to do with the crime, let us kill some magistrates so that at least we will be put in jail for something that we have actually done (testimony excerpted in Pezzino 1995, 320). Whether this reasoning was actually acted upon remains unclear in the testimony, but it does call to mind the danger of *summus jus, summa iniuria*. Against this backdrop, it is not surprising that many guilty verdicts reached in trials of first instance could not survive the scrutiny of other courts. A desire to surmount this problem further complicated the administration of justice.

By the end of the 1980s, pressures to secure guilty verdicts for real or reputed members of crime syndicates became so great in Italy as to take precedence over due legal process. It was somehow expected that the accused would not pursue the legal opportunities afforded by the system. The Supreme Court of Appeal section headed by Judge Corrado Carnevale was vigorously criticized by some left-leaning elected officials and by the elite mass media for what Judge Carnevale considered to be a careful discharge of his judicial duties (*Corriere della Sera* 1991e). By the end of 1991, a way was found to rotate the criminal cases among different sections of the Supreme Court of Appeal (Court of Cassation), with the intent of securing more guilty verdicts; and, as we noted in chapter 6, Judge Carnevale was eventually removed from the Court of Cassation and charged with collusion with the mafia, a criminal offense. What followed after 1992 is summarized in the words of an American magazine writer and reporter: "not only did the high court uphold the original convictions but it accepted the so-called Buscetta [theorem]. For the first time in history, the leadership of Cosa Nostra was faced with a nonappealable life sentence. Not only were dozens of major bosses unlikely ever to leave prison, but prosecutors could continue using the same tools to go after the rest of the organization. The decision was a clear signal that the age of impunity that had lasted forty-five years was over" (Stille 1995, 349).

By 1999, it was still unclear whether the former judge, Carnevale, who continued to maintain his innocence (*Corriere della Sera*, 1998b), did indeed collude with criminals, as some ex-mafiosi and journalists claim (Bolzoni and D'Avanzo 1995). As the discussion about judicial proceedings in the last chapter notes, his case may be *sub judice* for quite some time (*Corriere della Sera* 1998b; Stille 1995, 334, 348–9; see also Clark 1996).

It is also equally unclear whether "the age of impunity" was actually over, for impunity is not unique to the Italian justice system, even when allowances are made for the fact that Italian appeal courts have generally treated each case as though it had never been tried before, as we saw in the previous chapter. The United States has a high arrest rate for murders, but only about one-third of all murders result in conviction – leading one scholar to entitle his study of the American system of criminal trials as "trials without truth" (Pizzi 1998). In the Italian context, whenever courts did not confirm the sentences of lower courts, it was automatically assumed by many observers that the higher court judge or judges had been bought off. (See also the recent court decision finding the mafiosi accused of taking part in the murder of Judge Scopelliti in 1991 not guilty, in *Corriere della Sera* 1998c). The argument of critics of the Italian criminal justice system suffers from the same unavoidable weakness that Richard A. Posner, an American federal judge and law professor, has recently identified in the argument of critics of the American criminal justice system – "an inability to establish the magnitude of the problem they have identified" (Posner 1999, 10).

In addition, other stacked and nested issues related to prison and correctional institutions have helped to keep the price of crime relatively low for criminals. Some of these issues were vividly brought to light in 1991, in a case involving a Palermitan underworld boss, Pietro Vernengo. Vernengo was a reputed heroine trafficker. Arrested in 1986 for taking part in ninety-nine murders, he was found guilty for some and was twice condemned to life imprisonment. Since he suffered from a bladder tumour, Vernengo successfully used his medical situation to delay imprisonment. He became a patient in the urology ward of the Palermo Civic Hospital, where, in consideration of his ill health, he was left unguarded most of the time. In October 1991, an appeal court sustained the judgment of a lower court against him, increasing the prospect of imprisonment. As soon as he received the news, seeing perhaps no other prospect except life imprisonment, Vernengo literally walked out of the hospital. His flight was a profound embarrassment to central government officials.

Justice Minister Claudio Martelli called for the immediate transfer of the Palermo appeal court judge, Pasquale Barreca, who had earlier extended Vernengo's hospital stay. Martelli's frustration was understandable, but his call seemed *ultra vires*. He was sharply criticized by legal scholars and magistrates who expressed sympathy and support for Judge Barreca. An examination of Vernengo's flight from the hospital suggests a sequence of events and decisions more complex and less conspiratorial than what was suggested by the Justice minister and media commentators.

In October 1991, soon after Vernengo's flight, the central government ordered an inquiry to determine how many convicted underworld figures were spending time in hospital rather than in jail. In the course of this inquiry, a report written in March 1989 by the antimafia commissioner, Domenico Sica, was uncovered. Leaked to, and widely circulated by the news media, the 1989 report gave a new twist to the unfolding events (*Corriere della Sera* 1991f). In that two-year-old report, Sica had drawn attention to the fact that an unusually high number of convicted mafiosi were spending more time in hospital than in prison. Sica had wondered if they all really needed what they claimed – extensive hospital care. Vernengo was one such case. The main problem brought to light by Sica's 1989 report was this: neither the Socialist (PSI) Justice minister nor the DC Interior minister of the time – Giuliano Vassalli and Antonio Gava, respectively – had acted upon the report. It is still not clear whether the ministers and their staff had tried but failed to implement the report, or whether they were even aware of it altogether.

Other features in the organizational capabilities and administrative procedures of correctional services emerged to widen the spectrum of problems. Originally imprisoned in the Palermo Ucciardone Penitentiary, Vernengo had been expected to receive medical care for his bladder tumour there, but other unrelated factors intervened. Huge sums of money had been spent to equip the Ucciardone prison for the megatrials of the 1980s, but little or no money had been set aside to improve the penitentiary infirmary; thus Vernengo could not receive adequate care there. He was assigned to the special ward for penitentiary inmates at the Palermo Civic Hospital, but then another chain of organizational issues surfaced: there was no room for Vernengo; the special wing had only a twelve-bed surgical unit. A projected expansion of the security wing had not been built, largely because it was not clear which level of government – regional or central – should fund the project. As a result, the hospital admissions office assigned Vernengo to the regular urology ward, where he had been a patient for some years. Judicial authorities had approved the arrangement and had been kept routinely informed.

In short, what Judge Barreca had done was to uphold the earlier judicial decision. In the process, however, he had interpreted some newly issued precautionary detention measures by the government as not applicable to ongoing cases like that of Vernengo. Here was another problem. Barreca thought he was under no obligation to apply the new regulations retroactively. And it was this understanding that brought him on a collision course with the Justice minister and set in motion the government inquiry that exposed faults in the organizational capabilities and procedures of the justice system. But the inquiry revealed yet another puzzle that seems to have remained unsolved: Why was Vernengo without police guard or surveillance in the hospital, and who – judge, police station, or hospital director – should be held responsible for this omission?

Much of the public controversy surrounding the Vernengo case gave little no consideration to the complexly nested and stacked set of issues sketched above. Instead, most "elite press" commentators of the time unbridled their imaginations to search for a directing mind orchestrating both the failure of the general war on crime and the strength of the underworld. Few, if any, sought to understand that what was taking place reflected the independent output of several organizations that could not in practice be directed from above, through hierarchic arrangements and excessive adherence to the law.

NEW POLICE AND LEGAL REMEDIES

The analysis in part 3 has highlighted the challenge facing police and prosecutorial strategies against offenders involved in criminal and criminogenic markets. New police and legal remedies were devised in the early 1990s in response to the various constraints and options that structure prosecutorial work in organized crime cases. They began in March 1991, when Giovanni Falcone moved from Palermo to Rome to become the director of penal affairs at the Justice ministry and to work closely with the minister. In retrospect, Falcone's move was the beginning of the new war on organized crime that emerged by November 1991 and that was eventually to cost him his life in 1992.

To be sure, Falcone was not the only artificer of the new instruments in the war on crime (Pirani 1991). But what enticed him to leave Palermo was not just his disappointment about the office of investigating magistrate, discussed in the previous chapter. It was also the promise, made by the Justice minister, Claudio Martelli, that Falcone would have considerable latitude in helping to fashion a new institutional response to organized crime (see also Di Lello 1994, 221–2). Falcone was equally attracted by Martelli's "decisionism" as Justice minister. Personalities and decisionism aside, there were other factors that led to a new war on crime.

The August 1991 murders of Cassation magistrate Antonino Scopelliti in his native Calabria and of Libero Grassi in Sicily gave renewed vigour to the preparatory work for the new government war on crime. Other factors, internal to the administration of justice itself, were just as important. There was the problem of coordinating different efforts, which the Vernengo case had exposed. The inconsistency between the preferred solution and the actual behaviour of agencies of the penal system needed to be addressed. By now it was clear that the earlier establishment of the office of the antimafia commissioner had not resolved the problem of "animating" and coordinating information and activities among a myriad of supposedly allied organizations. Without denying the organizational skills, knowledge, and dedication of successive antimafia commissioners, the data gathering and dissemination they had achieved – and could achieve, in a democratic society with an excessive conception of the rule of law and with a judiciary extremely assertive of its constitutional independence – were at best modest, if not negligible. The office of the antimafia commissioner had made the world of bureaucratic politics messier by challenging – unsuccessfully, it turned out – the standard operating procedures of established organizations and their respective organizational jurisdictions. As a result, in the course of nine years of operation, the office had become just another institution in a hierarchic conglomerate of presumably allied organizations; each unit had sought to maintain a substantial administrative life and antimafia project of its own.

The new police and legal remedies emerged in the fall of 1991. They called for the creation of a special system of public administration to handle law enforcement and judicial investigations against the mafia, now broadly understood to include all forms of criminal entrepreneurship. Recourse to special administration has long been part of the central government repertoire of action programs to meet institutional weakness and failure in the ordinary administrative system. In this sense, the creation of a new set of institutional arrangements was not unusual. What was different now was that the new special system was made up of two units expressly designed to overcome previous organizational problems. These units were 1) an antimafia investigative directorate (*Direzione Investigativa Antimafia*, DIA); and 2) a national antimafia procurator's office (*Direzione Nazionale Antimafia*, DNA).

The creation of the DIA was an attempt to overcome the problem of coordination in law enforcement agencies and to animate and direct organized crime investigations. Public officials and media people spoke of DIA as the Italian FBI. Support for the new special judicial branch, the DNA, was grounded in the argument advanced by, among others, the Florence procurator, Pier Luigi Vigna. He understood that the DNA "will make it possible to undertake more effective investigations of mafia power and its plans. The basic idea is to oppose expert and skilled criminals with inquiring magistrates endowed with a high degree of professionalism and organization" (Pier Luigi Vigna, quoted in *Corriere della Sera* 1991g). As the DNA was taking shape, magistrates expressed considerable reservations about the parallel judicial system being set up to combat organized crime. These reservations were grounded in three fundamental concerns: 1) the DNA or *Superprocura* would be too dependent on the political executive, judged to be a grave danger by a judiciary exceedingly jealous of its independence vis-à-vis other branches of government; 2) it would come into jurisdictional conflict with the regular judicial administration; and 3) it would undermine the already difficult implementation of the new code of criminal procedure, which did not contemplate a special branch of the judiciary such as the *Superprocura* (Geraci 1991; *La Stampa* 1991c). In sum, the new police and legal remedies were not designed to tackle most dimensions of the political economy of crime and punishment highlighted in this chapter.

CONCLUSION

This survey of the political economy of crime and punishment reveals perplexing problems. Statutory legislation and its administrative complement challenge the very concept of a rule of law. As long as opportunities for illegal and criminal activities exist, and as long as people are locked into institutional arrangements that offer few prospects for legally pursuing individual and collective opportunities, it is difficult to anticipate positive changes. A new source of disappointment could come from the new police and legal remedies aimed at controlling or incapacitating crime market participants, but the DIA and DNA elicited far too many expectations, not always easy to match in practice. If they work to make the fast lane of crime more costly to professional criminals and to discourage others from entering it, they stand to succeed as deterrents. But the criminal underground, consisting of both illicit and criminogenic markets, cannot easily be dried up or eradicated by government fiat. Moreover, there are too many *res incognitae* in DIA and DNA, and the experience of past anticrime initiatives – and indeed of previous agencies and institutions of "special administration" (see Germino and Passigli 1968, ch. 6) – counsels a cautious optimism.

We now know that 1992 was a turning point in the war on crime as a fight for good government. It started not quite as planned, with the assassination of Giovanni Falcone and Paolo Borsellino, but an emerging wisdom began to see their deaths as acts of desperation by mafiosi – an *ex adverso* confirmation that the new police and legal remedies were working. Just as the kickback scheme uncovered in Milan in early 1992 brought down, in about two years, almost the entire postwar governing class, so the murders of the two crime fighters triggered a flurry of anticrime activities by law enforcement agencies that challenged to an unprecedented degree the view that crime pays in and beyond Sicily. But there remain troubling and unavoidable facts.

First, the expressed intention to craft institutions and policies of good government is not enough to overcome the constraints of translating institutional and policy designs into operational reality. A perverse emphasis on legalism is a major obstacle, and to do away with what it implies – the universality and uniformity of statutory legislation and administrative regulations – is to do away with a core feature of the *stato di diritto*, something not likely to happen in the near future. As long as the Italian legislators and the attentive public continue to insist that the greatest liberty of citizens depends on the intrusiveness or extension of the law, it will be almost impossible for the *stato di diritto* to cease to be, in Hobbes's words, "a trap for money" (Hobbes [1651] 1962, 254). Second, in such an environment the work of law enforcement agencies is much more difficult than is generally realized. Understanding the police and prosecutorial strategies used against offenders in criminal or criminogenic markets requires a systematic understanding of the practical options available to various subsets of decision makers involved in the day-to-day business of apprehending, prosecuting, and sentencing crime market participants. Finally, it is questionable to perceive organized crime issues as primarily matters of public morality ("if only the police and politicians were virtuous"). Remedial policies of crime markets that fail to recognize how the perverse emphasis on legality fosters its own system of illegalities will not have a high rate of success, irrespective of stated goals. The basic challenge that emerges from part 3 then, is part of the larger challenge: whether it is possible for people and public officials alike to break free of and reform a system of governance that produce outcomes which they do not value very highly as viable alternatives. This challenge is not unrealistic, after all. As the next part makes clear, people are not path-dependently or culturally doomed to bad government.

PART FOUR

Why People Are Not Culturally or Path Dependently Doomed to Bad Government

8 The Search for the Real Montegrano

A strong impression exists abroad that the "paradox of Italy" and the resultant poor government performance are chiefly attributable to particular beliefs and attitudes of Italians and, more generally, to Italian culture, ethos, or morality. This is why Italy united so late, in spite of Dante's and Machiavelli's appeals; this is why, the argument continues, Italian citizens and public officials have been unable to cope effectively with the collective problems that plague their society; this is why, noted the 1998 *Economist* editorial cited in the first chapter, contemporary Italy cannot be taken seriously as an advanced market economy and democratic state. Carlo Cattaneo strenuously challenged this culturalist interpretation in the nineteenth century (Cattaneo [1836b] 1964, 3: 230; [1845a] 1951, 2:80), just as the preceding chapters have tried to do for the post-1946 period, by focusing on how crafting constitutional and institutional arrangements can (and do) rig the game of life in particular ways. But there is force in the paradoxical view of Italian public life and the accompanying culturalist contention that has often fed "respectable bigotry." Intuitively they seem to carry the ring of truth, like many stereotypes.

A chief merit of Joseph LaPalombara's *Democracy Italian Style* (1987) was to challenge the conventional view of Italian politics. Unfortunately, LaPalombara's praise of postwar party politics and the national governing class has been seriously undercut by the very collapse of the postwar political order since 1992. By restating LaPalombara's argument more directly on facts – differential performance of regional government – Robert D. Putnam's *Making Democracy Work*

(1993) may have succeeded in toppling the exaltedly pessimistic view of Italy and demonstrating convincingly that good government does exist there. As noted in chapter 1, however, Putnam's path-dependent explanation of differential performance of regional government has also tended to reinforce the standard view, if only by confining it to southern Italy. This view, in turn, has served to give renewed standing to the descriptive and explanatory power enjoyed by Edward C. Banfield's *The Moral Basis of a Backward Society*, first published in 1958. It becomes all the more important, then, to reexamine Banfield's thesis. This is the aim of this chapter. Chapter 9 turns specifically to Putnam's work.

BANFIELD'S WORK IN COMPARATIVE ANALYSIS

Banfield developed the expression "amoral familism" to explain the collective inaction he perceived among the inhabitants of "Montegrano," a village located in the province of Potenza, Basilicata, during the eight or so months he spent there in 1954–55. The village's real name is Chiaromonte, and this is the one we shall use throughout.

Some Italian scholars, disturbed in part by the use of such terms as "amoral," have tended to dismiss Banfield's work as "populist American sociology" (Marselli 1963; Romeo 1965, ix). Others dismissed it as a form of respectable bigotry or racism to the point of preventing its author from speaking at a Canadian university (*Globe and Mail* 1974). However, the recognition that Banfield's effort had the merit of identifying some of the patterns of politics and culture within a microcosm of a single community, where it might be easier to disaggregate the elements of problematic situations, led to the publication of a second Italian-language edition of his study in 1976.

Banfield was careful not to claim too much, but quite a few readers have accorded even more status to amoral familism than did the author. Though Banfield's description and explanation date back to the 1950s, they have been widely cited in the comparative politics literature, and even beyond it, as a characterization of much of the history of southern Italy and as a lesson for understanding determinants of economic backwardness in other parts of Europe and the rest of the world (e.g., Fukuyama 1995, 9, 56, 98–100; Hildebrand 1965, 310). Some analysts continue to regard Italy across time and space as nothing but Banfield's village writ large (Bosworth 1979, 2; Gambino 1991; Kogan 1965, 37). The resurgence of cultural explanations since the late 1980s has given Banfield's account renewed standing and importance to the point that few English-language books on modern Italian politics and society published in the postwar period have become as well known and frequently cited or discussed among social scientists as Banfield's study.

On the empirical front, Robert D. Putnam's *Making Democracy Work* (1993) refined and expanded Banfield's thesis to explain differential performance among Italian regional governments. One of Putnam's collaborators elevated Banfield's account into a "systemic logic" for understanding the success and failure rate of European Union development programs (Leonardi 1995). On the more explicitly theoretical front, Michael Thomson, R. Ellis, and A. Wildavsky treated Banfield's study as "the finest study of fatalism" and gave amoral familism a formal conceptualization as a "fatalistic cultural bias impeding the collective action necessary to sustain economic development and a democratic political order" (1990, 223). Jon Elster did no less when he incorporated Banfield's amoral familism into his own philosophical investigations about what binds societies together and what leads them to disintegrate into chaos and war (Elster 1989, 147, 269).

In sum, more than forty years after it first appeared, Banfield's analysis of a southern Italian village continues to be an important scholarly reference. Curiously, there seems to have been no replication of Banfield's fieldwork, even when it was still somewhat possible to match his temporal conditions. Nor has there been much scholarly research on public and voluntary collective initiatives in Chiaromonte either before 1954 or after 1955.

What perhaps made verification seem unnecessary was that Banfield's thesis and construction of Chiaromonte reality confirmed a view of southern Italy that emerged after unification to become prevalent among Italian positivists and idealists alike – from Antonio Gramsci's general description of the south as "a great social disaggregation" (Gramsci [1926] 1967, 42) and Benedetto Croce's characterization of its people through history as "an inert and heavy reluctant mass" (Croce [1925] 1970, 195) to more recent Weberian accounts of Italian cultural backwardness (Tullio-Altan 1986). Even most of Banfield's critics – no matter how much they disagreed with him about the causal priority to be assigned to "culture" – accepted, albeit in varying degrees, the epistemological foundations and truth value of his description (see most of the article-length critiques of Banfield's work, published in the Italian edition, Banfield 1976). This may help to explain why hardly anyone has taken up Banfield's challenge to replicate his study (Banfield [1958] 1967, 11).

If Banfield's construction of Chiaromonte reality, a southern Italian village, were of little general relevance, the absence of replication would be a minor problem. As the popularity of Banfield's work suggests, this is not the case, however. Thus, it is of no small importance to determine the extent to which Banfield's thesis is consistent with the facts on the ground in Chiaromonte.

I attempted such an exploration in the summer of 1994, spending two weeks doing intense field work on Chiaromonte, its culture and history. Of course, not much can be accomplished – however intensely one may work – in such a brief time. But I did manage to collect some archival data in Rome and Potenza (while the latter's Archivio di Stato was being moved to a new location). I took note of, and eventually took hold of, other potential sources of historical and contemporary data, in part by visiting the regional offices in Potenza and by tracking down local histories written by villagers and some Italian scholarly accounts that discuss Chiaromonte. I travelled to the village for a one-day visit (which made me appreciate what Banfield, his wife, and children must have experienced to reach the village from Potenza more than forty years ago, without the benefit of the Salerno-Reggio Calabria "superhighway"), and met with, among others, the mayor, who was then also a national leftist politician. Field research in the fall of 1995 and the summer of 1998 for other projects provided an opportunity to augment material gathered earlier, to reduce uncertainties in written and oral accounts, and to fortify the analysis. Before considering an alternative description and explanation, I will present Banfield's analysis.

BANFIELD'S INQUIRY

Banfield set out in 1954 to find an answer to the question, What accounts for the political incapacity of the village? (Banfield [1958] 1967, 32). By political incapacity he meant "the inability of the villagers to act together for their common good or, indeed, for any end transcending the immediate, material interest of the nuclear family" (9–10). "To act together for their common good" is used throughout Banfield's book interchangeably with "concerted action," "organized action," "community action," "local action," and "group action." Thus, Banfield used the term "political incapacity" to refer to the lack of collective action undertaken either through individual or public initiative. The difference between individual voluntary initiative and public communal initiative in actions for the common good is of fundamental importance. Failure to make this distinction led Banfield to misconstruct social and political reality and to create confusion among his critics who missed or failed to appreciate the importance of the distinction (Davis 1970; Hancey 1977; Marselli 1963).

Banfield claimed that villagers acted as if they were following this rule: "Maximize the material, short-run advantage of the nuclear family; assume that all others will do likewise" (Banfield 1958 [1967], 83). Villagers following this individualistic rule were labelled "amoral familists" – that is, one who acts "without morality only in relation to persons outside the family – in relation to family members, he applied standards of right and wrong" (83). Banfield then proceeded to present seventeen logical implications of this individualistic rule relating to the absence of both voluntary and communal collective action. He was thus faced with the problem of how to explain collective inaction.

Aaron Wildavsky (1992, 15) observed that this is the key issue both in Banfield's work and in rational choice theory and institutional analysis. But, as noted in chapter 1, the work of Elinor Ostrom (1990, 1998) makes clear that there are empirical and logical difficulties with a view of society based on extreme rationality assumptions (see also M. Levi 1997a, 1997b). Moreover, a self-interested, rational actor is not necessarily nontuistic (i.e., not taking into account the interests of others) (V. Ostrom 1997, 89). Self-interested individuals who repeatedly interact with each other with an infinite time horizon may engage in cooperative behaviour if they can observe each other's actions and place a sufficiently high value on future transactions. In short, "rational individuals" do not necessarily have to result in "irrational society" and poor government performance. A view of society based on extreme rationality assumptions is as inconsistent with observed reality as Banfield's thesis is not fully consistent with observed facts in Chiaromonte. But, let us turn first to the explanation provided by Banfield.

Banfield's Culturalist Explanation

Banfield identified the basis of the political backwardness of Chiaromonte in the "sentiments, values, beliefs and ideas" of its villagers (Banfield, 1958 [1967], 103), the ethos of that community (10). Ethos was used interchangeably with "culture" and "morality" (8, 155–6); thus, the principal predictive hypothesis of amoral familism was taken as a manifestation of this ethos, culture, or morality. The sources of the Chiaromonte ethos were found in the particular system of land tenure, fear of premature death, and absence of the extended family. These, in turn, created a situation whereby the central theme of one's existence was the nuclear family. Villagers were amoral familists because, under the conditions in which they were living, their ideas of right and wrong related only to their immediate families and not to some universal or general principles that were felt to be obligatory outside the family. Thus, to the question, Why do villagers engage only in individualistic action for immediate personal or family gain? Banfield's answer was that they did so because they had backward values, because they lacked a broader or more general morality. The "moral basis" of that backward society was identified as "amoral familism."

In his introductory chapter, Banfield suggests a high degree of organization as a necessary condition to realizing a high level of economic development and a democratic political order in a human society. The inability of some human societies to achieve such a high degree of organization can be found in their ethos or culture, he argued. Thus culture becomes "the limiting factor which determines the amount and character of organization and therefore of progress in the less developed parts of the world" (9). Chiaromonte was part of this less-developed world.

Banfield used the term culture in several different ways. He referred to non-Western cultures and to Japanese culture. He also spoke of "the ability of a culture to maintain organization," and a culture that "is able to maintain an effective military force" (8, 9). At the individual level, culture is identified as ethos or morality – basic values, sentiments, beliefs. The problem is how culture as ethos or morality is related to the ability to maintain an organization or an effective military force. Banfield failed to connect individual preferences, beliefs, ethos, or morality to the conditions that apply to the organization of collective action. A sociologist with a deep knowledge of Chiaromonte has put Banfield's failure to connect the two this way: "Is a simple handshake between the people of Chiaromonte enough to build roads? Or is the arrival of a Protestant mission enough to turn the mountainous terrain into a plain? Or again, is it enough that the people of Chiaromonte bring up their children differently for water to arrive and the soil to become fertile? Or finally will the arrival of television transform the hoe into the latest tractor?" (Colombis 1983, 22).

The failure in Banfield's analysis can also be illustrated by calling up a quotation he made from Tocqueville's *Democracy in America*: "The most democratic country on the face of the earth is that in which men have, in our time, carried to the highest perfection the art of pursuing in common the objects of their common desires and have applied this new science to the greatest number of purposes" (Tocqueville [1840] 1962, 2:115, quoted in Banfield [1958] 1967, 7–8;). The high degree of organization suggested by Banfield refers to the society described by Tocqueville, but Tocqueville's analysis is based upon an assumption that people are self-interested. Indeed, Tocqueville feared that individuals would "adopt the doctrine of self-interest" as their rule of action "without adequate understanding of the science that puts it to use" (Tocqueville [1835] 1962, 1:11). One would expect in Banfield's work – but does not find – a reference to the conditions analyzed by Tocqueville that allowed American citizens to pursue their "enlightened self-interest" – that is, to resist selfish interest and nontuistic behaviour. At this point, Banfield could also have raised the question of what allowed the inhabitants of St George, Utah, to undertake "a buzz of activity [for] the advancement of community welfare" (Banfield [1958] 1967, 17). Instead, he simply used the events in that American community as an introduction and contrast with the events he was about to describe in Chiaromonte.

Not unlike Cattaneo, in his approach to the study of Italian cities, Tocqueville was less concerned with the federal government and its place in American society and more concerned with how the American tradition of self-government developed – first in the townships, then in the states, and finally in the national government (Tocqueville [1835] 1962, 1:49). Each level of government was based on the principle that every individual "is the best and sole judge of his own private interest and that society has no right to control a man's actions unless they are prejudicial to the common weal or unless the common weal demands his help" (Tocqueville [1835] 1962, 1: 64). In his analysis of the *ancien régime* in France, Tocqueville found a common origin for the old French parish system and the rural townships in North America. That common origin did not, however, insure similar developments. "Transported overseas from feudal Europe and free to develop in total independence, the rural parish of the Middle Ages became the township of New England. Emancipated from the seigneur, but controlled at every turn by an all-powerful government, it took in France ... the form of paternal government" (Tocqueville [1856] 1956, 48, 51). These developments had different results. "Thus the French government lends its agents to the *commune*; in America the township lends its agents to the government. This fact alone shows how widely the two nations differ ... The New Englander is attached to his township not so much because he was born in it, but because it is a free and strong community, of which he is a member, and which deserves the care spent in managing it." And echoing Cattaneo's view of communes sketched in chapter 3, Tocqueville continued: "In Europe the absence of local public spirit is a frequent subject of regret to those who are in power; everyone agrees that there is no surer guarantee of order and tranquility, and yet nothing is more difficult to create. If the municipal bodies were made powerful and independent, it is feared that they would become too strong and expose the state to anarchy. Yet without power and independence a town may contain good subjects, but it can have no active citizens" (Tocqueville [1835] 1962, 1: 68–9). By taking as given the institutional arrangements of the Italian state, Banfield did not consider the extent to which the consequences predicted by Tocqueville, as well as by Cattaneo and Ferrara, could be observed in Chiaromonte.

To sum up the argument thus far, Banfield did not consider how the design and structure of basic local institutions for the pursuit of communal and voluntary initiatives was linked to the values, norms, and attitudes held by the Chiaromontesi. He did not ask to what extent, if any, local people have had a part in the modelling and remodelling of basic local institutions: the problem, for Banfield, was not "political" but "cultural." Yet, for all his emphasis on a cultural explanation, Banfield gave no thick description of the moral and cultural basis of Chiaromonte village life. This puzzle is, I would argue, related to his choice of the term "amoral familism."

Banfield's "Amoral Familism"

"Amoral familism" is a loaded expression. Some puzzling aspects of the choice of such a term have been brought out by Alessio Colombis, the sociologist cited earlier. His comments may be worth reproducing at some length:

In the first moment, reading Banfield's critique of amoral familism one is tempted to believe that he intends to fight for the right of men to apply standards of right and wrong in their relations and hence one is somewhat surprised that an academic coming from a social system in which capitalism has imposed as the "normal" model of life, a model based on the logic of the growth of material consumption, should come to Chiaromonte and complain of the lack of altruistic sentiment in human relations ...

But, analyzing Banfield's theses in greater depth one discovers that he is not in the least interested in the disappearance or reduction of individualism and egoism. In fact, in his final chapter, he states that "In order for concerted action – and therefore economic development either in the village or elsewhere – to take place, it would not, of course, be necessary that amoral familism be replaced by altruism. Indeed, individualism (or familism) is a very good thing from an economic standpoint, provided it is not so extreme as to render concerted action altogether impossible." And Banfield continues asserting that to ensure concerted action requires a few persons to have the moral capacity to act as leaders. These need not act altruistically either; it is sufficient that they lead and they may do simply because they are paid to do so. (Colombis 1983, 17–8)

Much of Banfield's concern that causal priority be assigned to cultural variables as opposed to structural variables was misguided because it conflated different sources and types of ethos, morality, and concerted action. This problematic aspect of Banfield's work, which was extended to the study of urban America, has received considerable scholarly criticism (Banfield 1968, 161; Hennessey 1970; Hennessey and Feen 1973). In the case of Chiaromonte, the failure to distinguish different types of ethos and norms led Banfield to misdescribe the onto-logical nature of the problematic situation and to conflate individual, voluntary concerted action and public, communal concerted action (see also Gribaudi 1993). These problems are evident in the disjunc-tions between Banfield's culturalist explanation and his empirical observations. Before considering these disjunctions, let us see how some Chiaromontesi have reacted to Banfield's inquiry.

VILLAGERS' REACTIONS

During my visit to Chiaromonte (8 August 1994), I interviewed, among others, three leading villagers, including the newly elected sen-ator on the left-wing Olive Tree ticket, who had read the Italian ver-sion of Banfield's work. Two of the villagers – one a retired school teacher – were old enough to have met Banfield in some of his trips to the town; they remember him well.

These villagers averred that Banfield seriously misunderstood what he observed and that he did not even get at the basic structures of vil-lage life as they existed in 1954 and 1955. These villagers questioned Banfield's findings and interpretation, and suggested that opinion mak-ers who have relied on Banfield's account to advance their own argu-ments have built them on questionable grounds. In support of their argument, these Chiaromontesi contested the reliability of Banfield's informants and methodology, pointing me to two sources.

First, they called up the discussion of Banfield by an expatriate vil-lager, Francesco Elefante, in one of the three small volumes he has writ-ten on the history of Chiaromonte (Elefante 1989, 165–9; see also Ele-fante 1987, 1988). Then they drew attention to Alessio Colombis, whose work I have already cited. As a sociologist at the University of Salerno, Colombis has expanded and refined Elefante's criticisms by dedicating, as he noted to me in several telephone and epistolary exchanges in 1994 and 1995, much of his professional life to the study of Chiaromonte (Colombis 1974, 1979, 1982, 1983, 1989, 1992). Colombis' treatment can be taken as a scholarly summary of what vil-lagers say.

Colombis notes several problems with Banfield's sample of Chiaromonte interviewees. They were twenty-eight peasants, and yet, Colombis continues, "we know nothing about how they were selected, nor if the sample was composed of men, women, nor if it was mixed and in what proportions, nor the age of the interviewees nor whether they were married. This makes it much more difficult to understand the real meaning of their replies" (Colombis 1983, 18). More importantly, in Colombis' view, the sample was hardly representative of the inhabitants of Chiaromonte that Banfield himself in chapter 3 of his book divided into seven social categories on the basis of occupation: landless labourers, peasant farmers, artisans, merchants, clerks, professionals, and landowners. At best, the result of the interviews could demonstrate the existence of "amoral familism" among some village peasants, but could not be construed to represent the Chiaromonte way of life (Colombis 1983, 19; see also Gribaudi 1993, 13–16).

Serious reservations were voiced about the questionnaire that Banfield used (Elefante 1989, 165–9). In fact, Colombis calls it a "methodological trap." The trap consisted in this: the choice of response among the three alternatives arrayed was between a non-familist solution and an amoral familist one. The peasants of Chiaromonte fell right into the trap, "the more so because [they were] totally unaware that what (they said would) be used to stick a pejorative label on them." For "Banfield did not provide for the possibility that the Chiaromontese is a familist but not in an amoral sense, *i.e.*, that he feels attachments to his own family and will do all he can for it, without being egoistically closed towards others" (Colombis 1983, 19; see also Gribaudi 1993). In sum, villagers can and do make a strong case for not paying attention to Banfield's thesis. They see it as a caricature of village life. They are puzzled as to why outsiders, including intellectuals in America as in Italy, have taken Banfield's account so seriously.

Listening to these Chiaromontesi, one is reminded of similar local reactions elsewhere – for example, the Ik of northeastern Uganda pointing to fatal inaccuracies in Colin M. Turnbull's description in *The Mountain People* (see Heine 1985; but cf., Elster's use of Turnbull in his 1989, 112); and Javanese Muslims relishing the fact that, for all his commitment to interpretive analysis and in-depth "thick description," Clifford Geertz's discussion in *The Religion of Java* was based on a profound misreading of Javanese social and religious categories, giving rise to its own literature (see citations in Hefner 1985, 3n1). The Chiaromontesi who brought Elefante's and Colombis' publications to my attention showed, however, no animosity toward Banfield. Some, in fact, remembered him fondly. All were solicitous about his health. No one seemed to have any of the melancholy usually ascribed to villagers by outsiders. The problem is that, whatever village relationships Banfield relied upon in 1954 and 1955 to construct his story, these relationships cannot be easily reconstructed and independently reexamined. Like the Basilicata of the same period (see Zuckerman 1997), the Chiaromonte of 1954–55 is gone. In addition, the credibility of Banfield's descriptive and explanatory account can be doubted on other grounds.

DISJUNCTIONS IN BANFIELD'S ANALYSIS

Banfield confronted – but did not resolve – the problem of reconciling the lack of voluntary efforts with his acknowledgment that "the [Chiaromonte] economy would not develop dramatically even if villagers cooperated like bees" (Banfield 1958 [1967], 157). He also did not resolve the problem of the lack of public action with his acknowledgment that the mayor and the communal council had nothing to do with solving local problems – that "even to buy an ashtray for the city hall requires approval from Potenza" (21).

For Banfield, the opposite of a society of amoral familists is one that has a significant element of "public spiritedness or even of 'enlightened' self-interest" (11). Again, Banfield proceeded in a puzzling way. While lamenting the lack of "public spirited persons" to act for the welfare of the community rather than for themselves alone, he conceded that, should a Chiaromonte man try to do something, it was unlikely that his action would make any difference: "In fact, the officials would be likely to resent what they would consider interference in their affairs" (19–20). He concluded that "a private citizen can do nothing" (85).

Thus, Banfield's initial question, What accounts for the absence of organized action in the face of pressing problems? (31) can better be rendered as follows, Under what conditions would we expect villagers to engage in voluntary collective action? Moreover, as Cattaneo suggested, the question is not Is there a local government? but Is local government so constituted as to facilitate collective efforts on behalf of the common interests shared by villagers?

Banfield did not raise these questions in his field work of 1954–55. He assumed that when individuals share a common interest they will automatically undertake common efforts to advance that interest. He further assumed that the structures of local government in Chiaromonte made no difference in the way that villagers related to one another, nor in the quantity and quality of public services supplied to villagers. From this vantage point, it becomes easier to understand how Banfield misconstructed local social and political reality.

Voluntary Collective Inaction

Banfield assumed that individuals would automatically engage in concerted action and that the inducements for such action would, to an important degree, be "unselfish" ("identification with the purpose of the organization," as if that were not related to individual well being) and "non material" (just "the intrinsic interest of the activity as a 'game,'" 86–7). Of the seventeen logical implications of amoral familism, only three follow from the predictive hypothesis and relate to the absence of voluntary initiative. They are:

  1 No one will further the interest of the group or community except as it is to his private advantage to do so.

  4 Organization (i.e., deliberately concerted action) will be very difficult to achieve and maintain ...

  11 There will be no leaders and no followers. No one will take the initiative in outlining a course of action and persuading others to embark upon it (except as it may be to his private advantage to do so) and, if one did offer leadership, the group would refuse it out of distrust. (83–4, 86, 97; italics removed)

Banfield used proposition 1 to account for the absence of "civic improvement associations, organized charities, and leading citizens who take initiative in public service"; proposition 4 for "the inability to create and maintain organization [which] is clearly of the greatest importance in retarding economic development in the region"; and proposition 11 for the lack of "a peasant leader to other peasants" and the lack of leadership positions of the doctor, the midwife, and the agricultural agent (84, 87, 97).

Mancur Olson's analysis of the logic of collective action (Olson 1968) has been subject to considerable criticisms and modifications since it first appeared. But if it has done nothing else, it has laid to rest the view held by Banfield that individuals sharing a common interest can automatically be expected to undertake collective action to advance that interest (see also M. Levi 1997b, 20). Both Banfield and Olson developed their respective inquiries on an assumption that has been somewhat problematic in Italian development, as this book has attempted to suggest: they both assumed the presence of a legal order that would not hinder joint voluntary efforts. This led Banfield to miss the obvious: "organized charities" in Chiaromonte did exist when he was there. A survey of enduring institutions of self-governance in the south reveals that organized charities or pious associations have been standard features of local life in most southern Italian towns over many centuries (Sabetti 1999a). Locally organized pious associations underwent profound transformations in the course of the second half of the nineteenth century as state laws increasingly incorporated voluntary organized charities into the public service system, leaving little or no room for local residents to act as "coproducers" of such voluntary local undertakings (see also Sabetti 1984, ch.5). I will return to this point toward the end of this chapter, and in the next.

At the same time, Banfield's benign view of organizations glosses critical issues whose validity goes beyond any peasant society. Analyses of organizations in action since Robert Michels' study of political parties in 1911 suggest that the pattern of political inequality inherent in collective decision making is apt to create serious splits between the interests of the leaders and those of the led, and radical disjunctions between organizational goals and organizational actions. Appeals to organizational goals from leadership positions can become, in the words of Philip Selznick (1966, ix), "protective covers behind which uncontrolled discretion can occur." When viewed against this backdrop, Banfield's propositions appear grounded in serious theoretical misconceptions and lead to a misconstruction of local issues.

In the immediate postwar period, the problem of voluntary collective action in Chiaromonte was compounded by 1) the presence of institutional arrangements that discouraged, if not impeded, citizens' action on matters of common concern (Rose 1961, esp. 169; Pinna 1971); and 2) the organization of most agricultural activities, which precluded large-scale joint efforts on a long-term basis (cf., Silverman 1968). Banfield referred to forestry, but gave little or no attention to the organization required to use and maintain the communal forest whose wood was then practically the only source of fuel for fire in most households. A cursory reading of archival records of the time and observations gathered from villagers during my 1994 site visit lead me to suggest that villagers seemed to have successfully avoided the problem of deforestation – and they could have done so only by some form of collective effort to govern the use of the communal woods. Banfield's own empirical observations are limited, but they can be used to arrive at different conclusions about the "political incapacity" of villagers.

The economy of Chiaromonte depended on agriculture and forestry. Two-thirds of its inhabitants earned a living by working on the land. In turn, merchants and artisans depended for their income on earnings from agriculture. To some extent, the doctor, the pharmacist, and the two priests also depended on the earnings of the Chiaromonte land workers; with the lawyer, they owned small amounts of land, which were usually rented out to peasants. But with the exception of the lawyer, these were people who, together with the school, tax, and police officials, received a monthly salary from the state. The largest landowner was a diplomat who went to the village to collect his rents from farms leased to tenants (Banfield [1958] 1967, 47–9).

The land was stony, steep, and poorly watered. Twelve per cent of the Chiaromonte territory was unproductive. About 80 per cent of the farms consisted of holdings of less than fifteen acres; they occupied less cultivated land than some ninety farms that were fifteen acres or more. Most of the large farms were in several pieces scattered over the territory, a division that resulted from the law of inheritance. Wheat was a principal crop in the early 1950s. In a normal year, the value of farm production hardly exceeded the cost of production. Soil erosion, the gradual depletion of the fertile soil, and natural calamities had reduced the value of the land (45, 51–2, 56–7, 63, 105–6, 168). At the same time, Banfield found "the population ... supported by the reduced resources to be slightly larger than it was a generation ago" (60).

In 1954–55, according to Banfield, there was not sufficient work for farm labourers. An "upper income labourer" like Carlo Prato "seldom knew a week ahead whether he would find work" (53). A landowner was dependent upon a peasant to work his holdings and pay rent; but the landowner had a large labour surplus from which to select replacements. A labourer, on the other hand, depended on the landowner for his very survival. The division of labour and the inequalities of conditions among the various residents in the village in 1954–55 had created a system of interdependence that was markedly asymmetrical. "Artisans, merchants, clerks, landowners, and professionals all have opportunities of one kind or another to take the offensive against each other and against the peasant; they are 'exploiters' because they have the possibility of being such. The peasant, especially the landless one, is altogether without power" (118). And Banfield had noted earlier: "Frequently the worker is prevented by self-interest from taking his case to the *carabinieri* Marshal. He cannot afford to be on bad terms with the employer: it is better to be cheated than to be deprived of employment altogether" (90). For a landless worker to raise a family in such circumstances was indeed "a hard and unremitting struggle" (104).

The struggle was compounded by the problem of dealing with interdependencies through time in attaining intergenerational transfer of income from the adult to the young in one generation and from adult to the aged in another. After the collapse or destruction of local lay confraternities and other local mutual aid societies (which Banfield ignored completely) by the time of the Fascist regime and before the advent of social security and health schemes and the construction of a hospital by the 1970s, Chiaromonte families were required to provide for all intergenerational transfers of income and to care for sick relatives. Thus, not surprising, at the time when Banfield was in the village, he noted that villagers feared the consequences that would follow from a premature death, from leaving one's children "on the street," and from not being cared for in one's old age. Landless workers especially were aware that no matter how hard they worked, they and their children could not get ahead; that they lived in a culture in which it was important to be *civile*, yet they were not (64–5; cf., Liebow 1967, 57–65); that the possibilities to make a good living existed in northern Italy and North America, but they could not easily go there. Villagers appeared so respectful of the law that there was a sense in which, as a result of an anti-internal-emigration law dating from Fascist times, they felt legally trapped in Chiaromonte (Banfield [1958] 1967, 58–9, esp. 59n9).

Under these conditions, Chiaromontesi, could not "afford the luxury of charity, which is giving others more than their due, or even of justice, which is giving them their due" (110). Banfield did not, as noted earlier, carefully pursue the issue of charity, but he did notice some cooperation and justice. When labourers and peasants were out of work, they could always get credit from merchants and artisans without charge for a few weeks or months. And when the merchants could not give more credit, "the charity of relatives, friends, and neighbors [was] then the stricken family's only hope" (57). Whenever they could, peasants exchanged labour and made each other loans of bread and cash. They knew they could rely on each other; they valued friendship (115, 126, 130).

Public Collective Inaction

As we saw in chapters 2–4, amid changes from the Bourbon to the Savoy monarchy, and from Fascist to republican Italy, the underlying design principles affecting the organization and operation of communes like Chiaromonte remained invariant. Under these conditions, choices about basic policies and the availability of different organizational arrangements for pursuing developmental opportunities continued to reside only with members of the ruling class – in essence, a form of "development by administration" (Loveman 1975, 1976).

To what extent then did the conduct of communal affairs under this administrative arrangement lead to the realization of the "common good," or lead to the opposite effect? As Alessandro Pizzorno observed in his response to Banfield, "even if the [Chiaromontesi] busied themselves with public improvements, the officials would not listen to them, and they would have every right not to do so" (1971, 91). Unfortunately, Pizzorno was more interested in developing an argument about the (presumed) historical marginality of Chiaromonte; he did not examine Banfield's logical implications as they related to the conduct of communal affairs.

Of the seventeen logical implications that Banfield derived from his predictive hypothesis, propositions 2, 3, 5, 6, 7, 8, 9, 10, 13, 14, 15, 16, and 17 refer explicitly to office holders, political parties, and legal relationships. As we can now appreciate, those hypotheses derive more from constitutional and institutional arrangements that regulate local government and party activities than from the "ethos" of villagers and local culture. In fact, Cattaneo, Ferrara, and a host of other analysts like Napoleone Colajanni and Luigi Einaudi discussed in chapters 2, 4, 6 and 7, would have readily recognized them as empirical statements describing, first, the structure of communal organization and, then, the consequences that result from it for the conduct of local affairs. For instance:

2 Only officials will concern themselves with public affairs, for only they are paid to do so. For a private citizen to take a serious interest in a public problem will be regarded as abnormal and even improper ...

3 There will be few checks on officials, for checking on officials will be the business of other officials only ...

5 Office-holders, feeling no identification with the purposes of the organization, will not work harder than is necessary to keep their places or ... to earn promotion. Similarly, professional people and educated people generally will lack a sense of mission or calling. Indeed, official position and special training will be regarded by their possessors as weapons to be used against others for private advantage ...

9 The claim of any person or institution to be inspired by zeal for public rather than private advantage will be regarded as fraud ...

14 The voter will place little confidence in the promise of the parties. He will be apt to use his ballot to pay for favors already received (assuming, of course, that more are in prospect) rather than for favors which are merely promised. (Banfield [1958] 1967, 85, 86, 89, 95, 99; italics removed)

At the same time, it is doubtful that proposition 6 applies only to Chiaromonte villagers acting in the institutional context of postwar Italy: "the law will be disregarded when there is no reason to fear punishment. Therefore individuals will not enter into agreements ... unless it is likely that the law will be enforced and unless the cost of securing enforcement will not be so great as to make the undertaking unprofitable" (90).

Banfield did not consider the following: What possibilities are available to human beings within structures of government where only officials are presumed to be concerned with public affairs, where the business of checking on them is left to distant officials, and where villagers cannot make or enforce any claims on them? This question is not unlike that raised by Magistrate Falcone when he wondered why mafiosi are compelled to devise for themselves criminal careers in order to survive with dignity. Together these questions sharpen our sense of what individual and collective results can be expected to follow from such a system of governance.

I would argue that what prevented Banfield from raising the question is related to the serious disjunctions that exist between his empirical observations and his interpretation. These disjunctions have to do with an unstated premise of his work, namely, that the rules of the political order and the configuration of institutional arrangements either have no incentive structures or are not critical determinants of human values and behaviour. Institutional variables were presumed to be either value-free or simply mechanical devices for translating ideas and values – the will of the modern prince – into practice. By contrast, the argument advanced in this volume, and earlier by Cattaneo and others, is based on the assumption that institutions are critical formative variables in policy development and determinants of human behaviour.

A counterargument might take the following form. Even if we recognize that Banfield seriously misconstrued the facts on the ground in Chiaromonte, is it not the case that all Italians and all Italian communes work within similar institutional arrangements for the pursuit of individual and joint opportunities in the market economy and the public sector? If so, how do we explain differentials in individual and organizational behaviour across the north-south divide? Are really small villages pretty much the same everywhere across that divide?

We furnished an initial answer to these questions in chapter 4 in the discussion of how the system worked at the communal level in Bologna and Naples during the postwar period and at the regional level in light of the work of Robert D. Putnam. As we saw, the course and timing of institutional arrangements, together with constraints specific to particular contexts, including size, are critical in understanding how a similar system actually works in different cities and regions with different developmental experience. The ecological conditions of the Italian peninsula and islands is not one of uniformity, while, unfortunately, the mind set that goes with general statutory enactments and their administrative complements is one of the "omniscient observer" oriented to universalities and uniformities. We shall return to these aspects in some depth in the next chapter. Suffice it here to note three points that any counterargument needs to take into account.

First, there is a dearth of studies dealing with village politics in northern Italy in the same way that Banfield tackled Chiaromonte in the 1950s. However, the evidence gathered by Norman E. Cohen for a study of village politics in Tuscany identified the governance of communal affairs as the major impediment to public concerted action. As a result, villagers in that Tuscan community tended to withdraw from political activities, to describe all politicians as "bandits" and to call for "a strong leader who will do away with political bickering and politicians" (N. Cohen 1968, 186–7). Robert H. Evans's political history of a Venetian village revealed similar impediments to communal initiative (Evans 1976). Gabriella Gribaudi has suggested that similar dynamics could be observed in some Alpine villages (Gribaudi 1993, 14).

Second, the disjunctions between Banfield's culturalist explanation and his empirical observations take on renewed importance if we recall the villagers' reactions to Banfield's portrayal, discussed earlier. We briefly consider Chiaromonte history below to anticipate a third point, which will be developed at some length in the next chapter: differential behaviours under the same institutional arrangements cannot be explained unless one introduces the rich historical diversity that characterizes particular towns and regions of Italy. This, Banfield and Putnam were prevented from doing by the very method of analysis they used. I shall deal with Putnam in the next chapter. Let me turn here to what Banfield missed.

CHIAROMONTE IN HISTORY

Fieldwork conducted in the summer of 1994 leads me to affirm that there is a considerable amount of empirical evidence from Chiaromonte history that fits neither Banfield's description of community life nor his theory. Far from being cut off from history, as the argument of historical marginality would lead us to believe, Chiaromonte was, as early as medieval times, an important agricultural, government, and religious centre for the area.

The feudal lord of Chiaromonte was a grand peer of the Neapolitan realm; successive holders of that title had a hand in governing the realm itself. The recent study by Tommaso Astarita (1992) on the continuity of feudal power in one part of Lucania, and the collection of essays on "good government in Spanish Naples" put together by Antonio Calabria and John A. Marino (1990) seriously question the prevailing orthodoxies about feudalism and Spanish Naples. They point to a different, more productive way of knowing about the south. We shall expand on this different way of knowing in some depth in the next chapter. One problem remains, however: there is no comparative historical analysis of the transformations of the Chiaromonte political economy. By 1994, the community still served as a kind of district centre for several villages: it had a judicial court (*pretura*) and jail, a land registry and tax office, and a building which had earlier served as a diocesan seminary and seat for a bishopric.

Even a cursory examination of the historical record in the public archives at Potenza and Rome is sufficient to realize that Chiaromonte has had, in its long history, the usual panoply of voluntary community organizations that can be found in most villages and towns throughout the south and the north. Such enduring local ventures ranged from mutual aid societies, lay congregations of men and women, wheat banks, and cooperatives before Fascism to more recent farm workers' organizations and rural cooperatives. The more problematic aspects of these efforts relate to the abolition of feudalism in the first half of the nineteenth century (Archivio di stato, Intendenza di Basilicata; Archivio di Stato, Prefettura; see also Elefante 1988, 1989; Ivone 1979). We still need to know what happened in the second half of the nineteenth century to the enduring community associations from the *ancien régime*, and to the workers' association reported to be operating in Chiaromonte by 1880 (Ivone 1979, 103). If amoral familism is truly the moral basis of that southern town, how did successive generations of ordinary people in Chiaromonte, as presumed amoral familists or rational egoists, manage to overcome the logic of collective inaction and the oligarchical tendencies inherent in organizational life?

While we still do not know why some community efforts succeeded while others failed, one aspect of the history of Chiaromonte is clear enough: the village has had many long-lasting forms of concerted action among the common people, and these involve both success and failure (cf., Robert Wade 1988).

Banfield's predictive hypothesis cannot account for the presence of secondary associations and community organizations in the course of Chiaromonte history. As chapter 9 makes clear, this problem afflicts Putnam's analysis as well. When residing in the village, Banfield did notice some concern for charity, cooperation, and justice among villagers (Banfield [1958] 1967, 57, 115, 130). Unfortunately, he did not carefully explore the presence of horizontal bonds of reciprocity, trust and the ad hoc mutual aid and exchange of services among neighbours that are very much part of the local culture and ethos. These can be easily observed if a researcher knows how and what to look for.

Such contemporary village norms are not of recent origin. They are part of the cultural patrimony of previous generations of villagers. But let there be no misunderstanding. There is no attempt here to create a golden past. For example, problems of commanding the services of impartial government officials and of sustaining existing agreements against new demands or unilateral cancellations of contracts appear to have been serious in Chiaromonte history. But a perusal of archival documents and notarial papers points to the substantial trust and hope that ordinary Chiaromontesi had in written agreements (even when they could only barely sign their names with a cross), in negotiation and the law, when conflict has to be transformed into a context of ideas. As we shall see in the next chapter, norms of trust, charity, hope, justice, solidarity, and cooperation are as much a feature of the history of other southern towns as they are of Chiaromonte.

Strong indications allow the conjecture that the moral basis of such norms in Chiaromonte is traceable to what the Roman Catholic Church teaches about "Christian optimism" (Elefante 1988). *Pace* Carlo Levi (1963), Christ did not really stop at Eboli after all! But community affairs are always more complex than they appear to outside observers. A more recent event in Chiaromonte challenges the descriptive and explanatory power of amoral familism from another direction: in the 1974 referendum on divorce, almost half of the Chiaromonte voters (48.7 per cent) voted in favour.

CONCLUSION

There is no question that Banfield's book dealt with matters of great practical importance with considerable care, but our search for the real Montegrano suggests that his fit of theory with observed facts is not fully consistent. Also, the observed facts are superficial renditions of village life, and more is excluded than included about the structure of village life and relationships in the 1950s. Equally, for all his emphasis on voluntary efforts, Banfield failed to see them in his own time and in the rich history of Chiaromonte.

In Banfield's view, Chiaromontesi in the 1950s were "prisoners of their family-centred ethos" (Banfield [1958] 1967, 155). If indeed the Chiaromontesi of Banfield's fieldwork were "prisoners," an alternative explanation advanced here is that they were prisoners more of the institutional rules that governed their agricultural and communal activities than of their culture or ethos. In documenting the problems of translating intentions into outcomes of postwar policies in the south, a Swedish scholar and one-time associate of Danilo Dolci in western Sicily, Eyvind Hytten, reached similar conclusions (Hytten 1969, 13–36). Hytten went on to note then that "the raw material for a social awakening [in the south] is not missing. What is missing are the instruments and the institutions that could enhance it in a proper way, without exploitation from any quarter, left or right" (Hytten 1969, 64). But, as Cattaneo and Ferrara observed more than a century ago, designing institutions for good government requires first of all a resolution of the crisis of understanding about the relationship between principles and forms of government. The crisis of understanding is a chief source of disorientation for Banfield and those who relied on his analysis. This chapter has sought to emphasize that Banfield's culturalist explanation was more of a hindrance than a help in making sense of community problems in Chiaromonte and in understanding how to explain differences between preferred solutions and actual behaviour of public institutions. Difficulties in explanatory schemes and in the narrative form they take should not be passed on as the failure of ordinary people to play their assigned roles. Social scientists do grave harm when they misconstruct the social and political reality of one locality and then generalize that misconstruction to an entire area or country. This chapter has, I hope, removed "amoral familism" as a source of misunderstanding. The next chapter seeks to remove other more general sources of disorientation accompanying the resurgence of culturalist explanations.

9 Path Dependence, Civic Culture, and Differential Government Performance

Robert D. Putnam's *Making Democracy Work: Civic Traditions in Modern Italy* (1993) sought to account for differential performance of regional governments in terms of culture, and for systemic variance between north and south in terms of the medieval legacy of civic norms and networks. At a time when the study of comparative politics seemed increasingly to privilege cross-national analysis, *Making Democracy Work* stood out as an important reminder that "comparative political research of the broadest philosophical and theoretical implications can be executed within a single country" (LaPalombara 1993, 550). The study has been hailed as a "stunning breakthrough in political culture research" (Laitin 1995, 171), contributing to "a renaissance of political culture" beyond the Italian peninsula in ways that Banfield's work did not (e.g., Jackman and Miller 1996). Putnam's work made other contributions to comparative inquiry. It brought the study of Italian politics "back in" and broadened it, precisely at a time when favourite Italian research topics among comparativists – such as leftist parties and national trade unions – no longer seemed to have the old currency. *Making Democracy Work* further suggested that, contrary to the view often expressed, Italy's past need not always be viewed as a burden. Indeed, it was the use of the past to explain differential effectiveness in contemporary regional governments that made Putnam's study an important work. It is, in turn, path dependence analysis that sharply distinguishes *Making Democracy Work* from its earlier Italian-language version (Putnam, Leonardi, and Nanetti 1985), adds more lustre to the former, and endows

Putnam's argument with a strong sense of intellectual closure and a seemingly flawless protective belt.

Putnam stated some unremarkable findings when he reported that the medieval monarchical and republican regimes worked differently, that modern public institutions work better in some parts of Italy than in others, and that the south has fewer expressions of voluntary joint or collective efforts than does the north. But for Putnam's explanation of these findings to hold, three things must be true. The first is that the Italian regional experiment was a "natural" experiment, to be approached in the same way that "a botanist might study plant development by measuring the growth of *genetically identical seeds* sown in different plots" (Putnam 1993, 7, emphasis added). The second is that patterns of civic culture best explain differential effectiveness in regions. The third is that these modern social patterns are plainly traceable to the monarchical and republican regimes of medieval times.

One objective of this chapter is to show that neither logic nor evidence bears out such an interpretation. The regional experiment was hardly a "natural" experiment. Patterns of civic culture do not explain all of the story about regional government performance. As hinted in chapters 4 and 8, differential behaviours in different regions cannot be explained unless one introduces the rich historical diversity that characterizes each region – and this Putnam was prevented from doing by the very method of analysis he used. The other, more general objective of the chapter, then, is to show that the substantive claim about how development proceeds explains why some of Putnam's findings are unsurprising and the great majority of his other findings are either misleading or wrong (cf., Bagnasco 1994; Goldberg 1996; M. Levi 1996; Lupo 1993a, 1993b; Tarrow 1996).

To be sure, not all the problems in *Making Democracy Work* are attributable to the assumptions of path dependence. For example, Putnam began his inquiry with sketches of Bari and Bologna, the regional capitals of Apulia and Emilia-Romagna respectively. The stark contrast is an effective literary device. The problem is that his story does not match the facts on the ground, insofar as they can be independently verified; Putnam's narrative misleads readers who have to rely on the author for a description of those cities and for civic practices throughout Italy (Putnam 1993, 5–6).[1] It seems petty to point out inaccurate and exaggerated small details – minutiae in a rich story – but such details assume importance only because Putnam so effectively employed them to paint a picture that is not quite true to life.

It is my contention in this chapter that a path dependence *forma mentis* or mindset goes a long way in accounting for the flaws that disable *Making Democracy Work*. The strength of path dependence as a substantive claim about how development proceeds consists in combining fortuitous contingencies of an initial phase with a deterministic logic concerning the subsequent process – both people and their behaviours are locked in as a consequence of their past history (e.g., Hodgson 1991). In the first section of the chapter, I shall point to the problems that path dependence analysis created for Putnam's understanding of the medieval legacy; in the second, I shall advance the argument that institutions more modern than the medieval ones Putnam considered have shaped the civic society and constitute a south different from what Putnam and others took for granted. From this vantage point, it should be easier to see that the creation of regional governments and differences in regional government performance have been deeply misunderstood. Above all, I shall argue that Putnam has drawn the wrong lessons from history and from the creation and performance of regional government. This is not to suggest that there are no north-south differences, but rather to point out that differentials in development remain poorly understood.

THE MEDIEVAL LEGACY

Putnam's inquiry into the historic roots of contemporary problems is very much part of the tradition of Italian scholarship and public discourse. Perhaps one of the best-known practitioners in this tradition is Carlo Cattaneo, the Milanese publicist with the reputation of an uncompromising Risorgimento radical democrat whom we met in chapter 3. Cattaneo and Putnam share an interest in civic community and social capital. In Cattaneo's 1858 essays on "The City as an Organizational Principle for Understanding the Course of Italian History," he used the legacy of medieval Italy to place in sharp relief the Italian civic tradition, to argue against the creation of a unitary, monarchical regime, and to press for a federal, republican solution to the making of modern Italy in the 1860s (Cattaneo [1858] 1957, 2:383–437). The title of Putnam's co-authored 1985 book on the Italian regions, *La pianta e le radici*, was taken from Cattaneo's characterization of liberty as a plant of many roots; moreover, several passages from Cattaneo's work grace the frontispiece of the book, fittingly published under the aegis of the Cattaneo Research Institute of Bologna, a prestigious independent social science research centre. A consideration of how Cattaneo approached the past clarifies what is new and what is old in Putnam's thesis and where the two analysts differ.

Writing in 1839, in an essay setting out what became a lifelong research program, Cattaneo noted the challenge awaiting those interested in issues of political development: how to navigate between the doctrines of extreme rationalism of the past two centuries and the deterministic doctrines of his own time so as to understand how particular institutions emerge; how they change over time; and how institutional arrangements affect individual and institutional behaviours as well as development potentials more generally. The pressing task, he stressed, was to construct a "public science or economy" incorporating history, institutions, culture, and individuals – not as blind instruments of a particular time and culture, but as beings capable through their actions of destroying, derailing, or refashioning the heredity of the past (Cattaneo [1839a] 1960, 1:95–142). In the end, and after more than twenty volumes, Cattaneo did not quite succeed in fashioning this new "public science." He seldom had the time, or the inclination, to return to his ideas and develop them fully, so, for example, he did not pursue the implication of his (and his mentor, Gian Domenico Romagnosi's) insights about transaction analysis. But his dynamic view of the world and his appreciation that "the state" may be nothing but rules manipulated for public and private ends sharply differentiates his logic of inquiry from Putnam's. Cattaneo also shared little of Putnam's benign view of government.

As we saw in chapter 3, Cattaneo argued that the most productive way to make sense of the vicissitudes of more than two thousand years of recorded history of Italy is to examine the question of self-government as an empirical and theoretical question. Thus the 1858 essays on the Italian civic tradition can be read at different levels: the city as an historical community; as a manifestation of the struggle for self-governance over time; and as a conceptual variable on the basic human reality (*consorzio umano*) identifying "democracy" with the universality of the local community, not with parliamentary government or even representative assemblies.

Cattaneo went back to ancient times – to the civic culture of *Magna Graecia* in the south, and of the Etruscan communities in the centre and the north. He identified several periods in the history of Italian cities; drew no sharp differences between city and countryside, a feature of Italian life that has sharply differentiated its rural population from northern European counterparts; and ended his account with the city republics in the fourteenth century. Unlike Putnam, Cattaneo identified characteristics of civic traditions *throughout* Italy: the role of local community in the historic memory and consciousness of people; the importance of municipal institutions; and the cities as self-governing, law making entities adapted to local ecological niches.

As we saw, Cattaneo credited the municipal institutions in the south for keeping alive remnants of civic life in Italy after the fall of the Roman Empire, when municipal institutions had become nearly extinct in the north. Though the portrayal is generally considered accurate as far as it goes, it stops precisely when northern communes were declining as free cities.

Cattaneo drew attention to two dissimilar sources of ruptures that had roughly similar results: the creation of a medieval kingdom in the south; and the insufficiency of city republics in the north. The position of southern cities in the new political economy changed for the worse. Local communities, including the free cities of Amalfi and Naples (the latter, one of the oldest Greek cities), were now subordinated to the extraneous and adverse principle of domination. Soon they became powerless, servile, and dull, while their inhabitants became estranged and indifferent to the place in which they lived.

Cattaneo equally suggested the insufficiency of the northern civic tradition for the constitution of a self-governing society. He attributed this insufficiency to three factors that have been, better documented since his own time: 1) the opportunities provided by governmental institutions for the rise of self-perpetuating local oligarchies; 2) the practical absence of overlapping arrangements among city republics (i.e., a federal or polycentric system of governance); and 3) more importantly, the intellectual failure to conceptualize the possibility of federal arrangements. These factors led to the breakdown of fiduciary relationships among the people of communes, the transformation of differences into factional struggles, despotic governments (*signorie*) and, eventually, foreign domination and conquest. By the fourteenth century, deep ruptures in civic culture had occurred in varying degrees and, and for different reasons, throughout Italy.

Cattaneo and Putnam share a particular retrospective view of "feudalism" and both tend to use a very wide brush to paint their canvas. Contrary to what Cattaneo suggested, Amalfi continued to have a rich civic life well after it was incorporated into the medieval kingdom. The Amalfitan Table continued, well after the eleventh century, to regulate southern commercial practices and was freely adopted by northern city republics – not a small case of self-enforcing rules prevailing throughout the peninsula in spite of political divisions (Del Treppo and Leone 1977; see also Greif 1998; Sabetti 1999a). Putnam's method of analysis led him to exaggerate more than Cattaneo and to lock people and their behaviours into predetermined games of life for centuries. This absolved Putnam of the responsibility of looking at how and which history matters over time. Thus, Putnam presents us with sharply different political consequences over a long period: in the north the people were citizens – in the south, subjects; authority was dispersed in the north, monopolized by the king in the south; horizontal relations in one, vertical social hierarchy in the other; collaboration, mutual assistance, civic obligations and trust versus hierarchy, domination, mistrust, and *incivisme*. Whereas collective life in north Italy was viewed as almost always healthy and strong, in the south collective life was viewed as blighted for a thousand years and more (Putnam 1993, esp. 162–3). This characterization not only overstated the case, but also did several other things badly.

First, it endowed pre-1860 southern kings (or their respective viceroys) with monopoly powers they seldom had, in theory or practice. The Neapolitan parliament, while tamed to servility and silence, fell into desuetude only by 1642, without, however, losing the hold that it had in running the Naples city government (*Seggi*). Indeed, between 1642 and 1734, when Naples acquired its own Bourbon king, viceregal authority was compelled to come to terms with the *Seggi*, which functioned as a kind of new Neapolitan parliament. The Sicilian parliament, though weakened in its organization and powers, stubbornly clung to the last vestiges of authority in matters of taxation and its claim of representing the Sicilian nation (i.e., the baronial class) before the monarch as late as 1812.

Hence, whereas the Neapolitan aristocracy became a court nobility only after 1734, if at all (Astarita 1992; Galasso 1982) the Sicilian aristocracy that controlled parliament retained some of the functions inherent in the prerogatives of rule into the nineteenth century. The parliamentary barons' claim that they were "associates of the sovereign" in governing Sicily was no empty boast. Many different Sicilian parliamentary barons managed, over time, to be successful agrarian capitalists. Thus, just as the king's monopoly powers were checked by parliamentary barons, so the monopoly powers of parliamentary barons were checked by dynastic, community and market requirements that applied to the fiefs as political, social, and economic ventures. Both monarchs and parliamentary lords faced common constraints: the entrepreneurial skills required to manage each "family firm" and residual earnings could not always be passed on as an inheritance. The history of Sicilian fiefs as capitalist enterprises engaged in the production and sale of grain in Sicily and Europe as late as the seventeenth century – "the golden age of baronial jurisdiction" – has not yet been written, but one thing seems clear: the history of baronial jurisdiction is not simply the history of exploitative relationships of rulers to ruled, ruinous lordships, and antiquated agrarian economies (see also Astarita 1992, 108–58; Epstein 1992). A concern with how people create and maintain efficiency-enhancing and inefficiency-prone institutions led Cattaneo to suggest the need to compare the evolution of Norman institutions in England and Sicily in a set of notes on Britain, written in English around 1834 and published only in Murray 1959). The insight that the route to modern representative institutions in south Italy had the potential of passing through feudal institutions was one that Putnam's explanatory scheme did not allow him to pursue.

Second, and not surprising, Putnam's characterization of southern Italy tends to fuse long periods of time and to obscure the norms of generalized reciprocity and the network of civic engagement that could be found in the rich variety of self-governing collective efforts at the neighbourhood level and among guilds and mutual aid societies in the different southern cities, towns, and villages under varying political-economic regimes (Cochrane 1986; Sabetti 1999a).

Third, the characterization of perennial exploitation glosses over successive, sometimes successful efforts at overthrowing exploitation and dependence in the larger context in which ordinary people lived and worked. John A. Marino's research on pastoral economics in the Kingdom of Naples (1988) brings to life additional problems with Putnam's argument. Marino studied the *dogana di Foggia*, (Foggia customs house, 1447–1806) – the Neapolitan equivalent to the better-known Castilian *mesta* (guild) – located in Capitanata, the most fertile region of Apulia. It was through the Apulian *mesta*, representing some 4,300 square kilometres of winter pasture in one of the largest plains in the Italian peninsula, that the Kingdom of Naples became a major supplier of raw wool to Europe. Wool production was critical to the internal revenue of the kingdom and, until the early nineteenth century, the sheep customs house of Foggia served as one of the most important financial institutions of the state. Many worlds converged at Foggia, and their extraordinary permutations were ably traced by Marino in his analysis of three hundred and fifty years of continuity and change. I draw on his work only to emphasize facets of southern history generally missed.

The Foggia customs house received its definitive charter around 1447, but pastoralism and its accompanying council of grazers or *mesta* charged with the task of regulating matters of common concern in southern Italy as in the former Papal States (where they were part of the customs house of the pastures) can be traced back to ancient times. Grazier associations in Capitanata, in particular, antedate the feudal state. As Marino put it: "The sheep owners' organization ... was an indigenous invention to establish and enforce a set of norms to allow for continued economic cooperation among the pastoral population. From the Southern European transhumant cousins – Mesta and dogana – the centralized medieval state incorporated those already existent sheep owners' institutions as partners in the royal plan to pacify and profit from the marginal zone" (Marino 1988, 114). Class conflict among rich and poor sheep owners did exist; but what emerges from the historical record of the parliament of graziers is the rich associational life that allowed the graziers to put aside or resolve their differences and to confront their common enemies together, be they doganal officers or merchants. "Thus, the sheep customshouse of Foggia developed a model for participatory democracy from below – even within the hierarchical world of an Old Regime monarchy" (Marino 1988, 10). Marino made it evident that horizontal as well as vertical bonds of solidarity and relationships together with a fairly high degree of self-government did exist in one of the most important sectors of the political economy of the Kingdom of Naples for several centuries. Bonds of fellowship also extended to others: "ongoing works of mercy were part of the [graziers' organization's] pious duties and associational responsibilities" (Marino 1988, 111).

There was at least one important difference between the common people of Apulia and the common people living in central and northern *signorie*. Whereas commoners in the north did not have the right to bear arms, for fear they would cause disorder or rebellion, the graziers on the Apulian plain did have such a right, one of the oldest and dearest rights of citizenship. So what in the south was the right of the lowest of social classes, was in the north the prerogative of the highest of social classes and their retainers.[2]

In fact, one would never know this from reading almost any of the English-language texts on the "southern question," because Marino's history goes against the grain of the prevalent strands of the reigning orthodoxies about the south. In fairness, one would hardly know of it even by reading such Italian classic texts as Benedetto Croce's *The History of the Kingdom of Naples* (1925). This highlights a serious historiographical problem in Putnam's analysis. He used an approach that did not enable him to sense the antifeudal (and anti-Spanish) bias that has marked much of the literature on south Italy since the eighteenth century. If one is prepared to go beyond the vista interposed by this literature, as many others have done in the past thirty years (see review essay, Cochrane 1986), it is possible to discover an extraordinary quantity and variety of documents on civic traditions and the pursuit of collective or joint economic and political opportunities. This documentation suggests that, below the power of alternating monarchies, successive viceroys, and self-perpetuating oligarchies, there were, in the cities, towns, and villages of southern Italy, vestiges of communal self-governance that, although half-destroyed, were still distinguishable over the entire history of the Kingdom of Naples or the Two Sicilies. These vestiges represented small-scale *civitates*, or civil societies – dense patterns of social assets involving collaboration, mutual assistance, civic obligation and trust.

Civic norms of trust in the law, collaborations, and obligation were as much a feature of the history of southern communes as they were of the history of city republics – including the history of Banfield's Chiaromonte and Putnam's Pietrapertosa, if their notarial archives mean anything. Also, Paolo Grossi offers a rich documentary database in his important 1977 work on collective property, available in English since 1981 (Grossi 1981, 1992).

Unintentionally, Putnam presented evidence that undermined his own claim about how development proceeds. In chapter 55 of book one of Niccolò Machiavelli's *Discourses*, Putnam found what he said he might term the "iron law of civic community." Machiavelli, Putnam noted, has "a passage of remarkable relevance to my own task of understanding institutional success and failure" (Putnam 1993, 132). Putnam would have Machiavelli say that in provinces like Naples "there has never arisen any republic or any political life, for men born in such conditions are entirely inimical to any form of civic government. In provinces thus organized no attempt to set up a republic could possibly succeed" (Machiavelli 1970, 246). But what are the provinces that Putnam said Machiavelli regarded "like Naples"? This question goes to the heart of Putnam's argument.

Putnam failed to indicate that these provinces are the Papal States, Emilia-Romagna, and Lombardy – that is, provinces identified by Putnam as having an almost unbreakable civic tradition were identified by Machiavelli as having such an uncivic tradition that no attempt to set up a republic or "good government" could possibly succeed there! Typical of Machiavelli to think that good or virtuous citizens could be found only in Tuscany (and, possibly, Venice). But the main problem is that what Putnam was inclined to call Machiavelli's "iron law of civic community" is not supported by Machiavelli's own evidence. If Machiavelli was correct in his empirical observation, then he was mistaken in his "iron law" – and Putnam was mistaken in giving Machiavelli's observation the standing he did, since it contradicts the claim it was mustered to support.

To sum up, Putnam was correct in drawing attention to two distinctive types of political regimes in early medieval Italy and to the negative consequences of monarchical government. Cattaneo's work shows that this thesis is an old one. What is new in Putnam is, unfortunately, the fruit of some profound misunderstandings. A path dependence perspective prevented Putnam from considering 1) that the roots of civic cultures throughout Italy go much deeper than medieval times; 2) that civic traditions were not entirely extinguished in the south by the creation of the medieval kingdom, just as they were not entirely extinguished in the north by the dissolution of city republics; and 3) that the civic practices of any area are more fluctuating than the logic of path dependence would lead us to believe. Cattaneo's work shows more of an awareness that the interplay of complex factors over time cannot be accommodated by particular "iron laws," be they simplistic renderings of history or deterministic conceptions of development.

The work of Cattaneo and Marino can be brought together to advance an alternative argument about north-south differentials: grazers on the Apulian plain and water appropriators on the Lombard plain of the Po River operated *terra terra* with roughly similar norms and networks of civic engagement, but the critical difference in their exigencies of life and work had to do with the megaconstraints imposed by geography (earthquake areas in the south), economics, and politics (see also Epstein 1992). These larger constraints, more than civil society or civic norms and networks, are the keys to understanding differentials in development. Some of these constraints, such as geography, are constants; others are variables, and to these I specifically turn next to pinpoint their historical legacy for contemporary Italy.

A DIFFERENT KIND OF HISTORICAL LEGACY

If the medieval legacy portrayed in *Making Democracy Work* cannot provide the appropriate historical context for understanding regional government performance, which history matters then? I suggest that what matters in the history of Italian political economy are the growth of governmental institutions since the eighteenth century and the enduring presence of ecclesial infrastructures in civil society. Whereas the basic logic of governmental arrangements generally sought to dissolve local civic assets in the south, the basic logic of ecclesial arrangements sought to build them up. While church-affiliated organizations have a long history, they ceased to be the only major network in civil society by the 1890s. The growth of autonomous workers' solidarity leagues, not long after national governments stopped putting them down, suggests that horizontal norms and networks of solidarity can emerge under conditions that many analysts have steadfastly, and mistakenly, described as *culturally* infertile terrain for such norms and networks. I thus advance another argument: institutions of political economy more modern than the ones Putnam considers have shaped the civic society and constitute a south different from the north, and from the south Putnam and others have taken for granted.

The Role of Governmental Institutions

The growth of governmental institutions in Italy involved two transition periods; each transition period in turn shaped the subsequent structure of political and economic life. The cumulative impact or historical legacy of these transitions went into making a new south.

The first transition period was brought about by the Enlightenment, which Sicilian, Neapolitan, Lombard, and Tuscan intellectuals and statesmen (often one and the same) shared with their counterparts elsewhere in Europe. Italy gave the general clash between "utopia and reform" its own colour (Venturi 1971), as we noted in chapter 2.

When allowance is made for the constraining presence or liberating absence of foreign rule, the differential impact of the intellectual, political, and economic forces of the Enlightenment among the Italian states, including the Papal States, can be summarized as follows: the more abstract the ideas, the more sweeping the attempts to liquidate the heredity of the past, the least likely their prospect of success, as in the case of the South; the more practical the ideas, the more "marginal" the changes, the higher their prospect of success, as in the case of the Papal States, Tuscany and Lombardy. Sicily stood in relation to Naples almost exactly as Lombardy stood in relation to Austria. What explains the policy variance, then, given the fact that these regimes were both autocratic in nature and that "elite public opinion" in both Lombardy and Sicily favoured reforms?

Two critical variations explain the different attempts at reform. Drawing on Margaret Levi's conceptual elaboration (1988), the first variation was the relative bargaining power, transaction costs, and discount rates of Lombard and Sicilian "rulers" vis-à-vis their respective viceroys: the Sicilian parliamentary barons were stronger and more united than were their Lombard counterparts, who represented different and conflicting interests. The second had to do with alternative Enlightenment conceptions on how best to repair failings in government and agriculture: whereas Austrians and Lombards shared, for different reasons, the same "ideology" for remedial action, Sicilian barons looked to Britain, "Sicily's sister island," while Neapolitan viceroys looked to France. This is why the tabula rasa approach failed in Sicily, and why the more modest reforms in Lombardy and elsewhere succeeded.

Two important consequences are worth noting for pinpointing sources of modern regional diversity. The moderate reforms in land, as in the community-based enclosure movement in Tuscany; in taxation, as in the tax reform in Lombardy which drew praise from Adam Smith (Smith [1776] 1965, 886); and in local administration, as in the Papal States – all were evolutionary in nature and contained, in varying degrees, mechanisms for correcting problems as they emerged. By contrast, the second consequence was that neither constitutional nor secondary changes were possible, especially in Sicily. Its parliamentary barons had also, by the 1790s, acquired a new awareness of their constitutional rights. For these reasons, the second transition period brought more profound changes in the south than in the north.

In northern Italy, the impact of the French Revolution and the Napoleonic period was more in fostering the growth of Italian nationalism than in fundamentally recasting existing institutional arrangements. By contrast, in the two politically separate parts of the Kingdom of the Two Sicilies, the impact went much deeper, precisely because earlier successes in preventing an erasure of the past now made ancient institutions stand in sharper relief. Three profound ruptures took place in the political economy of the south between 1805 and 1865.

First, there was a basic restructuring of property rights in rural land, albeit for different reasons and by different actors. On the mainland south, French-inspired Neapolitan liberals abolished in 1806 remnants of feudal privileges of the nobility, transformed complex forms of property in land into private property – largely for themselves – and initiated what eventually took place in liberal Italy in 1865, the disbandment of the Apulian *mesta*. In Sicily, parliamentary barons went further. In 1812 they gave up all the former privileges of their rank, transformed fiefs into private property for themselves, and prevailed upon the Bourbon king to promulgate a new Sicilian constitution endowing Sicily with a system of parliamentary monarchy and taxation far more representative even than that of Britain.

A complex matrix of choices involving internal and external events brought a second rupture by 1816. A reformulated absolutist Kingdom of the Two Sicilies was established, with a system of government and administration borrowed from the French and supported by Austrian arms. All the kingdom was divided into provinces; Sicily lost almost all the vestiges of its nationhood and independence, including flag and parliament. The enforcement of regulations issued from Naples became subject to serious institutional weakness and failure; at the same time, control over agricultural resources now gave new southern landowners – Sicilian barons and their agents – a political power they had never had before.

The earlier economic and political ruptures weighted the constitutional outcome of the Risorgimento in the direction of a centralized system of government and administration. The making of liberal Italy fits Hobbes's Leviathan better than the making of the medieval monarchy: ordinary people had the constitutional right to say "yes" or "no" to the creation of the Italian state, but lost that right and became mere subjects as soon as the new commonwealth was proclaimed. The third rupture for the people in the south lay elsewhere, however, in the wholesale remodelling of secondary laws and other institutional arrangements that directly impinged on everyday life as well as on the intergenerational cycle of life – from state monopolies on tobacco, matches, fire arms, stamp paper, and salt (economies on which cities like Trapani depended) to military conscription; from a radically new system of excise duties to pay for the new national debt to numerous mutations in currency, weight, and land measures; and even in new linguistic meanings of common and juridical terms. It was these "mundane" changes, more than the new constitutional regime itself, that would make Sicily "the Ireland of Italy," as Sicilian political economist Francesco Ferrara was bold enough to tell Count Camillo Benso di Cavour in July 1860 (Ferrara [1860] 1949, 300).

Let me now bring the two transition periods and the ruptures in the second transition period together and sketch, in a brief and stylized fashion, their impact on civil society in the south. I shall then compare this sketch with Putnam's presentation.

One legacy is the creation of great estates under single proprietorship. Capitanata became the heart of latifundism in Apulia only by the late 1860s. Although these changes are much later than in Sicily and Calabria, the transformation was just as profound. The abolishment of the *dogana di Foggia* did away with all the infrastructures, including social capital, connected with wool production. It was the "scramble for land" affecting about 4,000 square kilometres of the plain that led Capitanata to be known as "the California of the South" and the "Texas of Apulia." Two classes of people could be found there by the end of the nineteenth century: large landowners and a proletarian workforce. The entire plain was now owned by no more than 500 landlords; up to 85 per cent of those who cultivated the land were landless daily labourers (see 1901 census figures in Snowden 1986, 10, 20–2).

The phenomenon of southern latifundism, far from being a relic of medieval times, is of more recent origin – the intended and unintended consequences of the political changes in the nineteenth century. In 1876 Sidney Sonnino (1847–1922), the Pisan nobleman and minister of foreign affairs during the First World War, observed in the classic study of Sicilian rural conditions he wrote with Leopoldo Franchetti, his travelling companion and fellow Tuscan nobleman that: "the situation we found in 1860 persists today ... We have legalized the existing oppression and are assuring the impunity of the oppressors. In modern societies, tyranny of the law is restrained by fears of remedies outside the law. In Sicily, with our institutions patterned on liberal formalism rather than informed by a true spirit of liberty, we have furnished the oppressing classes the legal means to defend their oppression and to take over all public positions by the use and abuse of power that was and continues to be in their hands" (Sonnino [1876] 1974). In sharp disagreement with the parliamentary commission on Sicilian conditions which had just reported that "in Sicily there exists neither a political question nor a social [i.e., agricultural] question" (R. Bonfadini 1876, quoted in Carbone and Grispo 1969, 2:1077), Sonnino continued,"we are now strengthening the oppressors' hands by reassuring them that, no matter how far they push their oppression, we will not tolerate any kind of illegal remedy, while there can be no legal remedy, for they have legality on their side" (quoted in Sabetti 1984, 48). Most ordinary people thus found themselves locked in what Sonnino called an "iron circle." On one hand, they suffered labour contracts imposed by the monopoly of large landowners or their agents and supported by the armed power of the state; on the other, they bore the cost of government – including more than three years of conscription for young males – without voice and with little benefit.

A logic of mutually destructive relationships came to dominate work and community life, and only in this period does Antonio Gramsci's characterization of the south as a great social disaggregation apply somewhat. It is this legacy that helps to situate historically the political economy of crime and punishment discussed in part 3 (see also Sabetti 1984). But it is still an open historical question whether local mafias were *ab origine* part of the oppressing classes, or whether such expressions of collective action developed as attempts by some ordinary people, after 1860, to alter a game of life rigged against them, resulting in the end only in new forms of predatory rule on other ordinary people, landowners, and the state. The extent to which antimafia forces, including political parties and social movements, managed *not* to become the mirror image of what they sought to destroy also remains to be determined (Sabetti 1984, 111–217; 1996). In the popular and scholarly literature, the latifundian legacy of southern Italy continued to exist even after a series of interconnected events – the growth of agricultural cooperatives by the 1890s, the "land invasions" between 1919 and 1921, market demands of grain with declining labour population (due to new exit, labour, and sharecropping laws in 1944–45) that placed considerable limits on the property rights of big landowners – had by 1947 largely relegated the latifundian legacy to the past.

A reliable survey of the National Institute of Agricultural Economics (INEA) conducted between 1946 and 1947 revealed the extraordinary number of private holdings, the very small size of most properties, and the relatively small extent of genuinely large holdings in the south. Moreover, the rapid industrialization then taking place in north

Italy and the demand for labour abroad provided powerful incentives for people to leave the rural areas and thus to undermine the prospect of land reforms premised on the assumption that a large number of southern people should "remain on the farm" as small landowners and cultivators. Nevertheless, under pressures from parties on the left, land reform came to be accepted by most Italian politicians as a major remedy for the ills affecting south Italy, and the year 1950 began a short period of land reform legislation in Sicily and other parts of the south. These reforms did, in time, do away with the few remaining truly large landholdings in Sicily and Calabria without, however, achieving the anticipated improvements in agricultural productivity and the working and living conditions of the rural population. The reforms also did little to improve the electoral success of the left, as they revealed that the Italian Way to Socialism itself was based more on myths about the south than facts (Sabetti 1984, 170–8, and the literature cited therein). At the same time, by extending social security legislation by the middle of the 1950s to farmowners who were middle-aged or elderly and had paid little or no contribution to social security, the DC-led national government did improve its electoral success among southern voters. But it also incurred the cost of encouraging an older, less productive generation of the farm population to remain on the land and, in effect, to raid the nascent social security funds, since they had contributed the least or not at all (Sabetti 1984, 186–9; Tarrow 1977, 90–1).

A second legacy is one that, as we noted in chapter 5 on problem solving by central planning, Italy shares with other countries with representative systems of government: the presupposition of parliamentary sovereignty, accentuated in the Italian case by the *stato di diritto*. Government policy-making since the postunification period confirms the view prevalent among both Italian radical democrats and public finance specialists after the 1860s, that "the monopolistic process of legislation is a spontaneous product of parliamentary regimes" (De Viti De Marco [1903] 1965, 249). The monopolistic process has produced, in fact, two parallel – if contradictory – tendencies in problem solving by legislation: nationalization and privatization. The effects have often been the same.

The disastrous effects in south Italy of nationalizing the rich horizontal and vertical mosaic of ventures in public beneficence that had existed from feudal times and of privatizing what previously had been a vast bundle of alternatives to private property are well documented by successive generations of Italian scholars. There is no intention here to idealize the status quo ante; most long-standing local ventures had developed serious failings as civic assets by the 1860s and were in need of reform. What I want to stress are two overlapping points. First, by retaining the greatest number of civic assets from its feudal past, the south was especially vulnerable to problem solving by national legislation. Second, by attempting to reform, direct, and supervise almost all those local undertakings, national legislators effectively excluded the possibility that communities of citizens – groups of principals – could take part in repairing institutional failings, and exposed those enduring civic ventures, often still endowed with considerable financial assets, to predatory rule by members of the national governing class itself.

Beginning in the 1880s, the Italian parliament attempted to rectify some of the problems that previous legislative measures had created, often through special laws for the south. But the earlier nationalization or privatization of civic assets could not be undone, while special or "exceptional" national laws for the south became increasingly standard practice, reaching dramatic proportions after the Second World War. Special laws and funds for the south have over time had the effect of bringing within the reach of most people amenities of modern life and standard of living unexampled in the history of the area. These laws have also enhanced the prerogatives of state and party officials and allowed them to dominate local and regional development (see Trigilia 1994, 1995a).

A third legacy is that members of the governing class -shown in the political career of Sidney Sonnino between 1880 and 1919, for example, as well as in many of the parliamentary debates until Fascist times – were themselves critically aware of the shortcomings in the structure of basic social institutions. As discussed in chapter 4, the problem was that changes in the instrumentalities of government would have given support to localized groups intent on asserting an inherent right of self-government in the whole area of political economy, and thus, it was feared, demolished the work of the creators of the Italian state. This problem – widely debated at least since Ferrara's memorandum to Cavour of July 1860, discussed in chapter 2 – persisted after the Second World War. The creation of a regionalist state was one solution. But another solution was put in place by 1896, and lasted almost until Fascist rule: keep the machinery of government as it is, but leave unenforced or apply leniently many unjust, harsh, and arbitrary laws. This, in the end, gave Giovanni Giolitti's "new liberalism" a bad reputation, especially among intellectuals. As will be recalled from chapter 1, Gaetano Salvemini labelled Giolitti the "minister of the underworld" (*ministro della malavita*), in direct contrast to how Giolitti saw himself, as the minister of good government, and to how he would appear some thirty years later to both Salvemini and the Communist leader Palmiro

Togliatti, (Salvemini [1945] 1960, xxi; Togliatti [1950] 1973). Under Giolitti's "new liberalism," many new forms of voluntary collective efforts emerged in the south as in the north, unimpeded by governmental action.

Norms of generalized reciprocity and networks of horizontal associations ranged from knitting circles, or "schools," to local musical bands and olive- and wine-producing consortia, and these have continued to present times. New and unprecedented associations were established with the purpose of interesting the greatest possible number of people in matters of the commonweal. By 1922 Sicily had the highest number of locally constituted and operated farmer cooperatives and the second-highest number of local (Catholic and non-Catholic) rural credit institutions in Italy; the three regions comprising what is now Calabria had as many rural credit institutions started and operated locally as did Tuscany (Caroleo 1976; Sabetti 1984, 6; *Bollettino* 1950–94). More recent quantitative fieldwork on the role of civic associations in the early years of Italian democracy (1900–24) shows, in fact, no significant differences between northern and southern Italy (Wellhofer 1998). But it was in the Capitanata region of Apulia that there emerged a labour movement more powerful, we now know, than its counterpart in Emilia-Romagna. This story is worth elaborating in some detail.

The land workers of Capitanata had been locked in Sonnino's "iron circle" with the disbandment of the *dogana di Foggia* in 1865 and the great social disaggregation that had followed the "scramble for land." But the data gathered by Frank M. Snowden (1986) show that by the turn of the century the landless workers on the Apulian plain had successfully learned to do three things: 1) extricate themselves from the logic of mutually destructive relationships; 2) organize themselves into a powerful peasant movement placing serious limits on the rights of large landowners; and 3) maintain a high degree of internal democracy in their local and provincial associations by insisting, among other things, that their leaders should come only from their ranks and that no political movement should possess a doctrine beyond the comprehension of its members. It took at least a generation for landless workers to extricate themselves from the "iron circle," but by 1911 they had created a strong and powerful labour movement. The Capitanata town of Cerignola became the centre and model of union activism throughout Apulia. In part because of this, it became known as "the Bologna of Apulia" (cited in Snowden 1986, 100).

The workers' movement in Apulia shared with that of Emilia-Romagna several common features, including a strong sense of worker solidarity. But the Apulian movement differed in one important respect. As it spread throughout the towns of Capitanata and beyond to other regions of Apulia, it maintained internal democracy, with a high degree of leaders' accountability. In contrast, by 1920 the workers' leagues in the Po River valley had become so centralized and hierarchical in nature as to be quite unresponsive to local members (Snowden 1986, 190–1; see also Cardoza 1982, 364–408, esp. 365). The differences between Apulian and northern workers' organizations were real and became critical as Fascists – Mussolini was Romagna's native son – sought power. In Apulia the workers' movement contested the advance of Fascism town by town and showed considerable resilience in the face of Fascist (squadrist) assaults on local headquarters of workers' leagues. By contrast, in the Po valley, including Emilia-Romagna, it was enough to strike only a few individuals to bring chaos to the workers' leagues, as happened in 1921–22. This is what made Apulia stand apart during the advent of Fascism (Cardoza 1982, chs. 7–8; Snowden 1986, 190). Norms of generalized reciprocity and networks of associations did not become entirely extinct under Fascist rule in Apulia; this allowed Giuseppe Di Vittorio to emerge as the most respected national workers' union leader after 1944. It seems evident that the Apulian land workers had built more solid foundations for generalized norms of reciprocity and networks of associations than had their counterparts in Emilia-Romagna.

Compare now this sketch of southern conditions with Putnam's claim of the continuity of a great social disaggregation and individual *scioltezza* or atomism from medieval times to Gramsci's era to contemporary times. Putnam's claim can be perpetuated only at great cost.

First, like Banfield's, Putnam's method of analysis did not allow him even to observe, let alone explain, what happened in the course of the nineteenth century to the rich and dense panoply of social assets that had been features of southern civil society since medieval times. Like Banfield, Putnam missed almost altogether the role that governmental action played in dissolving those small-scale *civitates*.

Second, the view of atomized southern individuals, or *scioltezza*, – held by Putnam and others he cited, from Pasquale Turiello and Leopoldo Franchetti in the nineteenth century to Gramsci, Sidney G. Tarrow, and Luigi Graziano for this century – has currency only if we either accept Putnam's benign view of government, or assume, as do the other analysts, that southern peasants and artisans should entrust their aspirations and needs to an enlightened and benevolent modern prince, be it a national parliament (for Turiello and Franchetti) or a Marxist-Leninist party (for Gramsci and others). Both strategies are questionable. They call for an examination of other key texts Putnam used to weave his story.

The statement in the 1863 Pasquale report (to the effect that society in Calabria *ulteriore* is not held together by economic bonds, but only by natural, civil, and religious bonds) can be reinterpreted as an indirect confirmation both of the upheaval created by the "abolition of feudalism" and of the still strong presence of civil and religious structures of village life characteristic of the *ancien régime*. In fact, Pasquale's last sentence in the paragraph that Putnam quoted from noted that "the propensity for mutual aid can be found everywhere [in Calabria], especially in villages" (quoted in Bevilacqua 1985, 296). Putnam uncomplicated his narrative by omitting this important sentence. Denis Mack Smith's discussion (in his modern history of Italy, 1959, 34–5) of the absence of community sense in liberal Italy did not refer, as Putnam seemed to suggest, to the absence of community spirit among southern villagers and the like; rather, it referred to the widespread lack of support for the post-1860 central government and policies throughout the entire country – an entirely different matter than what Putnam wished to convey (Putnam 1993, 143).

Even Franchetti's often-cited views about Sicilian *scioltezza* take on a different meaning when they are ranged alongside the analysis advanced by his travelling companion, Sonnino. Franchetti's description is "institutions free"; it tells us how individuals behave when they are locked in a many-person analogue to the prisoner's dilemma. Sonnino provided the missing links in Franchetti's account by telling us about the rules or constraints of the game. Gramsci's "great social disaggregation," then, does not mean a lack of community concern, or an inability to act, or a proclivity for vertical, clientelistic politics, but rather the presence of governmental institutions that create serious impediments to both voluntary and public initiatives. The "iron circle" sketched by Sonnino explains "great social disaggregation" better than the "ethos laws" advanced by Putnam and, as we saw in chapter 8, by Banfield.

Third, Putnam's explanatory schema did not allow him to recognize contradictions in his own argument. He cannot explain the network of secondary associations and community organizations that developed especially after the 1890s: If *scioltezza* is as universal as it is alleged, how have successive generations of ordinary people in the south, as presumed rational egoists or amoral familists, managed to overcome the logic of collective *inaction* and the oligarchical tendencies inherent in organizational life? North-south differences in group action and other joint voluntary undertakings are not really comparable unless we take into account the differential impact of governmental action. Indeed, as mentioned earlier, more recent quantitative research on the role of civic associations in the years between 1900 and 1924 found no significant differences between northern and southern Italy – that is, the findings do not support Putnam (Wellhofer 1998). By contrast, Sonnino's method of analysis gave him greater predictive capacity because he did not view ordinary people just as "prisoners" and because he understood better than Franchetti, Banfield and Putnam the rules of the game and how to change them.[3]

Fourth, Putnam's method of analysis allowed him to overlook similarities in civic practices throughout the country. He could observe horizontal bonds of reciprocity and trust, the mutual aid and exchange of services among neighbours (*aiutarella*) in north Italian communities, could call up similar practices among residents of Mexico City, Java, and other parts of the world – even among prisoners of some Latin American jail – but could not come to terms with the fact that the same social practices can be found in south Italian cities, towns, and villages. The tenacity of his presumptive knowledge did not prepare him well for his voyage of inquiry to Pietrapertosa; it led him to ignore visible facts on the ground.

Finally, just as Putnam's explanatory schema allowed him to take only a benign view of governmental action in promoting social capital, so it allowed him to ignore completely the role that a powerful institution of civil society has had in creating social capital in the south. I reserve a longer discussion below.

Organized Religion and Civil Society

The view is put forward in chapter 4 of *Making Democracy Work* that organized religion is an alternative to, or works against, the civic community in Italy. This view is advanced, however, on the strength of historical and contemporary events that suggest the opposite.

As portrayed by Putnam, the church in the north – from medieval times to unification – is only one civil institution among many, itself a local affair with horizontal religious allegiances and alignments. For the same period, by contrast, the church in the south is portrayed as a single entity, as a powerful and wealthy proprietor in the feudal order (Putnam 1993, 130), with presumably negative consequences for the civic community. It is not clear whether what is meant by "church" is the same in the two contexts; what is less ambiguous is that a unitary-actor model can produce gross distortions of the historical record.

The church was and is a single entity in spiritual and doctrinal matters, but it was not organizationally a single entity or proprietor in the south. Sicilian exceptionalism applies to the church as well. Sicilian churchmen and lay organizations enjoyed considerable autonomy from

Rome under the apostolic legateship as late as the nineteenth century. On the mainland south, it was only in 1867 that the system whereby local churches were run entirely by lay people, with appointed priests to administer the sacraments and say mass, and where the local bishop had no right of jurisdiction except in matters *quoad spiritualia* was abolished. Strong indications exist in the available literature that local parishes, known as *chiese ricettizie*, were more the norm than the exception throughout the mainland south for many centuries; quite a few of them were run like synagogues, each with its own common property regime – a tradition that can be traced back to medieval times. As a corrective to any tendency to idealize this particular tradition in retrospect, it would do well to emphasize that, over time, the *chiese ricettizie* developed critical failings that could not be easily repaired. The chief point remains, however: the church in the south was a complex and overlapping system of individual and local churches, lay confraternities and congregations of men and women[4], mutual aid societies and public-spirited societies (*opere pie*) operating hospitals. All were linked in different ways to all sorts of diocesan institutions and monastic orders – each with its own bundle of property rights and with considerable entrepreneurial initiative in providing material and spiritual benefits to distinct but often overlapping political communities.

For centuries and as late as the 1880s – when state regulations effectively destroyed their capacity to act as essential coproducers of many collective services – all those entities remained very visible neighbourhood institutions, passing on an ethic of community involvement, social responsibility, and mutual assistance among different classes and social equals.[5] It was in this sense that the church on the mainland south, in the words of a British analyst, "represented, in a curious form, the embryo of democratic institutions" (Johnston 1904, 1:13). Sonnino observed, paradoxically, that the key factor which made local parishes in Sicily stand out in community life was precisely that "civil society appears to the Sicilian peasant only in the form of rapacious landlords, tax collectors, conscription officers and police officials ... outside of [the church], he finds nothing but toil, sweat and misery" (quoted in Sabetti 1984, 90).

The papal *non expedit* ban that forbade Catholics from participating in Italian national life for some time after unification was also used to argue that Catholicism and civic involvement are antagonistic. Three aspects of the injunction, seldom noted, give a more nuanced, less negative interpretation of the ban. Keeping in mind the tense church-state relations of the post-1859 period, including the fall of papal Rome in 1870, the *non expedit* does not appear to be a strong

Vatican response to the nationalization of church properties in 1865 and the serious threats to the liberty of the church itself. Moreover, given the very limited franchise for the first thirty years of the new kingdom, the *non expedit* applied in practical terms to a relatively small portion of the population: for example, up until 1882 only 2 per cent of the population was eligible to vote (about 620,000 male voters). At the same time, the ban did not apply to local elections and, in fact, did not negatively affect Catholic community efforts and civic involvement. On the contrary, beginning in 1874 there took place a considerable renewal in Catholic social action that emerged with particular strength in Sicily and Calabria after the 1890s.

Church-sponsored associations allowed villagers to realize mutual benefits and to participate in self-governing efforts to a degree not possible in public, governmental affairs; membership in these associations also served to provide the primary political leadership and social capital for other types of concerted action. Far from negating or opposing civic involvement, the *non expedit* ban actually encouraged committed Catholics to renew their grassroots efforts just at the time when the central government was bent on dissolving social civic assets from the *ancien régime*. It was these grassroots efforts, undertaken as part of Luigi Sturzo's apostolic work, that had by 1919 propelled this Sicilian priest and nobleman to national prominence as leader of the newly formed (Catholic) Popular Party. Sturzo's commitment to self-governance was as strong as union leader Giuseppe Di Vittorio's.

A third line of contention that organized religion in Italy is an alternative to the civic community, and not a part of it, derives in particular from the period following Vatican II in the 1960s. Data drawn from aggregate Eurobarometer surveys in (1976, 1985, 1988, and 1989) and some qualitative accounts are used to suggest that "churchgoers seem more concerned about the city of God than the city of man" (Putnam 1993, 107). The conclusion follows: the civic community in today's Italy is a secular community (Putnam 1993, 109).

First, the Eurobarometer surveys for Italy are well known to be methodologically flawed and notoriously unreliable. In the absence of more reliable surveys, it might be argued that they are the best we have and thus should be used. There is, however, little or no evidence of caution in the way Putnam constructed his index of clericalism on the basis of Eurobarometer studies.[6] The Putnam index conflates religiosity with clericalism, civic community with secularism, and thus erects a false dichotomy between civic community and religious faith. Second, even if the cited sources correctly portray what they observed, it does not mean that they can be taken as accurate representations of Catholic theology, teaching, and practice. In fact, the play on words with the title of St Augustine's book, *The City of God*, reveals mistaken notions about Catholicism. The Roman Catholic Church teaches the inseparability of one's love of neighbour from the love of God, and not a substitution of one for the other. The journey onward toward salvation for the Christian begins – in Augustine's work as in the more recent Second Vatican Council document *Lumen gentium* no. 31 – not so much with the flight from the world as with self-examination and self-control, and with a commitment to sanctify the world from within through the ordinary circumstances of life and work. Third, the call to human dignity, solidarity, and the inseparability of one's love of neighbour from the love of God have served to build new infrastructures of collective efforts and community development in Apulian, Lucan, Calabrian, and Sicilian towns. A large part of the voluntary action sector throughout Italy is connected with social movements inspired by the teachings of the Catholic Church. Christian roots may not always be visible enough to account for social civic assets and community efforts in contemporary Emilia-Romagna, but it is a mistake to overlook those roots and civic assets in other parts of the country (e.g. Accattoli 1995; Alongi 1997; CENSIS 1994; Cestaro 1995; Donati 1993; De Leo 1991).

REGIONAL GOVERNMENT

I have shown that two of the three pillars on which Putnam's analytical and empirical scaffold rests cannot withstand close inspection: the historical legacy portrayed by Putnam's path dependence analysis is profoundly mistaken and cannot be used to explain differential effectiveness in regions. Cultural patterns and associational networks dissimilar from – and richer than – those Putnam describes have been at work in shaping the south. Moreover, taking the basic analytical perspective of representative government with a presupposition of parliamentary sovereignty places any inquiry about "making democracy work" at risk of drawing the wrong conclusions about legislative output. Whether the legislative output of regional governments is interpretable as Putnam suggested remains questionable. Can Putnam's other pillar withstand close inspection? Was the creation of regional government a "natural" experiment?

Putnam said that "the border of the new governments largely corresponded to the territories of historical regions of the peninsula, including such celebrated principalities as Tuscany and Lombardy" (Putnam 1993, 5). Though it is not clear from the text what he meant by "largely," he may have been somewhat correct in matching the present regional boundaries with the territories of Tuscany, Lombardy, and

Emilia-Romagna as representing political entities with historic identities. The situation in the south, beginning with what used to be called Abruzzi e Molise, is more complicated than Putnam allowed. The farther south one goes, the harder it is to find a historical equivalent of the regional states (see also Sabetti 1997, 403). Several facts stand out.

The regional governments created in 1970 do not match the regions that have existed in southern history, at least not in the same way that they match the historic regions in the north. For centuries, there were at least three Apulias, two Abruzzos, generally three Calabrias, and perhaps the same number for what is now known as Campania – each with its own territorial boundaries, capital, distinct political economy, historical consciousness, and cultural identity. This helps to explain why almost all these areas have been known in Italian in the plural – the Abruzzi, the Puglie, the Calabrie. The creation of regional governments made them singular. To be sure, the areas politically united shared the same name, but this did not give the regional experiment there a more spontaneous and less contrived nature (see also Barbera 1994, 46–7; Levy 1996, esp. chs. 1–3).

There were two exceptions: Lucania (or Basilicata), with its relatively small size and historically distinct boundaries, was left as it was; Molise was allowed to break away from Abruzzi and form its own regional government, even though the people of Abruzzi (or the Aquila and southern part of it) and Molise have been historically linked and share close identities. Putnam does not tell us why Molise was allowed to secede from Abruzzi and have its own regional government even though the historic reasons for such a move are not strong.[7] The fact that some Molisan intellectuals and politicians who favoured the creation of the Molise region were, or had close ties with, powerful leaders in the national center-left governing coalition may explain the Molise exception. This exception reinforces the view that the regional experiment was not a natural one: the borders of the new governments were as much political contrivances of national legislators as they were historical legacies. This point can be illustrated in another way.

National legislators also had authority over which cities should be regional capitals. This decision constituted a mere formality in the case of, say, Turin for Piedmont, Milan for Lombardy, and perhaps even Bologna for Emilia-Romagna, but not so for the southern regions, where more than one city often had equal claims to be the regional capital. There was even some opposition in Lucania and Campania, where it was difficult to question the historic importance and claims of Potenza and Naples, respectively. The choice of regional capitals elsewhere proved considerably more contentious. Mass protests were organized in cities with equal claims to be capitals – like Pescara in Abruzzi and

Reggio Calabria in Calabria. The protests in Reggio Calabria were strong, cutting across left-right party lines and trade union barriers; so intense did they become that some citizens lost their lives as police tried to contain demonstrators during the so-called revolt of Reggio Calabria in 1970–71. The riots against making Catanzaro the regional capital caught national legislators, including those from the region, by surprise. The mass revolt explains why Calabria is the only region to have its central machinery of government in two different cities: the de jure regional capital, where the regional government and its central administration are located, remained Catanzaro; but the regional assembly was moved to and now meets in Reggio Calabria.

The fact that Apulia and Calabria seemed, in Putnam's analysis, to be the worst-governed regions may, in part, be due to the way national legislators disregarded historic borders and regional identities and imposed what, from the perspective of ordinary people in Capitanata and Crotone, appeared to be one more consolidated – and distant – layer of government between localities, the provincial field services of the national system of public administration and Rome itself.[8] Putnam's evaluation of the institutional performance in Apulia and Calabria may have coincided with the constituency evaluation there (Putnam 1993, 76–81), but the *criteria* for the constituency evaluation may be grounded in an interpretative scheme that Putnam and his collaborators did not appear to have seriously explored. By paying little or no attention to the riots of Reggio Calabria and to the resultant regional government arrangements, Putnam misidentified Reggio Calabria as the regional capital when he said that "for many southerners ... being ruled from Bari or Reggio Calabria is not much better than being ruled from Rome" (Putnam 1993, 54). More importantly, he missed an opportunity to explore the suggestion advanced earlier by some Italian analysts – that the way the Calabrian regional experiment took effect had a negative impact on, or slowed down, its legislative performance (see Amato et al. 1975, 41).

The present regions are, then, in part historic entities and in part arbitrary administrative contrivances – a point already alluded to in chapter 4. This is to say that the design principles of regional government did not embody similar meanings everywhere and thus the creation of regional government cannot be reasonably construed as constituting a single, uniform political experiment across Italy.

This conclusion, which leaves no pillars in Putnam's analysis standing, would not have surprised many nineteenth-century publicists – from Cattaneo in the north to Napoleone Colajanni and Edoardo Pantano in the south – who took part in or followed the regionalist debate between 1860 and 1945 (see Ganci 1973; Ruffilli 1971). As we saw in chapters 2–4, these analysts did not assume that the extension of representative institutions built on a logic of parliamentary sovereignty could be equated with self-government; they, in fact, anticipated that central government decentralization, far from being a neutral policy instrument, would be a political contrivance more sensitive to the demands of the governing classes than to the regional diversities of Italy. This point was made by Cattaneo in the 1860s. About thirty years later Colajanni and Pantano amplified it, likening proposals to decentralize central government authority to attempts to shorten the handle of the hammer when the hammer of centralized government and administration itself was the problem. The southern analysts may have been too pessimistic in their predictions, but Putnam imperiled his own experiment by not profiting from the rich regionalist debate in Italy since 1860.

CONCLUSION

There is no question that Robert Putnam has written a powerful book. The widespread attention the book and the author have received in the media, among policy makers, and in academic circles has contributed to fostering a positive image of contemporary Italian politics and, more generally, has drawn attention to the importance that community and associational life can make in the politics of everyday life. At the same time, Putnam's work has given renewed standing to the culturalist explanation offered by Banfield more than forty years ago and has contributed to the resurgence of culturalist explanations of differential government performance more generally. Unfortunately, like Banfield's, Putnam's explanation of Italian regional government performance does not withstand close inspection. His analysis advanced a strong argument for path dependence and culturalist explanation but, as I have shown, also accentuated their fatal shortcomings.

The conclusions of this chapter are threefold. First, Putnam's model reminds us that history matters, and then proceeds to mess up how, when, and why it matters. A path dependence *forma mentis* can lead, and has led, to a caricature of the north and the south and to the neglect of nuances in both. Second, Putnam's explanatory scheme led him to draw the wrong conclusions from history and the regional experiment. I have shown that north-south differences are not really comparable unless we take into account the differential impact of governmental action, something which Putnam was prevented from doing by the explanatory scheme he uses. Third, the transitions and ruptures I have sketched in the growth of governmental institutions since the eighteenth century point to the constraints on development that have a structure other than path dependence. Crafting institutions for good government was not as determined and closed-ended a process as Putnam suggested. The transitions and ruptures support the argument that the continuing interplay of economic and political factors at the local, regional, and national levels has far more profound implications for development (or inertia) than any particular path-dependent structure.

Serious flaws thus disable *Making Democracy Work* both from making sense of the Italian regional experiment and from being a classic in comparative politics research. As we unlearn the lessons taught by the resurgence of culturalist explanations, we are challenged to provide less flawed accounts of how history, culture, institutions, and individuals come together to matter. Cattaneo's lifelong intellectual struggle and Putnam's own twenty-year poking around the regions of Italy suggest that the task is not an easy one. The search for good government surveyed in this book shows that the struggle is still worthwhile, no matter how elusive the dependent variable of good government turns out to be. The elusiveness of that variable offers reflections for the concluding chapter.

10 Good Government: The Elusive Dependent Variable

The preceding chapters have sought to construct an argument for rejecting the paradox of rational individuals and irrational society in contemporary Italian politics, and consequently for thinking differently about poor government performance. The argument was developed through an empirically grounded examination of four distinct but interconnected dimensions of the "paradox of Italy," involving different levels of analysis. The study attempted to provide answers to the following questions: What constitutional knowledge was available during the Risorgimento and informed the creation of the Italian state? What institutional learning shaped the reiteration of constitutional choice and design in 1946, and how did the system work at the local level? How can the government war on crime be seen as a fight for good government? What is wrong with the accepted view that some parts of Italy have been culturally or path dependently doomed to bad government?

This book shows that crafting institutions of good government can – and does – produce antithetical and counterintentional results. While the chapters in each part convey specific and multidimensional aspects, the overall argument can be summarized as follows: Italian politics should not be understood as some kind of sinkhole of misgovernment and corruption, but as a laboratory of what a search for good government can generate, or an illustration of why good government remains such an elusive dependent variable. The rest of this chapter summarizes the principal conclusions of the study and their implications for the politics of reform in the post-1992 period, then extends those implications to reflect on the study of Italian politics more generally, and, finally, looks at the prospects of overcoming the odds – something which Italians have successfully done in the past – in order to realize the fuller potentials of democracy in Italian public life.

THE PAST AS THE FUTURE? IMPLICATIONS FOR THE POST-1992 PRACTICE OF POLITICS

One argument of the study is that the sheer complexity of governmental structures, including the power of past decisions and the incentives they provide in the present, has made it very difficult, if at all possible, to bring about "good government" in Italy *sub species aeternitatis*. This theme is evident in different historical and administrative contexts – in the Risorgimento debate about systems of government (chapters 2 and 3), in the constraints on government services during the post-1945 period (chapter 4), problem solving by central planning (chapter 5), and in waging the government war on crime (chapters 6 and 7). The Meli-Falcone disputes, in particular, show that a lot of poor results in various sectors of the Italian public administration are due to a genuine difference of views on what is best and to the rational pursuit of interests by different professional groups. People in politics and public administration, then, invoke either "the war on crime" (*lotta alla criminalità*) or "the letter of the law" (*il garantismo*) to pursue their plans. The interplay of rational self-interest and genuine argument makes good government difficult to achieve and maintain.

This conclusion, important as it is, may seem unsurprising in comparative analysis and in more philosophical verdicts on the human condition. People the world over – not just contemporary Italians – face a difficult challenge regarding the place of statutory legislation and administrative regulations as the core of legal processes, which in turn presents a serious challenge to the concept of a rule of law. Statutory law and its administrative complement are much too arbitrary when linked with a presumption of universality requiring uniform application. We need adaptation to local ecological niches and room for variation in local and regional rules, laws that fit within municipal corporations and other types of associational realities. Unfortunately, contemporary Italian political and legal discourse, not unlike that of much of the world, identifies "democracy" with parliamentary government and representative assemblies rather than with the universality of the village and community as the basic human reality. When viewed against this backdrop, it is not surprising that much of the modern literature in rational choice institutionalism has persuasively – and perhaps conclusively – shown that collective action does not necessarily produce a collective good (M. Levi 1997b, 20), and that no system of government can guarantee good government, or even particular outcomes (Vibert 1995, 18). Almost two thousand years ago, writing about the city of God and free will (*de libero arbitrio*), Augustine of Hippo observed that human justice is fundamentally defective. Unsurprising as it may be, this conclusion is worth emphasizing, if only to restrain expectations of perfectionism or tendencies of self-denigration about Italian politics often voiced by some of the best foreign and Italian intellectuals (references in Barzini 1968; LaPalombara 1987; Mastropaolo 1996, 1997; Romeo 1965). It must be quickly added, however, that Augustine's conclusion alone does not explain why good government in contemporary Italy has remained an elusive dependent variable. Additional explanations are brought out in this study.

By the Risorgimento, Italy had such a rich heritage that the meaning of the past posed dilemmas about how to face the future. To institute uniform rules across a "united" Italy did not allow a synthesis to develop by mutual accommodation in a world of great cities. This is where Carlo Cattaneo's vision was of fundamental importance, and this is why we began the discussion of contemporary politics by going back to the creation of the Italian state. In additional to the general challenge shared by almost the whole world about the place of statutory legislation and administrative regulations as the core of legal processes, the troubles of governance in present-day Italy have also been due – just as Cattaneo and others like him anticipated – to traits specific to the constitutional and institutional arrangements and resultant political economy of decisions. These traits or core elements can be summarized as the *form* of government and the *ways* governments operate. They have kept public institutions from performing better or, to reprise the argument in chapter 1, at least not with the same degree of responsiveness, flexibility, and efficiency said to characterize millions of small private Italian enterprises.

The constitutional and institutional form of Italian government is based on the presumption that there exists a single system of rule (monocentric) and a single institutional paradigm (bureaucratic) applicable to all sorts of policy objectives, public issues, and collective problems. This characteristic of the Italian system has remained – in spite of modifications in the prefectoral administration so as not to be a mere replica of the French form (chapter 2, cf., Samuels 1997, 292), and even in spite of efforts to reform that practice of rule through the creation of neighbourhood and regional governments in the 1970s (chapters 4, 9). For these reasons, the full implementation of the republican constitution by the 1970s did, in the end, bring about the creation of a regionalist state, without, however, fundamentally altering the basic design or operational ways of the Italian system, as we shall recall shortly.

In the 1990s, renewed efforts were made to reform that state and the resultant practice of rule: in 1990 a new national law sought to restructure communal and provincial governments; in 1993 a new electoral law sought to free local politics and services from the oligopolistic control of national parties. Between 1992 and 1997, other structural reforms were put in place to improve service delivery in the local health units and to "decenter" state authority to regional and communal governments (Ferrera 1997; Gilbert 1998; Newell 1998). These changes can now be seen as part of the chain of events that moved Italian politics well beyond the postwar republican regime and put again on the public agenda a federalist option or project for Italy. By the late 1990s, the issue on the public agenda was not whether to reform the unitary state but, rather, who should decide what kind of federalism should replace it – with regional and municipal governments claiming an equal share in constitutional decision making with national legislators (see CINSEDO 1997, De Siervo 1999; Mariucci 1997; Vassallo 1998; the seven www home pages of Progetto Italia Federale; cf., Panebianco 1998). There can be little doubt that the practice of rule changed dramatically with the upheavals brought about by the Clean Hands operation in Milan, the renewed government war on organized crime since 1991, especially following the murders of Falcone and Borsellino in Palermo in 1992, and the election of the Berlusconi – and later – Prodi and D'Alema – governments. But whether the attempt to craft institutions of good government, moved along especially since 1996 by the government of Romano Prodi and by the parliamentary constitutional reform commission headed, at one point, by Massimo D'Alema (*bicamerale*), will solidify what some have termed "the end of politics, Italian style" (Gilbert 1995) or "the crisis of the Italian state" (McCarthy 1995) remains to be seen.

It is certainly premature to refer to the Italy of the late 1990s as the Second Republic. The Italian state persisted throughout the 1990s – as did the tendency among its governing class to identify democracy with parliamentary government and representative assemblies – in spite of the "revolution" of the early 1990s and the nearly unanimous agreement among public officials, elite opinion makers, and concerned citizens about the need to bring governments closer to the people and to encourage grassroots democracy in line with "the constitutional design that did not happen" in Cattaneo's time, discussed in chapters 2 and 3. Good people and good intentions are important, but they are not enough. To borrow what Stephen L. Elkin has said in another context, what is desirable is not always probable (Elkin 1987). It is hard, therefore, to make an optimistic prognosis concerning the political changes of the 1990s.

At the same time, there is no attempt here to reduce what is wrong with contemporary Italian politics to the issue of centralized government and administration, nor to suggest that if only Italy could establish a federal system everything would be all right. Even if I have succeeded in showing that a monocentric form of government leads to suboptimal performance, it does not follow that a polycentric – or indeed any other – form of government will automatically perform better. Federalism can just as easily exacerbate problems of efficiency, responsiveness, and probity as solve them. Observers like Michel Crozier have drawn attention to the fact that the American federal system is highly susceptible to institutional dysfunctions, "the vicious circle of decentralization" (Crozier 1984, 246). Other analysts, from Alexis de Tocqueville to Vincent Ostrom, have drawn attention to the fact that the American federal system is highly vulnerable to the tyranny of the majority and the problem of democratic despotism (V. Ostrom 1997; Tocqueville [1845] 1962, vol. 2, chps. 6–7). Still, the argument for a polycentric, federal system goes beyond the production and delivery of public services and related issues of efficiency, responsiveness, and probity. It also has to do with what Machiavelli called *vivere libero* – what it means to be a citizen in a self-governing society – and with the recognition that nonunitary, polycentric forms of rule provide greater opportunities for people to practise the art of self-governance, or covenanting with one another (see also E. Ostrom 1997; Viroli 1995, 29–37; Zincone 1992).

Luigi Einaudi's 1944 essay "Away with the Prefect!" may be worth recalling here, since it echoed both Machiavelli's idea of *vivere libero* and Cattaneo's discussion of the communal society as the foundational, covenanting basis for people to live as free citizens engaged in self-rule and shared rule. To those who feared moving away from the Napoleonic state, Einaudi would say that "democracy begins in the commune." To those who argued that the unity of the country was provided by the prefects, field services, and circulars of the central government, Einaudi might have reminded them that "the unity of the country is made by the Italian people. By the Italians who learn at their own expense, committing mistakes, to govern themselves" (Einaudi [1944] 1954, 59).

The other core feature of the crafting and recrafting of the machinery of government that has kept public institutions in republican Italy from performing better relates to *how* governments are expected to operate – that is, the *stato di diritto*. "The state based on law" means not so much the practice of restraining governments through judicial review as the public philosophy of applying to specific government tasks general universal principles with little or no consideration either to the specific ecologies of those tasks or to whether the basic principles (i.e., accountability, responsiveness, equality, and efficiency) contradict one another to the point that none of them can be served. This helps to explain why Italian legislators, unlike Hobbes's ruler, have often acted as if "the greatest liberty of subjects depends on the intrusiveness of the law." Not surprisingly, the *stato di diritto* has produced the following observable results in contemporary Italian politics: a policy process open to an extensive articulation of political demands, but with little prospect of translating most of those demands into effective government programs; public discussion of problems that has become increasingly misspecified, and public communications that have become systematically distorted, where rationalization has displaced rationality; a country whose national debt was about 125 per cent of the size of its gross domestic product by 1996; and a perverse emphasis on "the law" accommodated by either neglect, the wink of an eye, or the granting of exceptions. One dramatic way to illustrate these problems is to recall from chapter 5 how a one-time national minister of public works, Fiorentino Sullo, put matters: "the laws give [administrative officials] important sanctions, it is true, but since they cannot see and check on everything, to exercise these powers would be a form of discriminatory treatment." The administration of criminal justice, with more than 100,000 laws on its books and, frequently, vague definitions of criminal offenses, has also been susceptible to this problem, as we saw earlier (see also Guarnieri 1997, 167; Pederzoli and Guarnieri 1997).

As a way of dealing with illegalities, successive generations of Italian reformers, on the left and on the right, have pursued anticorruption projects by strengthening the *stato di diritto*, by seeking to expunge, in the famous words of Vittorio Emanuele Orlando, a leading constitutional law professor and one-time prime minister of liberal Italy, "all political, sociological, and economic consideration" from the design of public administration (quoted in Ferraresi 1982, 8). These well-intentioned attempts – not unlike American anticorruption attempts (see Anechiarico and Jacobs 1996) – did not produce the anticipated results. Instead, they have made the work of government in postwar Italy exceedingly cumbersome and unaccountable, while encouraging the practice of bureaucratic free enterprise and opportunistic behaviour. They also encouraged the (mistaken) view, noted by Gianfranco Pasquino (1997, 43–7), that nonpolitical leaders are more capable of pursuing general, less partisan interests. By contrast, Cattaneo's message is that if we go back to the city and the neighbourhood as the basic human reality, we have the possibility of escaping from the tyranny of uniform legislation and can begin to appreciate that universalities are always subject to accommodations to time and place specificities.

It would be wrong, however, to conclude that the *stato di diritto* or the tyranny of uniform legislation, has not brought considerable benefits to individual Italians. The rigid wage structure requiring the state and many businesses to pay the same salaries in all regions, irrespective of productivity and differentials in cost of living, has, among other things, dissuaded people from investing in southern industries, but has also brought considerable economic benefits to public employment in the south, where the cost of living is much cheaper. The result is that public functionaries, including teachers and police officers, are more well off living in, say, Isernia than in Milan. (The antisouthern prejudice among supporters of the Northern League cannot be understood if such issues are not considered.)

In sum, a chief problem in contemporary Italian public affairs is not the absence of law but rather the rule *by* law, or too many laws, with little or no emphasis on character and professional formation (*la formazione degli uomini*) and on adaptation to local ecological niches. Problematic aspects of Italian public affairs would have appeared more dramatic if we had extended the analysis to two features of postwar Italy: welfare state and party finance. Let us briefly consider them.

Maurizio Ferrera has written on the Italian welfare state from a sympathetic perspective (Ferrera 1997, 1998). But even from that vantage point, it is clear that, by adding the welfare state to the rule of law (*lo stato sociale di diritto*), Italian legislators in the postwar period succeeded in solidifying their political communities at the cost of compounding political, administrative, and financial problems beyond manageable limits for successive national governments, and for future generations of Italians as well (Matteucci 1993, 283–4). Martin Rhodes (1997) has emphasized that the 1974 national law, establishing a system of public subventions for parties receiving more than 2 per cent of the valid votes in general elections, encouraged both an additional raid on the public purse and the expansion of illicit funding, while giving immunity from prosecution to politicians and parties. It is this context that makes the exposure of massive political corruption by Milan magistrates in their Clean Hands operation truly revolutionary. As some have correctly noted (Burnett and Mantovani 1998, esp. chps 9, 12, 14, 16), by targeting only some politicians and not all others (say, Giulio Andreotti and *not* Amintore Fanfani), magistrates stand accused of misusing their discretion and of having "overthrown" the First Republic. Like officials in the Public Works ministry, officials in the Justice administration cannot see and check on everything criminal, as the laws require, so that in the end the exercise of their powers does amount to a form of discriminatory or preferential treatment. The approval of public financing of political parties by the national parliament in April 1998, and again in 1999, suggests that the problems associated with the 1974 law may reemerge in the future.

The conclusions advanced thus far can be rendered this way: the so-called impasse or crisis of the Italian state is not the result of an incapacity for internally generated institutional reform nor the relative absence of alternation in coalition government, as many observers claim (e.g., Bull and Rhodes 1997, 3–4; Mack Smith 1995, 10), but the difficulties under the present institutional arrangements of 1) facilitating rather than hindering individual and collective efforts on behalf of common interests shared by people, including opportunities for citizens to act as "coproducers" of many labour-intensive public services; 2) emphasizing service rather than control; 3) insuring the accountability of public officials; 4) establishing a closer fit between preferred solutions and the actual behaviour of public and elected officials, between policy intentions and policy performance; and 5) anticipating what are the characteristic results that can be expected to flow from the *form* of government and the *ways* governments operate. The commitment to good government and the resultant success stories of Emilia-Romagna, Lucania, Abruzzo, and Molise (highlighted, among others, by Robert Putnam, Alan Zuckerman, and Simona Piattoni respectively) are, as we saw in chapter 4, not sufficient to override the system as a whole. By the end of the 1990s, the center-left parties saw no contradiction between the diversity implied by their espousal of grassroots democracy (and even federalism) and the perverse emphasis on uniformity implied by their support of *lo stato sociale di diritto*, just as the center-right parties saw no contradiction between their insistence on grassroots democracy and the central-government trap implied by their "presidentialist" reform proposals.

Chapters 2–5 and 9 document that successive generations of analysts since Cattaneo and Ferrara, from Napoleone Colajanni to Sidney Sonnino and Luigi Einaudi, anticipated the very design of the Italian state to preclude the possibility of the system working as it should. Thus, successive generations of Italians have found themselves in a multiperson analogue of the prisoner's dilemma – working within a system that produces outcomes which they do not value very highly as viable alternatives. At the same time, those analysts saw, in different degrees, the potential for a gradual transformation of that state through decentralization efforts, though they had no illusion that the transformation of a highly centralized state into a state based upon a different design could occur except over a long period of time.

Thus, for all these reasons, good government at the constitutional, governmental, and operational levels in contemporary Italy has remained elusive. But this is not a story of unmitigated failure. Contemporary Italy remains a vibrant, if tumultuous, democracy. Why, then, have many informed observers tended to celebrate the backwardness of Italy and talk about Italian democracy as if it were not "a normal democracy"? (discussion in Barzini 1968; Bull and Rhodes 1997; Stille 1996; cf., Agnew 1996). In other words, what factors have blocked observers from seeing, and giving proper weight to, the underlying principles, institutional arrangements, and variegated contours of public life emphasized in this study?

IMPLICATIONS FOR THE STUDY OF ITALIAN POLITICS

In part 4, we dealt with tendency to resort to cultural explanations, to treat politics as a dependent variable, and in Giovanni Sartori's apt description, to do the sociology of politics rather than political sociology (Sartori 1969). In addition there are three separate but overlapping sets of factors that have blocked many observers from seeing what the preceding narrative has placed in sharp relief. First, there is self-colonization, the tendency of Italians, especially of elite opinion makers and intellectuals, to accept a view of themselves through the looking-glass of others. Another factor that invites negative characterization and lends mythic status to the paradox of Italy as the explanation for poor government performance is misfocused genius, the expectation that, for a country that has contributed so much to the advancement of human civilization and is as economically prosperous as postwar Italy, the quality of its public life and the character of its citizenry ought to be higher (Hine 1993, 255). This is compounded by the tendency among social scientists to evaluate Italy's development experience through a conception of a model history of nation states and, consequently, to consider successive generations of Italians as poor institutional artisans. Finally, there is the seemingly extraordinary and exceptional nature of clientelism, kickbacks, bribes, and the like in contemporary Italian public life.

Before taking up each one in turn, let me anticipate possible misunderstanding. I am not suggesting that all three sets of explanations are shared or accepted by the analyses and points of view I criticize. Nor am I interested in singling out for criticism specific elite opinion makers, scholars, or publications. My concern at all times is to identify tendencies that have, in my view, inoculated us from obtaining a fuller appreciation of the principal factors that generate suboptimal performance of public institutions. Paraphrasing Paul Diesing (1991, x), my aim is not to argue, except incidentally, but to promote greater self-awareness among social scientists.

Self-Colonization

Self-colonization refers to a situation whereby people justify their actions or begin to see themselves through the eyes of others. As people increasingly accept the images that others have of them, they become alienated from their own culture and ways of life – they willingly become colonized and thus stand to lose (or become demoralized about) their capacity, skills, and knowledge for self-governance, or, at least, become stuck with labels they do not deserve, like the people of Chiaromonte. The resurgence of cultural explanations suggests the poverty of our formulations and alerts us to a problem seldom considered by Anglo-American comparativists, and even historians, studying Italy: social science and elite opinion makers may not kill people, but they can certainly make life miserable. This is why Amilcar Cabral, the deceased leader of the national liberation struggle against the Portuguese in Guinea-Bissau, emphasized that the task of organizing a revolutionary movement requires above all a cultural revolution, a rejection of colonial dependency. He called this "a return to the source" (Morgado 1974). Drawing on his personal experience as an academic and public functionary in Israel, with professional experience in the process of decolonization in Africa, Dan V. Segre echoed similar concerns about the crisis of identity and self-colonization in modern Israel (Segre 1980; cf., Sternhell 1998, x–xii; Wurmser 1999).

All this to say that the problem of self-denigration is not a problem unique to Italy. Indeed, when modern Israel celebrated its fiftieth anniversary, the ongoing public debate about its "founding myths" (e.g., *Economist* 1997b; Sternhell 1998; Wurmser 1999), bore considerable similarities to the debate that occurred when united Italy reached its fiftieth year (chapters 1, 2, 4, and 9 offer glimpses of that debate; see also Croce [1925] 1970). The Italian case differs from the Israeli case in part because of the longer time span involved and in part because the state of Israel has become the secular "religion" of many diaspora Jews, who are very protective of the image of that state and its affairs; after all, the Jewish diaspora established the Jewish state (Sheffer 1996, 64). Italophobia (Harney 1985) may or may not be "respectable bigotry," still current in some academic circles and elite press as we saw in chapter 1, but it certainly does not have the same standing as anti-Semitism as a mechanism for prompting sober second thoughts about what is being written about Italian life. Still, the theme of failure in accounts of united Italy suggests that if the universalistic values and extreme rationality assumptions of "post-Zionism" and "post-Judaism" succeed in freeing the Israeli Risorgimento from its historical context and in gaining ground among the Israeli intellectual and political elite, Israel may in the next fifty years experience the problem that Italy has faced, and continues to face – a struggle with itself far more threatening than military threats from outside (Wurmser 1999).

Self-abnegation and self-destruction (*il piacere di compiangersi* and *autolesionismo*) have continued in united Italy since it turned fifty. They have been kept alive in part because of Fascism and the debacle in the Second World War (cf., Galli della Loggia 1996). The cold war that came after may have equally contributed to those negative perceptions, as citizens and public officials divided their loyalties and identities and even replaced their "love of country" (Viroli 1995) with a choice between Communism and what might be called Americanism. *Tertium non datur*, or so it appeared to many during the cold war (Duggan and Wagstaff 1995; Galli della Loggia 1996; Lanaro 1992, chps. 1–3; cf., Pavone 1991). The end of the cold war and the political upheavals of the early 1990s invigorated public life, but also renewed self-questioning and doubts.

Thus, complex chains of developments have helped to replace the view of Italians as "good people" (*brava gente*) with negative stereotypes to the point that it appears to some that Italians may be one of the few peoples to have only negative stereotypes; even norms of individualism, self-reliance, accommodation, consociationalism, and tolerance, generally praised as virtues in others, have been mostly viewed as vices among Italians (Cavalli 1994, 159). Sorting out these developments remains problematic, as the debate of the 1990s revealed.

That debate revealed that some people attribute problems of self-image ultimately to a lack (even death) of patriotism, brought about by Fascism and the Second World War; others even question how long Italy can continue as a national community (Galli della Loggia 1996, 1998; Rusconi 1993; cf., Viroli 1995, 172–5). There are still others who tend to look to this very debate itself as a source for "home-grown negative stereotypes" (Mastropaolo 1996, 1997; Sciolla 1997). Few, however, disagree that imported and "home-grown" negative stereotypes have become powerful epistemic sources of disorientation about what Italians as a people have achieved politically and economically since 1946 (Mastropaolo 1996). All the more since many expressions of self-colonization have increasingly been incorporated into the language of Italian public discourse and elite public opinion – from columnist Giorgio Bocca on the left to columnist Indro Montanelli on the right. Thus, it has become possible to argue that many opinion

makers and intellectuals have become so disorientated as to be unable
to react to foreign assessments in the same way that an earlier generation of scholars and intellectuals did – for example, to Edward C. Banfield's *The Moral Basis of a Backward Society* and *The Civic Culture*,
by Gabriel A. Almond and Sidney Verba (Mastropaolo 1996; Sciolla
1997; Sciolla and Negri 1996; see also Romeo 1965; Sani 1980). It
may be too early to tell whether the adverse response of several Italian
commentators to Robert D. Putnam's characterization of Italian history, politics, and society constitutes a reversal of established practices
(e.g., Lupo 1993b). What is clear is that analysts who tend to emphasize the positive aspects and achievements of postwar Italian political
economy also tend to look kindly on Joseph LaPalombara's assessment
of postwar Italian democracy and governing class (LaPalombara
1987). But LaPalombara's argument has been, for many, seriously
undermined by the upheavals of the early 1990s.

We have something to learn from Cattaneo in this ongoing debate,
for he thought that Italian history and the resultant public life had
made Italians especially vulnerable to misunderstandings, stereotypes,
and self-colonization. Cattaneo's assessment is worth examining in
some detail, if only because, unlike LaPalombara's, it has better with-
stood the test of experience.

To be sure, terms like "self-colonization" were not yet available in
most European languages of his time, and therefore, Cattaneo did not
make use of them. This may help to explain why almost all the secondary literature on Cattaneo, and even the current debate among Italian intellectuals, seems to have ignored this aspect of his work. Another reason for this neglect is that Cattaneo himself, though a strong
republican patriot, was hardly viewed as the paragon of Italian nationalism in his own time. Another reason still is that Cattaneo associated
Italian pride more with the city than with the nation-state, and he saw
Italy as a great civilization that needed to build on its cities as human
communities rather than to build a nation-state as such. But there is no
mistake that Cattaneo thought through the problem of self-colonization and the accompanying cultural alienation of citizens. He viewed
self-colonization as a source of disorientation that must be confronted
and overcome by people who aspire to be self-governing. Indeed, it
would have been quite surprising – for he grew up with the knowledge
of Metternich's dismissal of Italy as a mere geographic expression – if
he had not considered this problem.

As early as the 1830s, Cattaneo noticed that knowledge of Italian
life and events was appallingly limited and misleading among French,
English, and German opinion makers and public officials. "Grand
Tours" of Italy, still in vogue then, were often used to find support for

the presumptive knowledge about and disdain of natives that many tourists brought with them. The anti-Catholicism of most British observers led them to identify the source of most problems in Italy, including the failure of its history to conform to the model history of their own country, as a question of "moral fibre." As we saw in chapter 1, in the 1860s Matthew Arnold was reiterating prevailing Italo-phobic and anti-Catholic views. Others, mostly from Germany, were fond of depicting southern Italy as a fairyland (*il bel paese*) inhabited by devils, while others still, mostly from France, described northern Italy as rich in physical resources and poor – "decrepit" was the word often used – in human ingenuity and resources (see also West 1999).

Cattaneo also recognized that knowledge of Italy was just as appalling among literate Italians, living under despotic and illiberal regimes of the peninsula. As we saw in chapter 3, his reservations about building the nation-state also had to do with the negative consequences that the forced creation of unity would have on people's capacity to act as self-reliant coproducers of many public services. He feared that, prevented from undertaking ventures that appeared to diminish the powers of public monopolies, people would in time (as Tocqueville was then discovering in France) acquire a negative image of themselves to the point that they would have little or no confidence in their own capabilities and accomplishments. Lack of public spirit can directly result from the way the political game is rigged, and self-colonization can also derive from trying to emulate great imperial powers – something to which in Cattaneo's view Italians should not aspire, as this emulation had already had disastrous consequences in the self-image of Italians as far back as Dante (Cattaneo [1836b] 1964, 3:230; [1839a] 1960, 1:95–142).

His conclusion was that this state of affairs was due not so much to deliberate malevolence, respectable bigotry, or even self-hate as such. Rather, it was due to unthinking and unreflective habits by foreign and domestic observers alike, as well as a failure to appreciate the consequences of political life on the orientation and disposition of people. The cosmopolitanism encouraged by the Catholic Church was equally at fault (Cattaneo [1845a] 1957, 2:80). Cattaneo was of the view that this state of affairs could be changed on two fronts simultaneously. One way was to gain a better appreciation of what political and social realities Italians themselves have constructed in the past and could construct now. Just as important was to develop a logic of inquiry or public science for a comparative assessment of Italian history, institutions, and culture. Anticipating what later came to be known as methodological individualism, Cattaneo held the view that such a public science needed to built on the microfoundations of individuals, for he assumed that they were not always blind instruments of particular times and cultures but, rather, human beings capable of shaping the world around them.

There are several ways in which Cattaneo tackled the first strategy. He urged his interlocutors not to be paralyzed by hostile and inaccurate reporting. He invited those who read the foreign press to write well-crafted rebuttals in defence of Italy and the truth (Cattaneo [1836b] 1964, 3:230). He acted on his own advice. In the fall of 1848 he practically chained himself to a desk in a Paris apartment so that he could, in two months, write a book for the French public explaining in their own language the Milanese insurrection against the Austrians. In 1859 he wrote three "letters" each to the *Times* (London) and the *Daily News* (London), offering his interpretation of Italian developments (Cattaneo [1859] 1965, 2:483–519). At the same time, he was ever attentive to news from the foreign press that, however unintentionally, recognized the positive presence of his compatriots in and beyond the peninsula. At one point, for example, he put his anticlericalism aside to reprint in Italian a long news dispatch from Calcutta describing the dedication and good work of a Neapolitan priest in Burma for over thirty years. Though this missionary dedicated his life to the spiritual and material well-being of others abroad, he continued to love Naples and Italy (Cattaneo [1833a] 1957, 1:3–8; see also [1833b] 1964, 1:7; [1834] 1964, 1:66). In chapter 3, we saw that Cattaneo had publicly welcomed an engineer from the British East India Company who had, in the early 1850s, travelled to north Italy to learn from the success of the Po valley irrigation system.

Another way of overcoming self-denigration was the diffusion of knowledge of different parts of Italy among Italians themselves. The journal Cattaneo edited, *Il Politecnico*, was one such means in the late 1830s and early 1840s, but there were others he equally praised and encouraged. For example, the annual meetings of Italian scientists before 1848 were an important vehicle for a pan-Italian exchange of views, for scientific collaborations, as well as personal contacts. The growing vision of a politically united Italy also came from such meetings. Another medium was the annual Italian geography yearbook, which he went out of his way to describe in some detail, so as to "redeem the misrepresentations of foreigners" and the more specific concerns of Italian regional journals (Cattaneo [1845a] 1957, 2:79–96). Augmenting the stock of knowledge upon which people can draw was, for Cattaneo, an important requisite for overcoming self-colonization and for reaffirming the educative process of human liberation. This was what a true *risorgimento* was about, after all.

In constructing a public science appropriate to Italian renewal, Cattaneo adopted a comparative perspective. He recognized that self-colonization was not unique to Italians. He would have agreed with Cabral that, for an armed revolution to be a truly liberating experience, it must be grounded in a previous, cultural revolution of the people. This is a point that Giuseppe Mazzini, Giuseppe Garibaldi, and many others in Cattaneo's own democratic, republican current of the Risorgimento ignored or missed altogether. We have, suggested Cattaneo, allowed stereotypes about people expressed in some abstract ideology to get in our way. By "we" Cattaneo had in mind several groups of intellectuals and opinion makers: detractors from the different nationalities then making up the Austrian empire; those who at that time denied that people of African origins – in Africa as in the Americas – could govern themselves and act accordingly; philosophers like Hegel who had characterized non-European nations as being "outside history"; and historians like Heinrich Leo who had extended Hegel's characterization to the Chinese (Cattaneo [1846] 1965, 3:339–40). "Sterile idle talk" prevents us from seeing and appreciating what different people do as they seek to craft their own social and political realities and their own opportunities. As a result, we are often at a loss in understanding ways of life, exchange relationships, and communal organizations, even of those much closer to us, like the Flemish and the Polish, the Irish and the Tuscans, and the French and the Corsicans. For these are people like us, argued Cattaneo, who "share the same alphabet, are pulled by the same locomotive, and genuflect at the same altar," who belong to the same civilization (Cattaneo [1846] 1965, 3:344). In the same vein, he engaged in a property-rights analysis of the "Jewish question," looking to Jews in a way diametrically opposite to that advanced by Karl Marx about ten years later (Cattaneo [1836b] 1964, 178–342). (This helps to explain why perhaps the only conference on Cattaneo as a "prophet of toleration" ever held outside of Italy and Switzerland was held in Israel in 1980.) But Cattaneo did not stop there.

He recognized that "aspirations of *incivilimento*, of progress, of economic reforms, of public works, and above all of being taken seriously by foreigners who seldom spare reprimands and criticisms" are universal and not confined to a single people or civilization (Cattaneo [1833c] 1981, 1: 445). To make the point, he engaged in a thought experiment. Just consider, he noted, what an outline of a book on Italian life written by a careful foreign observer would look like? Such an observer would have to come to terms with the fact that people in Italy face basic contingencies of everyday and cyclical life not unlike those that other human beings face the world over. What Italians share with other peoples could fill volumes, while what makes them different and even unique could probably take up only a small part (Cattaneo [1838b] 1981, 1:309–14). Why is this so?

Cattaneo's answer went something like this. Much of the world inhabited by humans is artifactual – that is, the work of human hands shaped by human knowledge. If Italy and not just its south is the fairy-land (*il bel paese*) that tourists come to admire, it must not be forgotten – and this was a point that Cattaneo liked to stress – that successive generations of human beings made it so. He estimated that, like much of the peninsula of Italy, nine-tenths of the Lombard plain was an artifactual creation – in his own words, a *patria* or *stato artificiale*. Cattaneo's appreciation of the art and science of institutional arrangements went beyond the political constitution of a country narrowly understood to apply to all sorts of joint and collective undertakings, both voluntary and public. Lest his interlocutors misconstrue his remarks as an expression of narrow regionalist or nationalist pride, Cattaneo, following G.B. Vico, liked to recall that the artifactual nature of human existence applies to much of the world – historical and contemporary – whether irrigation systems and other human artifacts are in Lombardy, India, or China. And this is so, Cattaneo averred, without in any way denying critical differences in the level and type of knowledge between early and modern individuals and across nations, political regimes, and civilizations (Cattaneo [1844a] 1957, 1:424; [1845b] 1956, 3:5; [1857–58] 1960, 3:80).

In chapter 3 we saw that Cattaneo did not quite succeed in fashioning the public science he envisaged. The vicissitudes of his life were such that he was seldom able to return to his scattered ideas and develop them systematically. But his assessment of the creation of the Italian state and his elaboration of the constitutional design that did not happen (discussed in chapters 2, 3, and 9) point to a theory of institutional analysis and design that enabled him to reach important conclusions about the direction that the course of Italian political development would take. His ideas also inspired successive generations of analysts to become autonomous scholars in the face of no small political impediments – from liberal Luigi Einaudi to liberal-socialists Gaetano Salvemini and Norberto Bobbio.

Misfocused Genius

Another argument that makes Italy appear less than a "normal" country is the widespread view that Italians do not, as a rule, excel in the use of principled ways to analyze and reform institutional arrangements – that their genius for political artisanship is misfocused, and misapplied, for it does not include designing a modern democratic order. How widespread this view is may be glimpsed from the following.

In most anglophone histories of political ideas, Italian thought is generally portrayed as either soft or cynical, not really fit to address issues of political artisanship, at least not of the kind that we find in the anglophone tradition of political thought. As a popular academic text once put it: "The contribution of Italian writers to political thought has alternated between lofty ideals and cynical realism. On one hand, Dante, Vico, Mazzini; on the other hand, Machiavelli and Pareto" (Bowle [1954] 1964, 168). This view has been incorporated in a leading Italian account of political and constitutional thought (Alberghetti 1989). Writing about the creation of the Italian state, a distinguished American comparativist offered a variant of the same view when he noted that "Italian political genius lies less in the creation of new administrative structures or of symbols that can stir men's hearts than in the sharing out of public goods among a host of private claimants" (Tarrow 1977, 64). Elite anglophone public opinion is not far off. Reflecting on the 1997 report of an all-party parliamentary commission on constitutional reform (the so-called *bicamerale*), the *Economist* suggested that the proposed new constitution was more a triumph for the old politics of the First Republic than a serious attempt to reshape the state in some federalist fashion, to make the national government more efficient, the national parliament more effective, and to reform the judicial system – the presumed goals of the constitutional reform commission. The explanation was clear: "Too bad that the Italian genius for design stops short at shoes and cars and does not extend to constitutions" (*Economist* 1997c, 18). Thus, the argument goes, the crisis of the Italian state continues (McCarthy 1995).

Marsilio da Padua's characterization of the relationship between artisan and artifact suggests that there is more to the making of shoes than the *Economist* was willing to entertain. John Dewey expressed Marsilio's characterization this way: "The man who wears the shoe knows best that it pinches and where it pinches even if the expert shoemaker is the best judge of how the trouble is to be remedied" (Dewey 1927, 207). Indeed, the received view represents a highly selective reading of the history and practice of Italian political thought. A broader picture is painted by a former dean of the Harvard Law School, Harold Berman, who has drawn attention to the importance of the constitutions of Melfi, and not just for medieval times: "What is particularly striking about the solutions [to some issues of justice] provided by the *Liber Augustalis* of 1231 [i.e., the constitutions of Melfi] is their modernity" (Berman 1983, 432). Recent scholarship is making it difficult to view "the southern question" in the old parameters, by revealing that successive generations of people in the south were skilled artisans in fashioning institutions of self-governance that endured for centuries (Epstein 1992; Sabetti 1999a). The received view also fails to recognize the important contribution of the free cities of Italy to the problems of constitutional choice. As noted earlier, Jacob Burckhardt, in his study of the civilization of the Renaissance in Italy, unfortunately did not really show what he often proclaimed – "the state as a work of art." By contrast, Harold Berman in *Law and Revolution* (1983) indicated that the basic principles of constitutional government were worked out in the free cities of Italy and Germany long before the Americans confronted the problems of constitutional choice. Scott Gordon (1991) has given a great deal of attention to the checks and balances devised by the Republic of Venice in an effort to reconcile the exercise of political authority with freedom and justice – and Venice remains the oldest self-constituted republic (see also Lane 1973). In times of trouble, many British figures, John Milton included, looked to the Venetian institutional arrangements to argue the case for a republican form of government for England (Gordon 1991, 65–8). Historian Carlo Cipolla recently recalled the chauvinistic tendency among Anglo-American historians to deny that crafting institutions for public health originated in the Italian cities between the fifteenth and seventeenth centuries, as opposed to Jeremy Bentham's Britain (*Corriere della Sera* 1994).

As noted in chapters 1 and 2, Italian concern with the art and science of institutional arrangements did not stop with the Renaissance. Indeed, if we are willing to shift the focus of historical investigation from the making of Italy as a preordained unitary state to the making of Italy as an experiment in constitutional analysis and development (as we did in part 1), it becomes easier to appreciate the problems confronting the creators of the Italian state.

As late as the beginning of the eighteenth century, the Italian peninsula was, in Franco Venturi's apt characterization, "still a sort of microcosm of all Europe," where, more than in Germany, it was possible to compare and contrast "a great variety of political forms and varying constitutions – theocracy, monarchies, dukedoms and republics, from Venice to San Marino. The Italian setting was fertile ground for examining the clash between kings and republics and the tension between Utopia and Reform in the Enlightenment" (Venturi 1971, 20). Not unsurprising, and as we saw in part 1, a considerable, if contradictory, body of constitutional knowledge was accumulated during the Risorgimento about how different sets of principles articulated in correlative forms could be expected to yield different results. This is why the debate on what system of government was best suited to a united Italy is as important as the prognostications of Cattaneo and Ferrara about the constitutional order that finally emerged.

Chapters 2–4 raise a chief problem in constitutional political economy that is not unique to the founding and refounding of the Italian state: namely, that it is entirely possible for fallible human beings to formulate explanations and use them for undertaking political and social experiments that do not work in anticipated ways. Witness the attempts of French and Russian revolutionaries to create new societies and new political orders. The repeated application of fallacious conceptions of organization in France led Tocqueville in 1848 to the conclusion that "in France there is only one thing that we cannot make: a free government; and only one that we cannot destroy: centralization" (Tocqueville [1848] 1971, xviii; see also Mény 1987, 52, 66–8). The failed Communist experiments in command-type economies and politics represent a disaster of major proportions for the people of Eastern Europe.

At this point, a critic might raise a counterargument that could go something like this. Granted the limitations noted by Tocqueville and what has happened in Eastern Europe more recently, the fact remains that the French state has been very effective. In Eastern Europe and in many developing countries, some forms of command-type economies and politics have provided equal access to basic public services and met nutritional needs of human beings better than ever before. Therefore, poor government performance in Italy does not dispose of the case *for* centralized government and administration elsewhere. Rather, the central question is, Why has the Italian state been so inefficient and the French state so efficient? Let me respond in part by calling up some points I made in an earlier context (Sabetti 1984, 226–7).

To raise the question of efficiency and to supply the routine answer is to slide unwittingly into an unperceptive and unimaginative way of thinking. We should recall that "producer efficiency in the absence of consumer utility is without economic meaning" (V. Ostrom 1974, 62). The criterion of efficiency is necessary but insufficient for a proper evaluation of the performance of a French-type system of public administration in a democratic society. Responsiveness, error-correcting capabilities, political accountability, and justice as fairness are among the evaluative criteria that in a democratic society need to be employed simultaneously alongside administrative efficiency. Bureaucracy does *not* equal efficiency. This issue is all the more important since the French state is often viewed – arguably not just under President Charles de Gaulle – as "the most oppressive in all the democratic states of the West" (Tarrow 1977, 2). What should we make, then, of the five republics, two empires, and several monarchies of France, and of a cultural chauvinism that has historically neglected the place of different language communities in that country?

The discussion in chapters 2 and 4 suggests additional points that would have to be incorporated in an appropriate comparative analysis of France and Italy – namely, differences in their prefectoral administrations. Somehow we would also need to recognize how important has been the need for Italy to defend itself in relation to the imperial aspirations of Spain, France, and Germany. Somehow the comparison would also have to account for the fact that liberal Italy had nothing like the Dreyfus affair, while it did have at least one prime minister, several cabinet ministers, and even army generals of Jewish origin. We would have to explain why anti-Semitism has been as pervasive among the French governing class as philo-Semitism has been among the Italian governing class. Even the history of Fascist Italy suggests a tolerance in public life that cannot be ignored. At least until 1938, it was possible for Italians to be Fascist and Jewish at the same time. Failure to consider institutional differences and to apply the same set of multiple evaluative criteria have led some, mistakenly, to celebrate the French state while lamenting that the Italian state has often been incapable even of mounting effective repression.

All these observations suggest a need to balance the record of centralized government and administration in France and Italy in comparative inquiry. As for other parts of the world, centralized practices of government and administration have produced quite impressive results in mobilizing resources and human beings for industrialization and modernization, but the cost has been, more often than not, "nation destroying" rather than "nation building".

There is something to the arguments of Tarrow and the *Economist*, if we shift our analysis from the level of individuals engaged in constitutional choice and design to individuals pursuing their relative advantages within governmental structures. The hard fact remains, however: people engaged in crafting institutions of collective action of almost any type face design problems that cannot always be overcome, even with great effort. A united Italy *à la* Cattaneo, (even less *à la* Gramsci), could not have been established in 1860. We should not forget that the Italian Risorgimento furnished ideas and role models to several Zionist leaders and personalities, from Theodor Herzl's time to the War of Independence in 1948. But consider Lord Balfour's 1917 declaration about the establishment in Palestine of a national home for the Jewish people. That declaration carried with it a promise that proved difficult, if not impossible, to meet: "that nothing shall be done which may prejudice the civil and religious rights of existing non-Jewish communities in Palestine." (Balfour 1917, quoted in Stein 1961, frontispiece; see also *Economist* 1997b; Lustick 1980). Even if Zionism was indeed "the God that did not fail" (*New Republic* 1997), it is doubtful whether the creation of Israel could have taken place when it did if the leaders of the Jewish Risorgimento had waited to ensure that its realization would not become a catastrophe for others. If Zeev Sternhell (1998) is correct, it is equally doubtful that the creators of modern Israel would have succeeded had they put the goal of socialism ahead of the goal of nationalism.

When we turn to North America, other fundamental problems in constitutional artisanship emerge. Much of the history of Canada since 1867 is the history of a political system that did not work as its creators had intended, of constitutional reform efforts that ended in stalemate, and of analysts "fallen into speaking the language of doubt when describing their society" (Bell and Tepperman, cited in Sabetti 1982, 11). The end of the Macdonaldian constitution was evident well before John A. Macdonald died, as French Canadians began to reap the bitter fruits of "responsible party government" and the accompanying tyranny of the majority in provinces outside Quebec. The failure to extend the logic of the constitutional formula reached at the Philadelphia Convention to all people in the United States had the consequence of sustaining a "race problem" as a persistent issue in American history (V. Ostrom, 1987, 178–81). The "southern question" remains probably *the* American problem, and it has taken a Sicilian from Brooklyn, Eugene D. Genovese, to convey fully the rich, variegated, and contradictory tapestry of that problem (1965, 1995). Turning to less tragic matters, supporters of the Eighteenth Amendment predicted that prohibition would usher in a new era of clean thinking and clean living, but the results differed widely from those lofty objectives. As Americans have increasingly turned their back on the general theory of limited constitutions formulated in *The Federalist*, they appear unable to resist both the "central-government trap" of problem solving and the allure of democratic despotism (e.g., Elkin 1987, chps. 8–9; V. Ostrom 1991, 1997; Putnam 1995; Sandel 1996).

While the Italian "southern question" still awaits its Genovese, it must be acknowledged that Sicily, for all its characterization as "the Ireland of Italy," did not quite evolve into the problem that continued, at great human cost, to baffle British-Irish politics into the 1990s. Both Cavour and Cattaneo tried – unsuccessfully – to teach the British how beneficial outcomes could emerge through the art and science of institutional design. As will be recalled from chapter 2, Cavour wrote a whole book on how the British government could help resolve the "Irish question"; Cattaneo did no less with his commissioned letters to a British reformer and public official (Cattaneo [1847] 1956, 3:68–145).

To disagree with the conventional wisdom about "Italian genius," to argue for a more calibrated appreciation of the constitutional challenge awaiting the creators of the Italian state, and to suggest why the crisis of the state has continued to our own days are not other ways of justifying what has actually happened. It is possible to promote greater self-awareness about what we do as social scientists without either presenting an anachronistic view of the past or falling into the other extreme of rationalizing problems away. To compare is to understand, not to excuse.

As we saw in earlier chapters, the system of governance brought about by Italian unification gave rise to a situation whereby it became increasingly difficult for public officials and political analysts to discern the causes that prevented things from working as they should. The search for ways to reform the state so as to produce better laws and better citizens took the form of successive "historical coalitions," but without basic changes in the design principles and instrumentalities of government. After all, since the Italian state was not "a product of political unity, but only the means for achieving that unity," any basic change potentially posed a threat to national unity (Fioravanti 1995, 413). Thus *trasformismo* as a kind of constitutional arrangement gave way to Fascism and Fascism to democratic centrism, and, eventually in the 1960s, to the Opening to the Left. But the lack of a close fit between the theory and practice of Italian government remained, hastening by the early 1990s the collapse, or overthrow, of the postwar political order.

In turn, many political analysts, by grounding their work on the model of the French Revolution and the history of France, or by explaining government failures as though either the forms of government or the ways governments operate do not matter, have also been unable to offer proper diagnoses and remedies. The tendency has been to narrate the crisis of the Italian state and to speak of generations of people as path dependently doomed to bad government. Such overarching characterizations have, however, evoked contrary reactions. Joseph LaPalombara's praises of "democracy Italian style" are not groundless: considering that Italy was by the late 1980s the fifth-largest economy, he was correct in saying that "something about the way the country is governed must be right. It is impossible to square today's Italy, in every sense, with the stereotypes that abound about that country" (LaPalombara 1987, 19).

Thus, the difficulty of getting centralized government and administration to work as it should has been accompanied by the difficulty of developing an adequate appreciation of the relationship between the principles and forms used in the design of the Italian state and its operational characteristics under monarchical and republican forms. At the same time, it must be acknowledged that Denis Mack Smith was partly right when he noted that "flaws" in its original creation made the Italian state, in some important respects, highly unstable (Mack Smith 1954, 6; cf., Romeo 1965). Yet, the "flaws" that made the Italian state highly unstable also served to foster among its people a spirit of independence and self-reliance which kept alive their sense of personality and self-respect.

Most Italians retained the traditional sense of justice and humanity that are such a part of Italian culture and life even under Fascism and during the last year and a half of the Second World War. As Robert C. Fried observed in his study of urban planning in Rome, "the compassion that today spares from demolition the thousands of illegally built homes that cover the Roman suburban landscape is the same that once saved the lives of antifascists and Jews in Rome in the days of the Nazi Terror" (Fried 1973, 107; see also Michaelis 1979). A critical issue since the creation of the Italian state still stands: how to incorporate in the design of public institutions what Hannah Arendt once described as "the almost automatic general humanity of an old and civilized people" (quoted in Steinberg 1990, 6). This is, in the end, the chief question in constitutional political economy that confronts Italy in the new millennium and the new Europe.

As we have seen, the work of Carlo Cattaneo suggests that some possibilities already exist. Whether such possibilities will be acted upon remains problematic, but it should be self-evident that poor constitutional artisanship cannot be attributed either to lack of knowledge or misfocused genius.

Endemic Corruption

The kickback scheme uncovered in Milan in early 1992 (*Tangentopoli*) revealed a pattern of corruption that went much beyond what was publicly known or suspected about long-standing practices of institutionalized corruption and bureaucratic free enterprise in the Italian public sector. The magnitude of that kickback scheme and the drama accompanying the resultant decimation of Italy's postwar political class reinforced the view of Italy as being exceptionally corrupt – corruption as a way of life. This view has distracted most commentators from paying attention to the legal basis of corruption in Italy – in the language borrowed from the American context, how "the pursuit of absolute integrity" in Italian public life has become the chief source of corruption (Anechiarico and Jacobs 1996). We should not forget that what is considered illegal (or criminal) according to Italian law may pass as perfectly legitimate pracice in other Western industrial societies and polities. Fortunately, there is gradually developing a comparative appreciation of the difference particular constitutional and legal regimes do make:

There is a difference between unitary and federal states when it comes to corruption. Even with no idea what the scandals per capita ratio would be between Italy and the United States, we can safely say that the spread of the inkblot is different. Corruption in the letting of contracts for building the Milan subway went from high to low on both the paying side and the receiving side. On the other hand, President Clinton's problems with campaign donations have not engulfed state and city Democratic parties nor endangered Democratic mayors and governors. And conversely Boss Daley's troubles in Chicago did not threaten the Truman administration. A strongly federal system has firebreaks, not always perfect but largely effective. (Burnett and Mantovani 1998, 260)

Just as the very system of government helped to transform corruption at different levels of public life into a single, gigantic scheme, so it took the Clean Hands operation in Milan to bring it to a sudden and catastrophic collapse. The interesting question is why France is not faced with similar situations, given the widespread corruption in its public life and, in the words of some analysts, "the end of the Republican ethic" there (e.g., Bornstein 1990; Mény 1997).

It is true that words like "vendetta" and "mafia" have "come into universal currency from the Italian language" (Mack Smith 1995, 10), but this point may be misleading and needs elaboration. It is important not to forget that many other words conveying positive Italian contributions to everyday life have come into universal currency from the Italian language (see Barzini 1964, xi). The tendency among most people to adopt foreign terms rather than use their own linguistic terms to describe negative phenomena in their societies (even when people of southern Italian origins have nothing to do with such phenomena) is understandable. For example, many southern Italians have followed this practice themselves when they describe what they do not like or would like to see stopped. They describe disorderly, individualist conduct or lack of good form as something American, un'americanata: the standard expression is "let's not do like the Americans do." The problem with the universal currency given to Italian terms like mafia and vendetta is that such a currency tends to gloss over the fact that individual, family, and group vengeance, crime syndicates, and corruption rackets are neither unique to Italy nor products imported by diaspora Italians. Crime and vengeance are not copyrighted as brand names of particular nationalities. Crime syndicates, assassin gangs, and vengeance can be found in most societies and political regimes.

One of the earliest modern examples of a "family business" in North America goes back to the British colonial elite, known as the Family Compact, that illegally and legally ruled Upper Canada in the 1830s. Already by the 1970s, Israel had become a "normal" country with its own organized crime problems, though scholars have been debating why Georgian Jews seem to excel in the business of crime more than other immigrants (Begin 1986). The emergence of a Russian mafia in more recent times cannot be fully understood unless we come to terms with the political upheavals of the 1980s and 1990s and their consequences for property rights and economic activities (Varese in press). It still remains to be explained why countries like Argentina and Brazil, with a history of sizable southern Italian immigration since the nineteenth century, are not known to have experienced serious problems of mafia and the like. The chief issue with words like "vendetta" and "mafia" coming into universal currency is that they make us forget that the phenomena they describe are not constant but variable, specific to the political economy of crime and punishment of particular political systems.

The new anticrime policies that Giovanni Falcone helped to create in 1991 may have triggered his own death in 1992. But the arrests and punishment by law enforcement agencies between 1992 and 1996 challenged to an unprecedented degree the view that crime and illegality pay in and beyond Sicily. Whether these developments will affect the conventional wisdom about the widespread existence of mafia groups remains an issue, as does reorienting the war on crime toward a reduction of state laws as "traps for money."

OVERCOMING THE ODDS

If one measure of the strength of democracy is its capacity to undergo institutional change while remaining democratic, events in the early 1990s clearly demonstrated that Italian democracy remains an exciting democracy in the full sense of the word. The election of the Prodi government in 1996 was not "a rejection of liberal democracy but rather a search for more effective liberal-democratic government, and especially for a more stable relationship between government and parliamentary majority" (Hine 1996b, 315). The same description can apply to the D'Alema government that followed Prodi's. There can be no doubt that the commitments of the Prodi and D'Alema governments to a democratic, egalitarian, prosperous, and safe world is more deeply rooted than perhaps any of the national governments since the Opening to the Left in the 1960s. Another measure of change brought about by the two governments is revealed in something clearly unthinkable even a few years ago: a former Communist as the minister of the Interior in one government and another former Communist as prime minister of Italy!

Strong as it is, however, Italian democracy still faces a critical challenge: to transform the changes in government that resulted from the "magic moments" of the early 1990s into standard operational features of governance without a basic reformulation of the design principles that apply both to the constitution and exercise of political authority and to the standing of citizens vis-à-vis authority structures, to emphasize service rather than control and citizenship rather than servitude. What emerges from this study is that basic changes in the forms of government and the ways governments operate will not be successful without a reformulation of underlying principles of institutional and policy design. Crafting institutions for self-governance requires a calculus of consent and commitment as well as a love of country that cannot be imposed and must emerge from people willing to engage in a dialogue with one another and to practise the art of associating together. Talking is better than fighting, but discourse and deliberation do not necessarily lead to desirable results. Political transitions are time consuming and messy.

To put matters this way seems unduly pessimistic, just as minimizing the challenge altogether seems unduly optimistic. It is certainly premature to reach a judgment on whether the process of political and economic reform initiated by different governments in the late 1990s will prove successful. As Barbara Geddes notes, "political scientists spend much of their time explaining events that have not finished happening" (quoted in Trebilcock 1996, 9). Enough time has elapsed, though, to make it evident that postwar Italy did confound its critics to become an industrial nation. By the second half of the 1990s, Italy again confounded its critics and surpassed expectations with profound, if controversial, transformations in its political class and public economy.

The odds are that Italy may continue to confound critics and expectations. The combination of the move to the European Union and reform within Italy is likely to yield a transformation in which Italy and its cities assume a prominent place in the future of civilization. The constitutional design that did not happen in Cattaneo's time may or may not happen in ours. But if good government is not to remain just "wishful thinking" (Donolo 1992), it seems certain that the search for it will continue to challenge the understanding, knowledge and artisanship of Italians and social scientists alike in the Europe of the third millennium.

Notes

1   *Milazzismo* is a reference to the "unnatural" political coalition formed in the late 1950s in Sicily by Silvio Milazzo, which brought together Sicilian Fascists, Communists, Socialists, Monarchists, and Christian Democrats. The term then is a pejorative reference to any unusual right-left ideological coalition in Sicilian politics. This short-lived coalition is discussed under the rubric of central government decentralization in chapter 4.

CHAPTER NINE

1   For example, Putnam says of Bari: "Like visiting researchers, ordinary Pugliesi must first locate the nondescript regional headquarters beyond the railroad yards" (1993, 5). The regional headquarters may have been nondescript and hard to locate in 1970, but not so at least since the second half of the 1970s. Street signs in the area point to it; the building is clearly marked. Moreover, the regional headquarters is not located beyond the railroad yards, but on the back side of the Bari main railway station in downtown (*centro*) Bari. (The railway yards are more than four kilometres away.) Putnam does not stop long enough in Bari to tell us why the building that houses the regional government is still rented from private sources.

As for Bologna, Putnam refers to the central piazza "famous for its nightly debates among constantly shifting groups of citizens and political activists, and those impassioned discussions about issues of the day are echoed in the chambers of the regional council" (6). What he describes here is not unique to Bologna's central piazza and applies equally well to the central piazzas of the other regional capitals and of almost all the towns and villages in the south, his final destination, Pietrapertosa, included. It is also very likely that, among the constantly shifting groups of citizens and political activists that can be observed pacing up and down the Bologna piazza, one would find transplanted southerners continuing the civic tradition of their natal villages and towns.

2   The right of selected common people in the south to bear arms was the source of much misunderstanding especially after unification, when national leaders sought to suppress or strictly regulate it.

3   Sonnino noted a capacity among ordinary Sicilians for changing the constraints and breaking out of their iron circle. He reported on cases he observed of tenant farmers seeking to impose limits on the rights of large landowners in some western Sicilian towns and villages in the 1875–76 sowing season, even though the tenant associations and the strikes they proclaimed were illegal and were put down by the arms of the state (Sonnino [1876] 1974, 246–66). I have examined in some detail how one such agrarian association developed, how the social capital accruing from participation in church confraternities helped to overcome the logic of collective inaction among peasants – a point that Sonnino also seemed to be aware of – and how the association was forcibly put down (Sabetti 1984, 86–8, 90–1).

4   It is generally not well known that Catholic lay congregations of women were the first self-organized and self-governed collective women's groups throughout Italian society until the second half of the nineteenth century. For an initial elaboration of this point in a comparative context, see Ridolfi 1990.

5   There is a huge and growing literature on the topic. Most of the research is being done by historians (Delle Donne 1990, Galasso and Russo 1980, Santangelo 1984, and Volpe 1993) who have been deeply influenced by the historical research of Gabriele De Rosa, cited therein. By nonhistorians, see the extracts from *A Tour through Italy*, by John Chetwode Eustace 1815 (reprinted in Seward 1984, 279–81).

6   One would have equally liked to see some caution in accepting at face value a 1982 survey which suggests that fully half of the citizens of Sicily and Sardinia claimed to have heard nothing at all about their own regional governments, by then more than thirty-five years old (Putnam 1993, 214n52).

7   The *contado* of Molise emerged as a jurisdictional and administrative unit only around 1806. It was created by the French-inspired Neapolitan government as a kind of buffer zone or "Switzerland" where Campania, the Abruzzi, and the Apulian Capitanata meet. Molise ceased to be such

a unit after 1860; the Italian government, rather than returning the Molise territory to the different areas from which it had been taken, simply incorporated Molise into the larger Abruzzi administrative system (see Picardi 1967).

8   Historically, the people of Apulian Capitanata have had, by almost all measures, more ties with the inhabitants of Molise than with the other two Apulian parts to which Capitanata is now administratively and politically joined. Similarly, since the consolidation of the Calabrias into one regional government, the Crotonese area has succeeded in gaining recognition as a new political and administrative entity (the province of Crotone), as have the people of the new Isernia province in Molise.

References

ACIR (Advisory Commission on Intergovernmental Relations). 1987. *The Organization of Local Public Economies*. Paper A-109. Washington, D.C.: ACIR

Accattoli, Luigi. 1995. *Cerco fatti di Vangelo: Inchiesta di fine millennio sui cristiani d'Italia*. Turin: SEI

Adams, J.C., and Paolo Barile. 1972. *The Government of Republican Italy*. Boston: Houghton Mifflin

Agnew, John. 1995. *Rome*. New York: John Wiley & Sons

– 1996. "Time into Space: The Myth of 'Backward' Italy in Modern Europe." *Time & Society* 5, no. 1: 27–45

Alberghetti, N. 1989. *Profilo di storia costituzionale italiana: Individualismo e assolutismo nello stato liberale*. Bologna: Il Mulino

Albini, Joseph L. 1971. *The American Mafia: Genesis of a Legend*. New York: Appleton-Century-Crofts

Alexander, H.E. and G.E. Caiden, eds. 1986. *The Politics and Economics of Organized Crime*. Lexington, Mass.: Lexington Books

Allison, Graham T. 1971. *Essence of Decision: Explaining the Cuban Missile Crisis*. Boston: Little, Brown

Allum, P.A. 1973. *Politics and Society in Post-War Naples*. Cambridge: Cambridge University Press

Alongi, Nino. 1997. *Palermo: Gli anni dell'utopia*. Soveria Mannelli: Rubbettino

Amato, Giuliano. 1974. "Gli apparati centrali e le regioni." In *L'amministrazione pubblica in Italia*, ed. S. Cassese, 478–91. Bologna: Il Mulino

Amato, Giuliano, Sabino Cassese, Enzo Cheli, Stefano Rodotà and Donatello Serrani. 1975. "Materiali per una discussione sullo stato dell'attuazione delle regioni." In AA.VV., *Dalla parte delle regioni. Bilancio di una legislatura*, 25–120. Milan: Edizione Comunità

Anechiarico, Frank and James B. Jacobs. 1996. *The Pursuit of Absolute Integrity: How Corruption Control Makes Government Ineffective*. Chicago: University of Chicago Press

Ansaldo, Giovanni. 1963. *Il ministro della buona vita*. Milan: Longanesi

Archer, Margaret S. 1995. *Realist Social Theory: The Morphogenetic Approach*. New York: Cambridge University Press

Archivio di Stato. 1811–60. Intendenza di Basilicata. Affari Demaniali. Comune di Chiaromonte. Potenza

– 1861–87. Prefettura. Affari Demaniali. Comune di Chiaromonte. Potenza

Arlacchi, Pino. 1987. *Mafia Business: The Mafia Ethic and the Spirit of Capitalism*. (Trans. M. Ryle of *La mafia imprenditrice*). New York: Verso

– 1992. "Premessa" to *Gli uomini del disonore: La mafia siciliana nella vita del grande pentito Antonino Calderone*, v–x. Milan: Mondadori

– 1994. "Introduzione" to *Addio Cosa Nostra: La vita di Tommaso Buscetta*, vii–xii. Milan: Rizzoli

Arlacchi, Pino and Nando Dalla Chiesa. 1987. *La palude e la città*. Milan: Mondadori

Armani, Giuseppe. 1998. *Carlo Cattaneo: Il padre del federalismo italiano*. Milan: Garzanti

Arnold, Matthew. 1867. "Italian Art and Literature before Giotto and Dante." *Macmillan Magazine* 33 (January): 228

Asor Rosa, Alberto. 1975. *Storia d'Italia*. Vol. 4. Turin: Einaudi

Astarita, Tommaso. 1992. *The Continuity of Feudal Power: The Caracciolo di Brienza in Spanish Naples*. New York: Cambridge University Press

Bagnasco, Arnaldo. 1994. "Regioni, tradizione civica, modernizzazione italiana: Un commento alla ricerca di Putnam." *Stato e Mercato* no. 40 (April): 93–103

Baini, Alberto. 1974. "Roma: Radiografia d'una capitale in frantumi." *Epoca* (7 December): 86–92

Baldini, Gianfranco and Guido Legnante. 1998. "From Party Mayors to a Mayors' Party." In *Italian Politics: Mapping the Future*, ed. Luciano Bardi and Martin Rhodes, 37–56. Boulder: Westview Press

Baldissara, Luca. 1994. *Per una città più bella e più grande: Il governo municipale di Bologna negli anni della ricostruzione (1945–1956)*. Bologna: Il Mulino

– 1998. *Tecnica e politica nell'amministrazione: Saggio sulle culture amministrative e di governo municipale fra anni trenta e cinquanta*. Bologna: Il Mulino

Banfield, Edward C. [1958] 1967. *The Moral Basis of a Backward Society*. New York: The Free Press

– 1968. *The Unheavenly City*. Boston: Little, Brown

– 1976. *Le basi morali di una società arretrata.* Edited by D. De Masi. Bologna: Il Mulino

– 1979. "Reply to J. Davis." *Comparative Studies in Society and History* 12 (July): 354–9

Barbagli, Marzio. 1995. *L'occasione e l'uomo ladro: Furti e rapine in Italia.* Bologna: Il Mulino

Barbera, Augusto. 1991. *Una riforma per la repubblica.* Rome: Editori Riuniti

– 1994. "Federalismo democratico e regionalismo." In *Quale federalismo: Interviste sull'Italia del futuro,* ed. Marco Sabella and Nadia Urbinati, 29–50. Florence: Vallecchi

Barile, Paolo. 1975. *Istituzioni di diritto pubblico.* Padua: CEDAM

Barnes, Samuel H. 1974. "Decision-making in Italian politics." *Administration and Society* 6 (August): 179–204

Barry, Brian. 1978. *Sociologists, Economists and Democracy.* Chicago: University of Chicago Press

Barry, Brian and Russell Hardin. 1982. *Rational Man and Irrational Society? An Introduction and Source Book.* Beverly Hills: Sage

Barzini, Luigi. 1964. *The Italians.* New York: Bantam.

– 1968. "The Anatomy of Expertise." *Encounter* 30 (January): 32–41

Bates, Robert H., Avner Greif, Margaret Levi, Jean-Laurent Rosenthal, Barry R. Weingast. 1998. *Analytical Narratives.* Princeton: Princeton University Press

Beales, Derek. 1995. "Saint of Nationalism." *New York Review of Books* (2 March): 6–9

Begin, Menachem. 1986. "Organized Crime and Organized Criminality among Georgian Jews." In *Organized Crime,* ed. Robert J. Kelly, 172–91, Totowa, N.J.: Rowman & Littlefield

Bell, Daniel. 1960. *The End of Ideology.* Glencoe: Free Press

Berkeley, G.F.H. and J. Berkeley. 1936. *Italy in the Making.* 2 vols. Cambridge: Cambridge University Press

Berman, Harold. 1983. *Law and Revolution: The Formation of the Western Legal Tradition.* Cambridge: Harvard University Press

Bevilacqua, Piero. 1985. "Uomini, terre, economia." In *Calabria,* ed. Piero Bevilacqua and Augusto Placanica, 117–365. Turin: Einaudi

Blok, Anton. 1974. *The Mafia of a Sicilian Village.* New York: Harper & Row

Bobbio, Norberto. 1971. *Una filosofia militante: Studi su Carlo Cattaneo.* Turin: Einaudi

– 1984. "The Rule of Men or the Rule of Law." In his *The Future of Democracy,* 138–56. Minneapolis: University of Minnesota Press

– 1995. *Ideological Profile of Twentieth-Century Italy.* Princeton: Princeton University Press

Bock, Gisella, Quentin Skinner, and Maurizio Viroli, eds. 1990. *Machiavelli and Republicanism.* New York: Cambridge University Press

Bollettino dell'Archivio per la storia del movimento sociale cattolico in Italia.
1950–94. Milan: Catholic University of Milan

Bolzoni, Attilio. 1988a. "L'atto di accusa di Borsellino divide palazzo di giustizia." *La Repubblica* (21 July): 18

– 1988b. "Un "pentito" (Antonino Calderone) fa tremare la Sicilia." *La Repubblica* (11 March): 17

– 1988c. "Lo stato si è arreso: del pool antimafia sono rimaste macerie." *La Repubblica* (20 July): 20

– 1991a. "Catania. Il giudice fruga nell'urna: Ora l'inchiesta punta su Gunnella." *La Repubblica* (25 June): 7

– 1991b. "Non è stato il boss Madonia a far uccidere Libero Grassi." *La Repubblica* (5 October): 6

Bolzoni, Attilio and Giuseppe D'Avanzo. 1995. *La giustizia è Cosa Nostra: Il caso Carnevale tra delitti e impunità*. Milan: Mondadori

Bornstein, Stephen E. 1990. "The Politics of Scandal." In *Developments in French Politics*, ed. P.A. Hall, J. Hayward, and H. Machin, 264–81. London: Macmillan

Bosworth, R.J.B. 1979. *Italy, the Least of the Great Powers: Italian Foreign Policy Before the First World War*. New York: Cambridge University Press

Bowle, John. [1954] 1964. *Politics and Opinion in the Nineteenth Century*. New York: Oxford University Press

Brancato, Francesco. 1956. *La Sicilia nel primo ventennio del regno d'Italia*. Bologna: Cesare Zuffe Editore

– 1963. "Carlo Cattaneo e l'opposizione democratica in Sicilia e a Napoli nel 1860." *Nuovi quaderni del Meridione* 1:1–26

Brennan, Geoffrey and James M. Buchanan. 1985. *The Reason of Rules: Constitutional Political Economy*. New York: Cambridge University Press

Briggs, John W. 1978. *An Italian Passage*. New Haven: Yale University Press

Brignoli, Marziano and Danilo L. Massagrande. 1988. *Bibliografia degli scritti su Carlo Cattaneo*. Florence: Le Monnier

Bruccoleri, Giuseppe. 1913. *La Sicilia d'oggi*. Rome: Atheneum

Buchanan, James M. 1960. "*La scienza delle finanze*: The Italian Tradition in Fiscal Theory." In *Fiscal Theory and Political Economy*, 24–74 Chapel Hill: University of North Carolina Press

– 1968. "Congestion on the Common: A Case for Government Intervention." *Il Politico* 33 (December): 776–86

– 1970. "Public Goods and Public Bads." In *Financing the Metropolis*, ed. John P. Crecine. Urban Affairs Annual Reviews, vol. 4. Beverly Hills: Sage

– 1975. "Public Finance and Public Choice." *National Tax Journal* 28 (December): 383–94

– 1979. "Natural and Artifactual Man." In *What Should Economists Do?* Indianapolis: Liberty Fund

Buchanan, James M. and Gordon Tullock. 1962. *The Calculus of Consent:*

Logical Foundations of Constitutional Democracy. Ann Arbor: University of Michigan Press

Bull, Martin and Martin Rhodes. 1997. "Between Crisis and Transition: Italian Politics in the 1990s." *West European Politics* 20, no.1 (January): 1–15

Bullock, Kari and John Baden. 1977. "Communes and the Logic of the Commons." In *Managing the Commons*, ed. Garrett Hardin and John Baden, 182–99. San Francisco: Freeman

Burckhardt, Jacob. 1860. *The Civilization of the Renaissance in Italy*. 2 vols. New York: Harper

Burnett, Stanton H. and Luca Mantovani. 1998. *The Italian Guillotine: Operation Clean Hands and the Overthrow of Italy's First Republic*. Lanham, Md.: Rowman & Littlefield

Calabria, Antonio and John A. Marino, eds. 1990. *Good Government in Spanish Naples*. New York: Peter Lang

Cancila, Orazio. 1988. *Palermo*. Rome-Bari: Editori Laterza

Canosa, Romano. 1991. *Storia della criminalità in Italia 1845–1945*. Turin: Einaudi

Caponnetto, Antonino. 1993. *Mafia e sistema politico-istituzionale*. Lezione tenuta in occasione del conferimento della Laurea Honoris Causa il 6 maggio 1993. Turin: Dipartimento di Studi Politici, Università degli Studi di Torino

Cappelletti, L. 1963. "Local government in Italy." *Public Administration* 41: 247–64

Capurso, G.L. 1964. "Cronache amministrative: Palermo." *Nord e Sud* (July): 52–6

Carbone, George. 1956. "The Long Detour: Italy's Search for Unity." In *Studies in Modern European History in Honor of Franklin Charles Palm*, ed. Frederick J. Cox et al., 49–80. New York: Bookman Associates

Carbone, Salvatore and Renato Grispo, eds. 1969. *L'inchiesta sulle condizioni sociali ed economiche della Sicilia 1875–76*. 2 vols. Bologna: Cappelli

Carboni, Carlo. 1998. "L'Abruzzo: regione cerniera o modello di sviluppo per il Sud?" *Il Mulino* 375, no.1 (January–February): 46–52.

Cardoza, Anthony L. 1982. *Agrarian Elites and Italian Fascism. The Province of Bologna 1901–1926*. Princeton: Princeton University Press

Caroleo, Anna. 1976. *Le banche cattoliche dalla prima guerra mondiale al fascismo*. Milan: Feltrinelli

Cassese, Sabino. 1980. *Esiste un governo in Italia?* Rome: Officina Edizioni

Castelnuovo Frigessi, Delia. 1972. "Introduzione" to *Carlo Cattaneo, industria e scienza nuova: Scritti 1833–1839*. Turin: Einaudi

Catanzaro, Raimondo. 1988. "Il governo violento del mercato: Mafia, imprese e sistema politico." *Stato e Mercato* 23 (August):177–212

Cattaneo, Carlo. [1833] 1956. "Notizia sulla questione delle tariffe daziarie negli Stati Uniti d'America desunta da documenti ufficiali." In *Scritti economici*.Vol. 1, ed. A. Bertolino, 11–55. Florence: Le Monnier

- [1833a] 1957. "Giuseppe D'Amato di Napoli." In *Scritti storici e geografici*. Vol. 1, ed. G. Salvemini and E. Sestan, 3–8. Florence: Le Monnier
- [1833b] 1964. "Altre notizie interessanti sull'India." In *Scritti politici*. Vol. 1, ed. Mario Boneschi, 7–9. Florence: Le Monnier
- [1833c] 1981. "L'antologia." In *Scritti letterari*. Vol. 1, ed. P. Treves, 443–8. Florence: Le Monnier
- [1834] 1964. "Fondazione d'un giornale letterario anglo-italo-greco." In *Scritti politici*. Vol 1, ed. M. Boneschi, 66. Florence: Le Monnier
- [1836a] 1956. "Ricerche sul progetto di una strada di ferro da Milano a Venezia." In *Scritti economici*. Vol. 1, ed. A. Bertolino, 112–77. Florence: Le Monnier
- [1836b] 1964. "Memoria di Claro Malacarne sui combustili fossili dell'alta Italia." In *Scritti politici*. Vol. 3, ed. M. Boneschi, 229–30. Florence: Le Monnier
- [1836c] 1956. "Ricerche economiche sulle interdizioni imposte dalla legge civile agli Israeliti." In *Scritti economici*. Vol. 1, by A. Bertolino, 178–342. Florence: Le Monnier
- [1837] 1948. "Del nesso fra la lingua valica e l'italiana." In *Scritti letterari artistici, linguistici e vari*. Vol. 1, ed. A. Bertani, 209–37. Florence: Le Monnier
- [1838a] 1965. "Di vari scritti intorno alla strada ferrata da Milano a Venezia." In *Scritti politici*. Vol. 2, ed. M. Boneschi, 52–132. Florence: Le Monnier
- [1838b] 1981. "L'Italia vista dagli stranieri [Disegno d'un libro che non fù scritto]." In *Scritti letterari*. Vol. 1, ed. P. Treves, 309–14. Florence: Le Monnier
- [1839a] 1960. "Su la *Scienza nuova* di Vico." In *Scritti filosofici*. Vol. 1, ed. N. Bobbio, 95–142. Florence: Le Monnier
- [1839b]. "Frammenti di sette prefazioni." In *Scritti filosofici*. Vol. 1, ed. N. Bobbio, 228–66. Florence: Le Monnier
- [1840] 1964. "Continuazione e fine delle notizie sul congresso dei dotti francesi a Clermont." In *Scritti politici*. Vol. 1, ed. M. Boneschi, 151–8. Florence: Le Monnier
- [1844a] 1957. "Notizie naturali e civili su la Lombardia." In *Scritti storici e geografici*. Vol. 1, ed. G. Salvemini and E. Sestan, 309–433. Florence: Le Monnier
- [1844b] 1960. "Considerazioni sul principio della filosofia." In *Scritti filosofici*. Vol. 1, ed. N. Bobbio, 143–170. Florence: Le Monnier
- [1845a] 1957. "Annuario geografico italiano." In *Scritti storici e geografici*. Vol. 2, ed. G. Salvemini and E. Sestan, 79–96. Florence: Le Monnier
- [1845b] 1956. "Industria e morale." In *Scritti economici*. Vol. 3, ed. A. Bertolino, 3–30. Florence: Le Monnier
- [1846] 1965. "Prefazione al volume II di *Alcuni scritti*." In *Scritti politici*. Vol. 3, ed. Mario Boneschi, 322–45. Florence: Le Monnier

- [1847] 1956. "Di alcune istituzioni agrarie dell'alta Italia applicabili a sollievo dell'Irlanda." In *Scritti economici*. Vol. 3, ed. A. Bertolino, 68–145. Florence: Le Monnier
- [?1848] 1965. "Militarismo e centralizzazione in Francia. In *Scritti politici*. Vol. 2, ed. M. Boneschi, 448–50. Florence: Le Monnier
- [1850] 1957. "Considerazioni sulle cose d'Italia nel 1848." In *Scritti storici e geografici*. Vol. 2, ed. G. Salvemini and E. Sestan, 123–337. Florence: Le Monnier
- [1852] 1952. "A Carlo Pisacane a Genova, 4 agosto 1852." In *Epistolario*. Vol. 2, ed. S. Taddeo, 167–70. Florence: Barbera
- [1855] 1952. "A Gaetano Strambio a Milano, Castagnola, 3 gennaio 1855." In *Epistolario*. Vol. 2, ed. R. Caddeo, 239–40. Florence: Barbera
- [1857–58] 1960. "Ideologia." In *Scritti filosofici*. Vol. 3, ed. N. Bobbio, 3–215. Florence: Le Monnier
- [1858] 1957. "La città considerata come principio ideale delle istorie italiane." In *Scritti storici e geografici*. Vol. 2, ed. G. Salvemini and E. Sestan, 382–437. Florence: Le Monnier
- [1859] 1965. "Lettere al direttore del *Times*, Lettere al direttore del *Daily News*." In *Scritti politici*. Vol. 2, ed. M. Boneschi, 483–519. Florence: Le Monnier
- [1860] 1960. "La nuova serie del *Politecnico*." *Scritti filosofici*, Vol. 1, ed. N. Bobbio, 370–84. Florence: Le Monnier
- [1860] 1965. "Prefazione al volume IX del *Politecnico*." In *Scritti politici*. Vol. 4, ed. M. Boneschi, 65–82. Florence: Le Monnier
- [1861] 1965. "Corporazioni delle arti e scioperi in Inghilterra." In *Scritti politici*. Vol. 4, ed. M. Boneschi, 168–209. Florence: Le Monnier
- [1864] 1965. "Sulla legge comunale e provinciale." In *Scritti politici*. Vol. 4, ed. M. Boneschi, 414–40. Florence: Le Monnier
Cavalli, Alessandro. 1994. "Conclusioni: Gli italiani fra provincia ed Europa." In *La cultura degli Italiani*, ed. Saverio Vertone, 155–72. Bologna: Il Mulino
Cavour, Camillo. 1845. *Considerations on the Present State and Future Prospects of Ireland*. London: Longman and Co.
- 1949. *Carteggi: La liberazione del Mezzogiorno e la formazione del regno d'Italia*. Vol. 1. Bologna: Zanichelli.
Cazzola, Franco. 1988. *Della Corruzione: Fisiologia e patologia di una sistema politico*. Bologna: Il Mulino
- 1992. *L'Italia del Pizzo: Fenomenologia della tangente quotidiana*. Turin: Einaudi
Cecchini, M., P. Vasconi, and S. Vettraino eds. 1991. *Estorti and riciclati: Libro bianco della Confesercenti*. Milan: Angeli
CENSIS (Centro Studi Investimenti Sociali). 1982. *Bologna: Stili di vita e istituzioni in una società consolidata*. Bologna: Il Mulino

– 1994. *Inventare una società neo-competitiva*. Milan: Franco Angeli

Centro Studi Economici. 1972. *La sinistra al governo, Bologna: Riflessione e proposte alternative sulla gestione del potere in una città democratica.* Bologna: Edizioni del Centro Studi Economici

Cervellati, Pier Luigi. 1976. "Rendita urbana e trasformazioni del territorio." In *L'Italia contemporanea 1945–1975*, ed. V. Castronuovo, 337–78. Turin: Einaudi

Cestaro, Antonio, ed. 1995. *Chiesa e società nel Mezzogiorno moderno e contemporaneo*. Naples: ESI

Chianura, C. 1991. "La piovra, esercito d'occupazione." *La Repubblica* (25 April): 9

Chickering, A. Lawrence, ed. 1976. *The Politics of Planning*. San Francisco: Institute for Contemporary Studies

Chinnici, Giorgio and Ugo Santino. 1989. *La violenza programmata: Omicidi e guerre di mafia a Palermo dagli anni '60 ad oggi*. Milan: Angeli

Chubb, Judith. 1982. *Patronage, Power and Poverty in Southern Italy*. New York: Cambridge University Press

CINSEDO (Centro Interregionale studi e documentazione). 1997. *Proposta di riforma costituzionale in senso federalista*. Milan: Francoangeli

Ciuffoletti, Zeffiro. 1994. *Federalismo e regionalismo da Cattaneo alla Lega*. Bari: Laterza

Clark, Martin. 1996. "Accused by Murderers and Men of Honour." *Times Literary Supplement* (July 19): 7

Cloward, R.A. and L.E. Ohlin. 1960. *Delinquency and Opportunity: A Theory of Delinquent Gangs*. New York: Free Press

Cochrane, Eric. 1986. "Southern Italy in the Age of the Spanish Viceroy: Some Recent Titles." *Journal of Modern History* 58 (March): 194–217

Cohen, Norman E. 1968. "Unity and Disunity Politics in an Italian Village." Ph.D. diss., University of Pennsylvania

Cohen, Stephen S. 1969. *Modern Capitalist Planning: The French Model*. Berkeley: University of California Press

Coletti, Alessandro. 1995. *Mafie*. Turin: SEI

Colombis, Alessio. 1974. "Organizzazione sociale e familismo amorale a Chiaromonte: Critica della tesi di E.C. Banfield da parte di un familista." *Sociologia dell'organizzazione* no. 4 (December): 437–88

– 1979. "Ricerca sociale, marginalità del Mezzogiorno e imperialismo culturale." In *Marginalità e lotte dei marginali*, ed. F. Granato, and D. Zingarelli, 343–74. Milan: Franco Angeli

– 1982. "Riflessioni metodologiche su ricerca sociale: concetti e ideologie." *Basilicata* 24 (July–September): 62–75

– 1983. "Amoral familism and social organization in Montegrano: a critique of Banfield's thesis." *Domination et dépendance: Situations* 25 (October–December): 11–34

– 1989. "Riflessioni metodologiche su di un 'tipo ideale' di marginalità stori-
ca." *Sociologia urbana e rurale* 11, no.28: 103–22
– 1992. "'L'invenzione' del familismo amorale." In *Dopo il familismo, cosa?
Tesi a confronto sulla questione meridionale negli anni '90*, ed. F.P. Cerase,
201–21. Milan: Franco Angeli
Conso, Giovanni, ed. 1995. *Le legislazione dell'emergenza*. Milan: Giuffré
Corbi, Gianni. 1998. "Quando 'l'inciucio' si chiamava Milazzo." *La Repubblica* (23 October): Culture page
Cordeau, G. and P. Tremblay. 1989. "The Occupational Hazard of Doing
Crime." Paper presented at symposium, Department of Sociology, McGill
University
Corriere della Sera. 1970. "Il malessere della giustizia: I dibattiti del Corriere."
(10 January): 7
– 1988a. "Ecco la lettera (di Giovanni Falcone) inviata al CSM." (31 July): 7
– 1988b. "Lotta alla mafia (lo stato della polizia a Palermo)." (10 August): 7
– 1988c. "Omicidio Chinnici." (22 December): 11
– 1988d. "E nel teatro di Mondello mille persone 'condannano' un magistrato."
(30 July): 9
– 1991a. "L'agonia da mafia, paralisi contagiosa." (4 April): 10
– 1991b. "Referendum: Il vento del Sud rovescia le previsioni." (11 June): 7
– 1991c. "Mafia, mafia, solo sciocchezze." (2 October): 11
– 1991d. "Io (Libero Grassi), industriale di Palermo, mi ribello alle tangenti."
(11 January): 13
– 1991e. "Carnevale scarcera sei boss." (30 October): 1, 11
– 1991f. "Marzo 1989 Sica denuncia: ricoveri regalati." (17 October): 2
– 1991g. "Bertoni: Superprocura come la cupola." (27 October): 11
– 1994. "Cipolla: Mal di soldi? Una risata vi guarirà." (9 August): 21
– 1998a. "Rapporto Censis: gli italiani non credono nella giustizia." (18
April): 7
– 1998b. "Siino: cosi i boss arrivavano a Carnevale." (6 April): 12
– 1998c. "Scopelliti, Cupola assolta in appello." (29 April): 14
Cortese, Nino. 1956. *La prima rivoluzione separatista siciliana 1820–1821*.
Naples: Libreria Scientifica Editrice
Cotta, Maurizio and Pierangelo Isernia, eds. 1996. *Il gigante dai piedi di
argilla: La crisi del regime partitocratico in Italia*. Bologna: Il Mulino
Crea, P. 1965. "Sul decentramento amministrativo di grandi centri urbani." In
La regione e il governo locale, ed. G. Maranini, Vol. 2, 62–73. Milan: Edi-
zioni di Comunità
Croce, Benedetto. [1925] 1970. *A History of the Kingdom of Naples*. Chica-
go: University of Chicago Press
– 1929. *A History of Italy 1871–1915*. Oxford: Clarendon Press
Crozier, Michel. 1964. *The Bureaucratic Phenomenon*. Chicago: University of
Chicago Press

- 1984. *The Trouble with America: Why the System is Breaking Down*. Berkeley: University of California Press

Daolio, A. 1971. "L'esperienza Milanese dei consigli di zona." *Economia Pubblica* (October): 23–32

Davis, J. 1970. "Morals and Backwardness." *Comparative Studies in Society and History* 12 (July): 340–50

De Leo, Franco. 1991. "Volontariato e cooperative di solidarietà sociale in Basilicata." *Sociologia* 25:237–59

Della Pergola, G. 1974. *Diritto alla città e lotte urbane*. Milan: Feltrinelli

Della Peruta, Franco. 1958. *I democratici e la rivoluzione italiana*. Milan: Feltrinelli

Della Porta, Donatella. 1993. "Milano: Capitale immorale." In *La politica in Italia*, ed. S. Hellman and G. Pasquino. Bologna: Il Mulino

- 1996. "The System of Corrupt Exchange in Local Government." In *The New Italian Republic: From the Fall of the Berlin Wall Berlusconi*, ed. D. Gundle and S. Parker, 221–33. London: Routledge

Della Porta, Donatella and Alberto Vannucci. 1995. "Politics, the Mafia and the Market for Corrupt Exchange." Pp. 165–184. In *Italian Politics: Ending the First Republic*, ed. Carol Mershon and Gianfranco Pasquino, 165–84. Boulder: Westview

Delle Donne, Enrica. 1990. *Chiesa e potere nel Mezzogiorno: Istituzioni ed economia 1741–1815*. Salerno: Edisud

Del Treppo, Mario and Alfonso Leone. 1977. *Amalfi medievale*. Naples: Giannini

Dente, B. 1974. "L'organizzazione di governo degli enti locali: Rassegna di proposte ed esperienze 1961–1973." *Rivista trimestrale di diritto Pubblico* 1:150–99

de Ruggiero, Guido. 1927. *The History of European Liberalism*. London: Oxford University Press

De Siervo, Ugo. 1999. "Dal difficile regionalismo ai federalismi verbali." Paper presented at conference, Cinquant'anni di autonomia della Sardegna, 21–3 January

De Soto, Hernando. 1989. *The Other Path: The Invisible Revolution in the Third World*. New York: Harper & Row.

De Viti De Marco, Antonio. [1903] 1965. "La politica commerciale e l'interesse dei lavoratori." In *Nuova antologia della questione meridionale*, ed. Bruno Caizzi. Milan: Comunità

Dewey, John. 1927. *The Public and Its Problems*. New York: Holt

Di Bella, Saverio, Filippo Sabetti, and Pierre Tremblay, eds. Forthcoming. *Antologia sulla criminalità: Contributi nordamericani (Rethinking Organized Crime: Recent American Studies)*. Cosenza: Pellegrini

Diesing, Paul. 1993. *How Does Social Science Work? Reflections on Practice*. Pittsburgh: University of Pittsburgh Press

Di Federico, Giuseppe. 1989. "The Crisis of the Justice System and the Referendum on the Judiciary." In *Italian Politics: A Review*. Vol. 3, ed. Robert Leonardi and Piergiorgio Corbetta, 25–49. London: Pinter

Di Federico, Giuseppe and Carlo Guarnieri. 1988. "The Courts in Italy." In *The Political Role of Law Courts in Modern Democracies*, ed. Jerold L. Waltman and Kenneth M. Holland, 153–80. New York: St. Martin's Press

Di Lello, Giuseppe. 1994. *Giudici: Cinquant'anni di processi di mafia*. Palermo: Sellerio

Di Scala, Spencer. 1989. Review of *Prima e dopo Craxi*, by W. Merkel. *Italian Politics & Society* 26 (Winter):31–2

– 1995. *Italy from Revolution to Republic: 1700 to the Present*. Boulder: Westview

Donati, Pierpaolo. 1993. "Carità e solidarietà nella società post-moderna." *Acta philosophica* 2: 233–60

Donolo, Carlo. 1992. *Il sogno del buon governo: Apologia del regime democratico*. Milan: Anabasi

Dragone, U., ed. 1975. *Decentramento urbano e democrazia: Milano, Bologna, Roma, Torino, Pavia*. Milan: Feltrinelli

Duggan, Christopher. 1989. *Fascism and the Mafia*. New Haven: Yale University Press

– 1995. "Italy in the Cold War and the Legacy of Fascism." In *Italy in the Cold War: Politics, Culture and Society, 1948–1958*, ed. C. Duggan and C. Wagstaff, 1–24. Oxford: Berg

Duggan, C. and C. Wagstaff, eds. 1995. *Italy in the Cold War: Politics, Culture and Society, 1948–1958*. Oxford: Berg

Dupuy, Francois. 1985. "The Politico-Administrative System of the *Département* in France." In *Centre-Periphery Relations in Western Europe*, ed. Y Mény and Vincent Wright, 79–103. London: Allen & Unwin

Economist. 1996. "Letter from Naples: See It and Live." (12 October): 94

– 1997a. "A Survey of Italy: Many Mountains Still to Climb." (8 November) 3–26

– 1997b. "The Unchosen People: Did the Palestinians Go or Were They Pushed? The Debate among Historians Racks Israel." (19 July):73–5

– 1997c. "As You Were in Italy: The Proposed New Constitution Is a Triumph for the Old Politics." (5 July):18

– 1999. "Europe Has to Scratch its Head." (March 20):21–2, 27

Einaudi, Luigi. [1944] 1954. "Via al prefetto!" (Away with the prefect!) In *Il buongoverno: Saggi di economia e politica, 1897–1954*. ed. E. Rossi, 52–9. Bari: Laterza

Elazar, Daniel J. 1971. "Community Self-Government and the Crisis of American Politics." *Ethics* 81 (January):91–106

Elefante, Francesco. 1987. *Saggio storico su Chiaromonte: Il territorio dalle origini all'unità d'Italia*. Chiaromonte: Arti Grafiche Racioppi

– 1988. *Luoghi sacri, casali e feudi nella storia di Chiaromonte*. Chiaromonte: Amministrazione Comunale

– 1989. *Chiaromonte: Economia amministrazione pubblica cultura*. Chiaromonte: Amministrazione Comunale

Elkin, Stephen L. 1987. *City and Regime in the American Republic*. Chicago: University of Chicago Press

Elkin, Stephen L. and Karol E. Soltan, eds. 1993. *A New Constitutionalism*. Chicago: University of Chicago Press

Elster, Jon. 1989. *The Cement of Society: Studies in Rationality and Social Change*. New York: Cambridge University Press

Epoca. 1991. "Documento: Le Pagine Gialle della mafia." No. 2138 (October 2): 109–12.

Epstein, Stephan R. 1992. *An Island for Itself: Economic Development and Social Change in Late Medieval Sicily*. Cambridge: Cambridge University Press

Ericson, R.V. 1982. *Reproducing Order: A Study of Police Patrol Work*. Toronto: University of Toronto Press

Ertman, Thomas. 1997. *Birth of the Leviathan: Building States and Regimes in Medieval and Early Modern Europe*. New York: Cambridge University Press

Evans, Robert H. 1967. *Coexistence: Communism and Its Practice in Bologna, 1945–1965*. Notre Dame, Ind.: University of Notre Dame Press

– 1976. *Life and Politics in a Venetian Community*. Notre Dame: University of Notre Dame Press

Falcone, Giovanni. 1988. "Il fenomeno mafioso: dalla consuetudine secolare all'organizzazione manageriale." *Una città per l'uomo* 7 (August): 4–12

– 1991. *Cose di Cosa Nostra*, in collaborazione con Marcelle Padovani. Milan: Rizzoli

– 1994. *Interventi e proposte (1982–1992). Fondazione Giovanni e Francesca Falcone*. Milan: Sansoni Editore

Farneti, Paolo. 1985. *The Italian Party System 1945–1980*. Ed. S.E. Finer and Alfio Mastropaolo. London: Pinter

The Federalist. [1788] n.d.. New York: New American Library

Ferrara, Francesco. [1860] 1949. "Brevi note sulla Sicilia." In *Camillo Cavour. Carteggi: La liberazione del Mezzogiorno e la formazione del regno d'Italia*. Vol. 1. Bologna: Zanichelli

Ferraresi, Franco. 1982. "Bureaucrats, Clients and Politicians: The Deflection of Change in the Italian Bureaucracy." Paper presented at the Conference on Organizational Responses to Change, April, at Concordia University Montreal

Ferrera, Maurizio. 1996a. "La particrazia della salute." In *Il gigante dai piedi di argilla: La crisi del regime partitocratico in Italia*, ed. Maurizio Cotta and Pierangelo Isernia 53–72. Bologna: Il Mulino

– 1996b. "The 'Southern Model' of Welfare in Social Europe." *Journal of European Social Policy* 6, no. 1:17–37

– 1997. "The Uncertain Future of the Italian Welfare State." *West European Politics* 20 (January): 231–49

– 1998. *Le trappole del welfare*. Bologna: Il Mulino

Fiandaca, G. and S. Costantino, eds. 1986. *La legge antimafia tre anni dopo*. Milan: Franco Angeli

Fioravanti, Maurizio. 1995. "Le dottrine dello stato e della costituzione." In *Storia dello stato italiano dall'Unità a oggi*, ed. R. Romanelli, 408–58. Rome: Donzelli

Flyvbjerg, Bent. [1991] 1998. *Rationality & Power: Democracy in Practice*. Trans. Steven Sampson. Chicago: University of Chicago Press

Fontana, Biancamaria. 1994. *The Invention of the Modern Republic*. New York: Cambridge University Press

Fontana, Sandro. 1998. "Towards a History of Transformism (1883–1983)." Trans. Mark Donovan. In *Italy*, ed. Mark Donovan, 305–20. Aldershot: Ashgate

Fowler, Edmund. 1992. *Building Cities That Work*. Montreal: McGill-Queen's University Press

Frei, Matt. 1995. *Getting the Boot: Italy's Unfinished Revolution*. New York: Random House Times Books

Fried, Robert C. 1963. *The Italian Prefects: A Study in Administrative Politics*. New Haven: Yale University Press

– 1967. "Urbanization and Italian Politics." *Journal of Politics* 29 (August): 505–34

– 1971. "Communism, Urban Budgets and the Two Italies: A Case Study in Comparative Urban Government." *Journal of Politics* 33 (November): 1008–51

– 1973. *Planning the Eternal City: Roman Politics and Planning since World War II*. New Haven: Yale University Press

Fukuyama, Francis. 1995. *Trust: The Social Virtues and the Creation of Prosperity*. New York: The Free Press

Galasso, Giuseppe. 1982. *Napoli spagnola dopo Masaniello*. 2 vols. Florence: Sansoni

Galasso, Giuseppe and Carla Russo, eds. 1980. *Per la storia sociale e religiosa del Mezzogiorno d'Italia*. Naples: Guida

Galetti, Vincenzo. 1975. *Bologna non è un'isola rossa: Le ragioni nazionali del 'miracolo emiliano.'* Bari: De Donato

Galli, Giorgio and A. Prandi. 1970. *Pattern of Political Participation in Italy*. New Haven: Yale University Press

Galli, Paolo. 1999. "Prodi's Progress." Letter to the Editor. *Economist* (27 March): 8

Galli della Loggia, Ernesto. 1996. *La morte della patria: La crisi dell'idea di nazione tra Resistenza, antifascismo e Repubblica*. Bari: Laterza

- 1998. *L'identità italiana*. Bologna: Il Mulino

Galluzzo, Lucio, Francesco La Licata, and Saverio Lodato, eds. 1986. "Giovanni Falcone intervista-racconto." In *Rapporto sulla mafia degli anni '80: Gli atti dell'Ufficio Istruzione del Tribunale di Palermo*. Palermo: Flaccovio

Gambetta, Diego. 1988. "Fragments of an Economic Theory of the Mafia." *European Journal of Sociology* 29:127–45

- 1993. *La Sicilian Mafia*. Cambridge: Harvard University Press

Gambino, Antonio. 1991. "La mafia è una famiglia." *La Repubblica* (10 January): 10

- 1998. *Itinerario italiano*. Turin: Einaudi

Ganci, S. Massimo. 1968. *L'Italia antimoderata: Radicali, repubblicani, socialisti, autonomisti dall'Unità a oggi*. Parma: Guanda

- 1973. *Da Crispi a Rudinì: La polemica regionalista, 1894–1896*. Palermo: Flaccovio

Genovese, Eugene D. 1965. *The Political Economy of Slavery: Studies in Economy Society of Slave South*. New York: Pantheon

- 1995. *The Southern Tradition: The Achievement and Limitations of an American Conservatism*. Cambridge: Harvard University Press

Gentile, Panfilo. 1969. "Magistratura e democrazia." *Corriere della Sera* (18 December): 1

Geraci, Vincenzo. 1991. "Il progetto di 'Superprocura': Perchè quel no dei giudici." *Giornale di Sicilia* (November 1): 2

Germino, Dante and Stefano Passigli. 1968. *The Government and Politics of Contemporary Italy*. New York: Harper & Row

Gerschenkron, Alexander. 1962. *Economic Backwardness in Historical Pespective*. Cambridge: Harvard University Press

Gilbert, Mark. 1995. *The Italian Revolution: The End of Politics, Italian Style?* Boulder: Westview

- 1998. "The Bassanini Laws: A Half-Way in Local Government Reform." Paper presented in the Department of Politics, University of Bath, England.

Giolitti, Giovanni. [1922] 1967. *Memorie della mia vita*. Milan: Garzanti

Giornale di Sicilia. 1988. "La Cassazione: Tante mafie." (14 December): 4

- 1989a. "Conti: 'Il pool va salvato.'" (19 January): 3

- 1989b. "Una giustizia da ritrovare." (15 January): 4

- 1989c. "Vitalone: la mafia è piu forte." (25 January): 3

- 1991a. "La tangente non conosce confini." (8 December): 15

- 1991b. "Caccia ai bugiardi di stato: La Procura accusa, la polizia replica, il giallo resta." (6 October): 1

Glazer, Nathan and Daniel P. Moynihan. 1970. *Beyond the Melting Pot*. Cambridge, Mass.: M.I.T. Press

Globe and Mail (Toronto). 1974. "Protestors Block Talk by Professor [Banfield]." (14 March): 1–2

Goldberg, Ellis. 1996. "Thinking about How Democracy Works." *Politics & Society* 24 (March): 7–18

Golden, Miriam. 1997. *Heroic Defeat: The Politics of Job Loss*. New York: Cambridge University Press

Gordon, Scott. 1991. *The History and Philosophy of Social Science*. London: Routledge

Graldi, Paolo. 1988. "Troppi processi in attesa di giudizio." *Corriere della Sera* (21 December): 7

Gramsci, Antonio. [1926] 1967. "The Southern Question." In his *The Modern Prince and Other Writings*, 28–51. Trans. Louis Mark. New York: International Publishers

– 1978. *Selections from the Prison Notebooks*. Ed. and trans. by Quintin Hoare and Geoffrey Nowell Smith. New York: International Publishers

Greenfield, Kent R. 1965. *Economics and Liberalism in the Risorgimento: A Study of Nationalism in Lombardy, 1814–1848*. Rev. ed. Baltimore: Johns Hopkins University Press

Greif, Avner. 1998. "Self-Enforcing Political Systems and Economic Growth: Late Medieval Genoa." *Analytical Narratives*, ed. Robert H. Bates et al., 23–63. Princeton: Princeton University Press

Grew, Raymond. 1962. "How Success Spoiled the Risorgimento." In *Italy from the Risorgimento to Fascism*, ed. A. William Salomone, 38–55. Garden City, N.Y.: Doubleday

– 1963. *A Sterner Plan for Italian Unity: The Italian National Society in the Risorgimento*. Princeton: Princeton University Press

Gribaudi, Gabriella. 1993. "Familismo e famiglia a Napoli e nel Mezzogiorno." *Meridiana* 17:13–42.

Grossi, Paolo. 1981. *An Alternative to Private Property: Collective Property in the Juridical Consciousness of the Nineteenth Century*. Trans. Lydia Cochrane. Chicago: University of Chicago Press

– 1992. *Il dominio e le cose: Percezioni medievali e moderne dei diritti reali*. Milan: Giuffrè

– 1996. "Un diritto senza Stato (La nozione di autonomia come fondamento della costituzione giuridica medievale)." *Quaderni fiorentini per la storia del pensiero giuridico moderno* 25: 267–84.

Guarnieri, Carlo. 1995. "The Political Role of the Italian Judiciary." In *Deconstructing Italy: Italy in the Nineties*, ed. S. Sechi, 90–112. Berkeley: University of California at Berkeley International and Area Studies

– 1997. "The Judiciary in the Italian Political Crisis." *West European Politics* 20 (January):157–75

Guarrasi, Vincenzo. 1988. "Verso una nuova identità urbana." *Segno* 93 (April): 65–71

Guicciardini, Francesco. [1651] 1969. *A History of Italy*. Ed. and trans. Sidney Alexander. Princeton: Princeton University Press

Haller, Mark H. 1990. "Illegal Enterprise: A Theoretical and Historical Interpretation." *Criminology* 28, no. 2: 207–35

Hamilton, Richard F. 1996. *The Social Misconstruction of Reality: Validity and Verification in the Scholarly Community*. New Haven: Yale University Press

Hancey, James O. 1977. "The Politics of Familism in a Stateless Society: the Mezzogiorno." *Europa* 1: 51–66

Hancock, W. K. [1926] 1969. *Ricasoli and the Risorgimento in Tuscany*. New ed. New York: Howard Fertig

Harney, Robert F. 1985. "Italophobia: English-speaking Malady?" *Etudes Migrations/Studi emigrazione* 22 (March): 6–43

Hayek, F.A. [1944] 1972. *The Road to Serfdom*. Chicago: University of Chicago Press

– 1988. *The Fatal Conceit: The Errors of Socialism*. Ed. W.W. Bartley III. Chicago: University of Chicago Press

Hays, Denys. 1961. *The Italian Renaissance in Its Historical Background*. Cambridge: Cambridge University Press

Hefner, Robert W. 1985. *Hindu Javanese: Tengger Tradition and Islam*. Princeton: Princeton University Press

Heine, Bend. 1985. "The Mountain People: Some Notes on the Ik of Northeastern Uganda." *Africa* 55:3–16

Hellman, Stephen. 1988. *Italian Communism in Transition: The Rise and Fall of the Historic Compromise in Turin, 1975–1980*. New York: Oxford University Press

Hennessey, Timothy. 1970. "Problems in Concept Formation: The Ethos 'Theory' and the Comparative Study of Urban Politics." *Midwest Journal of Political Science* 14 (November): 537–64

Hennessey, Timothy and Richard Feen. 1973. "Social Science as Social Philosophy: Edward C. Banfield and the New Realism in Urban Politics." *American Behavioral Scientist* (November–December): 171–204

Hildebrand, George H. 1965. *Growth and Structure in the Economy of Modern Italy*. Cambridge, Mass.: Harvard University Press

Hine, David. 1993. *Governing Italy: The Politics of Bargained Pluralism*. Oxford: Clarendon Press

– 1996a. "Federalism, Regionalism and the Unitary State: Contemporary Regional Pressures in Historical Perspective." In *Italian Regionalism: History, Identity and Politics*, ed. Carl Levy, 109–30. Oxford: Berg

– 1996b. "Italian Political Reform in Comparative Perspective." In *The New Italian Republic: From the Fall of the Berlin Wall to Berlusconi*, ed. S. Gundle and S. Parker, 311–25. London: Routledge

Hirschman, Albert O. 1991. *The Rhetoric of Reaction: Perversity, Futility, Jeopardy*. Cambridge, Mass.: Harvard University Press.

Hobbes, Thomas. [1651] 1962. *Leviathan, or the Matter, Forme and Power of A Commonwealth Ecclesiastical and Civil*. New York: Collier Books

Hodgson, Geoffrey M. 1991. "Economic Evolution: Intervention contra Pangloss." *Journal of Economic Issues* 25 (June): 519–34

Hofmann, Paul. 1990. *That Fine Italian Hand.* New York: Henry Holt and Co.

Hytten, Eyvind. 1969. *Esperienze di sviluppo sociale nel Mezzogiorno.* Rome: SVIMEZ, Giuffrè

Ivone, Diomede. 1979. *Associazioni operaie: Clero e borghesia nel Mezzogiorno tra ottocento e novecento.* Milan: Giuffrè

Jackman, Robert W. and Ross A. Miller. 1996. "A Renaissance of Political Culture?" *American Journal of Political Science* 40 (August): 632–59

Jacobs, Jane. 1961. *The Death and Life of Great American Cities.* New York: Random House

Jaggi, Max, Roger Muller, and Sil Schmid. 1977. *Bologna.* London: Writers and Readers

Jardin, André. 1988. *Tocqueville: A Biography.* 2nd ed. New York: Farrar and Strauss

Johnson, Douglas. 1985. "The 'Brain' of Italy." *New York Review of Books* (13 June): 24–5

Johnston, R.M. 1904. *The Napoleonic Empire in Southern Italy and the Rise of Secret Societies.* 2 vols. London: Macmillan

Keates, Jonathan. 1999. Domestic Diaspora. Review of *Italian Culture in Northern Europe in the Eighteenth Century,* ed. Shearer West. *Times Literary Supplement* (30 July): 18

Kelly, Robert J. 1986. "Criminal Underworlds." In *Organized Crime,* ed. R.J. Kelly, 10–31. Totowa, N.J.: Rowman & Littlefield

Kertzer, David I. 1980. *Comrades and Christians: Religion and Political Struggle in Communist Italy.* New York: Cambridge University Press

King, Bolton. 1899. *History of Italian Unity.* 2 vols. London: James Nisbet

Kjellberg, Francesco. 1979. "A Comparative View of Municipal Decentralization: Neighbourhood Democracy in Oslo and Bologna." In *Decentralist Trends in Western Democracy,* ed. L.J. Sharpe, 81–118. Beverly Hills, Ca.: Sage

Kogan, Norman. 1965. *The Government of Italy.* New York: Thomas Y. Crowell

– 1975. "Impact of the New Italian Regional Government on the Structure of Power within the Parties." *Comparative Politics* 8 (April): 383–406

Lacaita, Carlo. 1975. *L'opera e l'eredità di Carlo Cattaneo.* Bologna: Il Mulino

Laitin, David D. 1995. "The Civic Culture at Thirty." *American Political Science Review* 89 (March): 168–73

Lanaro, Silvio. 1988. *L'Italia nuova: Identità e sviluppo 1861–1968.* Turin: Einaudi

– 1992. *Storia dell'Italia repubblicana.* Venice: Saggi Marsilio

– 1994. "Federalismo e tradizione nazionale." In *Quale Federalismo? Interviste sull'Italia del futuro,* ed. Marco Sabella and Nadia Urbinati, 115–34. Florence: Vallecchi

Lane, Frederic C. 1973. *Venice: A Maritime Republic*. Baltimore: Johns Hopkins University Press

LaPalombara, Joseph. 1966. *Italy: The Politics of Planning*. Syracuse: Syracuse University Press

– 1987. *Democracy Italian Style*. New Haven: Yale University Press

– 1993. Review of *Making Democracy Work*, by Robert D. Putnam. *Political Science Quarterly* 108 (Fall): 550

Legnani, Massimo, ed. 1975. *Regioni e Stato dalla Resistenza alla Costituzione*. Bologna: Il Mulino

Leonardi, Robert. 1995. "Regional Development in Italy: Social Capital and the Mezzogiorno." *Oxford Review of Economic Policy* 11, no.2:165–79

– 1998. *Coesione, convergenza ed integrazione nell'Unione Europea*. Bologna: Il Mulino

Leonardi, Robert, Robert D. Putnam, and Raffaella Y. Nanetti. 1987. *Il Caso Basilicata: L'effetto regione dal 1970 al 1986*. Bologna: Il Mulino

Lerner, Michael. 1969. "Respectable Bigotry." *American Scholar* 38, no.4 (Autumn): 606–16.

Letkemann, Peter. 1973. *Crime as Work*. Englewood Cliffs, N.J.: Prentice Hall

Levi, Carlo. 1963. *Christ Stopped at Eboli*. Trans. F. Frenaye. New York: Noonday Press

Levi, Margaret. 1988. *Of Rule and Revenue*. Berkeley: University of California Press

– 1993. Review of *Making Democracy Work*, by Robert Putnam. *Comparative Political Studies* 26 (October): 378

– 1996. "Social and Unsocial Capital: A Review Essay of Robert Putnam's *Making Democracy Work*." *Politics & Society* 24 (March): 45–55

– 1997a. *Consent, Dissent, and Patriotism*. New York: Cambridge University Press

– 1997b. "A Model, a Method and a Map: Rational Choice in Comparative and Historical Analysis." In *Comparative Politics: Rationality, Culture and Structure*, ed. Mark I. Lichbach and Alan S. Zuckerman, 19–41. New York: Cambridge University Press

Levy, Carl. ed. 1996. *Italian Regionalism*. Oxford: Berg

Libonati, M. and H. Edelhertz. 1991. "Study of Proprety Ownership and Devolution in the Organized Crime Environment." Organized Crime Research Program, Temple University School of Law, Philadelphia

Liebow, Elliot. 1967. *Tally's Corner*. Boston and Toronto: Little, Brown

Lindblom, Charles E. 1977. *Politics and Markets: The World's Political-Economic Systems*. New York: Basic Books

Loveman, Brian. 1973. "The Logic of Political Corruption." Bloomington, Ind.: Indiana University Workshop in Political Theory and Policy Analysis Publications

- 1975. "Can Development Be Administered?" Paper presented at the Annual Meetings of the American Political Science Association, 1–5 September, San Francisco, California

- 1976. "The Comparative Administration Group: Development Administration and Antidevelopment." *Public Administration Review* 36 (November–December): 616–21

Lovett, Clara M. 1972. *Carlo Cattaneo and the Politics of the Risorgimento 1820–1860*. The Hague: Nijhoff

- 1979. *Giuseppe Ferrari and the Italian Revolution*. Chapel Hill: University of North Carolina Press

Lupo, Salvatore. 1993a. *Storia della mafia dalle origini ai giorni nostri*. Rome: Donzelli

- 1993b. "Usi e abusi del passato: Le radici dell'Italia di Putnam." *Meridiana*, no.18:151–68

Lustick, Ian. 1980. *Arabs in the Jewish State: Israel's Control of a National Minority*. Austin: University of Texas Press

Machiavelli, Niccolò. 1970. *Discourses*. Ed. Bernard Crick. Trans. by Leslie J. Walker. London: Penguin

Mack Smith, Denis. 1950. "The Peasants' Revolt of Sicily in 1860." In AA. VV., *Studi in onore di Gino Luzzatto*. Milan: Giuffré

- 1954. *Cavour and Garibaldi 1860*. Cambridge: Cambridge University Press

- 1959. *Italy: A Modern History*. Ann Arbor: University of Michigan Press

- 1971. *Victor Emanuel, Cavour and the Risorgimento*. New York: Oxford University Press

- 1974. "Regionalism." In *Modern Italy: A Topical History since 1861*, ed. E.R. Tannenbaum and E.P. Noether, 125–46. New York: New York University Press

- 1994. *Mazzini*. New Haven: Yale University Press

- 1995. "Italy's Dirty Linen." *New York Review of Books* (30 November): 10, 12, 14–15

- 1998. *La storia manipolata*. Bari: Laterza

- ed. 1968. *The Making of Italy, 1796–1870*. New York: Walker

Macry, Paolo. 1998. "Bassolino, per esempio: I piccoli bassi di Napoli." *Il Mulino* 376, no. 2 (March–April): 341–52

Manfredi, Christopher P. 1998. "Court's 'Declaration of Independence' Should Be Tested." *Calgary Herald* (24 April), sec. A, p.7

Manno, M. 1991. "Falcone: difficile bloccare i soldi della mafia." *Corriere della Sera* (28 April):11

Maradei, Manlio. 1975. "I giudici fanno il compromesso storico." *L'Espresso* (20 April):22–3

Marino, John A. 1988. *Pastoral Economics in the Kingdom of Naples*. Baltimore: Johns Hopkins University Press

Mariucci, Luigi. 1997. *La Riforma Federale: Vademecum per la commissione bicamerale e il parlamento 'costituente.'* Rimini: Maggioli Editore

Mariucci, Luigi, Roberto Bin, Marco Cammelli, Adriano di Pietro, and Gian-domenico Falcon. 1996. *Il federalismo preso sul serio: Una proposta di riforma per l'Italia.* Bologna: Il Mulino

Marselli, Gilberto A. 1963. "American Sociologists and Italian Peasant Society." *Sociologia Ruralis* 3:319–36

Masi, Anthony C. 1987. "Organizations, Occupations and Markets." *Contemporary Sociology* 16 (July): 485–98

– 1989. "Deindustrialization, Economic Performance, and Industrial Policy: British and American Theories Applied to Italy." In *The Politics of Economic Adjustment*, ed. Richard E. Fogleson and Joel D. Wolfe, 127–52. New York: Greenwood Press

– 1998a. Personal communication, 15 March

– 1998b. Personal communication, 15 May

– 1999. Personal communication, 18 February

Mastrogiacomo, D. 1991. "Notte di contrabbando." *La Repubblica,* (4 May): 23

Mastropaolo, Alfio. 1988. "Il caso Palermo tra tendenze nazionali e variabili locali." *Segno* 93 (April): 41–56

– 1991. "Il consolidamento della democrazia italiana su scala municipale: Un'ipotesi e alcuni dati sui consiglieri comunale in Piemonte tra anni quaranta e anni cinquanta." In *Le élites politiche locali e la fondazione della Repubblica*, ed. A. Mastropaolo, 67–96. Milan: Franco Angeli

– 1992. "Machine Politics and Mass Mobilization in Palermo: Epitaph for a failed revolt." In *Italian Politics: A Review*, ed. R. Leonardi and F. Anderlini, 123–41. Vol. 6. London: Pinter

– 1996. *La Repubblica dei destini incrociati: Saggio su cinquant'anni di democrazia in Italia.* Florence: Nuova Italia

– 1997. "L'Italia d'oggi: Elogio dell'imperfezione." Paper presented at the Department of Political Science, University of Turin, Italy

– 1998. Personal communication, 1 October

Matteucci, Nicola. 1993. "Costituzione italiana e europea: La sovranità ripartita." In *La riconquista dell'Italia. Economia istituzioni politica*, ed. Fabio Luca Cavazza, 279–90. Milan: Longanesi

Matthew, Donald. 1992. *The Norman Kingdom of Sicily.* New York: Cambridge University Press

Mazzocchi, Silvana. 1974. "Colloquio con Marco Ramat: Giudici assoluti." *Il Mondo* (31 January): 5

McCarthy, Patrick. 1995. *The Crisis of the Italian State: From the Origins of the Cold War to the Fall of Berlusconi.* New York: St Martin's Press

Melloni, Alberto. 1997. "Giuseppe Dossetti, il senso delle sproporzioni." *Il Mulino* 46 (July–August): 612–26

Mény, Yves. 1987. "France: The Construction and Reconstruction of the Centre, 1945–86." *West European Politics* 10 (October): 52–69

– 1997. "France: The End of the Republican Ethic?" In *Democracy and Cor-*

ruption in Europe, ed. Donatella Della Porta and Yves Mény, 7–21. London: Pinter

Mershon, Carol A. 1996. "The Costs of Coalition: Coalition Theories and Italian Governments." *American Political Science Review* 90 (September): 534–54

Michaelis, Meir. 1979. *Mussolini and the Jews: German-Italian Relations and the Jewish Question in Italy 1922–1945*. New York: Oxford University Press

Michels, Robert. [1911] 1966. *Political Parties: A Sociological Study of the Oligarchical Tendencies of Modern Democracy*, ed. S.M. Lipset. New York: Free Press

Miglio, Gianfranco. 1994. "La prospettiva teorica del nuovo federalismo." *Federalismo & Società* 1 no. 2:27–38

Mignosi, Enzo. 1988. "Palermo: Meli accusa la Procura." *Corriere della Sera* (7 November): 11

Miller, R., D.M. Benjamin, and D.C. North. 1990. *The Economics of Public Issues*. 8th ed. New York: Harper & Row

Il Mondo. 1969. "I quantamila baraccati di Roma." (13 November): 16–17

– 1973. "Il marcio di Roma." (22 November): 4

– 1974. "Capitale del malvivere." (17 January): 14–15

– 1975. "Riforma regionale." (22 May): 67

– 1991. "Piovra: Padrona dell'economica. Tutte le attività lecite città per città." (11 November): 32–43

Montanelli, I., A. Cavallari, P. Ottone, G. Piazzesi, and G. Russo. 1965. *Italia sotto inchiesta: "Corriere della sera" 1963–65*. Florence: Sansoni

Monti, Antonio. 1922. *L'idea federalistica nel Risorgimento italiano*. Bari: Laterza

Moore, William H. 1974. *The Kefauver Committee and the Politics of Crime 1950–1952*. Columbia: University of Missouri Press

Morgado, Michael S. 1974. "Amilcar Cabral's Theory of Cultural Revolution." *Black Images* 3 (Summer): 3–14

Murray, Charles. 1994. *In Pursuit of Happiness and Good Government*. 2nd ed. San Francisco: ICS Press

Murray, Robert G. 1959. "Un inedito di Cattaneo sull'Inghilterra." *Rivista Storica Italiana* 71:611–52

Mutti, Antonio. 1994. "Il particolarismo come risorsa: Politica ed economia nello sviluppo abruzzese." *Rassegna italiana di sociologia* 35 (October–December): 451–518

Nanetti, Raffaella Y. 1977. "Municipal Planning Through Neighborhood Councils: A Case Study of Citizen Participation in the Planning Process in Bologna, Italy." 2 vols. Ph.D. diss., University of Michigan

– 1988. *Growth and Territorial Policies: The Italian Model of Social Capitalism*. London: Pinter

- 1998a. "The Role of Planning in Social Capital Formation: Lessons from Naples, Italy." Paper presented at the Urban Affairs Association Annual Meeting, 22–25 April Forth Worth, Texas
- 1998b. Personal communication, 1 May

Newell, James. 1998. "At the Start of a Journey: Steps on the Road to Decentralization." In *Italian Politics: Mapping the Future*, ed. L. Bardi and M. Rhodes, 149–68. Boulder: Westview

New Republic. 1997. "Zionism at 100: The God That Did not Fail." A symposium edited by Martin Peretz. 8, 15 September, 2–24

New York Times. 1988. "A Rift in the Anti-Mafia Connection," (7 August), sec. E, p. 2

Nicastro, Franco. 1988. "Da Boris Giuliano a Giuseppe Insalaco: I nostri terribili anni di piombo." *Segno* 93 (April): 16–40

Olson, Mancur Jr. 1968. *The Logic of Collective Action*. 2nd ed. New York: Schocken Books

L'Ora. 1988. "E Calderone parlò." (28 October): 17

Ordeshook, Peter. 1993. "Some Rules of Constitutional Design." *Social Philosophy and Policy* 10, no. 2:198–232

Orlando, Leoluca. 1988. "Dalla cultura dell'appartenenza al progetto trasversale e nazionale." *Segno* 93 (April): 178–82

- 1998. "Pentimento e politica [Introduzione dibattito]". *Segno* 190 (November–December): 7–8

Ornaghi, Lorenzo. 1979. "I progetti di stato (1945–1948)." In *Cultura politica e partiti nell'età della costituente*, ed. Roberto Ruffilli. Vol. 1, 39–102. Bologna: Il Mulino

Ornaghi, Lorenzo and Vittorio Emanuele Parsi. 1994. *La virtù dei migliori*. Bologna: Il Mulino

Ostrom, Elinor. 1989. "Multiconstitutional Change in Multiconstitutional Political Systems." *Rationality and Society* 1, no. 1 (July): 11–50.

- 1990. *Governing the Commons. The Evolution of Institutions for Collective Action*. New York: Cambridge University Press

- 1992. *Crafting Institutions for Self-Governing Irrigation Systems*. San Francisco: Institute for Contemporary Studies Press

- 1997. "The Comparative Study of Public Economies." Paper read in acceptance of the Frank E. Seidman Distinguished Award in Political Economy, 26 September, Rhodes College, Memphis, Tennessee

- 1998. "A Behavioral Approach to the Rational Choice Theory of Collective Action." *American Political Science Review* 92 (March): 1–22

Ostrom, Elinor, Larry Schroeder, and Susan Wynne. *Institutional Incentives and Sustainable Development: Infrastructure Policies in Perspective*. Boulder: Westview

Ostrom, Vincent. 1972. "Polycentricity." Paper presented at the annual meeting of the American Political Science Association, 5–9 September, Washington, D.C.

- 1974. *The Intellectual Crisis in American Public Administration*. University: Alabama University Press.
- 1980. "Artisanship and Artifact." *Public Administration Review* 40 (July–August): 309–17
- 1987. *The Political Theory of a Compound Republic*. Rev. ed. Lincoln: University of Nebraska Press
- 1988. "Cryptoimperialism, Predatory States and Self-Governance." In *Rethinking Institutional Analysis and Development*, ed. V. Ostrom, D. Feeny, and H. Picht, 43–68. San Francisco: Institute for Contemporary Studies
- 1991. *The Meaning of Federalism: Constituting a Self-Governing Society*. San Francisco: ICS Press
- 1997. *The Meaning of Democracy and the Vulnerability of Democracies: A Response to Tocqueville's Challenge*. Ann Arbor: University of Michigan Press
- 1998. Personal communication, 20 November

Pacini, Marcello, ed. 1996. *Un federalismo dei valori*. Turin: Edizioni Fondazione Giovanni Agnelli

Page, Edward C. 1991. *Localism and Centralism in Europe*. Oxford: Oxford University Press

Panebianco, Angelo. 1989. "Le scienze sociali e i limiti dell'illuminismo applicato." In *L'analisi della politica: Tradizioni di ricerca, modelli, teorie*, ed. Angelo Panebianco, 563–98. Bologna: Il Mulino
- 1998. "Federalismo eppur si muove." *Corriere della Sera* (29 April): 1

Pardo, Italo. 1996. *Managing Existence in Naples: Morality, Action and Structure*. Cambridge: Cambridge University Press

Pasquino, Gianfranco. 1997. "No Longer a 'Party State'"? Institutions, Power and the Problem of Italian Reform." *West European Politics* 20, no. 1 (January): 34–53

Passigli, Stefano. 1963. "Italy." *Journal of Politics* 25 (November): 718–36

Pavone, Claudio. 1964. *Amministrazione centrale e amministrazione periferica da Rattazzi a Ricasoli (1859–1866)*. Milan: Giuffrè
- 1991. *Una guerra civile: Saggio storico sulla moralità nella Resistenza*. Turin: Bollati Boringhieri

Pederzoli, Patrizia and Carlo Guarnieri. 1997. "The Judicialization of politics, Italian Style." *Journal of Modern Italian Studies* 2, no.3 (Fall): 321–36

Perez, Francesco. 1862. *La centralizzazione e la libertà*. Palermo: Stabilimento Tipografico di Francesco Lao

Pezzino, Paolo, ed. 1995. *Mafia: Industria della violenza*. Florence: Nuova Italia

Piattoni, Simona. 1996. "Local Political Classes and Economic Development: The Cases of Abruzzo e Puglia in the 1970s and 1980s." Ph.D. diss., Massachusetts Institute of Technology
- 1998a. "Clientelism Revisited: Clientelist Politics and Economic Development in Postwar Italy." *Italian Politics & Society*, no. 49 (Spring): 44–62

Piattoni, Simona. 1998b. "Clientelismo virtuoso: Una via di sviluppo nel Mezzogiorno?" *Rivista italiana di scienza politica* 28 (December): 483–514

Picardi, Luigi. 1967. "Il Molise centrifugo." *Nord e Sud* 14, no. 94 (October):
84–95

Pinna, Luca. 1971. *La famiglia esclusiva*. Bari: Laterza

Pintacuda, Ennio. 1986. *Palermo palcoscenico d'Italia*. Palermo: Accetta Editori

– 1988. *Breve corso di politica*. Milan: Rizzoli

Pirani, Mario. 1991. "Ma contro Cosa nostra occorrono superuomini: E Falcone chiede Procure anti-mafia e una FBI italiana." *La Repubblica* (3 October): 9

Pizzetti, Franco. 1996. *Federalismo regionalismo e riforma dello stato*. Turin:
Giappichelli

Pizzi, William T. 1998. *Trials Without Truth: Why Our System of Criminal
Trial has Become an Expensive Failure and What We Need to do to Rebuild
It*. New York: New York University Press

Pizzorno, Alessandro. 1971. "Amoral familism and historical marginality." In
European Politics: A Reader, ed. M. Dogan and R. Rose, 87–98. Boston:
Little Brown

Plunkitt, George Washington. [1905] 1963. *A Series of Very Plain Talks on
Very Practical Politics*. Ed. W.L. Riordon. New York: Dutton

Pombeni, Paolo. 1995. *La costituente: Un problema storico-politico*. Bologna:
Il Mulino

Porsken, Ume. 1989. *Plastic Words: The Tyranny of a Modular Language*.
University Park: Pennsylvania State University Press

Posner, Richard A. 1999. "Sentence first, verdict afterwards." *Times Literary
Supplement* (26 February): 9–10

Pryce, R. 1957. *The Italian Local Elections, 1956*. St Anthony's Papers, no. 3.
London: Chatto and Windus

Przeworski, Adam. 1991. *Democracy and the Market: Political and Economic Reforms in Eastern Europe and Latin America*. New York: Cambridge
University Press

Puccio, Umberto. 1977. *Introduzione a Cattaneo*. Turin: Einaudi

Putnam, Robert D. 1993. *Making Democracy Work: Civic Traditions in Modern Italy*. With Robert Leonardi and Raffaella Nanetti.Princeton: Princeton
University Press

– 1995. "Bowling Alone: America's Declining Social Capital." *Journal of
Democracy* 6, no. 1: 65–78

Putnam, Robert D., Robert Leonardi, and Raffaella Nanetti. 1985. *La pianta
e le radici: Il Radicamento dell'istituto regionale nel sistema politico italiano*.
Bologna: Il Mulino

Quadrio Curzio, Alberto. 1997. "Verso una Costituzione poco europea." *Il
Mulino* 374, no. 6 (November–December): 1100–10

Rebuffa, Giorgio. 1995. *La costituzione impossibile. Cultura politica e sistema parlamentare in Italia.* Bologna: Il Mulino

La Repubblica. 1988a. "Ayala spiega il business dei palermitani." (3 December): 5

– 1988b. "Document csm: Il modello attuale va salvato." (15 September): 3

– 1988c. "Cossiga: Una riposta risolutiva." (16 September): 7

– 1991. "I bugiardi di Palermo: Il capo della Procura accusa lo staff di Scotti." (4 October): 1–3

– 1998a. "Italiani, popolo di falsari: un pamphlet di Mack Smith." (12 November): Culture page

– 1998b. "Strage a Roma: Niente ferro, solo cemento." (17 December): 7

Reuter, Peter. 1983. *Disorganized Crime: The Economics of the Visible Hand.* Cambridge, Mass.: MIT Press

Reuter, Peter and J. Rubenstein. 1978. "Fact, Fancy and Organized Crime." *The Public Interest* 53 (Fall): 45–76

Rhodes, Martin. 1997. "Financing Party Politics in Italy: A Case of Systemic Corruption." *West European Politics* 20, no. 1 (Summer): 54–80

Ridolfi, Maurizio. 1990. *Il circolo virtuoso: Sociabilità democratica, associazionismo e rappresentanza politica nell'ottocento.* Florence: Centro Editoriale Toscano

Romanelli, Raffaele, ed. 1995a. *Storia dello Stato Italiano dall'Unità a oggi.* Rome: Donzelli.

– 1995b. "Centralismo e autonomie." In *Storia dello Stato Italiano dall'Unità a oggi,* ed. R. Romanelli, 126–86. Rome: Donzelli

Romano, Ruggiero. 1994. *Paese Italia: Venti secoli di identità.* Rome: Donzelli

Romeo, Rosario. 1965. "Introductory Essay." In *Economics and Liberalism in the Risorgimento: A Study of Nationalism in Lombardy, 1814–1848,* by R. Kent Greenfield. Rev. ed. Baltimore: Johns Hopkins University Press

– 1973. *Il Risorgimento in Sicilia.* New ed. Bari: Laterza

– 1974. *Dal Piemonte Sabaudo all'Italia liberale.* Bari: Laterza

– 1977. "Deformazioni di Cattaneo." In his *Italia moderna fra storia e storiografia,* 97–100. Florence: Le Monnier

Rose, Arnold. 1961."On Individualism and Social Responsibility." *European Journal of Sociology* 2:163–9

Rotelli, Ettore. 1973. "Le transformazioni dell'ordinamento comunale e provinciale durante il regime fascista." In *Il fascismo e le autonomie locali,* ed. Sandro Fontana, 73–156. Bologna: Il Mulino

– 1976. "Carlo Cattaneo e gli ordinamenti locali lombardi." In *L'opera e l'eredità di Carlo Cattaneo,* ed. Carlo Lacaita, 283–306 Bologna: Il Mulino

– 1991. *Il martello e l'incudine: Comuni e province fra cittadini e apparati.* Bologna: Il Mulino

Ruffilli, Roberto. 1971. *La questione regionale dall'Unificazione alla dittatura, 1862–1942.* Milan: Giuffrè

– , ed. 1979. *Cultura politica e partiti nell'età della Costituente*. 2 vols. Bologna: Il Mulino

Rusconi, Gian Enrico. 1993. *Se cessiamo di essere una nazione*. Bologna: Il Mulino

Sabella, Marco and Nadia Urbinati, eds. 1994. *Quale Federalismo? Interviste sull'Italia del futuro*. Florence: Vallecchi

Sabetti, Filippo. 1975. "Theory of Public Policy: European Contributions." In *Policy Studies in America and Elsewhere*, ed. S.Nagel, 41–9. Lexington: Lexington Books

– 1982. "The Historical Context of Constitutional Change in Canada." *Law and Contemporary Problems* 45 (Autumn): 11–32

– 1984. *Political Authority in a Sicilian Village*. New Brunswick, N.J.: Rutgers University Press

– 1990. "Un precursore siciliano di 'Public Choice'? Francesco Ferrara e lo sviluppo delle scienze sociali in Nord America." In *Francesco Ferrara e il suo tempo*, ed. P. Barucci and M. Ganci, 259–74. Rome: Bancaria Editrice

– 1993. *Politica e potere in un comune siciliano*. Cosenza: Pellegrini

– 1995. Review of *Italy: From Revolution to Republic, 1700 to the Present*, by Spencer Di Scala and of *The Italian Revolution: The End of Politics Italian Style?*, byMark Gilbert. *Italian Politics & Society*, no. 44 (Fall): 32–6

– 1996. Review of *Mafia: Industria della violenza. Scritti e documenti inediti sulla mafia dalle origini ai nostri giorni*, by Paolo Pezzino. *Journal of Modern Italian Studies* 1 (Summer): 479–82

– 1997. Review of *Italian Regionalism: History, Identity and Politics*, by Carl Levy. *Journal of Modern Italian Studies*, no. 3 (Fall): 403–4

– 1999a. "An Agenda for the Study of Long-Enduring Institutions of Self-Governance in the Italian South." Paper presented at the American Political Science Association Meetings, Atlanta, Georgia, 2–5 September

– 1999b. "Covenant Language in Canada: Continuity and Change in Political Discourse." 1980. Reprint, in *The Covenant Connection*, ed. Daniel J. Elazar, 259–83. Lanham, Md.: Rowman and Littlefield

Sabetti, Filippo and Raimondo Catanzaro. 1991. "The 1989 Events in Perspective: The End of an Era or the Past as the Future?" In *Italian Politics: A Review*. ed. F. Sabetti and R. Catanzaro, 1–7. Vol. 5, London: Pinter

Saladino, Giuliana. 1988. "Emerge un'ansia nuova: Riconoscersi in qualcosa di pulito." *Segno* 93 (April): 9–15

Salvatorelli, Luigi. 1970. *The Risorgimento: Thought and Action*. New York: Harper & Row

Salvemini, Gaetano. [1945] 1960. "Introductory Essay." In *Italy in the Giolittian Era: Italian Democracy in the Making, 1900–1914*, by A. William Salomone, xiii–xxii.Philadelphia: University of Pennsylvania Press

Samuels, Richard. 1997. "Tracking Democracies: Italy and Japan in Historical Perspective." *Journal of Modern Italian Studies* 2 (Fall): 283–320

Sandel, Michael J. 1996. *Democracy's Discontent: America in Search of a Public Philosophy*. Cambridge: Harvard University Press

Sani, Giacomo. 1980. "The Political Culture of Italy: Continuity and Change." In *The Civic Culture Revisited*, ed. Gabriel A. Almond and Sidney Verba, 273–324. Boston: Little, Brown

Santangelo, Annamaria. 1984. *Antiche confraternite a Venosa*. Venosa: Edizioni Osanna

Santino, Ugo. 1988. "The Financial Mafia: The Illegal Accumulation of Wealth and the Financial-industrial Complex." *Contemporary Crises* 12: 203–43

Santino, Ugo and G. La Fiura. 1990. *L'impresa mafiosa*. Milan: Franco Angeli

Sartori, Giovanni. 1962. "Constitutionalism: A Preliminary Discussion." *American Political Science Review* 54 (December): 855–64

– 1966. "European Political Parties: The Case of Polarized Pluralism." In *Political Parties and Political Development*, ed. Joseph LaPalombara and Myron Weiner, 137–76. Princeton: Princeton University Press

– 1969. "From the Sociology of Politics to Political Sociology." In *Politics and the Social Sciences*, ed. S.M. Lipset, 65–100. New York: Oxford University Press

– 1994. *Comparative Constitutional Engineering: An Inquiry into Structures, Incentives and Outcomes*. New York: New York University Press

Sassoon, Donald. 1977. "Introduction: Italy Today; A Society in Transition." In *Bologna*, by M. Jaggi, R. Muller, and S. Schmid, 7–28. London: Writers and Readers

Sbragia, Alberta. 1979. "Not All Roads Lead to Rome.: Local Housing Policy in the Unitary Italian State." *British Journal of Political Science* 9:315–39

Scalfari, Eugenio. 1991. "Beffe e sberleffi allo Stato pupazzo." *La Repubblica* (19 October): 1, 6

– 1994. "Il colpo di spugna su Mani Pulite." *La Repubblica* (30 October): 14

Schiera, Pierangelo, ed. 1993. *Le autonomie e l'Europa: Profili storici e comparati*. Bologna: Il Mulino

Sciacca, A. 1991. "Collega giudice, la mafia ha vinto." *Corriere della Sera* (29 April): 11

Sciolla, Loredana. 1997. *Italiani: Stereotipi di casa nostra*. Bologna: Il Mulino

Sciolla, Loredana and Nicola Negri. 1996. "L'isolamento dello spirito civico." In *Il paese dei paradossi: Le basi sociali della politica in Italia*, ed. N. Negri and L. Sciolla, 119–45. Roma: Nuova Italia Scientifica

Scott, James C. 1998. *Seeing Like a State: How Certain Schemes to Improve the Human Condition Have Failed*. New Haven: Yale University Press

Sechi, Salvatore. 1995. "Introduction" to *Deconstructing Italy: Italy in the Nineties*, ed. S. Sechi, 1–35. Berkeley: University of California at Berkeley International and Area Studies

Segno. 1997. "Per ricominciare il pentimento [Dibattiti]." 190 (November–December): 5–76

Segre, Dan V. 1980. *A Crisis of Identity: Israel and Zionism*. New York: Oxford University Press

Selznick, Philip. 1966. TVA *and the Grass Roots: A Study in the Sociology of Formal Organization*. New York: Harper & Row

Sergi, P. 1991. *La 'Santa' Violenza*. Cosenza: Edizioni Periferia

Serio, Ettore. 1966. "Burocrazia in Sicilia." *Nord e Sud* (June): 51–7

Seton-Watson, Christopher. 1967. *Italy from Liberalism to Fascism 1870–1925*. London: Methuen & Co.

Seward, Desmond, ed. 1984. *Naples: A Traveller's Companion*. New York: Atheneum

Sheffer, Gabriel. 1996. "Israel Diaspora Relations in Comparative Perspective." In *Israel in Comparative Perspective: Challenging the Conventional Wisdom*, ed. M. N. Barnett, 85–106. Albany: State University of New York Press

Silverman, Sydel F. 1968. "Agricultural Organization, Social Structure and Values in Italy: Amoral Familism Reconsidered." *American Anthropologist* 70: 1–20

Sinisi, Giuseppe. 1993. "Il decentramento urbano in Italia: Il ruolo dei consigli di quartiere a Catania dal 1980 al 1990." *Il politico* 58, nos. 1–2: 181–212

Skogan, Wesley G. 1992. *Disorder and Decline: Crime and the Spiral of Decay in American Neighborhoods*. Berkeley, Ca.: University of California Press

Smith, Adam. [1776] 1965. *The Wealth of Nations*. New York: Random House.

Snowden, M. Frank. 1986. *Violence and Great Estates in the South of Italy: Apulia 1900–1922*. Cambridge: Cambridge University Press

Solazzo, A. 1991. "Ex-collaboratore di Sica denuncia l'impreparazione di politici e toghe." *Corriere della Sera* (14 June): 15

Soltan, Karol E. 1996. "Introduction: Imagination, Political Competence and Institutions." In *The Constitution of Good Societies*, ed. Karol E. Soltan and Stephen L. Elkin, 1–18. University Park: Pennsylvania State University Press

Soltan, Karol E. and Stephen L. Elkin, eds. 1996. *The Constitution of Good Societies*. University Park: The Pennsylvania State University Press

Sonnino, Sidney. [1876] 1974. *I contadini di Sicilia*. Florence: Vallecchi Editore

Spotts, Frederic and Theodor Wieser. 1986. *Italy: A Difficult Democracy*. New York: Cambridge University Press

Sproule-Jones, Mark H. 1974. "An Analysis of Canadian Federalism." *Publius* 4 (Fall): 109–36

– 1993. *Governments at Work: Canadian Parliamentary Federalism and Its Public Policy Effects*. Toronto: University of Toronto Press

Spruyt, Hendrik. 1994. *The Sovereign State and Its Competitors: An Analysis of Systems Change*. Princeton: Princeton University Press

Stajano, Corrado. 1986. *Mafia: L'atto di accusa dei giudici di Palermo*. Rome: Editori Riuniti

La Stampa. 1991a. "La mafia, prima azienda d'Italia." (12 July): 8

- 1991b. "Inquisito un amministratore su sette: Un dossier di Sica sui reati di 17 mila politici." (14 May): 13
- 1991c. "La Superprocura ha sbagliato strada: Giovanni Conso." (12 November): 11

Stein, Leonard. 1961. *The Balfour Declaration*. New York: Simon and Schuster

Steinberg, Jonathan. 1990. *All or Nothing: The Axis and the Holocaust 1941–1943*. London: Routledge

- 1997. *Why Switzerland?* 2nd ed. Cambridge: Cambridge University Press

Steiner, H. A. 1939. "Italy: Communal and Provincial Government." In *Local Government in Europe*, ed. W. Anderson, 305–80. New York: D. Appleton Century

Stern, A.J. 1974. "The Italian CP at the Grass Roots." *Problems of Communism* 23 (March–April): 42–54

Sternhell, Zeev. 1998. *The Founding Myths of Israel: Nationalism, Socialism and the Making of the Jewish State*. 2nd ed. Princeton: Princeton University Press

Stille, Alexander. 1995. *Excellent Cadavers: The Mafia and the Death of the First Italian Republic*. New York: Pantheon

- 1996. "Italy: The Convulsions of Normalcy." *New York Review of Books* (June 6): 42–6

Stoppino, Mario. 1975. "Decentramento comunale e partecipazione politica." *Amministrare*, no. 4:489–505

SVIMEZ (Associazione per lo Sviluppo dell'industria nel Mezzogiorno). 1991. *Rapporto 1991 sull'economia del Mezzogiorno*. Bologna: Il Mulino

Talese, Gay. 1972. *Honor Thy Father*. Greenwich, Conn.: Fawcett Crest Book

Tarrow, Sidney G. 1977. *Between Center and Periphery: Grassroots Politicians in Italy and France*. New Haven: Yale University Press

- 1996. "Making Social Science Work across Space and Time: A Critical Reflection on Robert Putnam's *Making Democracy Work*." *American Political Science Review* 90 (June): 389–98

Taylor, A.J.P. 1934. *The Italian Problem in European Diplomacy 1847–1849*. Manchester: Manchester University Press

Taylor, Michael. 1996. "Good Government: On Hierarchy, Social Capital and the Limitations of Rational Choice Theory." *Journal of Political Philosophy* 4 (March): 1–28

Tendler, Judith. 1997. *Good Government in the Tropics*. Baltimore: Johns Hopkins University Press

Thoenig, J.C. 1987. "State Bureaucracies and Local Government in France." In *Interorganizational Policy Making and Limits to Coordination and Central Control*, ed. I. Hanf and Fritz W. Scharpf, 167–97. London: Sage

Thom, Martin. 1998. Review of *Carlo Cattaneo il padre del federalismo italiano*, by Giuseppe Armani. *Times Literary Supplement*, no. 4,970 (3 July): 25

Thomson, Michael, R. Ellis, and A. Wildavsky. 1990. *Cultural Theory*. Boulder: Westview Press

Tilly, Charles, ed. 1975. *The Formation of National States in Western Europe*. Princeton: Princeton University Press

Tocqueville, Alexis de. [1835 and 1840] 1962. *Democracy in America*. 2 vols. New York: Vintage Books

– [1848] 1971. *Recollections*. Ed. J.P. Mayer and A. P. Kerr. Garden City: Doubleday Anchor Books

– [1856] 1956. *The Old Regime and the French Revolution*. Garden City: Doubleday Anchor Books

Togliatti, Palmiro. [1950] 1973. "Discorso su Giolitti." In his *Momenti della storia d'Italia*, 79–116. Rome: Editori Riuniti

Trebilcock, Michael J. 1996. "What Makes Poor Countries Poor: The Role of Institutional Capital in Economic Development." wsp paper no. 6–1996. Toronto: University of Toronto Centre for the Study of State and Market

Tremonti, Giulio and Giuseppe Vitaletti. 1994. *Il federalismo fiscale: Autonomia municipale e solidarietà sociale*. Bari: Laterza

Trigilia, Carlo. 1994. *Sviluppo senza autonomia: Effetti perversi delle politiche nel Mezzogiorno*. Bologna: Il Mulino

– 1995a. "Economia e società nel Mezzogiorno contemporaneo." Paper presented at the "Convegno strutture e metodi del consenso nell'Italia repubblicana," 29 March–1 April, Pisa

– , ed. 1995b. *Cultura e sviluppo: L'associazionismo nel Mezzogiorno*. Catanzaro: Meridiana Libri

Tsebelis, George. 1990. *Nested Games: Rational Choice in Comparative Politics*. Berkeley: University of California Press

Tucci, B. 1991. "Reggio, 800 miliardi a spartire. Il sindaco Licandro." *Corriere della Sera* (16 July): 12

Tullio-Altan, Carlo. 1986. *La nostra Italia: Arretratezza socioculturale, clientelismo, trasformismo e rebellismo dall'Unità ad oggi*. Milan: Feltrinelli

Tullock, Gordon. 1965. *The Politics of Bureaucracy*. Washington, D.C.: Public Affairs Press

Varese, Federico. 1994. "Is Sicily the Future of Russia? Private Protection and the Rise of the Russian Mafia." *Archives europeennes de sociologie* 30, no. 2:224–58

– 1996. "What is the Russian Mafia?" *Low Intensity Conflict & Law Enforcement* 5, no. 2 (Autumn): 129–38

– 1997a. "The Transition to the Market and Corruption in Post-Socialist Russia." *Political Studies* 45, no. 3: 579–96

– 1997b. "Capo fear." *Times Literary Supplement* (7 November): 22

– 1997c. "The Structure of Criminal Groups in Perm' Compared." Working paper, Annual Conference of the British Association for Slavonic & East European Studies, 12–14 April, Cambridge, England

Varese, Federico. In press. *The Emergence of the Russian Mafia*. Oxford: Oxford University Press

Vassallo, Salvatore. 1998. "The Third Bicamerale." In *Italian Politics: Mapping the Future*, ed. L. Bardi and M. Rhodes, 111–32. Boulder: Westview

Venturi, Franco. 1971. *Utopia and Reform in the Enlightenment*. Cambridge: Cambridge University Press

Vibert, Frank. 1995. *Europe: A Constitution for the Millennium*. Aldershot, Eng.: Dartmouth

Villani, A. 1972. "La distribuzione di funzioni fra diversi livelli di governo." *Città e Società* 7 (March–April): 3–34

Viroli, Maurizio. 1995. *For Love of Country: An Essay on Patriotism and Nationalism*. Oxford: Oxford University Press

Viviano, Franco. 1988. "Vado via ma lascio a Palermo un team di giudici eccezionali." *La Repubblica* (15 March): 16

Volpe, Francesco, ed. 1993. *Studi e storia del Mezzogiorno offerti ad Antonio Cestaro da colleghi ed allievi*. Venosa: Edizioni Osanna

Wade, Richard C. 1959. *The Urban Frontier: The Rise of Western Cities, 1790–1830*. Cambridge: Harvard University Press

Wade, Robert. 1988. *Village Republics: Economic Conditions for Collective Action in South India*. San Francisco: ICS Press

Warren, Mark K. 1994. "Exploitation or Cooperation? The Political Basis of Regional Variation in the Italian Informal Economy." *Politics & Society* 22, no. 1 (March): 89–115

Weinberger, Otto. 1940. "The Importance of Francesco Ferrara in the History of Economic Thought." *Journal of Political Economy* 48:91–104

Wellhofer, E. Spencer. 1998. "Democracy, Fascism and Civil Society: Italy, 1900–1924." Paper presented at the Organization and State Building Workshop, 11 May, University of Chicago, Chicago

West, Shearer, ed. 1999. *Italian Culture in Northern Europe in the Eighteenth Century*. New York: Cambridge University Press

Wildavsky, Aaron. 1992. "Indispensable Framework or Just Another Ideology? Prisoner's Dilemma as an Antihierarchical Game." *Rationality and Society* 4 (January): 8–23

Woodcock, G. 1967. "Regional Government: The Italian Example." *Public Administration* 45 (Winter): 403–15

Wurmser, Meyfrav. 1999. "Israel's Struggle – with Itself." *National Post* (10 July): B7

Zincone, Giovanna. 1992. *Da sudditi a cittadini: Le vie dello stato e le vie della società*. Bologna: Il Mulino

Zuckerman, Alan S. 1979. *The Politics of Faction: Christian Democratic Rule in Italy*. New Haven: Yale University Press

– 1997. "Transforming a Peripheral Region: The Consolidation and Collapse of Christian Democratic Dominance in Basilicata." *Regional and Federal Studies* 7, no. 2 (Summer): 1–24

Index

Abruzzi, 104, 235, 246, 266–7n7
absolute integrity in American public sector: as anticorruption project, 244; as source of corruption, 261. *See also* corruption; *stato di diritto*
accountability: in unitary systems, 1, 12, 82, 86, 90, 100, 106–7, 140, 173–4, 241, 244–6; in self-organized workers' movement, 229. *See also* constitutional choice
administration, centralized: municipal, 86–90; national, 11, 13, 43–4, 49, 130; regional, 112–13, 122; special system of, 184–6, 229. *See also* centralized government and administration; Interior, Ministry of the; judiciary; prefects
Africa, 51, 253
Agnew, John, 118, 119, 123, 124, 247
agriculture, 57, 222. *See also* feudalism; land reform; property rights
Agriculture, Ministry of, 87
Alberghetti, N., 255
Allison, Graham T., 19, 159
Allum, P.A., 95, 98, 99, 100, 101
Almond, Gabriel, 16, 250
Alongi, Nino, 139, 152, 153, 154, 157, 159, 162, 234
Amalfi, 71, 216
Amari, Michele, 47
American: Civil War, 47, 259; Revolution, 59
amoral familism, 14; defined, 192, 195; as label, 248; as misconstruction of reality, 196–9, 211, 230; and rational

choice, 193; as respectable bigotry, 192. *See also* Banfield, Edward C.
Andreotti, Giulio, 245
antimafia: campaigns, 132, 139, 147, 225; commissioner, 176, 182, 184; forces, 132, 142, 149–50, 153; laws, 163, 167; parliamentary commission, 133, 138; "pool" and strategic thinking, 133, 143, 145–9; professionals, 152
anti-Semitism, 13, 253, 258; and Italo-phobia, 248
Apulia, 19, 164, 229, 266–7n7, 267n8; and *mesta*, 218–19
Archer, Margaret, 1
Arendt, Hannah, 261
aristocracy: as agrarian capitalists, 217; as governing class, 42, 219, 222–3
Arlacchi, Pino, 57, 134, 135, 163, 178
Armed Forces, Ministry of, 88. *See also carabinieri*
Arnold, Matthew, 8, 251
artifact-artisanship relationship, 1, 4, 5, 8, 11, 29, 46, 49, 55; and Cattaneo, 254–6; and Marsilio da Padua, 255. *See also* constitutional choice; ideas
Asia, 69–71
association: art and science of, 58, 69; as civic asset, 202, 204, 219, 226, 228; database on, 220; north-south differentials in, 230; in southern Italy, 209, 213, 218, 226–32, 234
Astarita, Tommaso, 208, 217
Austria, 29; as empire, 253; as ruler of Italy, 38, 41; as trustee of European peace, 32

Cavour, Camillo Benso Conte di, 10–11, 19, 20, 26, 40, 61, 166, 224; constitutional achievements of, 41–2 ; and Francesco Ferrara's regionalist proposal, 47; pragmatic liberalism of, 27, 44, 46, 47; statecraft of, 48, 52–3, 84, 115, 224; and Tocqueville, 10; view of Irish question, 45, 259

CENSIS, x, 14, 98, 104, 234

centralized government and administration: liberal conception of, 20, 26, 29, 40–1, 49, 141; and good government, 87, 90, 104; practice of, in France and Italy, 31, 197, 257–8; trap, 29, 246, 259. *See also* administration, centralized; constitutional choice; constitutional knowledge; ideas; political parties; *stato di diritto*; unintended consequences

Cerignola, 228

Chamber of Deputies, 92, 125

Charles Albert, King, 38, 39

Chiaromonte, 14, 192–211, 220, 248. *See also* Banfield, Edward C.; Montegrano

Chinnici, Rocco, 151, 152

Christian Democracy, 85

Christian Democrats (DC), 84, 85, 91, 94, 99, 100, 111–12, 148, 153, 156, 161; and mafia, 132; and Opening to the Left, 105; in Palermo, 153–5, 265n1 (ch 6)

Christian optimism, 210. *See also* Catholic Church

Chubb, Judith, 101, 132, 172

CINSEDO, 114, 242

Cipolla, Carlo, 256

cities: American, 64, 119; Asian, 70; as basic human reality in Italy, 57–64, 156–7; distinctiveness of Italian, 71, 72, 106–7, 115, 118, 121; origins of, 63. *See also* Cattaneo, Carlo; commune; decentralization; local government

citizenry, 2, 12, 243, 264; as coproducer of public services, 197, 203, 246, 252; formation of, 245. *See also* Cattaneo, Carlo; Tocqueville, Alexis de

City and Regime in the American Republic (Elkin), ix

City of God, The (St Augustine), 234

Ciuffoletti, Zeffiro, 26, 33, 84

civic assets. *See* association; norms

Civic Culture, The (Almond and Verba): Italian reactions to, 250

civic: community, 214, 231; culture in Italy, 66, 68, 71, 213, 215, 200, 218, 220; pride, 29, 56, 61, 64, 67, 77, 156–7, 250, 255–6; traditions, 96, 214–15, 219; virtues as vices, 13

Civilization of the Renaissance in Italy, The (Burckhardt), 65

class: baronial, 217; common, 219; middle, 30; social, 224

Clean Hands operation (*Tangentopoli*), 7, 93, 174, 242, 245, 260–1; *See also* corruption

clientelism: corrupt practice of, 7, 173–6, 247; enlightened practice of, 94, 104, 172–3; legal basis of, 172, 261; as strategy of rule, 51–2, 172, 261. *See also* coalition governments; elections; transformism

coalition governments, 94–5, 156

Cochrane, Eric, 218–19

Coexistence: Communism and Its Practice in Bologna, 1945–65 (Evans), 98

Cohen, Norman E., 207–8

Colajanni, Napoleone, 115–16, 140, 206, 236, 237, 246

cold war, 99, 249

collective-action dilemmas, 2–3,14–16, 39, 57, 65, 119, 130, 191, 211, 239, 247

Colombis, Alessio, 196, 198, 199, 200

Colonial Affairs, Ministry for, 111

commune, 62–74; Bologna and Naples, 98–105; Catania and Palermo, 134; French and Italian Communist administrations, 91–8; as electoral and administrative unit, 49–50, 74–6, 83–92, 205–8; in France, Lombardy, and Sicily, 67, 75; in Middle Ages and Renaissance, 71–2, 116–20; in Tocqueville, 197; in Cattaneo, 58–61; as villages, 204–5. *See also* decentralization; local government

Communists (PCI), 84, 91, 99, 101, 102, 111, 112, 139, 161, 242, 263–4, 265n1 (ch 6)

compliance. *See* bureaucratic free enterprise; law; *stato di diritto*

Comte, Auguste, 56

Confederation, Canadian, 47

Considerations on the Present State and

Putnam, Robert D., ix, 8, 20, 61, 82,
104, 114–15, 175, 191, 207–9, 212,
229, 231, 246, 250, 259, 266n6

rational choice institutionalism, 18, 193,
212–38, 240
rationality: in agents, 195, 215; extreme
forms of, 195, 215, 248. *See also*
methodological individualism; laws;
rule of law
Rebuffa, Giorgio, 86, 90
reciprocity, 49, 228, 231. *See also* association; norms
Redemptorist fathers, 153
referendum, 152, 210
Reggio Calabria, x, 131, 235–6
Reggio Emilia, 102
Regional Presidents, National Conference
of, 114
regions: as administrative contrivances,
236–7; bureaucratic organization of,
112–13; capitals of, 235–6; debate on,
237; as experiments, 114, 214, 234; as
historic entities, 235–6; performance,
114–15, 192, 214. *See also* decentralization
rent control, 122
Repubblica, La, 4, 124, 126, 138, 142,
146, 147, 179
Republicans, 91, 173
respectable bigotry, 2, 191–2, 248. *See
also* Italophobia
Rete, La, 160
Reuter, Peter, 137, 163
revolts: (1848), 30, 38, 40, 252, 257;
(1859–60), 41
revolution, 3; American, 59; French, 59,
223, 257, 260. *See also* ruptures
Rhodes, Martin, xi, 245–7
risk avoidance, 50, 80
Risorgimento, Israeli, 249, 259
Risorgimento, Italian: as cultural revival,
37; as Gramscian failed revolution, 28;
and constitutional design, 3, 29, 49, 65
Romagnosi, Gian Domenico, 215
Romanelli, Raffaele, 4, 49, 50, 85, 91
Roman Empire, 66, 68, 71. *See also*
empire
Romano, Ruggiero, 30, 32, 33, 35, 64
Roman plan of 1931. *See* Mussolini plan
Roman plan of 1962, 117–18; difficulties
in formulation, 122–3; importance of,

119; and party politics, 123; adoption
of, 123; record of implementation,
123. *See also* Mussolini plan
Rome, x, xi, 10, 40, 41, 66, 118–26
Romeo, Rosario, 8, 40–1, 52, 53, 57,
192, 241, 250, 261
Rotelli, Ettore, 74, 86–7, 95
Ruffini, Cardinal Ernesto, 153
Ruggiero, Guido de, 57
rule of law, 9, 11; vs rule by law, 11,
244–6. *See also* law; *stato di diritto*
rules, self-enforcing, 216. *See also* self-
governance
ruptures, 44, 71, 224. *See also* Enlightenment; property rights; revolts; revolution; transition periods
Russia, 29, 69

St Augustine, 234, 241
Salvatorelli, Luigi, 33
Salvemini, Gaetano, 8, 9, 51, 227–8, 254
Sardinia, 31, 40, 84. *See also* Savoy,
House of; Victor Emmanuel II
Sartori, Giovanni, 5, 6, 29, 38, 93, 247
Savonarola, Girolamo, 7
Savoy, House of, 34, 35, 47, 84, 205. *See
also* Sardinia; Victor Emmanuel II
Sbragia, Alberta, 93
Scaglione, Pietro, 151
Scelba, Mario, 90
Sciascia, Leonardo, 152
Scopelliti, Antonino, 181, 184
Scotti, Enzo, 163–4
Sechi, Salvatore, 15
Segre, Dan V., 248
self-colonization, 248–54
self-governance, ix, 20, 37, 46, 48, 69,
73, 197, 219, 233, 243, 248, 253. *See
also* Cattaneo, Carlo; commune; con-
stitutional choice; democracy
self-interested actor, 11–12, 37, 195–7, 201
Sica, Domenico, 182
Sicilian: Catholic Social Union, 112; con-
stituency revolt, 112–13; exceptional-
ism, 111; revolt of 1848, 41
Sicily, 19, 32, 41–3, 47, 84; as Ireland of
Italy, 45, 160, 224, 259. *See also* Ferrara, Francesco
Siena, 106
size principle, 58, 74–6, 87, 207
Smith, Adam, 222
Snowden, Frank, 224, 228, 229